Learn C# Programming

A guide to building a solid foundation in C# language for writing efficient programs

Marius Bancila

Raffaele Rialdi

Ankit Sharma

BIRMINGHAM—MUMBAI

Learn C# Programming

Commissioning Editor: Richa Tripathi
Acquisition Editor: Alok Dhuri
Senior Editor: Storm Mann
Content Development Editor: Ruvika Rao
Technical Editor: Pradeep Sahu
Copy Editor: Safis Editing
Language Support Editor: Safis Editing
Project Coordinator: Francy Puthiry
Proofreader: Safis Editing
Indexer: Pratik Shirodkar
Production Designer: Jyoti Chauhan

First published: April 2020
Production reference: 1280420

Published by Packt Publishing Ltd.
Livery Place
35 Livery Street
Birmingham
B3 2PB, UK.

ISBN 978-1-78980-586-4

www.packt.com

*To my smart boys, Cristian and Bogdan, who love learning
new things every day.*

– Marius

*To my mom and dad, who ignited my passion with a Sinclair ZX81
when I was a child, and to my beautiful wife, Valeria, who has always
supported me in my adventures. I love you!*

– Raffaele

To my mother, Vibha Sharma, for everything she did for me.

– Ankit

`Packt.com`

Subscribe to our online digital library for full access to over 7,000 books and videos, as well as industry leading tools to help you plan your personal development and advance your career. For more information, please visit our website.

Why subscribe?

- Spend less time learning and more time coding with practical eBooks and Videos from over 4,000 industry professionals

- Improve your learning with Skill Plans built especially for you

- Get a free eBook or video every month

- Fully searchable for easy access to vital information

- Copy and paste, print, and bookmark content

Did you know that Packt offers eBook versions of every book published, with PDF and ePub files available? You can upgrade to the eBook version at `packt.com` and as a print book customer, you are entitled to a discount on the eBook copy. Get in touch with us at `customercare@packtpub.com` for more details.

At `www.packt.com`, you can also read a collection of free technical articles, sign up for a range of free newsletters, and receive exclusive discounts and offers on Packt books and eBooks.

Foreword

As a developer of the 2020s, it's hard to believe that there was a time in which the choice of programming language was crucial for the success of a software project, with each programming language coming with its own set of libraries defining the range of possible actions. Data access, for example, was a no-brainer in Visual Basic but hard to do in C++, for example. By the same token, calling into low-level Windows API functions was easy in C but sometimes impossible in Visual Basic.

Then came the .NET platform made of two distinct pillars. One pillar was an object-oriented framework defining a wide range of predefined behaviors. The other pillar was a language runtime able to support a variety of programming languages, including Visual Basic and the new C#. Over the years, C# has then become the primary language for the whole .NET platform.

So, what does it mean to learn C# today, two decades after .NET 1.0? Learning the sole syntax and semantics of a programming language makes little to no sense these days, whether it is C#, Java, or Python. A programming language is a largely interchangeable tool with limited real programming power without the backbone of a solid framework.

Subsequently, learning the plain syntax of a programming language is a small fraction of the job and a book that intends to cover any programming language has to go well beyond data types, operators, and control statements. This is precisely what this book does and in addition, in it, you will also explore the authors' well-known obsession through clear and precise topics.

This book is not simply a technical guide about using the C# language. It covers statements, data types, classes, generics, concurrency, and even functional and dynamic programming, plus the array of new features in the latest C# language. However, if you are only armed with these tools, you won't go too far even with building *toy* applications. It is also important for you to know about the foundational aspects of the .NET platform, such as reflection, collections, regular expressions, files, streams, serialization, and LINQ.

Anything else? You bet!

Error handling, exceptions, garbage collection, and memory management also have a reserved chapter, before ending with an overview of C#8 in the context of .NET Core 3 and unit testing.

In spite of the title, this is not simply the umpteenth book on a popular programming language. It is a book about how to use a popular programming language to its fullest for building .NET applications on a solid foundation.

Dino Esposito
Digital Strategist, Youbiquitous.net

Contributors

About the authors

Marius Bancila is a software engineer with almost two decades of experience in developing solutions for the industrial and financial sectors. He is the author of *Modern C++ Programming Cookbook* and *The Modern C++ Challenge*. He works as a software architect and is focused on Microsoft technologies, mainly developing desktop applications with C++ and C#, but not solely. He is passionate about sharing his technical expertise with others and, for that reason, he has been recognized as a Microsoft MVP for C++ and later developer technologies since 2006.

> *I would like to thank everybody that made this book possible. To Raffaele and Ankit for laboring on this project together and making it a great book. To Omprakash for his useful comments. To Ruvika for all her support and patience during the project. To Alok, Storm, and all the other people at Packt that helped turn this book from an idea to reality.*

Raffaele Rialdi is a senior software architect working as a consultant, speaker, and trainer. Since 2003, he is a Microsoft MVP in the Developer Security category. His passion for the community leads him to be a member of the board of UGIdotNET, president of DotNetLiguria, and co-founder of the Italian C++ user group. Currently, he is working as an architect and developer on the backend of an enterprise project with a specific focus on code generation, and working on cross-platform mobile and IoT development in both C# and C++. You can find him on Twitter with the handle @raffaeler.

> *A big thank you goes to my fellow co-authors, Marius and Ankit, for their great work; Omprakash for his valuable reviews; the entire Packt team, who did a great job in letting me work with peace of mind; and, last but not least, Ruvika for her great patience in coordinating with all of us.*

Ankit Sharma is a software engineer currently working as Senior Member Technical with ADP in Hyderabad, India. He has over six years of extensive experience with Microsoft technologies, including C#, ASP.NET, and SQL Server, and UI technologies such as jQuery, Angular, and Blazor. Ankit is a technical author and speaker and loves to contribute to the open source community. He writes articles for multiple platforms, including c-sharpcorner, Dzone, Medium, and freeCodeCamp. For his dedicated contribution to the developer's community, he has been recognized as c-sharpcorner MVP, Dzone MVB, and a top contributor in the technology category on Medium. He is also the author of the first ever book on Blazor – *Blazor Quick Start Guide*. You can tweet him at `@ankitsharma_007`.

I would like to thank my mother for her continuous support throughout the process of writing this book.

I would also like to thank my co-authors, Marius and Raffaele, for their constructive feedback throughout the writing process, which was crucial in enhancing the quality of the content.

About the reviewer

Omprakash Pandey is a seasoned software technology professional associated with Synergetics. He has provided innovative solutions on C, C++, Java (Core, Intermediate, and Advanced), .NET (Basic), ADO.NET, WCF, WF, ASP.NET MVC, Microsoft 365, Microsoft Azure, infrastructure management for portal development and deployment, and services development.

Packt is searching for authors like you

If you're interested in becoming an author for Packt, please visit `authors.packtpub.com` and apply today. We have worked with thousands of developers and tech professionals, just like you, to help them share their insight with the global tech community. You can make a general application, apply for a specific hot topic that we are recruiting an author for, or submit your own idea.

About the reviewer

Packt is searching for authors like you

Table of Contents

3

Control Statements and Exceptions

4

Understanding the Various User-Defined Types

5

Object-Oriented Programming in C#

6

Generics

7

Collections

8

Advanced Topics

9

Resource Management

10

Lambdas, LINQ, and Functional Programming

11

Reflection and Dynamic Programming

12

Multithreading and Asynchronous Programming

16

C# in Action with .NET Core 3

17
Unit Testing

Assessments

Other Books You May Enjoy

Preface

C# is a general-purpose, multi-paradigm programming language that combines object-oriented, imperative, generic, functional, declarative, and dynamic programming. Soon after its release, C# became one of the top choices for developers for writing a large variety of types of applications. Although it is not the only language targeting the CLI (the others include VB.NET and F#), it is the primary choice for writing .NET applications for desktop, web, cloud, and mobile platforms.

Over the years, the language has evolved gradually but steadily. Although initially it was an object-oriented programming language, new versions have opened up the language to new paradigms such as generic, functional, and dynamic programming. New language features and more concise syntax have also been added regularly. With its release as an open source project of the .NET Compiler Platform, also known as Roslyn, which is a set of compilers and code analysis APIs for C# and VB.NET, the language has entered a new open era with the community deeply involved in the development of the language.

The current version of the language is known as C# 8. This was released in September 2019 for .NET Core 3.0 and requires Visual Studio 2019 16.3 or a newer version. C# 8 can also be used with .NET Framework, although not all features are available. That is because they required runtime changes, which was something Microsoft did not want to do due to its intent to no longer invest in .NET Framework (other than long-time support) and turn .NET Core into the one framework used to target all platforms and types of applications. This framework will be known simply as .NET.

This book is designed to help you learn the language from scratch and eventually master all its multi-paradigm programming aspects. We start with the very basics: data types, statements, and other building blocks. We then continue with object-oriented concepts such as classes, interfaces, inheritance, and polymorphism. We cover generics, functional programming and LINQ, reflection and dynamic programming, and more advanced topics, such as resource management, pattern matching, concurrency and asynchronous programming, error handling, and serialization. Toward the end of the book, we give special attention to the new features introduced in C# 8. Last, but not least, we discuss unit testing and how you can write unit tests for your C# code. At the end of each chapter, we provide you with a set of questions to help you assess what you learned in that chapter.

The book contains many code snippets that are designed to help you easily understand and learn all the language features. All of them are available in the source code that accompanies the book. You will need either Visual Studio or Visual Studio Code to try them. Alternatively, you can use an online compiler, the primary choice in this case being `https://sharplab.io/`.

Who this book is for?

If you are a passionate programmer and want to learn C#, this book is for you. If you want to start learning to program and want to do that with C# and .NET, you will also find the book valuable. However, we assume you have some basic knowledge of programming concepts, such as what a compiler is, what classes and methods are, and so on. On the other hand, if you are an experienced C# programmer but want to learn about the latest features of C# 8 or how to work with .NET Core and migrate from .NET Framework, this book will be handy for you, too.

What this book covers

Chapter 1, Starting with the Building Blocks of C#, gives an introduction to the language, its history, and its relationship with the Common Language Infrastructure and .NET Framework, as well as providing an introduction to the family of .NET frameworks used today. At the end, you learn about assemblies, how to create a project in Visual Studio, and how to write a Hello World program in C#.

Chapter 2, Data Types and Operators, walks you through the basic elements of the language, including the built-in data types, variables and constants, reference, and value types, nullable types, and array types, as well as type conversions and built-in operators.

Chapter 3, Control Statements and Exceptions, looks in depth at how to write selection statements and loops and briefly at working with exceptions.

Chapter 4, Understanding the Various User-Defined Types, provides information about classes, fields, properties, methods, constructors, how to pass arguments to methods, what access modifiers are, and other aspects related to classes. Toward the end, you will learn about structures and how they compare to classes, as well as enumerations.

Chapter 5, Object-Oriented Programming in C#, continues on the foundation built with the previous chapter and teaches you the core pillars of object-oriented programming and how you achieve them using C# language features such as interfaces, virtual members, method overloading, and others.

Chapter 6, Generics, covers all the aspects of generic programming in C# and teaches you how to write generic types and methods and use constraints for type parameters.

Chapter 7, Collections, provides a walk-through of the generic collections from the .NET base class library that you typically use when writing C# programs. The chapter ends with an overview of the concurrent collections used in multithreading scenarios.

Chapter 8, Advanced Topics, contains a variety of more advanced features, such as delegates and events, tuples, extension methods, pattern matching, and regular expressions.

Chapter 9, Resource Management, explains how the garbage collector works and how you should handle resources deterministically. Also, in this chapter, you learn how to make system or, in general, native API calls with Platform Invocation Services, as well as how to write unsafe code.

Chapter 10, Lambdas, LINQ, and Functional Programming, provides an overview of functional programming concepts and details pertaining to lambda expressions in C#. You learn how to uniformly query various data sources using Language Integrated Query (or LINQ). At the end of the chapter, we cover several typical functional programming concepts: partial function application, currying, closures, monoids, and monads and how they work in C#.

Chapter 11, Reflection and Dynamic Programming, teaches you what reflection services are and how they can be used to write extensible applications, how to dynamically load assemblies and execute code, how to use attributes, and how to use the Dynamic Language Runtime and the dynamic type to interop with dynamic languages.

Chapter 12, Multithreading and Asynchronous Programming, provides an in-depth look at threads, tasks, and synchronization mechanisms and uncovers the details of the async-await pattern for writing asynchronous programs in C#.

Chapter 13, Files, Streams, and Serialization, explains how to work with paths, files, and directories, and how to use streams for reading and writing data from and to a variety of storage options, such as files and memory. In the second part of the chapter, you will learn about data serialization with XML and JSON.

Chapter 14, Error Handling, builds on the concepts concerning exception handling introduced in *Chapter 3, Control Statements and Exceptions,* and teaches you the inner workings of exceptions and how exception handling differs from error handling. You will learn valuable information about debugging and monitoring as well as best practices for working with exceptions.

Chapter 15, *New Features of C# 8*, covers in detail all the new language features introduced in C# 8, including nullable reference types, async streams, ranges and indices, pattern matching, and default implementations of interface members.

Chapter 16, *C# in Action with .NET Core 3*, teaches you about using the .NET CLI for building .NET Core applications, how you can target and develop for Linux, what .NET Standard is and how it can help application design, how to consume NuGet packages, and how you can migrate .NET Framework applications to .NET Core.

Chapter 17, *Unit Testing*, covers unit testing, the Microsoft tools for unit testing your C# code, how to create unit testing projects using Visual Studio, and how to write unit tests and data-driven unit tests.

To get the most out of this book

This is a book that covers C#, from its building blocks to its most advanced features. This book is intended for people who want to learn C#. Therefore, we do not expect you to have any prior knowledge of the language. However, we do expect you to have some basic exposure to programming concepts, such as what a compiler is, the difference between compile time and runtime, the difference between stack and heap, and others.

All the code samples in this book have been written using C# 8 and a modern programming style (such as using expression-bodied members, interpolated strings, local functions, and so on). All these samples are available together with the book in projects targeting .NET Core 3.1.

The following table lists the software and platform requirements for running these samples:

Software/Hardware covered in the book	OS Requirements
C# 8	Windows, macOS X, and Linux (any)
.NET Core 3.1	
Visual Studio 2019 16.3 or newer	

In order to run the source code, you need Visual Studio 2019 16.3 or newer, any edition, or Visual Studio Code. Most of the samples can also be tested using an online compiler. Should you prefer this option, we recommend that you use `https://sharplab.io/`.

If you are using the digital version of this book, we advise you to type the code yourself or access the code via the GitHub repository (link available in the next section). Doing so will help you avoid any potential errors related to the copying/pasting of code.

Download the example code files

You can download the example code files for this book from your account at
www.packt.com. If you purchased this book elsewhere, you can visit www.packtpub.
com/support and register to have the files emailed directly to you.

You can download the code files by following these steps:

1. Log in or register at www.packt.com.
2. Select the **Support** tab.
3. Click on **Code Downloads**.
4. Enter the name of the book in the **Search** box and follow the onscreen instructions.

Once the file is downloaded, please make sure that you unzip or extract the folder using
the latest version of:

*   WinRAR/7-Zip for Windows
*   Zipeg/iZip/UnRarX for Mac
*   7-Zip/PeaZip for Linux

The code bundle for the book is also hosted on GitHub at https://github.com/
PacktPublishing/Learn-C-Sharp-Programming. In case there's an update to
the code, it will be updated on the existing GitHub repository.

We also have other code bundles from our rich catalog of books and videos available at
https://github.com/PacktPublishing/. Check them out!

Code in Action

Code in Action videos for this book can be viewed at https://bit.ly/2VaAls9.

Download the color images

We also provide a PDF file that has color images of the screenshots/diagrams used
in this book. You can download it here: https://static.packt-cdn.com/
downloads/9781789805864_ColorImages.pdf.

Conventions used

There are a number of text conventions used throughout this book.

`Code in text`: Indicates code words in text, database table names, folder names, filenames, file extensions, pathnames, dummy URLs, user input, and Twitter handles. Here is an example: "In this example, we are creating an `Employee` class with three fields to represent the ID, first name, and last name of an employee."

A block of code is set as follows:

```
class Employee
{
    public int    EmployeeId;
    public string FirstName;
    public string LastName;
}
```

When we wish to draw your attention to a particular part of a code block, the relevant lines or items are set in bold:

```
public struct Vector
{
    public float x;
    public float y;
    private readonly float SquaredRo => (x * x) + (y * y);
    public readonly float GetLengthRo() => MathF.
Sqrt(SquaredRo);
    public float GetLength() => MathF.Sqrt(SquaredRo);
}
```

Any command-line input or output is written as follows:

```
cd HelloSolution
dotnet new console -o Hello
dotnet sln add Hello
```

Bold: Indicates a new term, an important word, or words that you see on screen. For example, words in menus or dialog boxes appear in the text like this. Here is an example: "When creating a new project, select **Console App (.NET Core)**."

Tips or important notes
Appear like this.

Get in touch

Feedback from our readers is always welcome.

General feedback: If you have questions about any aspect of this book, mention the book title in the subject of your message and email us at customercare@packtpub.com

Errata: Although we have taken every care to ensure the accuracy of our content, mistakes do happen. If you have found a mistake in this book, we would be grateful if you would report this to us. Please visit www.packtpub.com/support/errata, selecting your book, clicking on the Errata Submission Form link, and entering the details.

Piracy: If you come across any illegal copies of our works in any form on the internet, we would be grateful if you would provide us with the location address or website name. Please contact us at copyright@packt.com with a link to the material.

If you are interested in becoming an author: If there is a topic that you have expertise in, and you are interested in either writing or contributing to a book, please visit authors.packtpub.com.

Reviews

Please leave a review. Once you have read and used this book, why not leave a review on the site that you purchased it from? Potential readers can then see and use your unbiased opinion to make purchase decisions, we at Packt can understand what you think about our products, and our authors can see your feedback on their book. Thank you!

For more information about Packt, please visit packt.com.

1
Starting with the Building Blocks of C#

C# is one of the most widely used general-purpose programming languages. It is a multi-paradigm language that combines object-oriented, imperative, declarative, functional, generic, and dynamic programming. C# is one of the programming languages designed for the **Common Language Infrastructure (CLI)** platform, which is an open specification developed by Microsoft and standardized by the **International Organization for Standardization (ISO)** and **European Computer Manufacturers Association (ECMA)** that describes executable code and a runtime environment to be used on different computer platforms without being rewritten for specific architectures.

Over the years, C# has evolved with powerful features released version by version. The most recent version (at the time of writing) is C# 8, which has introduced several features to empower developers to be more productive. These include nullable reference types, ranges and indices, asynchronous streams, default implementations of interface members, recursive patterns, switch expressions, and many others. You will learn about these features in detail in *Chapter 15, New Features of C# 8*.

In this chapter, we will introduce you to the language, the .NET Framework, and the basic concepts around them. We have structured the contents of this chapter as follows:

- Learning the history of C#
- Understanding the CLI

- Knowing the .NET family of frameworks

- Assemblies in .NET

- Understanding the basic structure of a C# program

At the end of this chapter, you will learn how to write a `Hello World!` program in C#.

The history of C#

C# development started at Microsoft in the late 1990s by a team led by Anders Hejlsberg. Initially, it was called **Cool**, but when the .NET project was first publicly announced in the summer of 2002, the language was renamed C#. The use of the sharp suffix was intended to denote that the language is an increment of C++, which, along with Java, Delphi, and Smalltalk, acted as an inspiration for the CLI and the C# language design.

The first version of C#, called **1.0**, was made available in 2002 bundled with .NET Framework 1.0 and Visual Studio .NET 2002. Since then, major and minor increments of the language have been released together with new versions of .NET Framework and Visual Studio. The following table lists all of the versions and some of the key features for each of these releases:

C# version	Release date	.NET Framework version	Visual Studio version	Features
1.0	Jan 2002	1.0	Visual Studio .NET 2002	Initial release
1.1	Apr 2003	1.1	Visual Studio .NET 2003	Stability update
2.0	Nov 2005	2.0	Visual Studio 2005	Generics, partial types, anonymous methods, iterators, nullable types, getter/setter separate accessibility, method group conversions (delegates), co- and contra-variance for delegates, static classes, and delegate inference
3.0	Nov 2007	3.0	Visual Studio 2008	Implicitly typed local variables, object and collection initializers, auto-implemented properties, anonymous types, extension methods, query expressions, lambda expressions, expression trees, and partial methods

C# version	Release date	.NET Framework version	Visual Studio version	Features
4.0	Apr 2010	4.0	Visual Studio 2010	Dynamic binding, named and optional arguments, generic co- and contravariance, and embedded interop types (NoPIA)
5.0	Aug 2012	4.5	Visual Studio 2012	Asynchronous methods and caller information attributes
6.0	Jul 2015	4.6	Visual Studio 2015	Compiler-as-a-service (Roslyn), import of static type members into the namespace, exception filters, `await` in `catch`/`finally` blocks, auto property initializers, default values for getter-only properties, expression-bodied members, null propagator (null-conditional operator, succinct null checking), string interpolation, the `nameof` operator, and dictionary initializers
7.0	Mar 2017	4.6.2	Visual Studio 2017	Out variables, pattern matching, tuples, deconstruction, local functions, digit separators, binary literals, `ref` returns and locals, generalized async return types, expression-bodied constructors and finalizers, and expression-bodied getters and setters
7.1	Aug 2017	4.7	Visual Studio 2017 15.3	Async Main, default literal expressions, and inferred tuple element names

C# version	Release date	.NET Framework version	Visual Studio version	Features
7.2	Nov 2017	4.7.1	Visual Studio 2017 15.5	Reference semantics with value types, non-trailing named arguments, leading underscores in numeric literals, and private protected access modifier
7.3	May 2018	4.7.2	Visual Studio 2017 15.7	Accessing fixed fields without pinning, reassigning `ref` local variables, using initializers on `stackalloc` arrays, using fixed statements with any type that supports a pattern, and using additional generic constraints
8.0	Sept 2019	.NET Core 3.0	Visual Studio 2019	Nullable reference types, ranges and indices, asynchronous streams, default implementations of interface members, recursive patterns, switch expressions, and target-typed new expressions

The latest version of the language at the time of writing, 8.0, is being released with .NET Core 3.0. Although most features will also work in projects targeting .NET Framework, some of them will not because they require changes in the runtime, which is something Microsoft will no longer do as .NET Framework is being deprecated in favor of .NET Core.

Now that you have an overview of the evolution of the C# language over time, let's start looking at the platforms that the language is targeting.

Understanding the CLI

The CLI is a specification that describes how a runtime environment can be used on different computer platforms without being rewritten for specific architectures. It is developed by Microsoft and standardized by ECMA and ISO. The following diagram shows the high-level functionality of the CLI:

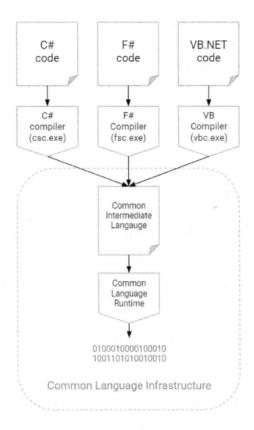

Figure 1.1 – Diagram of the high-level functionality of the CLI

The CLI enables programs written in a variety of programming languages (that are CLS-compliant) to be executed on any operating system and with a single runtime. The CLI specifies a common language, called the **Common Language Specification (CLS)**, a common set of data types that any language must support, called the **Common Type System**, and other things such as how exceptions are handled and how the state is managed. The various aspects specified by the CLI are described in more detail in the following sections.

Information box

Because of the limited scope of this chapter, a deep dive into the specification is not possible. If you want more information about the CLI, you can visit the ISO site at `https://www.iso.org/standard/58046.html`.

There are several implementations of the CLI and among these, the most important ones are .NET Framework, .NET Core, and Mono/Xamarin.

Common Type System (CTS)

The CTS is a component of the CLI that describes how type definitions and values are represented and memory is intended to facilitate the sharing of data between programming languages. The following are some of the characteristics and functions of the CTS:

- It enables cross-platform integration, type safety, and high-performance code execution.

- It provides an object-oriented model that supports the complete implementation of many programming languages.

- It provides rules for languages to ensure that objects and data types of objects written in different programming languages can interact with each other.

- It defines rules for type visibility and access to members.

- It defines rules for type inheritance, virtual methods, and object lifetime.

The CTS supports two categories of types:

- **Value types**: These contain their data directly and have copy semantics, which means when an object of such a type is copied its data is copied.

- **Reference types**: These contain references to the memory address where the data is stored. When an object of a reference type is copied, the reference is copied and not the data it points to.

Although it is an implementation detail, value types are usually stored on the stack and reference types on the heap. Conversion between value types and a reference type is possible and known as **boxing**, while the other way around is called **unboxing**. These concepts will be explained in further detail in the next chapter.

Common Language Specification (CLS)

The CLS comprises a set of rules that any language that targets the CLI needs to adhere to, to be able to interoperate with other CLS-compliant languages. CLS rules fall into the broader rules of the CTS and therefore it can be said that the CLS is a subset of CTS. All of the rules of CTS apply to the CLS unless the CLS rules are stricter. Language constructs that make it impossible to easily verify the type safety of the code were excluded from the CLS so that all languages that work with the CLS can produce verifiable code.

The relationship between the CTS and CLS as well as the programming languages targeting the CLI is conceptually shown in the following diagram:

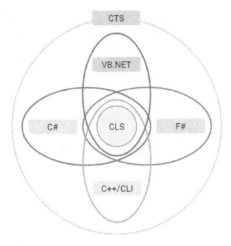

Figure 1.2 – A diagram showing the conceptual relationship between the CTS and CLS and the programming languages that target the CLI

Components built using only the rules of the CLS are called **CLS-compliant**. An example of such components is the framework libraries that need to work across all of the languages supported on .NET.

Common Intermediate Language (CIL)

CIL is a platform-neutral intermediate language (formerly called **Microsoft Intermediate Language** or **MSIL**) that represents the intermediate language binary instruction set defined by the CLI. It is a stack-based object-oriented assembly language that represents the code in byte-code format.

Once the source code of an application is compiled, the compiler translates it into the CIL bytecode and produces a CLI assembly. When the CLI assembly is executed, the bytecode is passed through the **Just-In-Time** compiler to generate native code, which is then executed by the computer's processor. The CPU and the platform-independent nature of the CIL make it possible that the code is executed on any environment supporting the CLI.

To help us to understand the CIL, let's look at an example. The following listing shows a very simple C# program that prints a `Hello, World!` message to the console:

```
using System;

namespace chapter_01
{
    class Program
    {
        static void Main(string[] args)
        {
            Console.WriteLine("Hello World!");
        }
    }
}
```

It is possible to view the content of the assembly produced by the compiler using various utility tools, such as `ildasm.exe`, which comes with .NET Framework, or ILSpy, which is an open source .NET assembly browser and decompiler (available at `http://www.ilspy.net/`). The `ildasm.exe` file shows a visual representation of the program and its components, such as classes and members:

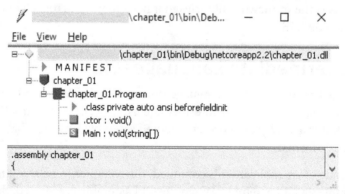

Figure 1.3 – A screenshot of the ildasm tool showing the content of an assembly

You can also see the content of the manifest (which includes assembly metadata) as well as the CIL code for each method if you double-click on it. The following screenshot shows the disassembled code of the `Main` method:

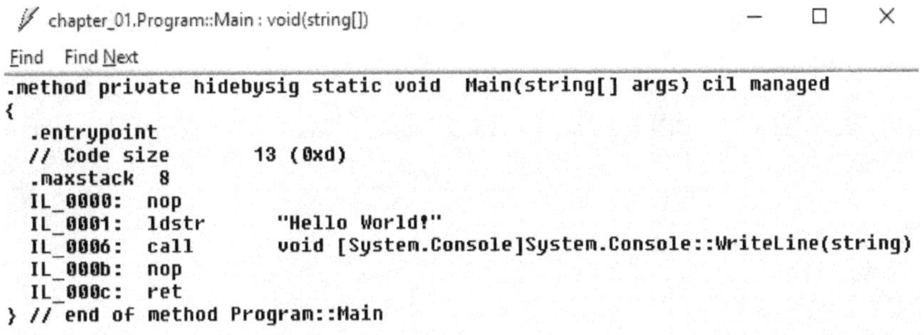

```
⚡ chapter_01.Program::Main : void(string[])                    —   □   ×

Find  Find Next
.method private hidebysig static void  Main(string[] args) cil managed
{
  .entrypoint
  // Code size       13 (0xd)
  .maxstack  8
  IL_0000:  nop
  IL_0001:  ldstr      "Hello World!"
  IL_0006:  call       void [System.Console]System.Console::WriteLine(string)
  IL_000b:  nop
  IL_000c:  ret
} // end of method Program::Main
```

Figure 1.4 – A screenshot of the ildasm tool showing the IL code of the Main method

A human-readable dump of the CIL code is also available. This starts with the manifest and continues with the class member's declarations. A partial listing of the CIL code for the preceding program is shown here:

```
// Metadata version: v4.0.30319
.assembly extern System.Runtime
{
  .publickeytoken = (B0 3F 5F 7F 11 D5 0A 3A )
// .?_....:
  .ver 4:2:1:0
}
.assembly extern System.Console
{
  .publickeytoken = (B0 3F 5F 7F 11 D5 0A 3A )
// .?_....:
  .ver 4:1:1:0
}
.assembly chapter_01
{

}
.module chapter_01.dll
// MVID: {1CFF5587-0C75-4C14-9BE5-1605F27AE750}
.imagebase 0x00400000
.file alignment 0x00000200
.stackreserve 0x00100000
.subsystem 0x0003       // WINDOWS_CUI
.corflags 0x00000001    //  ILONLY
// Image base: 0x00F30000


// =============== CLASS MEMBERS DECLARATION
===================
```

```
.class private auto ansi beforefieldinit chapter_01.Program
        extends [System.Runtime]System.Object
{
   .method private hidebysig static void  Main(string[] args)
cil managed
   {
     .entrypoint
     // Code size        13 (0xd)
     .maxstack  8
     IL_0000:  nop
     IL_0001:  ldstr       "Hello World!"
     IL_0006:  call        void [System.Console]System.
Console::WriteLine(string)
     IL_000b:  nop
     IL_000c:  ret
   } // end of method Program::Main

   .method public hidebysig specialname rtspecialname
          instance void  .ctor() cil managed
   {
     // Code size        8 (0x8)
     .maxstack  8
     IL_0000:  ldarg.0
     IL_0001:  call        instance void [System.Runtime]System.
Object::.ctor()
     IL_0006:  nop
     IL_0007:  ret
   } // end of method Program::.ctor

} // end of class chapter_01.Program
```

An explanation of the code here is beyond the scope of this chapter, but you can probably identify at a glance parts of it such as classes, methods, and instructions executed in each method.

Virtual Execution System (VES)

VES is a part of the CLI that represents a runtime system that provides the environment for executing the managed code. It has several built-in services to support the execution of code and handling of exceptions, among other things.

The Common Language Runtime is .NET Framework's implementation of the
Virtual Execution System. Other implementations of the CLI provide their own
VES implementations.

The .NET family of frameworks

.NET is a general-purpose development platform developed by Microsoft for writing
a variety of types of applications for desktop, cloud, and mobile. .NET Framework was
the first implementation of the CLI but, over time, a series of other frameworks have
been created, such as .NET Micro Framework, .NET Native, and Silverlight. While .NET
Framework works on Windows, other current implementations, such as .NET Core and
Mono/Xamarin, are cross-platform and run on other operating systems, such as Linux,
macOS, iOS, or Android.

The following screenshot shows the main characteristics of the current top .NET
frameworks. .NET Framework is intended for developing .NET applications for Windows
and is distributed with the operating system. .NET Core, which is cross-platform and
open source, is optimized for modern application requirements and developer workflows
and is distributed with the application. Xamarin, which uses a Mono-based runtime, is
also cross-platform and open source. It is intended for developing mobile applications for
iOS, macOS, Android, and Windows, and is distributed with the application:

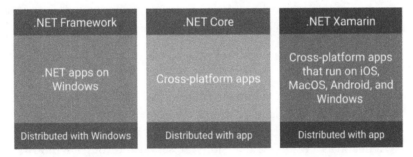

Figure 1.5 – A diagram with the main characteristic of the most important .NET frameworks

All of these implementations are based on a common infrastructure that includes languages, compilers, and runtime components and supports a variety of application models, some of which are shown in the following screenshot:

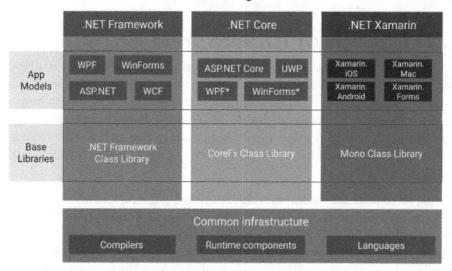

Figure 1.6 – A high-level diagram of the .NET frameworks infrastructure and the application models they support

Here, you can see that each framework resides on top of the common infrastructure and provides a set of base libraries as well as different application models.

.NET Framework

.NET Framework was the first implementation of the CLI. It is the primary development platform for Windows Server and client developers. It contains a large class library that supports many types of applications. The framework is distributed as a part of the operating system and as a result, new versions are serviced through **Windows Update**, although standalone installers are also available. Initially, .NET Framework was proprietary software developed by Microsoft. In recent years, parts of .NET Framework have been open-sourced.

The following table shows the history of .NET Framework, as well as the major features available in each release:

Version	Release data	Features
1.0	Feb 2002	Initial release
1.1	Apr 2003	Enables code access security in ASP.NET applications, built-in support for mobile ASP.NET controls, built-in support for ODBC and Oracle Database, enables Windows Forms assemblies to execute in a semi-trusted manner from the internet, .NET Compact Framework, and **Internet Protocol version 6 (IPv6)** support
2.0	Jan 2006	Membership provider, partial classes, nullable types, anonymous methods, iterators, data tables, Microsoft SQL Server integration, new personalization features for ASP.NET, .NET Micro Framework, language support for generics built directly into the .NET CLR, a new hosting API for native applications wishing to host an instance of .NET runtime, and full 64-bit computing support for both the x64 and the IA-64 hardware platforms
3.0	Nov 2006	**Windows Presentation Foundation (WPF)**, **Windows Communication Foundation (WCF)**, **Windows Workflow Foundation (WF)**, and Windows CardSpace
3.5	Nov 2007	LINQ, 3.5 SP1 (Entity Framework, WCF Data Services, System.Web.Abstraction, System.Web.Routing)
4.0	Apr 2010	**Parallel LINQ (PLINQ)**, Task Parallel Library, `System.Numerics.BigInteger`, and `System.Numerics.Complex`
4.5	Aug 2012	.NET for Windows Store apps, **Managed Extensibility Framework (MEF)**, and enhancement to ASP.NET, networking, and parallelism
4.5.1	Oct 2013	Async-aware debugging in the Call Stack and Tasks windows, debugger support for seeing managed return values, debugger support for X64 **edit and continue (EnC)**, and ADO.NET idle connection resiliency
4.5.2	May 2014	High DPI for Windows Forms applications and higher reliability HTTP header inspection and modification methods in ASP.NET
4.6	Jul 2015	New JIT called RyuJIT and improvements to WPF, Win Forms, WCF, and cryptography

Version	Release data	Features
4.6.1	Nov 2015	Enhanced support for **Elliptic Curve Digital Signature Algorithm (ECDSA)** X509 certificates; WPF improvements for spell check; support for per-user custom dictionaries and improved touch performance; support in SQL connectivity for AlwaysOn, distributed transactions, and Always Encrypted; improved connection open resiliency support for Azure SQL Database; and other performance, stability, and reliability related fixes in RyuJIT, GC, WPF, and WCF
4.6.2	Aug 2016	Support for localization of data annotations in ASP.NET; support for paths longer than 260 characters; TLS 1.1/1.2 support for ClickOnce; enabling .NET desktop apps with Project Centennial; soft keyboard and per-monitor DPI support for WPF; and support for FIPS 186-3 DSA in X.509 certificates
4.7	May 2017	Improve TLS support, especially for version 1.2; enhanced cryptography with elliptic curve cryptography; more support for touch and stylus in **Windows Presentation Foundation WPF**; new print APIs for WPF; and support for High-DPI awareness in Windows Forms
4.7.1	Oct 2017	Fix for the d3dcompiler dependency issue and compatibility with the .NET Standard 2.0 out of the box
4.7.2	Apr 2018	Improvements to BCL, CLR, ASP.NET, networking, SQL, WCF, Workflow, WPF, Windows Forms, and ClickOnce
4.8	Apr 2019	JIT and NGEN improvements, accessibility enhancements in WinForms, service behavior enhancements in WCF, high DPI enhancements, and UIAutomation improvements in WPF

In the future, Microsoft intends to unify all .NET frameworks into a single one. At the time of writing this book, this is planned to be named .NET 5.

.NET Framework includes the **Common Language Runtime** (**CLR**), which is the execution engine of the framework that provides services such as memory management, type safety, garbage collection, exception handling, thread management, and others. It also includes an implementation of the CLI foundational standard libraries. The following is a list of the components of the standard libraries (although not all of them):

- **Base Class Library** (**BCL**): It provides types to represent the CLI built-in types, simple file access, custom attributes, string handling, formatting, collections, streams, and others.

- **Runtime Infrastructure Library**: It provides services to dynamically load types from a stream and other services that allow the compiler to target the CLI.

- **Reflection Library**: It provides services that make it possible to examine the structure of types at runtime, instantiate objects, and invoke methods.

- **Network Library**: It provides networking services.

- **Extended Numerics Library**: It provides support for floating-point and extended-precision data types.

- **Parallel Library**: It provides parallelism in simple forms.

Apart from these libraries, the **.NET Framework Class Library** (**FCL**) includes many other libraries, such as WPF, WinForms, WCF, LINQ, and others. Most of these are in the `System.*` or `Microsoft.*` namespaces.

A key aspect of developing in C# for the .NET platform is how memory is managed. In general, developers do not have to worry about the lifetime of objects and the disposal of memory. Memory management is automatically done by the CLR through the **Garbage Collector** (**GC**). The GC handles the allocation of objects on the heap and the disposal of memory when heap objects are no longer used.

The garbage collection is a *non-deterministic process* because it happens on a per-need basis and not at some deterministic moments. A detailed description of the way the garbage collection works is provided in *Chapter 9, Resource Management*.

.NET Core

.NET Core is a new implementation of the CLI that is cross-platform, open source, and modular. It is intended for developing a variety of applications, such as web apps, micro-services, libraries, or console apps that run on Windows, Linux, and macOS. The .NET Core framework is packaged using NuGet; as a result, it is either compiled directly into an application or put into a folder inside the application. Therefore, .NET Core applications distribute the framework components directly, although a cache system for a centralized deployment, called **runtime package store**, is also available starting with version 2.0.

The implementation of the VES for .NET Core is called **CoreCLR**. Similarly, the implementation of the CLI foundational standard libraries is called **CoreFX**.

ASP.NET Core is a part of .NET Core but also runs on the .NET Framework CLR. However, an ASP.NET Core app is cross-platform only when targeting .NET Core.

With the release of version 3.0 in September 2019, developers can create web apps, micro-services, desktop applications, machine learning, and AI applications, IoT applications, libraries, and console applications using .NET Core.

You will learn more about .NET Core in *Chapter 16, C# in Action with .NET Core 3*.

Xamarin

Xamarin is a CLI implementation based on **Mono**, which is a cross-platform, open source .NET framework. In general, Mono APIs followed the progress of .NET Framework and not .NET Core. The framework is intended for writing mobile applications that can run on iOS, Android, macOS, and Windows devices.

Applications developed with Xamarin are *native*, which provides similar performance to those developed with Objective-C or Swift for iOS and Java or Kotlin for Android. Xamarin also provides facilities to directly invoke Objective-C, Java, C, and C++ libraries.

Xamarin applications are written in C# and use the .NET Base Class Library. They can share most of the code, with only a small portion needed to be platform-specific.

Detailed information about Xamarin is beyond the scope of this book. If you want to learn more about this implementation, you should use additional resources.

Assemblies in .NET

An assembly is a basic unit for deployment, versioning, and security. Assemblies come in two forms, either as an **executable file** (`.exe`) or a **dynamic-linked library** (`.dll`). An assembly is a collection of types, resources, and meta-information that forms a logical unit of functionality. Assemblies are loaded into memory only if needed. For .NET Framework applications, assemblies could either be located in the application private folder or shared in the Global Assembly Cache, provided they are strongly-named. For .NET Core applications, this latter solution is not available.

Each assembly contains a manifest that contains the following information:

- The identity of the assembly (such as name and version)
- A file table describing the files that make up the assembly, such as other assemblies or resources (such as images)
- A list of assembly references that contains the external dependencies that the application needs

The identity of an assembly is composed of several parts:

- The **name** of the file where the name should be compliant with the Windows Portable Executable file format
- A **version** of the form of `major.minor.build.revision`, such as 1.12.3.0
- The **culture** that should be locale-agnostic except in the case of satellite assemblies (which are locale-aware assemblies)
- The **public key token**, which is a 64-bit hash of the private key used to sign the assembly; signed assemblies have strong names that are meant to provide a unique name

You will learn more about assemblies in *Chapter 11*, *Reflection and Dynamic Programming*.

Global Assembly Cache (GAC)

As mentioned in the preceding section, .NET Framework assemblies could either be stored *locally*, in the application folder, or in *GAC*. This is a machine-wide code cache that enables the sharing of assemblies between applications. Since the release of .NET Framework 4, the default location for the GAC is `%windir%\Microsoft.NET\assembly`; however, previously, the location was `%windir%\assembly`. GAC also enables storing multiple versions of the same assembly, which is not actually possible in a private folder, since you cannot store multiple files with the same name in the same folder.

To deploy an assembly to the GAC, you could use the Windows SDK utility tool called `gacutil.exe` or an installer that is able to work with the GAC. However, an assembly must have a strong name to be deployed to the GAC. A **strong-name assembly** is an assembly cryptographically signed with a private key that corresponds to a public key distributed with the assembly. You can sign an assembly using the **Strong Name tool** (`sn.exe`).

> **Note**
>
> For more details about how to sign an assembly, please refer to the following document, which describes how to sign an assembly with a strong name: `https://docs.microsoft.com/en-us/dotnet/framework/app-domains/how-to-sign-an-assembly-with-a-strong-name`.

When you add an assembly to GAC, integrity checks are performed on all of the files contained by the assembly. This is done to ensure that the assembly has not been tampered with. The cryptographic signing ensures that any change to any of the files in the assembly invalidates the signature and only someone that has access to the private key can resign the assembly.

Runtime package store

The GAC is not used for .NET Core assemblies. These are assemblies that can run on any platform and not just Windows. Prior to .NET Core 2.0, the only option for deployment was the application folder. Since version 2.0, however, it is possible to package and deploy applications against a known set of packages that exist in the target environment. This enables faster deployment and lower disk space requirements. Typically, this store is available at `/usr/local/share/dotnet/store` on macOS and Linux and `C:/Program Files/dotnet/store` on Windows.

The packages available in the runtime package store are listed in a target manifest file that is used while publishing an application. This file has a format that is compatible with the project file format (`.csproj`).

Detailing the targeting process is beyond the scope of this chapter, but you can learn more about the runtime package store by visiting the following link: `https://docs.microsoft.com/en-us/dotnet/core/deploying/runtime-store`.

Understanding the basic structure of a C# program

So far, we have learned about the basics of C# and the .NET runtime. In this section, we will write a simple C# program so that we can have a short introduction to some of the key elements of a simple program.

Before writing a program, you must create a project. For this purpose, you should use Visual Studio 2019; alternatively, you could use any other version for most of the content of this book. The source code accompanying this book was written in Visual Studio 2019 using .NET Core projects. When creating a new project, select **Console App (.NET Core)** and call the project `chapter_01`:

Figure 1.7 – Select the Console App (.NET Core) template when creating a new project in Visual Studio

A project with the following content will be automatically created for you:

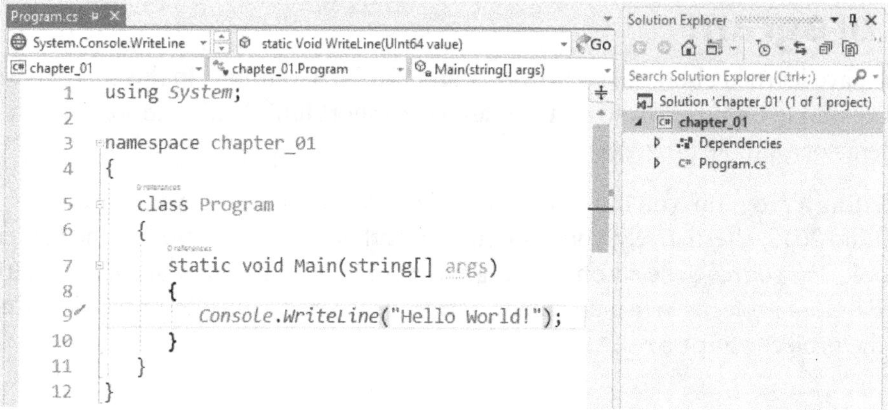

Figure 1.8 – Screenshot of Visual Studio and the code generated for the selected template

This code represents the minimum a C# program must contain: a single file with a single class having a single method called `Main`. You can compile and run the project and the message **Hello World!** will be displayed to the console. However, to better understand it, let's look at the actual C# program.

The first line of the program (`using System;`) declares the namespaces that we want to use in this program. A namespace contains types and the one used here is the core namespace of the base class library.

On the following line, we define our own namespace, called `chapter_01`, which contains our code. A namespace is introduced with the `namespace` keyword. In this namespace, we define a single class called `Program`. A class is introduced with the `class` keyword. Furthermore, this class contains a single method called `Main`, with a single argument that is an array of strings called `args`. The code within namespaces, types (whether it's a class, struct, interface, or enum), and methods is always provided within curly braces { }. This method is the entry point of the program, which means it's where the execution of a program starts. A C# program must have one and only one `Main` method.

The `Main` method contains a single line of code. It uses the `System.Console.WriteLine` static method to print a text to the console. A static method is a method that belongs to a type and not an instance of the type, which means you do not call it through an object. The `Main` method is itself a static method, but furthermore, it is a special method. Every C# program must have a single static method called `Main`, which is considered the entry point of the program and the first to be called when the execution of the program begins.

Throughout the next chapters, we will learn about namespaces, types, methods, and other key features of C#.

Summary

In this chapter, we looked in short at the history of C#. We then explored the basic concepts behind the CLI and its constituents, such as CTS, CLS, CIL, and VES. Then, we looked at the .NET family of frameworks and briefly discussed .NET Framework, .NET Core, and Xamarin. We also talked about assemblies, the GAC (for .NET Framework) and the runtime package store (for .NET Core). Finally, we wrote our first C# program and looked at its structure.

This overview of the frameworks and the runtime will help you to understand the context of writing and executing a C# program and will provide a good background when we talk about more advanced features such as reflection, assembly loading, or look at the .NET Core framework.

In the next chapter, we will explore the basic data types and operators in C# and learn how to work with them.

Test what you learned

1. When was C# first released and what is the current version of the language?
2. What is the Common Language Infrastructure? What are its main components?
3. What is the Common Intermediate Language and how is it related to the Just-In-Time compiler?
4. What tools can you use to disassembly and explore the assemblies produced by the compiler?
5. What is the Common Language Runtime?
6. What is the Base Class Library?
7. What are currently the major .NET frameworks? Which one will no longer be developed?
8. What is an assembly? What constitutes the identity of an assembly?
9. What is the Global Assembly Cache? What about the runtime package store?
10. What is the minimum a C# program must contain to be executed?

2

Data Types and Operators

In the previous chapter, we learned about .NET Framework and understood the basic structure of a C# program. In this chapter, we will learn about data types and objects in C#. Alongside control statements, which we will explore in the next chapter, these are the building blocks of every program. We will discuss built-in data types, explain the difference between value types and reference types, and learn how to convert between types. We will also discuss the operators defined by the language as we move on.

The following topics will be covered in this chapter:

- Basic built-in data types
- Variables and constants
- Reference types and value types
- Nullable type
- Arrays
- Type conversion
- Operators

By the end of this chapter, you will be able to write a simple C# program using the aforementioned language features.

Basic data types

In this section, we will explore the basic data types. The **Common Language Infrastructure** (**CLI**) defines a set of standard types and operations that are supported by all programming languages targeting the CLI. These data types are provided in the System namespace. All of them, however, have a *C# alias*. These aliases are keywords in the C# language, which means they can only be used in the context of their designated purpose and not elsewhere, such as variable, class, or method names. The C# name and the .NET name, along with a short description of each type, are listed in the following table (listed alphabetically by the C# name):

C# type name	.NET type name	Description
bool	System.Boolean	Represents a Boolean value. It can be set to true or false
byte	System.Byte	Represents an 8-bit unsigned integer
char	System.Char	Represents a UTF-16 code unit
decimal	System.Decimal	128-bit data type suitable for financial calculations
double	System.Double	Double-precision floating-point value
float	System.Single	Single precision floating-point value
int	System.Int32	Represents a 32-bit integer value
long	System.Int64	Represents a 64-bit integer value
sbyte	System.SByte	Represents an 8-bit signed integer
short	System.Int16	Represents a 16-bit signed integer
uint	System.UInt32	Represents a 32-bit unsigned integer
ulong	System.UInt64	Represents a 64-bit unsigned integer
ushort	System.UInt16	Represents a 16-bit unsigned integer

The types listed in this table are called **simple types** or **primitive types**. Apart from these, there are two more built-in types:

C# type name	.NET type name	Description
object	System.Object	The base type for all reference and value types
string	System.String	A string of UTF-16 code units

Let's explore all of the primitive types in detail in the following sections.

The integral types

C# supports eight integer types that represent various ranges of integral numbers. The bits and range of each of them are shown in the following table:

Type	Bits	Range
byte	8	0 to 255
sbyte	8	-128 to 127
short	16	-32,768 to 32,767
ushort	16	0 to 65,535
int	32	-2,147,483,648 to 2,147,483,647
uint	32	0 to 4,294,967,295
long	64	-9,223,372,036,854,775,808 to 9,223,372,036,854,775,807
ulong	64	0 to 18,446,744,073,709,551,615

As shown in the preceding table, C# defines both signed and unsigned integer types. The major difference between signed and unsigned integers is the way in which the high order bit is read. In the case of a signed integer, the high order bit is considered the sign flag. If the sign flag is 0, then the number is positive but if the sign flag is 1, then the number is negative.

The default value of all integral types is 0. All of these types define two constants called MinValue and MaxValue, which provide the minimum and maximum value of the type.

Integral literals, which are numbers that appear directly in code (such as 0, -42, and so on), can be specified as decimal, hexadecimal, or binary literals. Decimal literals do not require any suffix. Hexadecimal literals are prefixed with 0x or 0X, and binary literals are prefixed with 0b or 0B. An underscore (_) can be used as a digit separator with all numeric literals. Examples of such literals are shown in the following snippet:

```
int dec = 32;
int hex = 0x2A;
int bin = 0b_0010_1010;
```

An integral value without any suffix is inferred by the compiler as int. To indicate a long integer, use l or L for a signed 64-bit integer and ul or UL for an unsigned 64-bit integer.

The floating-point types

The floating-point types are used to represent numbers having fractional components. C# defines two floating-point types, as shown in the following table:

Type	Bits	Range
float	32	1.5E-45 to 3.4E+38
double	64	5E-324 to 1.7E+308

The `float` type represents a 32-bit, single-precision floating-point number, whereas `double` represents a 64-bit, double-precision floating-point number. These types are implementations of the **IEEE Standard for Floating-Point Arithmetic (IEEE 754),** which is a standard established by the **Institute of Electrical and Electronics Engineers (IEEE)** in 1985 for floating-point arithmetic.

The default value for floating-point types is 0. These types also define two constants called `MinValue` and `MaxValue` that provide the minimum and maximum value of the type. However, these types also provide constants that represent not-a-number (`System.Double.NaN`) and infinity (`System.Double.NegativeInfinity` and `System.Double.PositiveInfinity`). The following code listing shows several variables initialized with floating-point values:

```
var a = 42.99;
float b = 19.50f;
System.Double c = -1.23;
```

By default, a non-integer number such as `42.99` is considered a double. If you want to specify this as a float type, then you need to suffix the value with the `f` or `F` character, such as in `42.99f` or `42.99F`. Alternatively, you can also explicitly indicate a double literal with the `d` or `D` suffix, such as in `42.99d` or `42.99D`.

Floating-point types store fractional parts as inverse powers of two. For this reason, they can only represent exact values such as `10`, `10.25`, `10.5`, and so on. Other numbers, such as `1.23` or `19.99`, cannot be represented exactly and are only an approximation. Even if `double` has 15 decimal digits of precision, as compared to only 7 for `float`, precision loss starts to accumulate when performing repeated calculations.

This makes `double` and `float` difficult or even inappropriate to use in certain types of applications, such as financial applications, where precision is key. For this purpose, the `decimal` type is provided.

The decimal type

The `decimal` type can represent up to 28 decimal places. The details for the decimal type are shown in the following table:

Type	Bits	Range
decimal	128	1E-28 to 7.9E+28

The default value for the decimal type is 0. `MinValue` and `MaxValue` constants that define the minimum and maximum value of the type are also available. A `decimal` literal can be specified using the m or M suffix as shown in the following snippet:

```
decimal a = 42.99m;
var b = 12.45m;
System.Decimal c = 100.75M;
```

It is important to note that the `decimal` type minimizes errors during rounding but does not eliminate the need for rounding. For instance, the result of the operation 1m / 3 * 3 is not 1 but 0.9999999999999999999999999999. On the other hand, `Math.Round(1m / 3 * 3)` yields the value 1.

The `decimal` type is designed for use in applications where precision is key. Floats and doubles are much faster types (because they use binary math, which is faster to compute), while the `decimal` type is slower (as the name implies, it uses decimal math, which is slower to compute). The `decimal` type can be an order of magnitude slower than the `double` type. Financial applications, where small inaccuracies can accumulate to important values over repeated computations, are a typical use case for the `decimal` type. In such applications, speed is not important, but precision is.

The char type

The character type is used to represent a 16-bit Unicode character. Unicode defines a character set that is intended to represent the characters of most languages in the world. Characters are represented by enclosing them in single quotation marks (' '). Examples of this include 'A', 'B', 'c' and '\u0058':

Type	Bits	Range
char	16	U+0000 - U+FFFF

Character values can be literals, hexadecimal escape sequences that have the form `'\xdddd'`, or Unicode representations that have the form `'\udddd'` (where dddd is a 16 hexadecimal value). The following listing shows several examples:

```
char a = 'A';
char b = '\x0065';
char c = '\u15FE';
```

The default value for the `char` type is decimal 0, or its equivalents, `'\0'`, `'\x0000'`, or `'\u0000'`.

The bool type

C# uses the `bool` keyword to represent the Boolean type. It can have two values, `true` or `false`, as shown in the following table:

Type	Range
bool	true or false

The default value for the bool type is `false`. Unlike other languages (such as C++), integer values or any other values do not implicitly convert into the `bool` type. A Boolean variable can be either assigned a Boolean literal (`true` or `false`) or an expression that evaluates to `bool`.

The string type

A string is an array of characters. In C#, the type for representing a string is called `string` and is an alias for the .NET `System.String`. You can use any of these two types interchangeably. Internally, a string contains a read-only collection of `char` objects. This makes strings immutable, which means that you cannot change a string but need to create a new one every time you want to modify the content of an existing string. Strings are not *null-terminated* (unlike other languages such as C++) and can contain any number of null characters (`'\0'`). The string length will contain the total number of the `char` objects.

Strings can be declared and initialized in a variety of ways, as shown here:

```
string s1;                         // unitialized
string s2 = null;                  // initialized with null
string s3 = String.Empty;          // empty string

string s4 = "hello world";         // initialized with text
```

```
var s5 = "hello world";
System.String s6 = "hello world";

char[] letters = { 'h', 'e', 'l', 'l', 'o'};
string s7 = new string(letters); // from an array of chars
```

It is important to note that the only situation when you use the `new` operator to create a string object is when you initialize it from an array of characters.

As mentioned before, strings are immutable. Although you have access to the characters of the string, you can read them, but you cannot change them:

```
char c = s4[0];    // OK
s4[0] = 'H';       // error
```

The following are the methods that seem to be modifying a string:

- `Remove()`: This removes a part of the string.

- `ToUpper()`/`ToLower()`: This converts all of the characters into uppercase or lowercase.

Neither of these methods modifies the existing string, but instead returns a new one.

In the following example, `s6` is the string defined earlier, `s8` will contain `hello`, `s9` will contain `HELLO WORLD`, and `s6` will continue to contain `hello world`:

```
var s8 = s6.Remove(5);       // hello
var s9 = s6.ToUpper();       // HELLO WORLD
```

You can convert any built-in type, such as integer or floating-point numbers, into a string using the `ToString()` method. This is actually a virtual method of the `System.Object` type, that is, the base class for any .NET type. By overriding this method, any type can provide a way to serialize an object to a string:

```
int i = 42;
double d = 19.99;
var s1 = i.ToString();
var s2 = d.ToString();
```

Strings can be composed in several ways:

- It can be done using the concatenating operator, +.

- Using the `Format()` method: The first argument of this method is the format, in which each parameter is indicated positionally with the index specified in curly braces, such as {0}, {1}, {2} and so on. Specifying an index beyond the number of arguments results in a runtime exception.

- Using string interpolation, which is practically a syntactic shortcut for using the `String.Format()` method: The string must be prefixed with $ and the arguments are specified directly in curly braces.

An example of all of these methods is shown here:

```
int i = 42;
string s1 = "This is item " + i.ToString();
string s2 = string.Format("This is item {0}", i);
string s3 = $"This is item {i}";
```

Some characters have a special meaning and are prefixed with a backslash (\). These are called escaped sequences. The following table lists all of them:

Escape sequence	Name	Unicode encoding
\'	Single quote	0x0027
\"	Double quote	0x0022
\\	Backslash	0x005C
\0	Null	0x0000
\a	Alert	0x0007
\b	Backspace	0x0008
\f	Form feed	0x000C
\n	New line	0x000A
\r	Carriage return	0x000A
\t	Horizontal tab	0x0009
\v	Vertical tab	0x000B
\u	UTF-16 escape sequence	\uHHHH (0000 - FFFF)
\U	UTF-32 escape sequence	\U00HHHHHH (000000 - 10FFFF)
\x	Unicode escape sequence with variable length	\xH[H][H][H] (0 - FFFF)

Escape sequences are necessary in certain cases, such as when you specify a Windows file path or when you need a text that spawns multiple lines. The following code shows several examples where escape sequences are used:

```
var s1 = "c:\\Program Files (x86)\\Windows Kits\\";
var s2 = "That was called a \"demo\"";
var s3 = "This text\nspawns multiple lines.";
```

You can, however, avoid using escape sequences by using verbatim strings. These are prefixed with the @ symbol. When the compiler encounters such a string, it does not interpret escape sequences. If you want to use quotation marks in a string when using verbatim strings, you must double them. The following sample shows the preceding examples rewritten with verbatim strings:

```
var s1 = @"c:\Program Files (x86)\Windows Kits\";
var s2 = @"That was called a ""demo""";
var s3 = @"This text
spawns multiple lines.";
```

Prior to C# 8, if you wanted to use string interpolation with verbatim strings, you had to first specify the $ symbol for string interpolation and then @ for verbatim strings. In C# 8, you can specify these two symbols in any order.

The object type

The `object` type is the base type for all other types in C#, even though you do not specify this explicitly, as we will see in the following chapters. The `object` keyword in C# is an alias for the .NET `System.Object` type. You can use these two interchangeably.

The `object` type provides some basic functionalities to all other classes in the form of several virtual methods that any derived class can override, if necessary. These methods are listed in the following table:

Method	Description
Equals()	Determines whether a specified object is equal to the current one
Finalize()	Allows an object to free resources and do other cleanup operations before it is reclaimed by the garbage collector
GetHashCode()	Retrieves a hash value for the current object to support the use of hash tables
ToString()	Returns a string that represents a serialization of the current object

Apart from these, the `object` class contains several other methods. An important one to note is the `GetType()` method, which is not virtual and which returns a `System.Type` object with information about the type of the current instance.

Another important thing to notice is the way the `Equals()` method works because its behavior is different for reference and value types. We have not covered these concepts yet but will do so later in this chapter. For the time being, keep in mind that, for reference types, this method performs reference equality; this means it checks whether the two variables point to the same object on the heap. For value types, it performs value equality; this means that the two variables are of the same type and that the public and private fields of the two objects are equal.

The `object` type is a reference type. The default value of a variable of the `object` type is `null`. However, a variable of the `object` type can be assigned any value of any type. When you assign a value type value to `object`, the operation is called **boxing**. The reverse operation of converting the value of `object` into a value type is called **unboxing**. This will be detailed in a later section in this chapter.

You will learn more about the `object` type and its methods throughout this book.

Variables

Variables are defined as a named memory location that can be assigned to a value. There are several types of variables, including the following:

- **Local variables**: These are variables that are defined within a method and their scope is local to that method.

- **Method parameters**: These are variables that hold the arguments passed to a method during a function call.

- **Class fields**: These are variables that are defined in the scope of the class and are accessible to all of the class methods and depending on the accessibility of the field to other classes too.

- **Array elements**: These are variables that refer to elements in an array.

In this section, we will refer to local variables, which are variables declared in the body of a function. Such variables are declared using the following syntax:

```
datatype variable_name;
```

In this statement, `datatype` is the data type of the variable and `variable_name` is the name of the variable. Here are several examples:

```
bool f;
char ch = 'x';
int a, b = 20, c = 42;

a = -1;
f = true;
```

In this example, `f` is an uninitialized `bool` variable. Uninitialized variables cannot be used in any expression. An attempt to do so will result in a compiler error. All variables must be initialized before they are used. A variable can be initialized when declared, such as with `ch`, `b`, and `c` in the preceding example, or at any later time, such as with `a` and `f`.

Multiple variables of the same type can be declared and initialized in a single statement, separated by a comma. This is exemplified in the preceding code snippet with the `int` variables `a`, `b`, and `c`.

Naming convention

There are several rules that must be followed for naming a variable:

- Variable names can consist of letters, digits, and underscore characters (_) only.

- You cannot use any special character other than underscore (_) when naming a variable. Consequently, *@sample*, *#tag*, *name%*, and so on are illegal variable names.

- The variable name must begin with a letter or an underscore character (_). The name of the variable cannot start with a digit. Therefore, `2small` as a variable name will throw a compile-time error.

- Variable names are case-sensitive. Therefore, `person` and `PERSON` are considered two different variables.

- A variable name cannot be any reserved keyword of C#. Hence `true`, `false`, `double`, `float`, `var`, and so on are illegal variable names. However, prefixing a keyword with @ enables the compiler to treat them as identifiers, rather than keywords. Therefore, variables names such as `@true`, `@return`, `@var` are allowed. These are called **verbatim identifiers**.

- Apart from the language rules that you must follow when naming variables, you should also make sure the names you choose are descriptive and easy to understand. You should always prefer that over short, abbreviated names that are hard to comprehend. There are various coding standards and naming conventions and you should adhere to one. These promote consistency and make the code easier to read, understand, and maintain.

When it comes to naming conventions, you should do the following when programming in C#:

- Use *pascal case* for classes, structures, enums, delegates, constructors, methods, properties, and constants. In Pascal case, each word in a name is capitalized; examples include `ConnectionString`, `UserGroup`, and `XmlReader`.
- Use *camel case* for fields, local variables, and method parameters. In camel case, the first word of a name is not capitalized, but all of the others are; examples include `userId`, `xmlDocument`, and `uiControl`.
- Do not use *underscore* in identifiers unless to prefix private fields, such as in `_firstName`, and `_lastName`.
- Prefer *descriptive name* over abbreviations. For example, prefer `labelText` over `lbltxt` or `employeeId` over `eid`.

You can learn more about coding standards and naming conventions in C# by consulting additional resources.

Implicity-typed variables

As we have seen in previous examples, we need to specify the type of a variable when we are declaring it. However, C# provides us with another way to declare variables that allows the compiler to infer the variable type based on the value assigned to it during initialization. These are known as **implicitly typed variables**.

We can create an implicitly typed variable using the `var` keyword. Such variables must always be initialized on the declaration because the compiler infers the type of the variable from the value that it is initialized with. Here is an example:

```
var a = 10;
```

Since the `a` variable is initialized with an integer literal, `a` is considered as an `int` variable by the compiler.

When declaring variables with `var`, you must keep in mind the following:

- An implicitly typed variable must be initialized to a value at the time of declaration, otherwise, the compiler has no reference to infer the variable type and it results in a compile-time error.

- You cannot initialize it to null.

- The variable type cannot be changed once it is declared and initialized.

> **Information box**
>
> The `var` keyword is not a datatype but a placeholder for an actual type. Using `var` to declare variables is useful when the type name is long and you want to avoid typing a lot (for example, `Dictionary<string, KeyValuePair<int, string>>`) or you do not care about the actual type, only the value.

Now that you learned how you can declare variables, let's look at a key concept: the scope of variables.

Understanding the scope and lifetime of variables

A **scope** in C# is defined as a block between an opening curly brace and its corresponding closing curly brace. The scope defines the visibility and lifetime of a variable. A variable can be accessed only within the scope in which it is defined. A variable that is defined in a particular scope is not visible to the code outside that scope.

Let's understand this with the help of an example:

```
class Program
{
    static void Main(string[] args)
    {
        for (int i = 1; i < 10; i++)
        {
            Console.WriteLine(i);
        }

        i = 20; // i is out of scope
    }
}
```

In this example, the i variable is defined inside the for loop, hence it cannot be accessed outside the for loop as it goes out of scope once the control exits the loop. You will learn more about the for loop in the next chapter.

We can also have nested scopes. This means a variable defined in a scope can be accessed in another scope that is enclosed in that scope. However, the variables from the outer scope are visible to the inner scope but the inner scope variables are not accessible in the outer scope. The C# compiler won't allow you to create two variables with the same name within a scope.

Let's extend the code in the previous example to understand this:

```csharp
class Program
{
    static void Main(string[] args)
    {
        int a = 5;
        for (int i = 1; i < 10; i++)
        {
            char a = 'w';                    // compiler error
            if (i % 2 == 0)
            {
                Console.WriteLine(i + a); // a is within the
                                          // scope of Main
            }
        }

        i = 20;                              // i is out of scope
    }
}
```

Here, the integer variable a is defined outside the for loop but within the scope of Main. Hence, it can be accessed within the for loop as it is in the scope of this. However, the i variable, which is defined inside the for loop, cannot be accessed inside the scope of Main.

If we try to declare another variable with the same name in the scope, we will get a compile-time error. Consequently, we cannot declare a character variable a inside the for loop as we already have an integer variable with the same name.

Understanding constants

There are some scenarios in which we do not want to change the value of a variable after it is initialized. Examples can include mathematical constants (pi, Euler's number, and so on), physical constants (Avogadro's number, the Boltzmann constant, and so on), or any application-specific constants (the maximum allowed number of logins, the maximum number of retries for a failed operation, status codes, and many others). C# provides us with constant variables for this purpose. Once defined, the value of a constant variable cannot be changed during its scope. If you try to change the value of a constant variable after it is initialized, the compiler will throw an error.

To make a variable constant, we need to prefix it with the `const` keyword. The constant variables must be initialized at the time of declaration. Here is an example of an integer constant initialized with the value `42`:

```
const int a = 42;
```

It is important to note that only the built-in types can be used to declare constants. User-defined types cannot be used for this purpose.

Reference types and value types

The data types in C# are divided into value types and reference types. There are several important differences between these two, such as **copy semantics**. We will look at these in detail in the following sections.

Value types

A variable of a value type contains the value directly. When a value type variable is assigned from another, the stored value is copied. The primitive data types we have seen earlier are all value types. All user-defined types declared as structures (with the `struct` keyword) are value types. Although all types are implicitly derived from the `object`, type value types do not support explicit inheritance, which is a topic discussed in *Chapter 4, Understanding the Various User-Defined Types*.

Let's see an example here:

```
int a = 20;
DateTime dt = new DateTime(2019, 12, 25);
```

Value types are typically stored on the stack in memory, although this is an implementation detail and not a characteristic of value types. If you assign the value of a value type to another variable, then the value is copied to the new variable and changing one variable will not affect the other:

```
int a = 20;
int b = a;   // b is 20
a = 42;      // a is 42, b is 20
```

In the preceding example, the value of a is initialized to 20 and then assigned to the variable b. At this point, both variables contain the same value. However, after assigning the value 42 to the a variable, the value of b remains unchanged. This is shown, conceptually, in the following diagram:

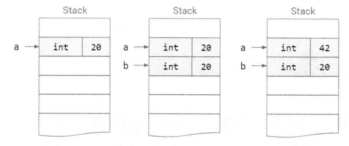

Figure 2.1 – A conceptual representation of the changes in the stack during the execution of the previous code

Here, you can see that, initially, a storage location corresponding to the a integer was allocated on the stack and had the value 20. Then, a second storage location was allocated and the value from the first was copied to it. Then, we changed the value of the a variable and therefore, the value available in the first storage location. The second one was left untouched.

Reference types

A variable of a reference type does not contain the value directly but a reference to a memory location where the actual value is stored. The built-in data types object and string are reference types. Arrays, interfaces, delegates, and any user-defined type defined as a class are also called **reference types**. The following example shows several variables of different reference types:

```
int[]  a = new int[10];
string s = "sample";
object o = new List<int>();
```

Reference types are stored on the heap. Variables of a reference type can be assigned the null value that indicates that the variable does not store a reference to an instance of an object. When trying to use a variable assigned the null value the result is a runtime exception. When a variable of a reference type is assigned a value, the reference to the actual memory location of the object is copied and not the value of the object itself.

In the following example, a1 is an array of two integers. The reference to the array is copied to the a2 variable. When the content of the array changes, the changes are visible both through a1 and a2, since both these variables refer to the same array:

```
int[] a1 = new int[] { 42, 43 };
int[] a2 = a1;      // a2 is { 42, 43 }
a1[0] = 0;          // a1 is { 0, 43 }, a2 is { 0, 43 }
```

This example is explained conceptually in the following diagram:

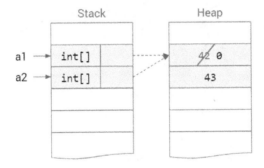

Figure 2.2 – The conceptual representation of the stack and the heap during the execution of the preceding snippet

You can see in this diagram that a1 and a2 are variables on the stack pointing to the same array of integers allocated on the heap. When the first element of the array is changed through the a1 variable, the changes are automatically visible to the a2 variable because a1 and a2 refer to the same object.

Although the string type is a reference type, it appears to behave differently. Take the following example:

```
string s1 = "help";
string s2 = s1;     // s2 is "help"
s1 = "demo";        // s1 is "demo", s2 is "help"
```

Here, s1 is initialized with the "help" literal and then the reference to the actual array heap object is copied to the s2 variable. At this point, they both refer to the "help" string. However, s1 is later assigned a new string, "demo". At this point, s2 will continue to refer to the "help" string. The reason for this is that strings are immutable. That means when you modify a string object, a new string is created, and the variable will receive the reference to the new string object. Any other variables referring to the old string will continue to do so.

Boxing and unboxing

We briefly mentioned boxing and unboxing earlier in this chapter when we talked about the object type. Boxing is the process of storing a value type inside an object, and unboxing is the opposite operation of converting the value of an object to a value type. Let's understand this with the help of an example:

```
int a = 42;
object o = a;    // boxing

o = 43;
int b = (int)o; // unboxing

Console.WriteLine(x);   // 42
Console.WriteLine(y);   // 43
```

In the preceding code, a is a variable of the type integer that is initialized with the value 42. Being a value type, the integer value 42 is stored on the stack. On the other hand, o is a variable of type object. This is a reference type. That means it only contains a reference to a heap memory location where the actual object is stored. So, when a is assigned to o, the process called **boxing** occurs.

During the boxing process an object is allocated on the heap, the value of a (which is 42) is copied to it, and then a reference to this object is assigned to the o variable. When we later assigned the value 43 to o, only the boxed object changes and not a. Lastly, we copy the value of the object referred by o to a new variable called b. This will have the value 43 and, being an int, is also stored on the stack.

The process described here is shown graphically in the following diagram:

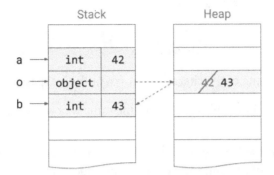

Figure 2.3 – Conceptual representation of the stack showing the boxing and unboxing
process described previously

Now that you understand the difference between value and reference types, let's look at
the topic of nullable types.

Nullable types

Reference types have the default value `null`, which indicates that a variable is not
assigned to the instance of any object. Value types do not have such an option. However,
there are cases when no value is a valid value for a value type too. To represent such cases,
you can use a nullable type.

A **nullable type** is an instance of `System.Nullable<T>`, a generic value type that can
represent the values of an underlying `T` type, which can only be a value type, as well as an
additional `null` value. The following sample shows a few examples:

```
Nullable<int> a;
Nullable<int> b = null;
Nullable<int> c = 42;
```

You can use the shorthand syntax, `T?`, instead of `Nullable<T>`; these two are
interchangeable. The following examples are alternatives for the preceding ones:

```
int? a;
int? b = null;
int? c = 42;
```

You can use the `HasValue` property to check whether a nullable type object has a value, and `Value` to access the underlying value:

```
if (c.HasValue)
    Console.WriteLine(c.Value);
```

The following is a list of some of the characteristics of nullable types:

- You assign values to a nullable type object the same way you would assign to the underlying type.

- You can use the `GetValueOrDefault()` method to get either the assigned value or the default value of the underlying type if no value is assigned.

- Boxing is performed on the underlying type. If the nullable type object has not assigned any value, the result of boxing is a `null` object.

- You can use the null-coalescing operator, `??`, to access the value of the object of a nullable type (for example, `int d = c ?? -1;`).

In C# 8, nullable reference types and non-nullable reference types have been introduced. That is a feature that you must opt for in the project properties. It allows you to make sure that only objects of reference types that are declared nullable, using the `T?` syntax can be assigned the `null` value. Attempts to do so on non-nullable reference types will result in a compiler warning (not an error, because that has the potential to affect large portions of existing code):

```
string? s1 = null; // OK, nullable type
string s2 = null;  // error, non-nullable type
```

You will learn more about nullable reference types in *Chapter 15, New Features of C# 8.*

Arrays

An array is a data structure that holds multiple values (including zero or a single one) of the same data type. It is a fixed-size sequence of homogeneous elements that are stored in contiguous memory locations. Arrays in C# are zero-indexed, meaning that the position of the first element of an array is zero and the position of the last element of the array is a total number of elements minus one.

The array type is a reference type and therefore arrays are allocated on the heap. The default value for the elements of numeric arrays is zero and for arrays of reference types, the default value is `null`. The type of the elements of an array can be of any type, including another array type.

Arrays in C# can be one-dimensional, multi-dimensional, or jagged. Let's explore these in detail.

One-dimensional arrays

A one-dimensional array can be defined using the syntax datatype[] variable_name. Arrays can be initialized when they are declared. If an array variable is not initialized, its value is null. You can specify the number of elements of the array when you initialize it, or you can skip this and let the compiler infer it from the initialization expression. The following sample shows various ways of declaring and initializing arrays:

```
int[] arr1;
int[] arr2 = null;
int[] arr3 = new int[6];
int[] arr4 = new int[] { 1, 1, 2, 3, 5, 8 };
int[] arr5 = new int[6] { 1, 1, 2, 3, 5, 8 };
int[] arr6 = { 1, 1, 2, 3, 5, 8 };
```

In this example, arr1 and arr2 have the value null. arr3 is an array of six integer elements all set to 0 because no initialization was provided. arr4, arr5, and arr6 are arrays of six integers, all containing the same values.

Once initialized, the size of the array cannot be changed. If you need to do so, you must either create a new array object or instead use a variable-size container, such as List<T>, which we will look at in *Chapter 7, Collections*.

You can access the elements of the array using the indexer, or with an enumerator. The following snippets are equivalent:

```
for(int i = 0; i < arr6.Length; ++i)
  Console.WriteLine(arr6[i]);

foreach(int element in arr6)
  Console.WriteLine(element);
```

Although the effect of these two loops is the same, there is a subtle difference—using an enumerator does not make it possible to modify the elements of the array. Accessing the elements by their index using the index operator does provide write access to the elements. Using an enumerator is possible because array types derive implicitly from the base type, System.Array, which implements IEnumerable and IEnumerable<T>.

This is shown in the following example:

```
for (int i = 0; i < arr6.Length; ++i)
    arr6[i] *= 2;   // OK

foreach (int element in arr6)
    element *= 2;   // error
```

In the first loop, we access the elements of the array by their index and can modify them. However, in the second loop, an iterator is used, and this provides read-only access to the elements. Trying to modify them produces a compile-time error.

Multi-dimensional arrays

A multi-dimensional array is an array with more than one dimension. It is also called a **rectangular array**. This can be, for instance, a two-dimensional array (a matrix) or a three-dimensional array (a cube). The maximum number of dimensions is **32**.

A two-dimensional array can be defined using the following syntax: `datatype[,] variable_name;`. Multi-dimensional arrays are declared and initialized in a similar fashion with single-dimensional arrays. You can specify the rank (which is the number of elements) of each dimension or you can leave it to the compiler to infer it from an initialization expression. The following snippet shows different ways of declaring and initializing two-dimensional arrays:

```
int[,] arr1;
arr1 = new int[2, 3] { { 1, 2, 3 }, { 4, 5, 6 } };
int[,] arr2 = null;
int[,] arr3 = new int[2,3];
int[,] arr4 = new int[,] { { 1, 2, 3 }, { 4, 5, 6 } };
int[,] arr5 = new int[2,3] { { 1, 2, 3 }, { 4, 5, 6 } };
int[,] arr6 = { { 1, 2, 3 }, { 4, 5, 6 } };
```

In this example, arr1 is initially null and then assigned a reference to an array of two rows and three columns. Similarly, arr2 is also null. On the other hand, arr3, arr4, arr5, and arr6 are arrays of two rows and three columns; arr3 has all of the elements set to zero, while the others are initialized with the specified values. The arrays in this example have the following form:

```
1 2 3
4 5 6
```

You can retrieve the number of elements of each dimension using the `GetLength()` or `GetLongLength()` methods (the first returns a 32-bit integer, the second a 64-bit integer). The following example prints the content of the `arr6` array to the console:

```
for (int i = 0; i < arr6.GetLength(0); ++i)
{
    for (int j = 0; j < arr6.GetLength(1); ++j)
    {
        Console.Write($"{arr6[i, j]} ");
    }
    Console.WriteLine();
}
```

Arrays with more than two dimensions are created and handled in a similar way. The following example shows how to declare and initialize a three-dimensional array of *4 x 3 x 2* elements:

```
int[,,] arr7 = new int[4, 3, 2]
{
    { { 11, 12}, { 13, 14}, {15, 16 } },
    { { 21, 22}, { 23, 24}, {25, 26 } },
    { { 31, 32}, { 33, 34}, {35, 36 } },
    { { 41, 42}, { 43, 44}, {45, 46 } }
};
```

Another form of multi-dimensional arrays is the so-called **jagged array**. We will learn about this next.

Jagged arrays

Jagged arrays are arrays of arrays. These consist of other arrays, and each array inside a jagged array can be of a different size. We can declare a two-dimensional jagged array, for instance, using the syntax `datatype [] [] variable_name;`. The following snippet shows various examples of declaring and initializing jagged arrays:

```
int[][] arr1;
int[][] arr2 = null;
int[][] arr3 = new int[2][];
arr3[0] = new int[3];
arr3[1] = new int[] { 1, 1, 2, 3, 5, 8 };
int[][] arr4 = new int[][]
{
    new int[] { 1, 2, 3 },
    new int[] { 1, 1, 2, 3, 5, 8 }
```

```
};
int [] [] arr5 =
{
    new int [] { 1, 2, 3 },
    new int [] { 1, 1, 2, 3, 5, 8 }
};
int [] [,] arr6 = new int [] [,]
{
    new int [,] { { 1, 2}, { 3, 4 } },
    new int [,] { {11, 12, 13}, { 14, 15, 16} }
};
```

In this example, arr1 and arr2 are both set to null. On the other hand, arr3 is an array of two arrays. Its first element is set to an array of three elements that are initialized with zero; its second element is set to an array of six elements initialized from the provided values.

The arr4 and arr5 arrays are equivalent, but arr5 uses the shorthand syntax for array initialization. arr6 mixes jagged arrays with multi-dimensional arrays. It is an array of two arrays, the first one being a two-dimensional array of *2x2*, and the second a two-dimensional array of *2x3* elements.

The elements of a jagged array can be accessed using the arr [i] [j] syntax (this example is for two-dimensional arrays). The following snippet shows how to print the content of the arr5 array shown earlier:

```
for(int i = 0; i < arr5.Length; ++i)
{
    for(int j = 0; j < arr5[i].Length; ++j)
    {
        Console.Write($"{arr5[i][j]} ");
    }
    Console.WriteLine();
}
```

Now that we have looked at the type of arrays we can use in C#, let's move to another important topic, which is conversion between various data types.

Type conversion

Sometimes we need to convert one data type into another, and that is where **type conversion** comes in picture. Type conversion can be classified into several categories:

- Implicit type conversion

- Explicit type conversion

- User-defined conversions

- Conversions with helper classes

Let's explore these in detail.

Implicit type conversion

For built-in numeric types, when we assign the value of a variable to one of another data type, implicit type conversion occurs if both types are compatible and the range of destination type is more than that of the source type. For example, int and float are compatible types. Therefore, we can assign an integer variable to a variable of the float type. Similarly, the double type is large enough to hold values from any other numerical type, including long and float, as shown in the following example:

```
int i = 10;
float f = i;

long l = 7195467872;
double d = l;
```

The following table shows the implicit type conversion between numeric types in C#:

Source type	Target type
sbyte	short, int, long, float, double, decimal
byte	short, ushort, int, uint, long, ulong, float, double, decimal
char	ushort, int, uint, long, ulong, float, double, decimal
short	int, long, float, double, decimal
ushort	int, uint, long, ulong, float, double, decimal
int	long, float, double, decimal
uint	long, ulong, float, double, decimal
long	float, double, decimal
ulong	float, double, decimal
float	double

There are several things to note about implicit numeric conversions:

- You can convert any integral type to any floating-point type.

- There is no implicit conversion to the `char`, `byte`, and `sbyte` types.

- There is no implicit conversion from `double` and `decimal`; this includes no implicit conversion from `decimal` to `double` or `float`.

For reference types, the implicit conversion is always possible between a class and one of its direct or indirect base classes or interfaces. Here is an example with an implicit conversion from `string` to `object`:

```
string s = "example";
object o = s;
```

The `object` type (which is an alias for `System.Object`) is the base class for all .NET types, including `string` (which is an alias for `System.String`). Therefore, an implicit conversion from `string` into `object` exists.

Explicit type conversion

When an implicit conversion between two types is not possible because there is a risk of losing information (such as while assigning the value of a 32-bit integer to a 16-bit integer), explicit type conversion is necessary. **Explicit type** conversion is also called a **cast**. To perform casting, we need to specify the target data type in parentheses in front of the source variable.

For example, `double` and `int` are *incompatible types*. Consequently, we need to do an explicit type conversion between them. In the following example, we assign a `double` value (d) to an integer using explicit type conversion. However, while doing this conversion, the fractional part of the `double` variable will be truncated. Hence, the value of i will be `12`:

```
double d = 12.34;
int i = (int)d;
```

The following table shows the list of predefined explicit conversions between numeric types in C#:

Source type	Target type
`sbyte`	`byte, ushort, uint, ulong, char`
`byte`	`sbyte, char`
`dhort`	`sbyte, byte, ushort, uint, ulong, char`
`ushort`	`sbyte, byte, short, char`
`int`	`sbyte, byte, short, ushort, uint, ulong, char`
`uint`	`sbyte, byte,  short,  ushort,  int,  char`
`long`	`sbyte, byte, short, ushort, int, uint, ulong, char`
`ulong`	`sbyte, byte, short, ushort, int, uint, long, char`
`char`	`sbyte, byte, short`
`float`	`sbyte, byte, short, ushort, int, uint, long, ulong, char, decimal`
`double`	`sbyte, byte, short, ushort, int, uint, long, ulong, char, float, decimal`
`decimal`	`sbyte, byte, short, ushort, int, uint, long, ulong, char, float, double`

There are several things to note about explicit numeric conversions:

- An explicit conversion may result in precision loss or in throwing an exception, such as `OverflowException`.

- When converting from an integral type to another integral type, the result depends on the so-called **checked context** and may result either in a successful conversion, which may discard extra most-significant bytes, or in an overflow exception.

- When you convert a floating-point type to an integral type, the value is rounded toward zero to the nearest integral value. The operation may, however, also result in an overflow exception.

C# statements can execute either in a *checked* or *unchecked* context, which is control either with the `check` and `unchecked` keywords or with the compiler option, `-checked`. When none of these are specified, the context is considered unchecked for non-constant expressions. For constant expressions, which can be evaluated at compile time, the default context is always checked. In a checked context, overflow checking is enabled for integral-type arithmetic operations and conversions. In an unchecked context, these checks are suppressed. When overflow checking is enabled and overflow occurs, the runtime throws a `System.OverflowException` exception.

For reference types, an explicit cast is required when you want to convert from a base class or interface into a derived class. The following example shows a cast from an `object` to a `string` value:

```
string s = "example";
object o = s;            // implicit conversion
string r = (string)o;    // explicit conversion
```

The conversion from `string` into `object` is performed implicitly. However, the opposite requires an explicit conversion in the `(string)o` form, as shown in the preceding snippet.

User-defined type conversions

A user-defined conversion can define an implicit or explicit conversion or both from one type into another. The type that defines these conversions must be either the *source* or the *target type*. To do so, you must use the `operator` keyword followed by `implicit` or `explicit`. The following example shows a type called `fancyint`, which defines implicit and explicit conversions from and to `int`:

```
public readonly struct fancyint
{
    private readonly int value;
    public fancyint(int value)
    {
        this.value = value;
    }
    public static implicit operator int(fancyint v) => v.value;
    public static explicit operator fancyint(int v) => new
fancyint(v);

    public override string ToString() => $"{value}";
}
```

You can use this type as follows:

```
fancyint a = new fancyint(42);
int i = a;                 // implicit conversion
fancyint b = (fancyint)i;  // explicit conversion
```

In this example, a is an object of the fancyint type. The value of a can be implicitly converted into int, because an implicit conversion operator is defined. However, the conversion from int to fancyint is defined as explicit, therefore a cast is necessary, as in (fancyint)i.

Conversions with helper classes

Conversion with a helper class or method is useful to convert between incompatible types, such as between a string and an integer or a System.DateTime object. There are various helper classes provided by the framework, such as the System.BitConverter class, the System.Convert class, and the Parse() and TryParse() methods of the built-in numeric types. However, you can provide your own classes and methods to convert between any types.

The following listing shows several examples of conversion using helper classes:

```
DateTime dt1 = DateTime.Parse("2019.08.31");
DateTime.TryParse("2019.08.31", out DateTime dt2);

int i1 = int.Parse("42");              // successful, i1 = 42
int i2 = int.Parse("42.15");           // error, throws exception
int.TryParse("42.15", out int i3);     // error, returns false,
                                       // i3 = 0
```

It is important to note the key difference between Parse() and TryParse(). The former tries to perform parsing and if that succeeds, it returns the parsed value; but if it fails, it throws an exception. The latter does not throw an exception, but returns bool, indicating the success or failure, and sets the second out parameter to the parsed value if successful or to the default value if it fails.

Operators

C# provides an extensive set of operators for built-in types. Operators are broadly classified in the following categories: arithmetic, relational, logical, bitwise, assignment, and other operators. Some operators can be overloaded for user-defined types. This topic will be further discussed in *Chapter 5, Object-Oriented Programming in C#*.

When evaluating an expression, operator precedence and associativity determine the order in which the operations are performed. You can change this order by using *parentheses*, just like you would do with a mathematical expression.

The following table lists the order of the operators with the highest precedence at the top and the lowest at the bottom. Operators that are listed together, on the same row, have equal precedence:

Operators	Category / name

`x.y, x?.y, x?[y], f(x), a[i], x++, x--,`
`new, typeof, checked, unchecked,`
`default, nameof, delegate, sizeof,`
`stackalloc, x->y`
	Primary

`+x, -x, !x, ~x, ++x, --x, (T)x, await, &x,` `*x, true and false`	Unary
`*, /, %`	Multiplicative
`+, -`	Additive
`<<, >>`	Shift
`<, >, <=, >=, is, as`	Relational and type-testing
`==, !=`	Equality
`&`	Boolean logical AND or bitwise logical AND
`^`	Boolean logical XOR or bitwise logical XOR
`|`	Boolean logical OR or bitwise logical OR
`&&`	Conditional AND
`||`	Conditional OR
`??`	Null-coalescing operator
`? :`	Conditional operator
`=, +=, -=, *=, /=, %=, &=, |=, ^=, <<=, >>=, =>`	Assignment and lambda declaration

For operators with the same precedence, associativity determines which one is evaluated first. There are two types of associativity:

- **Left-associativity**: This determines operators to be evaluated from *left to right*. All of the binary operators are left-associative except for the assignment operators and the null coalescing operators.

- **Right-associativity**: This determines operators to be evaluated from *right to left*. The assignment operator, the null-coalescing operator, and the conditional operator are right-associative.

In the following sections, we will take a closer look at each category of operators.

Arithmetic operators

Arithmetic operators perform arithmetic operations on the numerical type and can be unary or binary operators. A unary operator has a single operand, and a binary operator has two operands. The following set of arithmetic operators are defined in C#:

Operator	Meaning
+	Addition
-	Subtraction
*	Multiplication
/	Division
%	Modulus
++	Increment
--	Decrement

+, -, and * will work as per the mathematical rules of addition, subtraction, and multiplication respectively. However, the / operator behaves a bit differently. When applied to an integer, it will truncate the remainder of the division. For example, 20/3 will return 6. To get the remainder, we need to use the modulus operator. For example, 20%3 will return 2.

Among these, the increment and decrement operators require special attention. These operators have two forms:

- A postfix form
- A prefix form

The increment operator will increase the value of its operand by 1, whereas the decrement operator will decrease the value of its operand by 1. In the following example, the a variable is initially 10, but after applying the increment operator, its value will be 11:

```
int a = 10;
a++;
```

The prefix and the postfix variants differ in the following way:

- The prefix operator first performs the operation and then returns the value.
- The postfix operator first retains the value, then increments it, and then returns the original value.

Let's understand this with the help of the following code snippet. In the following example, a is 10. When a++ is assigned to b, b takes the value 10 and a is incremented to 11:

```
int a = 10;
int b = a++;
```

However, if we change this so that we assign ++a to b, then a will be incremented to 11, and that value will be assigned to b, so both a and b will have the value 11:

```
int a = 10;
int b = ++a;
```

The next category of operators that we will learn about is the relational operator.

Relational operators

Relational operators, also called **comparison operators**, perform a comparison on their operands. C# defines the following sets of relational operators:

Operator	Meaning
==	Equal to
!=	Not equal to
>	Greater than
<	Less than
>=	Greater than or equal to
<=	Less than or equal to

The result of a relational operator is a bool value. These operators support all of the built-in numerical and floating-point types. However, enumerations also support these operators. For operands of the same enumeration type, the corresponding values of the underlying integral types are compared. Enumerations will be later discussed in *Chapter 4, Understanding the Various User-Defined Types*.

The next code listing shows several relational operators being used:

```
int a = 42;
int b = 10;
bool v1 = a != b;
bool v2 = 0 <= a && a <= 100;
if(a == 42) { /* ... */ }
```

The <, >, <=, and >= operators can be overloaded for user-defined types. However, if a type overloads < or >, it must overload both of them. Similarly, if a type overloads <= or >=, it must overload both of them.

Logical operators

Logical operators perform a logical operation on `bool` operands. The following set of logical operators are defined in C#:

Operator	Meaning
&&	Logical AND
||	Logical OR
!	Logical NOT

The following example shows these operands in use:

```
bool a = true, b = false;
bool c = a && b;
bool d = a || !b;
```

In this example, since a is `true` and b is `false`, c will be `false` and d will be `true`.

Bitwise and shift operators

A bitwise operator will work directly on the bits of their operands. A bitwise operator can only be used with integer operands. The following table lists all of the bitwise and shift operators:

Operator	Meaning
&	Bitwise AND
|	Bitwise OR
^	Bitwise XOR
<<	Left shift
>>	Right shift

In the following example, a is `10`, which in binary is `1010`, and b is `5`, which in binary is `0101`. The result of the bitwise AND is `0000`, so c will have the value `0`, and the result of bitwise OR is `1111`, so d will have the value `15`:

```
int a = 10;    // 1010
int b = 5;     // 0101
int c = a & b; // 0000
int d = a | b; // 1111
```

The left-shift operator shifts the left-hand operand to the left by the number of bits defined by the right-hand operand. Similarly, the right-shift operator shifts the left-hand operand to the right by the number of bits defined by the right-hand operand. The left-shift operator discards the higher-order bits that are outside the range of the result type and sets the lower-order bits to zero. The right-shift operator discards the lower-order bits and the higher-order bits are set as follows:

- If the value that is shifted is `int` or `long`, an arithmetic shift is performed. That means the sign bit is propagated to the right on the higher-order empty bits. As a result, for a positive number, the higher-order bits are set to zero (because the sign bit is *0*) and for a negative number, the higher-order bits are set to one (because the sign bit is *1*).

- If the value that is shifted is `uint` or `ulong`, a logical shift is performed. In this case, the higher-order bits are always set to `0`.

The shift operations are only defined for `int`, `uint`, `long`, and `ulong`. If the left-hand operand is of another integral type, it is converted to `int` before the operation is applied. The result of a shift operation will always contain at least 32 bits.

The following listing shows examples of shifting operations:

```
// left-shifting
int x = 0b_0000_0110;
x = x << 4;  // 0b_0110_0000

uint y = 0b_1111_0000_0000_0000_1111_1110_1100_1000;
y = y << 2;  // 0b_1100_0000_0000_0011_1111_1011_0010_0000;

// right-shifting
int x = 0b_0000_0000;
x = x >> 4;  // 0b_0110_0000

uint y = 0b_1111_0000_0000_0000_1111_1110_1100_1000;
y = y >> 2;  // 0b_0011_1100_0000_0000_0011_1111_1011_0010;
```

In this example, we initialized the x and y variables with binary literals to make it easier to understand how shifting works. The value of the variables after shifting is also shown in binary in the comments.

Assignment operators

An assignment operator assigns a value to its left operand based on the value of its right operand. The following assignment operators are available in C#:

Operator	Meaning
=	Simple assignment
+=	Add assignment
-=	Subtract assignment
*=	Multiply assignment
/=	Divide assignment
%=	Modulus assignment
<<=	Left shift assignment
>>=	Right shift assignment
&=	Bitwise AND assignment
^=	Bitwise exclusive OR
|=	Bitwise inclusive OR

In this table, we have the simple assignment operator (=) that assigns the right-hand value to the left operand, and then we have compound assignment operators, that first perform an operation (arithmetical, shifting, or bitwise) and then assign the result of the operation to the left operand. Therefore, operations such as a =   a + 2 and a += 2 are equivalent.

Other operators

Apart from the operators discussed so far, there are other useful operators in C# that work both on built-in types and user-defined types. These include the conditional operator, the null-conditional operators, the null-coalescing operator, and the null-coalescing assignment operator. We will look at these operators in the following pages.

The ternary conditional operator

The **ternary conditional operator** is denoted by ? : and often simply referred to as the *conditional operator*. It allows you to return a value from two available options based on whether a Boolean condition evaluates to true or false.

The syntax of the ternary operator is as follow:

```
condition ? consequent : alternative;
```

If the Boolean condition evaluates to true, the consequent expression will be evaluated, and its result returned. Otherwise, the alternative expression will be evaluated, and its result returned. The ternary conditional operator can also be perceived as a shorthand for an if-else statement.

In the following example, the function called max () returns the maximum of two integers. The conditional operator is used to check whether a is greater or equal to b, in which case the value of a is returned; otherwise, the result is the value of b:

```
static int max(int a, int b)
{
    return a >= b ? a : b;
}
```

There is another form of this operator called **conditional ref expression** (available since C# 7.2) that allows returning the reference to the result of one of the two expressions. The syntax, in this case, is as follows:

```
condition ? ref consequent : ref alternative;
```

The result reference can be assigned to a ref local or ref read-only local variable and uses it as a reference return value or as a ref method parameter. The conditional ref expression requires the type of consequent and alternative to be the same.

In the following example, the conditional ref expression is used to select between two alternatives based on user input. If an even number is introduced, the v variable will hold a reference to a; otherwise, it will hold a reference to b. The value of v is incremented and then a and b are printed to the console:

```
int a = 42;
int b = 21;
int.TryParse(Console.ReadLine(), out int alt);
ref int v = ref (alt % 2 == 0 ? ref a : ref b);
v++;
Console.WriteLine($"a={a}, b={b}");
```

While the conditional operator checks whether a condition is true or not, the null-conditional operator checks whether an operand is null or not. We will look at this operator in the next section.

The null-conditional operators

The **null-conditional operator** has two forms: ?. (also known as the **Elvis operator**) to apply member access and ?[] to apply element access for an array. These operators apply the operation to their operand if and only if that operand is not null. Otherwise, the result of applying the operator is also null.

The following example shows how to use the null-conditional operator to invoke a method called run() from an instance of a class called foo, through an object that might be null. Notice that the result is a nullable type (int?) because if the operand of ?. is null, then the result of its evaluation is also null:

```
class foo
{
    public int run() { return 42; }
}

foo f = null;
int? i = f?.run()
```

The null-conditional operators can be *chained* together. However, if one operator in the chain is evaluated to null, the rest of the chain is *short-circuited* and does not evaluate.

In the following example, the bar class has a property of the foo type. An array of bar objects is created and we try to retrieve the value from the execution of the run() method from the f property of the first bar element in the array:

```
class bar
{
    public foo f { get; set; }
}

bar[] bars = new bar[] { null };
int? i = bars[0]?.f?.run();
```

We can avoid the use of a nullable type if we combine the null-conditional operator with the null-coalescing operator and provide a default value in case the null-conditional operator returns null. An example is shown here:

```
int i = bars[0]?.f?.run() ?? -1;
```

The null-coalescing operator is discussed in the following section.

The null-coalescing and null-coalescing assignment operators

The **null-coalescing operator**, denoted by ??, will return the left-hand operand if it is not null; otherwise, it will evaluate the right-hand operand and return its result. The left-hand operand cannot be a non-nullable value type. The right-hand operand is only evaluated if the left-hand operand is null.

The **null-coalescing assignment operator**, denoted by ??=, is a new operator added in C# 8. It assigns the value of its right-hand operand to its left-hand operand, if and only if the left-hand operand evaluates to null. If the left-hand operand is not null, then the right-hand operand is not evaluated.

Both ?? and ??= are *right-associative*. That means, the expression a ?? b ?? c is evaluated as a ?? (b ?? c). Similarly, the expression a ??= b ??= c is evaluated as a ??= (b ??= c).

Take a look at the following code snippet:

```
int? n1 = null;
int n2 = n1 ?? 2;   // n2 is set to 2
n1 = 5;
int n3 = n1 ?? 2;   // n3 is set to 5
```

We have defined a nullable variable, n1, and initialized it to null. The value of n2 will be set to 2 as n1 is null. After assigning n1 a non-null value, we will apply the conditional operator on n1 and integer 2. In this case, since n1 is not null, the value of n3 will be the same as that of n1.

The null-coalescing operator can be used multiple times in an expression. In the following example, the GetDisplayName() function returns the value of name if this is not null; otherwise, it returns the value of email if it is not null; if email is also null, then it returns "unknown":

```
string GetDisplayName(string name, string email)
{
    return name ?? email ?? "unknown";
}
```

The null-coalescing operator can also be used in argument checking. If a parameter is expected to be non-null, but it is in fact null, you can throw an exception from the right-hand operand. This is shown in the following example:

```
class foo
{
    readonly string text;

    public foo(string value)
    {
        text = value ?? throw new
        ArgumentNullException(nameof(value));
    }
}
```

The null-coalescing assignment operator is useful in replacing code that checks whether a variable is `null` before assigning it with a simpler, more succinct form. Basically, the `??=` operator is syntactic sugar for the following code:

```
if(a is null)
    a = b;
```

This can be replaced with a `??= b`.

Summary

In this chapter, we learned about built-in data types in C#, which are the numerical types, floating-point types, Boolean and character types, string, and object. Moreover, we also covered nullable types and array types. We learned about variables and constants and looked at the differences between value types and reference types. In addition to this, we covered the concepts of type conversion and casting. At the end of this chapter, we learned about the various types of operators available in C#.

In the next chapter, we will explore control statements and exceptions in C#.

Test what you learned

1. What are the integral built-in types in C#?
2. What are the differences between the floating-point types and the `decimal` type?
3. How do you concatenate strings?
4. What are escape sequences and how are they related to verbatim strings?
5. What is an implicitly typed variable? Can these variables be initialized with `null`?
6. What are value types? What are reference types? What are the main differences between them?
7. What are boxing and unboxing?
8. What is a nullable type and how do you declare a nullable integer variable?
9. How many types of arrays exist and what is the difference between them?
10. What are the available type conversions and how do you provide user-defined type conversion?

3

Control Statements and Exceptions

In the previous chapter, we discussed data types and operators in C#. In this chapter, we will explore control statements in C#. Control statements allow us to implement conditional execution paths in our code. We will also learn how to implement exception handling, which will help us to handle errors that might occur while executing our application.

In this chapter, we will cover the following concepts:

- Control statements
- Exception handling

By the end of this chapter, we will have seen how to implement these statements and clauses practically. Let's look at each of these topics in detail using examples.

Understanding control statements

Control statements allow us to control the flow of execution of a program. They also allow us to execute a particular block of code based on a certain condition. C# defines three categories of control statements, as mentioned here:

- **Selection statements**: if and switch
- **Iteration statements**: for, while, do-while, and foreach
- **Jump statements**: break, continue, goto, return, and yield

We will explore each of these statements in detail in the following sections.

Selection statements

Selection statements allow us to change the execution flow based on whether a condition is true or not. C# provides us with two types of selection statements: if and switch.

The if statement

The following snippet shows the syntax of an if statement:

```
if (condition1)
    statement1;
else if(condition2)
    statement2;
else
    statement3;
```

If condition1 evaluates to true, then statement1 will be executed. Else, if condition2 evaluates to true, then statement2 will be executed. Otherwise, statement3 will be executed.

The else-if and else clauses are *optional* and either of them, or both, can be *omitted*. On the other hand, you can have as many else-if clauses as you'd like.

In this example, we have only one statement to be executed for both the `if` and `else` clauses. If we have to execute a series of statements, we need to add curly braces ({ }) to make it a block. This is optional for single statements, although it is often a good way to make the code clearer or less prone to errors. In this case, the syntax will change as follows:

```
if (condition)
{
    statement 1;
    statement 2;
}
else
{
    statement 3;
    statement 4;
}
```

If `condition` evaluates to `true`, then both `statement1` and `statement2` will be executed. Otherwise, `statement3` and `statement4` will be executed. Let's try to understand the `if-else` statement with the help of the following code snippet:

```
class Program
{
    static void Main(string[] args)
    {
        Console.WriteLine("Enter a positive integer");
        var line = Console.ReadLine();
        int.TryParse(line, out int number);

        if (number % 2 == 0)
        {
            Console.WriteLine("Even number");
        }
        else
        {
            Console.WriteLine("Odd number");
        }
    }
}
```

The preceding program checks if a positive integer is even or odd. We are reading an integer from the console as input. As the value entered on the console is considered a string, we need to convert it to an integer. We will then find the remainder of division by 2 by applying the modulus (%) operator. If the remainder is 0 then the number is *even*, if not, the number is *odd*.

The `if` statements can be nested. We can put an `if` statement inside another `if` or an `else` statement. The following syntax shows an example of nested `if` statements:

```
if (condition1)
{
    if(condition2)
        statement 1;
    if(condition3)
        statement 2;
    else
        statement 3;
}
else
{
    if(condition4)
        statement 4;
    else
        statement 5;
}
```

In this example, if `condition1` evaluates to `true`, then the control will enter into the `if` block and execute the statement based on the evaluation of the nested `if` statements. If `condition1` is `false`, then the nested `if` statements inside the `else` clauses will be executed.

In a nested `if` statement, each `else` clause belongs to the last `if` statement that doesn't have a corresponding `else` statement. To avoid confusion and errors, it is recommended that you use curly braces when nesting `if` statements to pair `if` and `else` clauses correctly. Take, for instance, the following example:

```
if(condition1)
    if(condition2)
        statement1;
    else
        statement2;
```

The preceding example is not the same as the following:

```
if(condition1)
{
    if(condition2)
        statement1;
}
else
{
    statement2;
}
```

In the first example, the else clause belonged to the second, inner if clause. On the other hand, in the second example, the else clause belonged to the first, outer if clause.

The switch statement

The switch statement provides us with a way to execute a set of instructions from several available alternatives. It will match the value of an expression against a list of available values. If a match is found, the code associated with that value is executed.

The switch statement is an alternative to the cascading if-else-if statements. If there is a small number of matches, an if statement may be preferred. However, if the number of matching conditions is larger, a switch statement is preferred to an if statement for its better readability and maintainability.

The syntax of a switch statement is as follows:

```
switch (expression)
{
  case value1:
    statement 1;
    break;
  case value2:
    statement 2;
    statement 3;
    break;
  default:
    statement 4;
    break;
}
```

A `switch` statement contains one or more sections and each section has one or more `case` labels. Each `case` label can have one or more statements. Each `case` label specifies a value that will be matched with the `switch` expression. If a match is found, the control will be transferred to the matching `case` label.

The statements present in the `case` label will be executed until a `break` statement is encountered. If no match is found, the control will go to the `default` case. After the execution of a particular `case` label, the control will exit the switch. The `default` case is optional. If no `default` case is present and no match is found for any case labels, the control will fall outside of the `switch` statement.

Note that we have not used curly braces ({ }) inside the case labels. The `default` case can appear anywhere on the list. It is always evaluated last after all the `case` labels have been evaluated.

You can place multiple case labels in the same switch section; in this case, the matching of any of the case labels will trigger the execution of the switch section. In a `switch` statement, only one switch section may execute. It is not possible to fall through from one section to another. Each `switch` statement must be followed by a `break`, `goto`, or `return` statement.

The following example shows a `switch` statement with multiple switch sections, some of them with multiple `case` labels. The `default` case is placed at the end, as you would usually do. Each section is exited with a `break` statement:

```
Console.WriteLine("Enter number (1-10)");
var line = Console.ReadLine();
int.TryParse(line, out int number);

switch(number)
{
    case 1:
        Console.WriteLine("Smallest number");
        break;
    case 2: case 3: case 5: case 7:
        Console.WriteLine("Prime number");
        break;
    case 4: case 6: case 8:
        Console.WriteLine("Even number");
        break;
    case 9:
        Console.WriteLine("Odd number");
        break;
    default:
```

```
        Console.WriteLine("Not in the range");
        break;
}
```

The `switch` statement supports various forms of pattern matching. However, this is a more advanced topic that will be detailed in *Chapter 8, Advanced Topics,* and in *Chapter 15, New Features of C# 8.*

Iteration statements

Iteration statements allow us to execute a set of code in a loop as long as a certain condition is satisfied. C# provides us with four different kinds of loop:

- `for`
- `while`
- `do-while`
- `foreach`

Let's explore them in detail.

The for loop

The `for` loop allows us to execute a code block as long as a Boolean expression evaluates to `true`. The following snippet shows the general syntax of a `for` loop:

```
for(initializer; condition; iterator)
{
    statement1;
    statement2;
}
```

The `initializer` section consists of one or more initialization statements intended to initialize the counter to control the loop. This will be executed only once before entering the loop for the first time. If there are multiple statements in the `initializer` section, they must be separated by a comma. However, the `initializer` section is *optional and can be left empty.*

The loop controlling counter is also known as the loop control variable. This variable is local to the loop and cannot be accessed outside the scope of the `for` loop.

`condition` is a Boolean expression that will determine if the loop will execute or not. It will be evaluated for every iteration of the loop. If it evaluates to `true`, the loop will be executed. Once the Boolean condition evaluates to `false`, the loop will terminate, and the program control will fall out of the loop. This statement is optional and can be left empty.

`iterator` is an expression to change (increment/decrement) the loop control variable after each iteration of the loop. It can have multiple statements separated by a comma. This statement is also *optional and can be left empty*. In fact, all three of these statements (`initializer`, `condition`, and `iterator`) can be omitted, in which case we have an infinite loop, as in the following snippet:

```
for(;;)
{
    /* infinite loop, unless a break, goto, return, or throw
    executes */
}
```

The `for` loop is an entry controlled loop, which means the Boolean condition will be evaluated before entering into the loop. If the condition evaluates to `false` in the first iteration, then the code block inside the loop will not be executed at all.

Let's understand the `for` loop with the help of the following code snippet:

```
for (int i = 0; i <= 10; i++)
{
    if (i % 2 == 0)
    {
        Console.WriteLine($"{i} is an even number");
    }
    else
    {
        Console.WriteLine($"{i} is an odd number");
    }
}
```

Here, we are running a `for` loop to check which integers between 0 and 10 are even or odd. When you execute this code, you will see the following output screen:

```
C:\Program Files\dotnet\dotnet.exe    —    □    ×
0 is an even number
1 is an odd number
2 is an even number
3 is an odd number
4 is an even number
5 is an odd number
6 is an even number
7 is an odd number
8 is an even number
9 is an odd number
10 is an even number
```

Figure 3.1 – A screenshot of the console showing the output of the preceding snippet

We can also put a `for` loop inside another `for` loop. In this case, the inner loop will execute completely for each iteration of the outer loop. Look at the following code snippet. Here, all of the values of the j variable (that is, 1 and 2) will be printed against each value of the i variable (that is, 1, 2, 3, and 4):

```
for (int i = 1; i < 5; i++)
{
    for (int j = 1; j < 3; j++)
    {
        Console.WriteLine($"i = {i},j = {j}");
    }
}
```

Upon execution, you can see the following output of the program:

```
C:\Program Files\dotnet\dot...    —    □    ×
i = 1,j = 2
i = 2,j = 1
i = 2,j = 2
i = 3,j = 1
i = 3,j = 2
i = 4,j = 1
i = 4,j = 2
```

Figure 3.2 – The console output from the execution of the preceding snippet

A typical example of nested `for` loops is multi-dimensional array traversal. In the following example, we have an array of integers with three rows and two columns initialized during its declaration. The nested `for` loops are used to print the value of its elements to the console:

```
var arr = new int[3, 2] { { 1, 2, }, { 3, 4 }, { 5, 6 } };
for (int r = 0; r <= arr.GetUpperBound(0); r++)
{
    for (int c = 0; c <= arr.GetUpperBound(1); c++)
    {
        Console.Write($"{arr[r, c]} ");
    }
    Console.WriteLine();
}
```

Notice that we used the `GetUpperBound()` method to retrieve the index of the last element of the specified dimension to avoid hard-coded values for the size of the array.

You can exit a loop iteration while the condition is still `true` using a `break`, `goto`, `return`, or `throw` statement. You can skip the execution of the loop block for the current iteration with a `continue` statement. This is also true for the other loops—`while`, `do`, and `foreach`. The `jump` statements will be explored in detail later on in this chapter.

The while loop

The `while` loop is an *entry controlled loop*. It executes a block of statements as long as a specified Boolean expression evaluates to `true`. The syntax of a `while` loop is as follows:

```
while (condition)
{
    statement1;
    statement2;
}
```

Here, `condition` is a Boolean expression and it controls the loop. The code block inside the loop will be executed while `condition` evaluates to `true`. When `condition` becomes `false`, the program control will fall outside of the loop. Because `condition` is evaluated first, the `while` loop may not execute at all if `condition` is initially `false`.

A `while` loop is very similar to a `for` loop. In fact, you can rewrite any `while` loop as a `for` loop and vice versa. You can see in the following snippet how we can re-rewrite the syntax of a `for` loop using a `while` loop:

```
initializer;
while(condition)
{
    statement1;
    statement2;
    iterator;
}
```

In the following code snippet, we have rewritten the example from the previous session that prints even and odd numbers to the console with the help of a `while` loop:

```
int i = 0;
while (i <= 10)
{
    if (i % 2 == 0)
    {
        Console.WriteLine($"{i} is an even number");
    }
    else
    {
        Console.WriteLine($"{i} is an odd number");
    }
    i++;
}
```

The result of the execution of the program is unchanged. In fact, there is yet another way to achieve the same result, and that is through using a `do` statement.

The do-while loop

The do-`while` loop is an *exit-controlled loop*. This means the Boolean condition will be checked at the end of the loop. This ensures that the `do-while` loop will always be executed at least once, even if the condition evaluates to `false` in the first iteration. That is the key difference between a `while` and a `do-while` loop; the former may not execute at all, but the latter is always executed at least once.

The syntax of a do-while loop is as follows:

```
do
{
    statement1;
    statement2;
} while (condition);
```

In the following code snippet, we are printing all the numbers between 0 and 10 using a do-while loop, specifying which is odd and which is even. This code will have the same output as the example shown for the while loop:

```
int i = 0;
do
{
    if (i % 2 == 0)
    {
        Console.WriteLine($"{i} is an even number");
    }
    else
    {
        Console.WriteLine($"{i} is an odd number");
    }
    i++;
}
while (i <= 10);
```

The loops we have learned about so far allow us to execute one or more statements repeatedly, such as iterating through the elements of a collection based on an index. Another sort of loop statement, such as foreach, simplifies this iterating in all cases where we are interested in the element but not the index. Let's take a look at foreach next.

The foreach loop

The foreach loop allows us to iterate through the items of a collection that implements the System.Collections.IEnumerable or System.Collections.Generic. IEnumerable<T> interface. Collections are discussed in detail in *Chapter 7, Collections*.

The syntax of the `foreach` loop is as follows:

```
foreach(datatype iterator in collection)
{
   statement1;
   statement2;
}
```

Here, `datatype` denotes a valid type in C# and it must be the same data type as the collection, or a type for which an implicit conversion exists. You can also use `var` instead of an actual type name, in which case the compiler will infer the type of the `iterator` variable from the type of the collection elements.

The `iterator` variable is a loop iteration variable. The loop iteration variable in a `foreach` loop is read-only. This means we cannot change its value inside the body of the loop. In each iteration of the loop, the iterator is assigned a value from the collection. When all of the elements of the collection have been iterated, the loop exits. Exiting the loop can also be done with a `break`, `goto`, `return`, or `throw` statement.

Let's take a look at the `foreach` loop with the help of the following code snippet:

```
string[] languages = { "Java", "C#", "Python", "C++",
"JavaScript" };

foreach (string lang in languages)
{
    Console.WriteLine(lang);
}
```

In this example, we have defined a string array that contains a list of programming languages. We are using a `foreach` loop to iterate through it and print each element of the array on the console. The output for this code is as in the following screenshot:

Figure 3.3 – The output of printing to the console the content of an array of strings using a foreach statement

The preceding `foreach` statement is semantically equivalent to the following:

```
var enumerator = languages.GetEnumerator();
while(enumerator.MoveNext())
{
    Console.WriteLine(enumerator.Current);
}
```

The collection type may not necessarily implement the `IEnumerable` or `IEnumerable<T>` interfaces, but it must have a public method called `GetEnumerator()`, that takes no parameters and returns a class, struct, or interface, and has a return type that contains a public property called `Current` and a public parameterless method called `MoveNext()` that returns `bool`.

If the `Current` property of the enumerator type returns a reference return value (which is made possible with C# 7.3), then you can declare the iteration variable with the `ref` or `ref only` modifier. An example of this is shown in this snippet:

```
Span<int> arr = stackalloc int[]{ 1, 1, 2, 3, 5, 8 };
foreach(ref int n in arr)
{
    n *= 2;
}

foreach(ref readonly var n in arr)
{
    Console.WriteLine(n);
}
```

Here, the `arr` variable is `System.Span<int>`. The return type of its `GetEnumerator()` method, which is `Span<T>.Enumerator`, satisfies the condition mentioned earlier. The first `foreach` loop iterates through the elements of the array (a `stackalloc` array is allocated on the stack and disposed of as the function call returns) and doubles the initial value of each element. The second `foreach` loop iterates again through the elements but in a read-only fashion. An attempt to change the value of the iterator variable in a read-only loop would result in a compiler error.

The jump statements

Jump statements allow us to immediately transfer the control from one point in the application to another. C# provides us with five different jump statements:

- break
- continue
- goto
- return
- yield

We will explore them in detail in the following sections.

The break statement

We already saw how to use break to exit out of a switch case. We can also terminate the execution of a loop using the break statement. Once the program control encounters a break statement inside a loop, the loop terminates immediately, and the control falls out of the loop.

Take a look at the following code snippet:

```
for (int i = 0; i <= 10; i++)
{
    Console.WriteLine(i);
    if (i == 5)
        break;
}
```

Here, we are iterating from 0 to 10 and writing the current value to the console. If the value of the loop control variable becomes 5, the loop will break, and no further element will be printed to the console. Although the loop is expected to run 10 times, the break statement makes it terminate immediately as the value of the iterator becomes 5. Upon execution, you can see the following output:

Figure 3.4 – A screenshot of the console showing the output of the preceding snippet

The `break` statement is not the only statement that can control the execution of a loop. Another one is `continue`, which we will look at in the next section.

The continue statement

The `continue` statement passes control to the next iteration of an enclosing loop, be it `for`, `while`, `do`, or `foreach`. It is used to terminate the execution of the loop body in the current iteration and skip to the next one. The `continue` statement does not determine the return from the loop statement, but only aborts the execution of the current iteration and moves the control to the evaluation of the loop condition.

Take a look at the following code snippet:

```
for (int i = 0; i <= 10; i++)
{
    if (i % 2 == 0)
        continue;
    Console.WriteLine(i);
}
```

In this example, we iterate from 0 to 10; if the value is an even number, then we skip the current iteration loop and continue to the next one. This code will print only the odd numbers between 0 and 10. The output is as follows:

Figure 3.5 – The output of the previous snippet that prints to the console the odd numbers smaller than 10

The `break` and `continue` statements control the execution of loops. The next statement is used to end the execution of functions.

The return statement

The `return` statement terminates the current execution flow and returns the control to the calling method. Optionally, we can also return a value to the calling method. If the method has a return type defined, we need to return a value. Otherwise, when the return type is void, we can return without specifying any value.

The following example shows a possible implementation of a function that returns the nth Fibonacci number:

```
static int Fibonacci(int n)
{
    if (n > 1)
        return Fibonacci(n - 1) + Fibonacci(n - 2);
    else
        return n;
}
```

The `return` statement triggers the stopping of the current function execution and the return of the control to the calling function.

The goto statement

The `goto` statement is an unconditional jump statement. When the program control encounters a `goto` statement, it will jump to the location specified by it. The target for `goto` is specified using a *label*, which is an identifier followed by a colon (`:`). We can also use `goto` to exit from a loop. In this case, it will behave similarly to a `break` statement.

Consider the following code snippet:

```
for (int i = 0; i <= 10; i++)
{
    Console.WriteLine(i);
    if (i == 5)
    {
        goto printmessage;
    }
}

printmessage:
    Console.WriteLine("The goto statement is executed");
```

In this example, we are iterating from 0 to 10. If the value of the iterator becomes 5, we will use a `goto` statement to jump out of the loop. The output for this code snippet is shown here:

Figure 3.6 – The console output from the preceding code snippet

The use of a `goto` statement is generally avoided as a good programming practice because it can lead to code that is unstructured and hard to maintain.

The yield statement

`yield` is a contextual keyword (that is, a word that provides a specific meaning in code without being a reserved word). It indicates that the method, operator, or `get` accessor, where it appears preceding a `return` or `break` statement, is an iterator. The sequence returned from an iterator method can be consumed using a `foreach` statement. The `yield` statement makes it possible to return values as they are produced and consume them as they are available, which is especially useful in an asynchronous context.

To better understand the use of `yield`, let's consider the following example. We have a function, let's call it `GetNumbers()`, that returns a collection with all the numbers from `1` to `100`. A possible implementation is shown in the following snippet:

```
IEnumerable<int> GetNumbers()
{
    var list = new List<int>();
    for (int i = 1; i <= 100; ++i)
    {
        list.Add(i);
    }

    return list;
}
```

The problem with this implementation is that we cannot consume the numbers before all of them are produced. On one hand, in a real example, this could be time consuming and we might want to consume the numbers as they are produced. On the other hand, we might be only interested in some of the numbers, but not all of them.

With this implementation, we have to first produce all of them before using those that we need. In the following example, we only print the first five numbers to the console:

```
var numbers = GetNumbers().Take(5);
Console.WriteLine(string.Join(",", numbers));
```

A `yield return` statement returns an item as soon as it is available. It is shorthand for creating an iterator, something that would make the code more laborious.

The implementation of `GetNumbers()` would change to the following:

```
IEnumerable<int> GetNumbers()
{
    for (int i = 1; i <= 100; ++i)
    {
        yield return i;
    }
}
```

We return each number as it is available and do this only as long as we iterated through the enumerator, such as with a `foreach` statement. The preceding example, which prints the first five numbers to the console, remains unchanged. However, the execution is different because only five iterations in the `for` loop will be executed.

To understand this better, let's change the example a bit so that a message is displayed to the console before every item is produced and consumed respectively:

```
IEnumerable<int> GetNumbers()
{
    for (int i = 1; i <= 100; ++i)
    {
        Thread.Sleep(1000);
        Console.WriteLine($"Produced: {i}");
        yield return i;
    }
}

foreach(var i in GetNumbers().Take(5))
{
    Console.WriteLine($"Consumed: {i}");
}
```

A call to `Thread.Sleep()` is used to simulate a one-second delay in producing the next number. The result of the execution of this code is shown in the following image:

Figure 3.7 – The result of the execution of the preceding code

Now that we've seen how we can return from the normal execution of the code, let's take a quick look at how we can handle abnormal situations when unexpected errors occur during the execution of the code.

Exception handling

There are scenarios where our code produces an error. The error might occur because of a logical issue in the code, such as trying to divide by zero or access an element in an array beyond the bounds of the array. For example, trying to access the fourth element in an array of size three. Errors can also occur because of external factors, such as trying to read a file that does not exist on a disk.

C# provides us with a built-in exception-handling mechanism to handle these types of errors at the code level. The syntax for exception handling is as follows:

```
try
{
    Statement1;
    Statement2;
}
catch (type)
{
    // code for error handling
}
finally
{
    // code to always run at the end
}
```

The `try` block can contain one or more statements. The `catch` block contains the error handling code. The `finally` block contains the code that will execute after the `try` section. This happens regardless of whether the execution resumed normally, or the control left the `try` block because of a `break`, `continue`, `goto`, or `return` statement.

If an exception occurred and a `catch` block exists, the `finally` block is also guaranteed to execute. If the exception is unhandled, the execution of the `finally` block depends on how the exception unwind operation is triggered, which depends on how the running machine is set up. The `finally` block is optional.

Upon execution, the program control will execute the code inside the `try` block. If no error occurs in the `try` block, the execution continues normally and control transfers to the `finally` block, if it exists. When an exception occurs inside the `try` block, program control will transfer to a `catch` block, if one exists. After the execution of a `catch` block, the program control will transfer to the `finally` block, if it exists.

Multiple `catch` clauses may exist for the same `try` block. The order they are listed in is important because they are evaluated in that given order. This means more specific exceptions should be caught before more general ones. It is possible to specify a `catch` clause without an exception type in order to catch all exceptions. However, this is considered rather a bad practice because you should only catch exceptions that you know how to handle and recover from.

When an exception occurs, the **Common Language Runtime (CLR)** checks if there is a `catch` block to handle it in the method that is currently executing. If one does not exist, it looks in the method that called the current method, and so on up the call stack. If no matching `catch` block is found, an unhandled exception message is displayed, and the execution of the program is aborted.

Let's try to understand exception handling with the help of the following code snippet:

```
class Program
{
    static void Main(string[] args)
    {
        try
        {
            int a = 10;
            int b = a / 0;
        }
        catch (Exception ex)
        {
            Console.WriteLine(ex);
        }
    }
}
```

Here, we are trying to simulate a *division by zero error*. When an error occurs inside the `try` block, it will create an instance of the `Exception` class and throw the exception. In the `catch` block, we are specifying an argument of the `Exception` type. The exception provides us with an error message but also with information about where the error occurred (filename and path) as well as the call stack.

If we only want the message associated with the exception, we can use the `Message` property of the `Exception` class. The output of this code snippet is as follows:

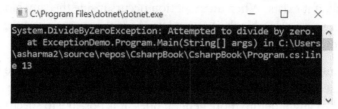

Figure 3.8 – The console showing the message of a division by zero exception

Exceptions are thrown with the `throw` statement. You must specify an instance of the `System.Exception` class or a class derived from it. Classes will be discussed in *Chapter 4, Understanding the Various User-Defined Types*, and inheritance in *Chapter 5, Object-Oriented Programming in C#*, but for the time being keep in mind that there are many exception types and they are all based on `System.Exception`. The `throw` statement can be used in a `catch` block without any argument to re-throw the exception, preserving the call stack. This is useful when you want to do something in the case of an exception, such as logging, but also want to pass the exception forward to be fully handled in a different place.

In the following example, a function called `FunctionThatThrows()` does something, but not before checking its input argument. If the `object` argument is `null`, it throws an exception of the `ArgumentNullException` type. However, if the argument is not null but of a type other than `string`, it throws an exception of the `ArgumentException` type. This is the base class for `ArgumentNullException`. When invoking the method, we catch multiple exception types:

- `ArgumentNullException`
- `ArgumentException`
- `Exception`

The order is important because it starts with the most-derived class and ends with the base class of all exceptions. A `finally` block is used to display a message at the end of the execution:

```
void FunctionThatThrows(object o)
{
    if (o is null)
        throw new ArgumentNullException(nameof(o));

    if (!(o is string))
        throw new ArgumentException("A string is expected");

    // do something
}

try
{
    Console.WriteLine("executing");
    FunctionThatThrows(42);
}
catch (ArgumentNullException e)
{
    Console.WriteLine($"Null argument: {e.Message}");
}
catch (ArgumentException e)
{
    Console.WriteLine($"Wrong argument: {e.Message}");
}
catch(Exception e)
{
    Console.WriteLine($"Error: {e.Message}");
}
finally
{
    Console.WriteLine("done");
}
```

The output of the execution of this program is as follows:

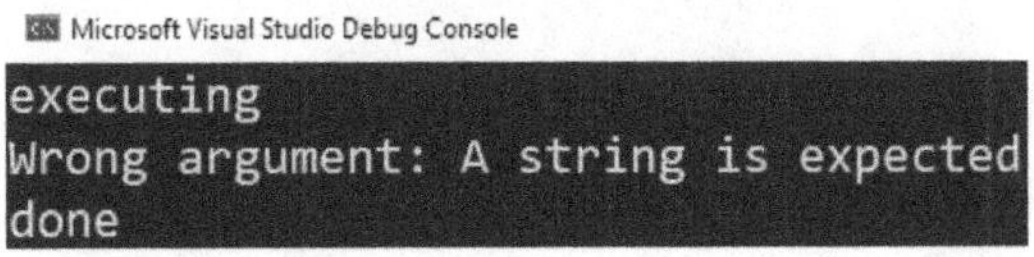

Figure 3.9 – The console output from the execution of the previous snippet

The topic of exception handling will be discussed in greater detail in *Chapter 14, Error Handling*. If you want to learn more about exceptions at this point, you can go ahead and read this chapter before continuing with the next one.

Summary

In this chapter, we explored control statements in C#. We learned how the different types of loops and jump statements work with the help of examples. We also looked briefly at how to throw and catch exceptions.

In the next chapter, we will look at user-defined types and explore what fields, properties, methods, indexers, and constructors are in a class.

Test what you learned

1.   What are the selection statements available in the C# language?

2.   Where can the default case of a `switch` statement appear and when it is evaluated?

3.   What is the difference between a `for` and a `foreach` statement?

4.   What is the difference between a `while` and a `do-while` statement?

5.   What statements can you use to return from a function?

6.   Where can you use a `break` statement and how does it work?

7.   What does the `yield` statement do and in which scenarios is it used?

8.   How do you catch all the exceptions from a function call?

9.   What does the `finally` block do?

10. What is the base class for all exceptions in .NET?

4
Understanding the Various User-Defined Types

In the previous chapter, we learned about control statements and exceptions in C#. In this chapter, we will explore the user-defined types in C#. We will learn how to create custom user types using classes, structures, and enumerations. We will explore what fields, properties, methods, indexers, and constructors are in a class. We will study the access modifiers in C# and learn how to use them to define the visibility of types and members. We will also learn about two important keywords in C#—this and static—and understand the ref, in, and out parameter modifiers for methods.

We will explore the following topics in detail:

- Classes and objects
- Structures
- Enumerations
- Namespaces

Good knowledge of these concepts is necessary to understand the **object-oriented programming (OOP)** concepts that we will cover in the next chapter.

Classes and objects

Before we go further, it is important that you understand these two key concepts. A class is a template or a blueprint that specifies the form of an object. It contains both data and code that operates on that data. An object is an instance of a class. Classes are defined using the `class` keyword and a type that is a class is a reference type. The default value for a variable of a reference type is `null`. You can assign it as a reference to an instance of the type. Instances—that is, objects—are created using the `new` operator.

> **Information box**
>
> The terms *class* and *object* are often used interchangeably in different technical documentations. They are not the same and it is improper to use them as so. The class is the blueprint that specifies the memory layout of objects and defines functionalities that operate with that memory. Objects are the actual entities created and operated according to the blueprint.

Take a look at the following code snippet to understand how a class is defined. In this example, we are creating an `Employee` class with three fields to represent the ID, first name, and last name of an employee:

```
class Employee
{
    public int    EmployeeId;
    public string FirstName;
    public string LastName;
}
```

We will use the `new` keyword to create an instance of the class. The `new` operator allocates memory for an object and returns a reference to it at runtime. This reference is then stored in the variable that specifies the object's name. The object is stored on the heap, and the reference to the object is stored in the stack storage location corresponding to the named variable.

To create an object of the `Employee` class, we will use the following statement:

```
Employee obj = new Employee();
```

To access the members of a class (fields, properties, methods) using an object, we use the dot (.) operator. Hence, to assign values to the fields of the object (obj), we will use the following statements:

```
obj.EmployeeId = 1;
obj.FirstName = "John";
obj.LastName = "Doe"
```

The following diagram shows, conceptually, what is happening here:

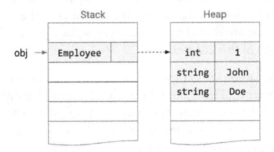

Figure 4.1 – The conceptual memory layout for the preceding Employee object

The **obj** variable of the **Employee** type is allocated on the stack. However, the stack does not contain the actual **Employee** object but only a reference to it. The object is allocated on the heap and the address of the object is stored on the stack so that by using the **obj** variable we can access the object that is located on the heap.

Two different instances of a class are two different objects. A reference to an object can be assigned to multiple variables. In this case, modifications to the object through one variable will be visible through the other variable. This is shown in the following example:

```
Employee obj1 = new Employee();
obj1.EmployeeId = 1;

Employee obj2 = obj1;
obj2.FirstName = "John";      // obj1.FirstName == "John"
obj2.LastName = "Doe";        // obj1.LastName == "Doe"
```

Here, we have created a first instance of the Employee class and only assigned a value to EmployeeId. Then, we created a second instance and assigned values to the first and last name, skipping the identifier. These are two different objects, residing in different locations in memory.

The properties of an employee are stored in the class in member fields. These will be discussed next.

Fields

These are variables declared directly inside a class and are, therefore, members of the class. Fields are used for storing the state of the object, which is data that must live for more than the period of the execution of a class method and that should be accessible from multiple methods. Variables that are not used outside the scope of a single method should be defined as local variables and not class fields.

In the preceding section, `EmployeeId`, `FirstName`, and `LastName` are the mentioned fields. These are called **instance fields** because they belong to the instance of the class, meaning that each object has its own instance of these fields. On the other hand, *static fields* belong to the class and are shared by all instances of the class. Static members will be discussed in a later section of this chapter.

These fields have been declared `public`, which means they can be accessed by anyone. This is, however, a bad practice. Fields should usually be declared as either `private` (to be accessible only to the class members) or `protected` (to also be accessible to the derived classes). This ensures better encapsulation, which will be discussed further in the next chapter. Fields can be accessed both for reading and writing using methods, properties, and indexers. We will discuss these in the following sections.

Fields that are declared with the `const` specifiers are called **constants**. Only built-in types can be constants. Constants are always initialized with a literal and are values known at compile time that cannot be changed at runtime:

```
class Employee
{
    public const int StartId = 100;
}
```

Constant fields are substituted for their literal value in the intermediate language code, which means you cannot pass a constant field by reference. But this has another, more subtle implication: if the constant value is referred in assemblies other than the one in which the type is defined and the literal value of the constant is changed in a future version, the assemblies referring the constant will continue to have the old version until they are recompiled.

For instance, if an integer constant defined in assembly A was initially set to 42 and it was referred in assembly B, then the value 42 will have been stored in assembly B. Changing the value of the constant to something else (let's say 100) will not be reflected in assembly B, which will continue to store the old value until it is recompiled with the new version of assembly A.

Fields can also be declared with the `readonly` specifier. These fields can only be initialized in a constructor and their value cannot be changed later on. They can be thought of as **runtime constants**.

In the following example, the `EmployeeId` field is a `readonly` field that is initialized in the constructor. Only the first and last name fields can be changed for an instance of the class:

```
class Employee
{
    public readonly int EmployeeId;
    public string       FirstName;
    public string       LastName;

    public Employee(int id)
    {
        EmployeeId = id;
    }
}

Employee obj = new Employee(1);
obj.FirstName = "John";
obj.LastName = "Doe";
```

Now that we have seen how to work with fields, let's learn about methods.

Methods

Methods are a series of one or more statements that are executed when the method is invoked. Instance methods require an object in order to be called. Static methods belong to the class and are not called using an object.

A method has a so-called *signature* that consists of several parts:

- **An access modifier**: This specifies the visibility of the method. This is optional and `private` by default.

- **Modifiers** such as `virtual`, `abstract`, `sealed`, or `static`: These are all optional and will be discussed in later sections.

- **A return type**: This could be `void` if the method does not return any value.

- **A name**: This must be a valid identifier.

- **Zero, one, or more parameters**: These are specified with a type, name, and optionally, the `ref`, `in`, or `out` specifier.

In the following example, we will add a method to our `Employee` class:

```
class Employee
{
    public int    EmployeeId;
    public string FirstName;
    public string LastName;

    public string GetEmployeeName()
    {
        return $"{FirstName} {LastName}";
    }
}
```

Here, we have added a method called `GetEmployeeName()`. The access modifier is `public`, which allows this method to be called from any part of the code. The return type is `string` as the method is returning the name of the employee by concatenating the `FirstName` and `LastName` fields separated by a space.

Methods that simply consist of evaluating an expression, and perhaps returning the result of the evaluation, can be written using an alternative syntax called **expression body definitions**. These have the `member => expression;` form and are supported for all class members, not just methods, but also fields, properties, indexers, constructors, and finalizers. The type of the result value of the expression evaluation must match the return type of the method.

The following code shows the implementation of the `GetEmployeeName()` method using an expression body definition:

```
public string GetEmployeeName() => $"{FirstName} {LastName}";
```

Overloaded methods are multiple methods that have the same name but a different signature. Such methods can exist. The return type of these methods is not a part of the signature in the context of method overloading. This means that you cannot have two methods with the same list of parameters but with different return values.

In the following example, `GetEmployeeName(bool)` is an overloaded method for the previous `GetEmployeeName()` method:

```
public string GetEmployeeName(bool lastNameFirst) =>
lastNameFirst ? $"{LastName} {FirstName}" :
                $"{FirstName} {LastName}";
```

This method has the same name but a different list of parameters. It takes a Boolean value that indicates whether the last name should be put first, or else returns the name with the first name followed by the last name, just like the previous method did.

Constructors

A constructor is a special method defined in a class that is called when we instantiate an object for the class. Constructors are used to initialize the members of the class upon the object's creation. A constructor cannot have a return type and has the same name as the class. Multiple constructors with different parameters may exist.

A constructor without any parameters is called a *default constructor*. Such a constructor is provided by the compiler to all classes. The default constructor is created at compile time and initializes the member variables to their default value. The default value is 0 for numeric data types, `false` for `bool`, and `null` for reference types. If we define our own constructor, the compiler will no longer provide the default constructor.

A constructor can have an access modifier. The default access modifier of a constructor is `private`. However, this modifier makes it impossible to instantiate the class from outside the class itself. In most cases, the access modifier of a constructor is defined as `public` since a constructor is generally called from outside of the class.

A private constructor is useful in certain situations. An example is when implementing the singleton pattern.

Let's try to understand all the concepts covered so far with the help of the following example:

```
class Employee
{
    public int EmployeeId;
    public string FirstName;
    public string LastName;

    public Employee(int employeeId,
                    string firstName, string lastName)
    {
        EmployeeId = employeeId;
        FirstName = firstName;
        LastName = lastName;
    }

    public string GetEmployeeName() =>
            $"{FirstName} {LastName}";
}
```

We have extended our `Employee` class and included a constructor in it. This constructor will accept three parameters to initialize the value of all three fields: `EmployeeId`, `FirstName`, and `LastName`. When creating an instance of the class, you must specify proper arguments for the class constructor:

```
Employee obj = new Employee(1, "John", "Doe");

Console.WriteLine("Employee ID is: {0}", obj.EmployeeID);
Console.WriteLine("The full name of employee is: {0}",
                    obj.GetEmployeeName());
```

Upon execution, this program will give the output shown in the following screenshot:

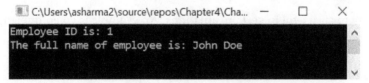

Figure 4.2 – A screenshot of the console showing the output of the preceding snippet

Objects can be initialized in a declarative manner using the so-called *object initializer*. You invoke a constructor and, apart from providing the necessary arguments to the constructor, you also provide a list of initialization statements for accessible members, such as fields, properties, or indexers, within curly braces.

Considering the `Employee` class without a user-defined constructor, having the default (parameterless) constructor provided by the compiler, we can write the following code to initialize an instance of the class:

```
Employee obj = new Employee()
{
    EmployeeId = 1,
    FirstName = "John",
    LastName = "Doe"
};
```

So far in this chapter, we have used fields to store the state of an object. The C# language provides an alternative to fields: properties, which is the topic of the next section.

Properties

A property is a combination of a field and a method to access that field. They look like fields but are actually methods called **accessors**. Properties make it possible to read or write the class state in a simple manner and hide the implementation details, including verification code.

The two accessors that properties define are called `get` (which is used to return a value from the property) and `set` (which is used to assign a new value). Within the context of the `set` accessor, the `value` keyword defines the value being accessed (which is the value assigned from the user code).

In the following example, the `Employee` class shown earlier in this chapter is rewritten so that the employee ID, first name, and last name are private fields made available to the class clients using properties:

```
class Employee
{
    private int employeeId;
    private string firstName;
    private string lastName;

    public int EmployeeId
    {
        get { return employeeId; }
        set { employeeId = value; }
    }
```

```
public string FirstName
{
    get { return firstName; }
    set { firstName = value; }
}

public string LastName
{
    get { return lastName; }
    set { lastName = value; }
}
}
```

Using the property's `get` and `set` accessors is actually transparent. You do not invoke them explicitly, but use the properties just as though they were fields. The following example shows how the three properties of the `Employee` class are to be accessed for both writing and reading:

```
Employee obj = new Employee();
obj.EmployeeId = 1;
obj.FirstName = "John";
obj.LastName = "Doe";

Console.WriteLine($"{obj.EmployeeId} - {obj.LastName}, {obj.FirstName}");
```

The implementation of the properties shown in the preceding code is straightforward—it just returns or sets the value of a private field. However, accessors are just like any other method, so you can write any code, such as parameter verification, as in the following example:

```
public int EmployeeId
{
    get { return employeeId; }
    set {
        if (value < 0)
            throw new ArgumentException(
                "ID must be greater than zero.");
        employeeId = value;
    }
}
```

On the other hand, a property is not required to refer to a corresponding field. A property may return values that are not read from one field or that are calculated from evaluating different fields. The following example shows a property, `Name`, that concatenates the value of the `FirstName` and `LastName` properties:

```
public string Name
{
    get { return $"{FirstName} {LastName}"; }
}
```

Notice that in the case of this property, the `set` accessor is missing. Both the `get` and `set` accessors are optional. However, at least one must be implemented. On the other hand, a write-only property does not have much value and you might want to implement such functionalities as a regular method. Also, the `get` and `set` accessors may have different access modifiers.

Implementing properties in this manner is cumbersome because you need to explicitly define private fields that you do not use elsewhere other than in the properties. Moreover, each property has to explicitly implement the `get` and `set` accessors, basically repeating the same code over and over again. It is possible to achieve the same result with a shorter syntax using *auto-implemented properties*. These are properties for which the compiler will provide a private field and the implementation of the `get` and `set` accessors, as we did earlier.

The `Employee` class is re-written with auto-implemented properties, as in the following code. This very much resembles our first implementation where we were using public fields:

```
class Employee
{
    public int EmployeeId { get; set; }
    public string FirstName { get; set; }
    public string LastName { get; set; }
}
```

If you do not want to set the values of these properties, you can declare only the `get` accessor `public`. In such cases, the `set` accessor would probably be `private` and you would provide values through the constructor. Such an example is shown here:

```
class Employee
{
    public int EmployeeId { get; private set; }
    public string FirstName { get; private set; }
    public string LastName { get; private set; }
```

```
    public Employee(int id, string firstName, string lastName)
    {
        EmployeeId = id;
        FirstName = firstName;
        LastName = lastName;
    }
}
```

Properties can be implemented using expression body definitions. The Name property shown earlier can be implemented as follows:

```
public string Name => $"{FirstName} {LastName}";
```

This is a read-only property that only has the get accessor. However, you can explicitly implement both the get and set accessors as expression body members. This is shown in the following listing:

```
class Employee
{
    private int employeeId;
    public int EmployeeId
    {
        get => employeeId;
        set => employeeId = value > 0 ? value :
                throw new ArgumentException(
                    "ID must be greater than zero.");
    }
}
```

Auto-implemented properties can also be initialized using the syntax shown in the following example:

```
class Employee
{
    public int EmployeeId { get; set; } = 1;
    public string FirstName { get; set; }
    public string LastName { get; set; }
}
```

The value of the EmployeeId property is initialized with 1. Unless otherwise explicitly set, all instances of the Employee class will have EmployeeId set to 1.

If you are implementing a read-only property using an expression body definition, you do not need to specify the `get` accessor. The syntax, in this case, is as follows:

```
class Employee
{
    public int EmployeeId => 1;
    public string FirstName { get; set; }
    public string LastName { get; set; }
}
```

This, however, looks very similar to the following:

```
class Employee
{
    public int EmployeeId = 1;
    public string FirstName { get; set; }
    public string LastName { get; set; }
}
```

There is a big difference between these syntaxes:

- In the former example, where `=>` is used, `EmployeeId` is a *read-only public property* with an *expression body definition*.

- In the latter example, where `=` is used, `EmployeeId` is a *public field* with an *initializer*.

There is a special form of property that can take parameters and allow access to class instances using the operator `[]`. These are called **indexers** and are discussed in the following section.

Indexers

An indexer allows an object to be indexed like an array. An indexer defines a `get` and `set` accessor, similar to a property. An indexer does not have an explicit name. It is created by using the `this` keyword. An indexer has one or more parameters, which can be of any type. As in the case of properties, the `get` and `set` accessors are usually simple and consist of a single statement that returns or sets a value.

In the following example, the `ProjectRoles` class contains a mapping of the project IDs and roles that an employee has in each project. This mapping is private but access to it is available through an indexer:

```
class ProjectRoles
{
    readonly Dictionary<int, string> roles =
        new Dictionary<int, string>();

    public string this[int projectId]
    {
        get
        {
            if (!roles.TryGetValue(projectId, out string role))
                throw new Exception("Project ID not found!");
            return role;
        }
        set
        {
            roles[projectId] = value;
        }
    }
}
```

The indexer is defined with the `public string this[int projectId]` syntax, which contains the following:

- An access modifier

- The type of the indexer, which is `string`

- The `this` keyword and the list of parameters in square brackets `[]`

The `get` and `set` accessors are implemented in the same way as for a regular property. This `ProjectRoles` class can be used as follows within the `Employee` class:

```
class Employee
{
    public int          EmployeeId { get; set; }
    public string       FirstName { get; set; }
    public string       LastName { get; set; }
    public ProjectRoles Roles { get; private set; }

    public Employee() => Roles = new ProjectRoles();
}
```

We can access the employee roles using the `Roles[i]` syntax, just as if `Roles` was an array. In this example, the parameter is not an index in the array but a project identifier, which is actually the key to the dictionary of projects and roles. The parameters can be of any type, not just numerical types:

```
Employee obj = new Employee()
{
    EmployeeId = 1,
    FirstName = "John",
    LastName = "Doe"
};

obj.Roles[1] = "Dev";
obj.Roles[3] = "SA";

for(int i = 1; i <= 3; ++i)
{
    try
    {
        Console.WriteLine($"Project {i}: role is {obj.
Roles[i]}");
    }
    catch(Exception ex)
    {
        Console.WriteLine(ex.Message);
    }
}
```

The output from executing this sample code is shown in the following screenshot:

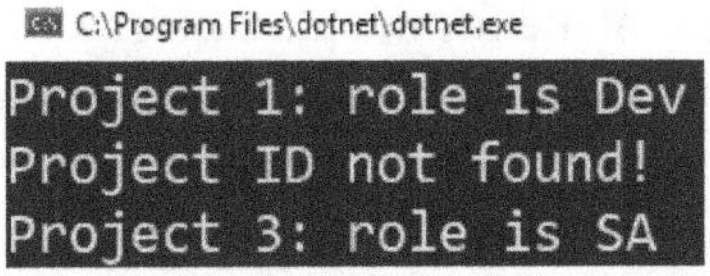

Figure 4.3 – Console output from executing the preceding code snippet

Indexers, including read-only indexers, can be implemented with expression body definitions. However, there are no auto-implemented indexers; they have to be implemented explicitly.

As mentioned, indexers are defined using the `this` keyword. However, this keyword has other meanings outside the scope of indexers. This topic will be discussed in the next section.

The this keyword

The `this` keyword is used to represent the current instance of a class. When a method is called, the reference of the calling object is passed to it using `this`. This is not done explicitly, but behind the scenes by the compiler.

The `this` keyword has two important purposes:

- To qualify class members when parameters or local variables with the same name exist

- To pass a reference to the current instance as a parameter to another method

Let's look at the following implementation of the `Employee` class:

```
class Employee
{
    public int EmployeeID;
    public string FirstName;
    public string LastName;

    public Employee(int EmployeeID,
                    string FirstName, string LastName)
    {
        this.EmployeeID = EmployeeID;
        this.FirstName = FirstName;
        this.LastName = LastName;
    }
}
```

In this example, the parameters of the constructor have the same name as the fields of the class. C# allows us to use the same name for the parameter and instance variable. Since the parameter name is local to a method, the local name takes precedence over the instance variable. To alleviate this situation, we use the `this` keyword to refer to the instance variable for the current method invocation.

So far, we have seen the `this` keyword used for referring to the current instance of a class and for declaring indexes. However, it is used for yet another purpose, and that is declaring extension methods. These will be discussed in *Chapter 8, Advanced Topics*. For now, let's look at another important keyword: `static`.

The static keyword

The `static` keyword can be used to declare classes or class members. These differ from what we have seen so far because you do not create instances of static classes or do not need objects to access static members. We will explore these in detail in the following subsections.

Static members

Fields, properties, methods, and constructors can be declared `static`. Indexers and finalizers cannot be declared `static`. A static member does not belong to the object (as in the case of an instance member) but rather to the type itself. Therefore, you cannot access a static member through an object but through the type name.

In the following example, we have an implementation of the `Employee` class that has a static field called `id` and a static method called `Create()`. The static field is storing the value of the next employee ID, and the static method is used to create a new instance of the class because the constructor is `private` and therefore it can only be called from within the class:

```
class Employee
{
    private static int id = 1;

    public int EmployeeId { get; private set; }
    public string FirstName { get; private set; }
    public string LastName { get; private set; }

    private Employee(int id, string firstName, string lastName)
    {
        EmployeeId = id;
        FirstName = firstName;
        LastName = lastName;
    }

    public static Employee Create(string firstName,
                                  string lastName)
    {
        return new Employee(id++, firstName, lastName);
    }
}
```

We can call the `Create()` method as follows to instantiate a new object of this class:

```
Employee obj1 = Employee.Create("John", "Doe");
Employee obj2 = Employee.Create("Jane", "Doe");
Console.WriteLine($"{obj1.EmployeeId} {obj1.FirstName}");
Console.WriteLine($"{obj2.EmployeeId} {obj2.FirstName}");
```

The first object created like this will have `EmployeeID` set to 1, the second one will have `EmployeeID` set to 2, and so on. Notice that we used the `Employee.Create()` syntax to call the static method.

Static classes

A `static` class is also declared using the `static` keyword. A `static` class cannot be instantiated. Since we cannot create instances of a `static` class, we access the class members using the class name itself. All members of a static class must themselves be static. A static class is basically the same as a non-static class, with a `private` constructor and all members declared as `static`.

A `static` class is typically used to define methods that operate only on their parameters (if any) and do not rely on class fields. This is often the case with utility classes.

The following example shows a static class called `MassConverters`, which contains static methods to convert between kilograms and pounds:

```
static class MassConverters
{
    public static double PoundToKg(double pounds)
    {
        return pounds * 0.45359237;
    }

    public static double KgToPound(double kgs)
    {
        return kgs * 2.20462262185;
    }
}

var lbs = MassConverters.KgToPound(42.5);
var kgs = MassConverters.PoundToKg(180);
```

Because static classes cannot be instantiated, the `this` keyword has no meaning within the context of such a class. An attempt to use it would result in a compiler error.

The static constructor

A class can have a static constructor, whether the class itself is static or not. A static constructor has no parameters or access modifiers and cannot be called by the user. A static constructor is called by the CLR automatically in the following instances:

- In a static class when the first static member of the class is accessed for the first time

- In a non-static class when the class is instantiated for the first time

Static constructors are useful for initializing static fields. For instance, a `static` `readonly` field can only be initialized during declaration or in the static constructor. This is useful especially when the values are taken from configuration files, for writing entries to a log file, or for writing wrappers for unmanaged code, when the static constructor can call the `LoadLibrary()` API.

In the following example, the previous implementation of the `Employee` class is modified such that a static constructor is provided to initialize the value of the static `id` field. This constructor is reading the ID of the next employee from an application file or initializes it with `1` if the file is not found. Every time a new instance of the class is created, the value of the next employee ID is written to this file:

```
class Employee
{
    private static int id;

    public int EmployeeId { get; private set; }
    public string FirstName { get; private set; }
    public string LastName { get; private set; }

    static Employee()
    {
        string text = "1";
        try
        {
            text = File.ReadAllText("app.data");
        }
        catch { }
        int.TryParse(text, out id);
    }

    private Employee(int id, string firstName, string lastName)
    {
        EmployeeId = id;
        FirstName = firstName;
```

```
        LastName = lastName;
    }

    public static Employee Create(string firstName,
                                  string lastName)
    {
        var employee = new Employee(id++, firstName, lastName);
        File.WriteAllText("app.data", id.ToString());
        return employee;
    }
}
```

If you run the following code several times, the first time the IDs of the two employees will be 1 and 2, then 3 and 4, and so forth:

```
Employee obj1 = Employee.Create("John", "Doe");
Employee obj2 = Employee.Create("Jane", "Doe");
Console.WriteLine($"{obj1.EmployeeId} {obj1.FirstName}");
Console.WriteLine($"{obj2.EmployeeId} {obj2.FirstName}");
```

So far, we have seen how to create methods and constructors. In the next section, we will learn about the different ways you can pass parameters to them.

The ref, in, and out parameters

When we pass an argument to a method, it is passed by a value. This means a copy is made. If the type is a value type, then the value of the argument is copied into the method parameter. If the type is a reference type, then the reference is copied to the method parameter. When you change the parameter value, it changes the local copy. This means changes in arguments of value types are not propagated to the caller. As for arguments of reference types, you can change the referred object on the heap but you cannot change the reference itself. This behavior can be altered using the ref, in, and out keywords.

The ref keyword

The ref keyword allows us to create a *call-by-reference mechanism* rather than a call-by-value mechanism. A ref keyword is specified when we declare and invoke the method. The use of the ref keyword alters the parameter so that it becomes an alias for an argument, which must be a variable. This means you cannot pass a property or an indexer (which is actually a method) as an argument for a ref parameter. A ref parameter must be initialized prior to the method call.

Let's take a look at the following code sample:

```
class Program
{
    static void Swap(ref int a, ref int b)
    {
        int temp = a;
        a = b;
        b = temp;
    }

    static void Main(string[] args)
    {
        int num1 = 10;
        int num2 = 20;

        Console.WriteLine($"Before swapping: num1={num1},
num2={num2}");
        Swap(ref num1, ref num2);
        Console.WriteLine($"After swapping:  num1={num1},
num2={num2}");
    }
}
```

In this program, we have defined a `Swap` method to swap two integer values. We are using the `ref` keyword to declare the method parameters. We defined this method as `static` so that we can invoke it without an object reference. Inside the `Main` method, we have initialized two integer variables.

While invoking the `Swap` method, we have also used the `ref` keyword with argument names. These `ref` parameters are passed as a reference and the actual value of the `num1` and `num2` variables will be swapped. The change is reflected in the variables in the `Main` method. The output of this program is shown in the following screenshot:

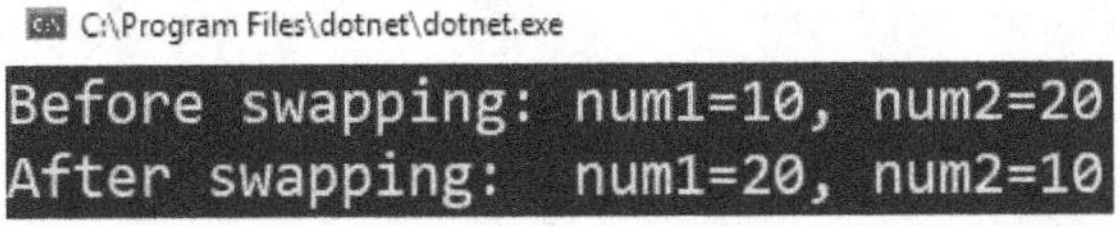

Figure 4.4 – Console showing the values of num1 and num2 before and after swapping

The `ref` keyword can be used to specify a reference return value. In this case, it must be present in the following:

- In the method signature, before the return type.

- In the return statement, between the `return` keyword and the returned value. Such a value is called a *ref return value*.

- In the declaration of a local variable that will receive the returned reference, before the variable's type. Such a variable is called a *ref local variable*.

- Before the call to the method with a `ref` return.

In the following example, the `Project` class has a member field of the `Employee` type. A reference to an `Employee` instance is set in the constructor. The `GetOwner()` method returns a reference to the member field:

```
class Project
{
    Employee owner;

    public string Name { get; private set; }

    public Project(string name, Employee owner)
    {
        Name = name;
        this.owner = owner;
    }

    public ref Employee GetOwner()
    {
        return ref owner;
    }

    public override string ToString() =>
        $"{Name} (Owner={owner.FirstName} {owner.LastName})";
}
```

This can be used as follows to retrieve and change the owner of a project. In the following code, notice the use of the `ref` keyword in the declaration of the local variable and the invocation of the `GetOwner()` method:

```
Employee e1 = new Employee(1, "John", "Doe");
Project proj = new Project("Demo", e1);
Console.WriteLine(proj);

ref Employee owner = ref proj.GetOwner();
owner = new Employee(2, "Jane", "Doe");
Console.WriteLine(proj);
```

The output of this program is shown in the following screenshot:

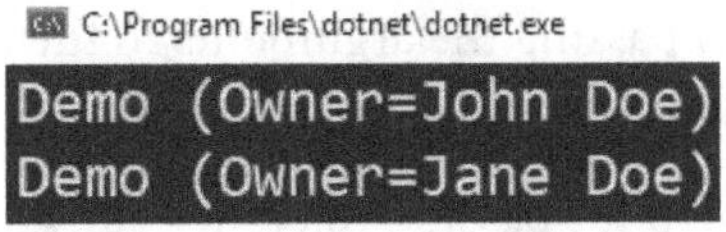

Figure 4.5 – A screenshot of the output from the previous snippet

When using `ref` to return a value, you must be aware of the following:

- It is not possible to return a reference to a local variable.
- It is not possible to return a reference to `this`.
- It is possible to return references to class fields but also to properties without a `set` accessor.
- It is possible to return a reference to `ref`/`in`/`out` parameters.
- Returning by reference breaks the encapsulation because the caller gets full access to the state, or parts of the state, of an object.

Let's now look at the `in` keyword.

The in keyword

The `in` keyword is very similar to the `ref` keyword. It causes an argument to be passed by reference. However, the key difference is that an `in` argument cannot be modified by the called method. An `in` parameter is basically a `readonly ref` parameter. Should the called method try to modify the value, the compiler will issue an error. A variable that is passed as an `in` argument must be initialized before being passed as an argument in a method called.

The following sample shows a method that takes two `in` arguments. Any attempt to change their value results in a compiler error:

```
static void DontTouch(in int value, in string text)
{
    value = 42;   // error
    ++value;      // error
    text = null;  // error
}

int i = 0;
string s = "hello";
DontTouch(i, s);
```

Specifying the `in` keyword when passing the arguments to the method is optional. In the preceding example, this is omitted.

The `in` specifier is mostly intended for passing references to value type objects on hot paths, that is, functions that are called repeatedly. When you pass a value type object to a function, a copy of the value is made on the stack. Typically, this does not pose any performance concerns but, when it is happening over and over again, performance issues arise. By using the `in` specifier, a read-only reference to the object is passed, thereby avoiding the copy.

Another benefit of the `in` specifier is the communication of the clear design intent that a parameter is not supposed to be modified by a method.

The out keyword

The `out` keyword is similar to the `ref` keyword. The difference is that a variable passed as an `out` argument does not have to be initialized before the method called, but the method taking an `out` parameter must assign a value to it before returning. The `out` keyword must be present both in the method definition and in the invocation of the method, before the argument.

Returning an output value is useful in situations when a method needs to return more than one value, or when it needs to return a value but also information about whether the execution was successful or not. An example is `int.TryParse()`, which returns a Boolean indicating whether the parsing was successful and the actual parsed value as an `out` parameter.

To see how it works, let's take a look at the following example:

```
static void Square(int input, out int output)
{
    output = input * input;
}
```

We have defined a `static` method to return the square of an integer. The `Square` method will accept two parameters. The `int` parameter will be an integer value and it will return the square of the input number via the `out` parameter output. It can be used as follows:

```
int num = 10;
int SquareNum;
Square(num, out SquareNum);
```

Upon execution, the output of this program will be `100`.

A variable that is used as an `out` argument can be declared inline in the method invocation. This produces simpler and more compact code. The scope of the inline variable is the scope in which the method is being invoked.

The preceding code can be simplified as follows:

```
int num = 10;
Square(num, out int SquareNum);
```

There are some restrictions when using these parameter specifiers, which will be explained in the following section.

Understanding their limitations

When using the `ref`, `in`, and `out` parameters, you must be aware of several limitations. These keywords cannot be used with the following:

- Async methods, defined with the `async` modifier.
- Iterator methods, which include either `yield return` or `yield break`.

On the other hand, the `ref`, `in`, and `out` keywords are not considered a part of the method signature in the context of overload resolution. That means you cannot have two overloads of the same method: one that takes a `ref` argument and one that takes the same argument as an `out` parameter. However, it is possible to have overloaded methods if one has a value parameter, and the other has a `ref`, `in`, or `out` parameter:

```
class foo
{
  public void DoSomething(ref int i);
  public void DoSomething(out int i); // error: cannot overload
}

class bar
{
  public void DoSomethingElse(int i);
  public void DoSomethingElse(ref int i);  // OK
}
```

All the methods that we have seen so far in this book have a fixed number of arguments. The language, however, allows us to define methods that can take a variable number of arguments. This topic is discussed next.

Methods with a variable number of arguments

So far, we have only seen methods that take zero or a fixed number of arguments. However, it is also possible to define methods that take any number of arguments of the same type. To do so, you must have an argument that is a single-dimensional array preceded by the `params` keyword. This parameter does not have to be the only parameter of the method, but no further parameters are allowed after it.

In the following example, we have two methods—Any() and All()—that take a variable number of Boolean values and return a Boolean value, indicating whether any of them is `true`, and respectively, whether all of them are `true`:

```
static bool Any(params bool [] values)
{
    foreach (bool v in values)
        if (v) return true;
    return false;
}

static bool All(params bool[] values)
{
    if (values.Length == 0) return false;
```

```
    foreach (bool v in values)
        if (!v) return false;
    return true;
}
```

Both of these methods can be invoked with zero, one, or any other number of arguments, as shown here:

```
var a = Any(42 > 15, "text".Length == 3);   // a=true
var b = All(true, false, true);              // b=false
var c = All();                               // c=false
```

The way the arguments are provided for a method call is flexible. We will look at existing possibilities next.

Named and optional arguments

In all of the examples we have seen so far, the arguments for a method call were provided in the order of the parameter declaration in the method signature. These are called *positional arguments* because they are evaluated based on the position they are given. Moreover, all the parameters were mandatory, which means that an invocation cannot occur unless an argument is supplied for each parameter in the parameters list.

However, C# supports two more types of arguments: *optional arguments* and *named arguments*. These are often used together and enable us to supply only some arguments for the parameters in a list of optional parameters. These can be used with methods, indexers, constructors, and delegates.

Optional arguments

When declaring a method, constructor, indexer, or delegate, we can specify a default value for a parameter. When such a parameter exists, supplying an argument for it upon the member invocation is optional. If none is provided, the compiler will use the default one. A default value for a parameter must be one of the following:

- A constant expression
- An expression of the new T() form, where T is a value type
- An expression of the default(T) form, where T is also a value type

A method can have both required and optional parameters. If optional parameters are present, they must follow all the non-optional parameters. A non-optional parameter cannot follow an optional parameter.

Let's consider the following implementation of the `Point` structure:

```
struct Point
{
    public int X { get; }
    public int Y { get; }

    public Point(int x = 0, int y = 0)
    {
        X = x;
        Y = y;
    }
}
```

The constructor takes two parameters, both of them having the default value 0. This means they are both optional. We can invoke the constructor in any of the following forms:

```
Point p1 = new Point();      // x = 0, y = 0
Point p2 = new Point(1);     // x = 1, y = 0
Point p3 = new Point(1, 2); // x = 1, y = 2
```

In the first example, no argument to the constructor of `Point` is supplied, so the compiler will use 0 for both x and y. In the second example, a single argument is supplied and that will be used to bind to the first constructor parameter. Therefore, x will be 1 and y will be 0. In the third and last example, two arguments are supplied, and they are bound to x and y in this order. Therefore, x is 1 and y is 2.

Named arguments

Named arguments enable us to invoke a method specifying the arguments by their name and not by their position in the parameters list. Arguments can be specified in any order and, in combination with default arguments, we can specify only some arguments for a method invocation. Named arguments are provided by specifying the parameter name followed by a colon (:) and the value.

Let's consider the following examples:

```
Point p1 = new Point(x: 1, y: 2); // x = 1, y = 2
Point p2 = new Point(1, y: 2);    // x = 1, y = 2
Point p3 = new Point(x: 1, 2);    // x = 1, y = 2

Point p4 = new Point(y: 2);       // x = 0, y = 2
Point p5 = new Point(x: 1);       // x = 1, y = 0
```

The first three constructor invocations are equivalent; p1, p2, and p3 represent the same point. The invocation of the constructor uses one or more named arguments but the effect is the same. When constructing p4, on the other hand, only the value for y is specified. Therefore, x will be 0 and y will be 2. Lastly, p5 is created by specifying only a named argument for x. Therefore, x will be 1 and y will be 0.

Access modifiers

An access modifier is used to define the visibility of a type or member in C#. It specifies what other parts of the code in the assembly or other assemblies can access the type or the type member. C# defines six types of access modifiers, as follows:

- public: A public field can be accessed by any part of the code in the same assembly or in another assembly.

- protected: A protected type or member can be accessed only in the current class and in a derived class.

- internal: An internal type or member is accessible only within the current assembly.

- protected internal: This is a combination of protected and internal access levels. A protected internal type or member is accessible in the current assembly or in a derived class.

- private: A private type or member can be accessed only inside the class or struct. This is the least-accessible level defined in C#.

- private protected: This is a combination of private and protected access levels. A private protected type or type member is accessible by code in the same class, or in a derived class, but only within the same assembly.

Trying to access a type or type member outside its access level will result in a compile-time error.

There are different kinds of rules for accessibility that apply to types and type members:

- **Class and struct accessibility**: When declared directly in a namespace, a class or a struct can only be declared public or internal (which is the default). Derived classes, on the other hand, cannot have greater accessibility than their base types. That means if you have an internal class B, you cannot derive from it a public class D.

- **Class and struct member accessibility**: Class members can have any of the six access modifiers. However, struct members can only be `public`, `internal`, or `private`. These rules apply to nested structs and classes. The default access level for class and struct members is `private`. A nested type that is `private` is accessible only from the enclosing type. The accessibility of a member cannot be greater than the type that contains it.

Moreover, the type of a field, property, or event must be at least as accessible as the field itself. Similarly, the return type of a method, indexer, or delegate, as well as the type of its parameters, cannot be less accessible than the member itself.

- **Other types and members**: User-defined operators are always `public` and `static`. Finalizers cannot have accessibility modifiers. Interfaces defined directly in a namespace can be `public` or `internal` (which is the default). Access modifiers cannot be applied to any interface members, which are implicitly `public`. In a similar manner, enumeration members are implicitly `public` and cannot have access specifiers. Delegates are like classes and structs – their default access is `internal` when defined directly in a namespace, and `private` when nesting in another type.

The following code shows various uses of access modifiers for types and type members:

```
public interface IEngine
{
    double Power { get; }

    void Start();
}

public class DieselEngine : IEngine
{
    private double _power;
    public double Power { get { return _power; } }

    public void Start() { }
}
```

We have learned in this chapter how to define custom classes. In all the examples so far, the entire class was defined in a single place. However, it is possible to split a class across several different definitions, in the same or different files, which is what we will look at in the next section.

Partial classes

A partial class allows us to divide our class into multiple class definitions, which is useful when a class becomes very large or when we want to separate a class logically into multiple parts. This enables technologies such as WPF to work better because the user code and the code written by the IDE designers are separated into different source files.

Each part can be defined in a different source file using the partial keyword. This keyword must appear immediately before the class keyword. The parts must be available at compile time. During compilation, the parts are combined into a single type.

The partial keyword can be applied not only to classes, but also structures, interfaces, and methods. The same rules apply to all of them.

An example of the partial class is shown here:

```
partial class Employee
{
    partial void Promote();
}

partial class Employee
{
    public int EmployeeId { get; set; }
}

partial class Employee
{
    public string FirstName { get; set; }
    public string LastName { get; set; }

    partial void Promote()
    {
        Console.WriteLine("Employee promoted!");
    }
}
```

Here, we split the class definition into two `partial` classes. Both `partial` classes contain some properties. We can instantiate the `partial` class and use its properties similar to a normal class. Refer to the following code snippet:

```
Employee obj = new Employee()
{
    EmployeeId = 1,
    FirstName = "John",
    LastName = "Doe"
};

obj.Promote();
```

The following list contains properties of partial types, as well as rules for them:

- All the parts must have the same accessibility.
- Different parts may specify a different base interface. The final type will implement all the listed interfaces.
- If multiple parts specify a base class then it must be the same base class, as multiple inheritances are not supported in C#. A base class can be specified only on one part. It is optional on the others.
- Attributes of all the parts are merged together at compile type. The final type will have all the attributes used on all the part declarations.
- Nested classes can also be partial.

Methods can also be partial. This enables us to provide the signature in one part of a `partial` class or structure and the implementation in another. This is useful in IDEs to provide method hooks that developers may or may not implement. If a partial method does not have an implementation, it is removed from the class definition at compile time. Partial methods cannot have an access modifier and are implicitly private. Also, a partial method cannot return a value; the return type of a partial method must be `void`.

Structures

The content of this chapter so far has been focused on classes. Types that are defined as classes are reference types. However, in .NET and C#, there is another category of types: **value types**. Value types have value semantics, meaning that the value of the object, and not a reference to the object, is copied on assignment.

Value types are defined using the struct keyword instead of class. In most aspects, structures are identical to classes and the characteristics presented in this chapter for classes apply to structures too. However, there are several key differences:

- Structures do not support inheritance. Although a structure can implement any number of interfaces, it cannot derive from another structure. For this reason, structure members cannot have the protected access modifier. Also, a structured method or property cannot be abstract or virtual.

- A structure cannot declare a default (parameterless) constructor.

- Structures can be instantiated without using the new operator.

- In a structure declaration, fields cannot be initialized unless they are declared const or static.

Let's consider the following example where we define a structure called Point with two integer fields:

```
struct Point
{
    public int x;
    public int y;
}
```

We can instantiate this either using the new operator, which would call the default constructor initializing all the member fields with their default value, or directly, without the new operator. In this case, the member fields would remain uninitialized. This could be useful for performance reasons, but such an object cannot be used until all of its fields are properly initialized:

```
Point p = new Point()
{
    x = 2,
    y = 3
};
```

The preceding code uses the new operator to create an instance of the type. On the other hand, in the following example, the object is created without the new operator:

```
Point p;
p.x = 2;
p.y = 3;
```

While structures and classes have many things in common, they also differ in several key aspects. It is important to understand when you should use classes and when you should use structures. A structure should be used in the following cases:

- When it represents a single value (such as a point, a GUID, and so on)
- When it is small (typically no larger than 16 bytes)
- When it is immutable
- When it is short-lived
- When it is not used frequently in boxing and unboxing operations (which alter performance)

In all the other cases, types should be defined as classes.

A variable of a value type cannot be assigned a `null` value. However, for situations when no value is a valid value for a value type, a nullable value type (denoted as `T?` using shorthand syntax) can be used. Nullable types were discussed in *Chapter 2, Data Types and Operators*.

The following shows an example of a nullable `Point` variable assigned with `null`:

```
Point? p = null;
```

It is often mentioned in the literature that instances of value types are stored on the stack. This statement is only partially true. The stack is an implementation detail; it is not part of the characteristics of value types. Local variables or temporaries of value types are indeed stored on the stack (unless they are not closed over outer variables of a lambda or an anonymous method) and not part of an iterator block.

Otherwise, they are typically stored on the heap. However, this is entirely an implementation and compiler detail and, in fact, value types can be stored in many places: in the stack, in a CPU register, on the FPU frame, on the heap managed by the garbage collector, on the loader heap of the AppDomain, or in the thread-local storage (if the variable has the `ThreadStorage` attribute).

When a value type object (the storage location contains the value directly) is assigned to a reference type object (the storage location contains a reference to the actual value), the process of boxing occurs. The other way around the process is called unboxing. We have discussed these two previously in this book, in *Chapter 2, Data Types and Operators*.

Take a look at the following example:

```
struct Point
{
    public int X { get; }
    public int Y { get; }

    public Point(int x = 0, int y = 0)
    {
        X = x;
        Y = y;
    }
}

Point p1 = new Point(2, 3);
Point p2 = new Point(0, 3);

if (p1.Equals(p2)) { /* do something */ }
```

Here, we have two variables of the `Point` value type and we want to check whether they are equal. To do so, we invoke the `Equals()` method that is defined in the `System.Object` base class. When we do this, boxing occurs because the parameter of `Equals` is an object, that is, a reference type. Boxing may become a performance issue if it is performed very often. There are two ways to avoid boxing for a value type.

The first solution is to implement the `IEquatable<T>` interface that contains a single `Equals(T)` method. This method allows both value and reference types to implement a way that determines whether two objects are equal. This interface is used by generic collections for testing for equality in various methods. Therefore, for performance reasons, it should be implemented by all types that might be stored in generic collections.

The implementation of the `Point` structure that implements `IEquatable<T>` is as follows:

```
struct Point : IEquatable<Point>
{
    public int X { get; }
    public int Y { get; }

    public Point(int x = 0, int y = 0)
    {
        X = x;
        Y = y;
    }
```

```
    public bool Equals(Point other)
    {
        return X == other.X && Y == other.Y;
    }

    public override bool Equals(object obj)
    {
        if (obj is Point other)
        {
            return this.Equals(other);
        }
        return false;
    }

    public override int GetHashCode()
    {
        return X.GetHashCode() * 17 + Y.GetHashCode();
    }
}
```

In this example, you should notice that the generic type parameter for `IEquatable` is the type itself, `Point`. This is a technique called the *curiously recurring template pattern*. The class implements `Equals(Point)`, checking the properties of the type. However, it also overrides the `System.Object` virtual methods, `Equals()` and `GetHashCode()`, making sure the two implementations are consistent.

When implementing the `IEquatable<T>` interface, you should keep the following in mind:

- `Equals(T)` and `Equals(object)` must return consistent results.
- If the value is comparable, then it should implement `IComparable<T>` too.
- If the type implements `IComparable<T>`, then it should implement `IEquatable<T>` too.

The second solution is to overload the == and != operators. This can be done as follows:

```
struct Point
{
    public int X { get; }
    public int Y { get; }

    public Point(int x = 0, int y = 0)
    {
        X = x;
        Y = y;
    }

    public override bool Equals(object obj)
    {
        if (obj is Point other)
        {
            return this.Equals(other);
        }
        return false;
    }

    public override int GetHashCode()
    {
        return X.GetHashCode() * 17 + Y.GetHashCode();
    }

    public static bool operator !=(Point p1, Point p2)
    {
        return p1.X != p2.X || p1.Y != p2.Y;
    }

    public static bool operator ==(Point p1, Point p2)
    {
        return p1.X == p2.X && p1.Y == p2.Y;
    }
}
```

In this case, we will no longer use Equals() to compare values, but the two operators == and !=:

```
Point p1 = new Point(2, 3);
Point p2 = new Point(0, 3);

if (p1 == p2) { /* do something */ }
```

It is, however, possible to both implement `IEquatable<T>` and overload the comparison operators, if you want to be able to check for equality both ways. We will discuss operator overloading in more detail in *Chapter 5, Object-Oriented Programming in C#*.

Enumerations

An enumeration is a set of named integral constants. We use the `enum` keyword to declare an enumeration. An enumeration is a value type. Enumerations are useful when we want to use a limited number of integral values for some particular purpose. Defining and using an enumeration has several advantages:

- We use named constants instead of literal values. This makes the code more readable and easier to maintain.

- When you use IDEs, such as Visual Studio, you can see the list of possible values that can be assigned to a variable.

- It enforces type safety for using numerical constants.

The following example shows an enumeration called `Priority` with four possible values:

```
enum Priority
{
    Low,
    Normal,
    Important,
    Urgent
}
```

Each element of an enumeration stands for an integer value. By default, the first identifier is assigned to zero (`0`). The value of each successive identifier will increase by one. It is also possible to specify explicit values for each element. The following rules apply:

- These values must be within the range of the underlying type.

- The values do not have to be consecutive or in order.

- Multiple identifiers with the same numerical value can be defined.

The enumeration, as defined, is semantically equivalent to the following, where values are specified explicitly:

```
enum Priority
{
    Low = 0,
    Normal = 1,
    Important = 2,
    Urgent = 3
}
```

As mentioned earlier, each element of the enumeration can have any numerical value. The following example shows a definition of the `Priority` enumeration. Where some elements do have explicit values, others are calculated based on them:

```
enum Priority
{
    Low = 10,
    Normal,
    Important = 20,
    Urgent
}
```

In this implementation, `Low` is 10, `Normal` is 11, `Important` is 20, and `Urgent` is 21.

The default underlying type of an enumeration is `int`, but any integral type can be specified as the underlying type. The `char` type cannot be the underlying type for an enumeration. In the following example, `byte` is the underlying type for `Priority`:

```
enum Priority : byte
{
    Low = 10,
    Normal,
    Important = 20,
    Urgent
}
```

To use an element of an enumeration, you specify the enumeration name followed by a dot (`.`) and the element name, such as `Priority.Normal`:

```
Priority p = Priority.Normal;
Console.WriteLine(Priority.Urgent);
```

Any value of the underlying type can be assigned to an enumeration variable, even if an element with a corresponding numerical value does not exist. This is only possible with a cast. However, the literal 0 is implicitly convertible to any enumeration type without the need for a cast:

```
Priority p1 = (Priority)42;    // p1 is 42
Priority p2 = 0;               // p2 is 0
Priority p3 = (int)10;         // p3 is Low
```

On the other hand, there is no implicit conversion between an enumeration and an integral type. To obtain the integer value of an enum identifier, we must use an explicit cast, as shown here:

```
int i = (int)Priority.Normal;
```

Because all the references to the elements of an enumeration are replaced at compile time with their literal values, changing the values of the enumeration elements will affect referencing assemblies. When the enum type is used in other assemblies, the numerical values will be stored in those assemblies. Changes in the enumeration will not be reflected in the dependent assemblies unless they are recompiled.

Should you need to parse an enumeration value from a string, you can use the generic Enum.TryParse() method, as in the following example:

```
Enum.TryParse("Normal", out Priority p); // p is Normal
```

However, if you want to parse from a string ignoring the case, then you need to use a non-generic overload of the same method, as shown here:

```
Enum.TryParse(typeof(Priority), "normal", true, out object o);
Priority p = (Priority)o;    // p is Normal
```

In this example, the string "normal" is parsed, ignoring the case to identify a possible value of the Priority enumeration. The value returned in the output parameter is Priority.Normal.

Namespaces

We have mentioned namespaces several times in this book already without explaining what they really are. Namespaces are used to organize your code in logical units. A namespace defines a declaration space that contains types. This declaration space has a name that is part of a type's name. For instance, the .NET type String is declared in the System namespace. The complete name of the type is System.String. This is called the fully-qualified name of the type. Typically, we use only the unqualified name of the type (String, in this case), because we use using directives to bring declarations into the current scope from a particular namespace.

Namespaces are used for two main purposes:

- To help organize the code. Typically, types that belong together are declared in the same namespace.

- To avoid possible name collisions for types. A program may rely on different libraries and it's not unlikely that types with the same name exist in two or more of these libraries. By using namespaces with a high degree of uniqueness, the chance for name collisions is drastically reduced.

- Namespaces are introduced with the namespace keyword. They are implicitly public and you cannot use access modifiers when declaring them. A namespace can contain any number of types (classes, structures, enumerations, or delegates).

The following example shows how to define a namespace, called chapter_04:

```
namespace chapter_04
{
    class foo { }
}
```

Namespaces can be nested; one namespace can contain other namespaces. An example is shown in the following snippet, where the chapter_04 namespace contains a nested namespace called demo:

```
namespace chapter_04
{
    namespace demo
    {
        class foo { }
    }
}
```

In this example, the fully qualified name of the `foo` type is `chapter_04.demo.foo`.

For brevity, nested namespaces can be declared with a shorthand syntax: instead of multiple namespace declarations, only one is necessary. The name of the namespace is the concatenation of all the namespace names, separated by a dot. The previous declaration is equivalent to the following:

```
namespace chapter_04.demo
{
    class foo { }
}
```

To use an instance of this `foo` type, you would have to use its fully-qualified name, as follows:

```
namespace chapter_04
{
    class Program
    {
        static void Main(string[] args)
        {
            var f = new chapter_04.demo.foo();
        }
    }
}
```

To avoid this, you can use a `using` directive, specifying the namespace name as follows:

```
using chapter_04.demo;
namespace chapter_04
{
    class Program
    {
        static void Main(string[] args)
        {
            var f = new foo();
        }
    }
}
```

A using directive can only be present at a namespace level (not locally to a method or type). Typically, you put them at the beginning of a source file, in which case its types are available throughout the entire source code defined in that file. Alternatively, you can specify them in a particular namespace, in which case its types will only be available to that namespace.

A namespace is said to be open-ended. This means that you can have multiple namespace declaration with the same name, either in the same or different source files. In this case, all these declarations represent the same namespace and contribute to the same declaration space. The following snippet demonstrates an example of this case:

```
namespace chapter_04.demo
{
    class foo { }
}
namespace chapter_04.demo
{
    class bar { }
}
```

There is an implicit namespace that is the root of all namespaces (and contains all namespaces and types that are not declared in a named namespace). This namespace is called global. If you need to include it to specify a fully qualified name, then you must separate it with :: and not with a dot, as in global::System.String. This can be necessary in situations where namespace names collide. Here is an example:

```
namespace chapter_04.System
{
    class Console { }

    class Program
    {
        static void Main(string[] args)
        {
            global::System.Console.WriteLine("Hello, world!");
        }
    }
}
```

In this example, without the global:: alias, the user-defined chapter_04.System.Console type would be used in the Main() function, instead of the expected System.Console type.

Summary

In this chapter, we have learned about the user-defined types in C#. We learned about classes and structures that help us to create custom user types in C#. We also learned how to create and use fields, properties, methods, indexers, and constructors inside a class, and we learned about the `this` and `static` keywords.

We explored the concepts of access modifiers and understood how we can define various levels of access to types and members. We also learned about `ref`, `in`, and `out` parameter modifiers, as well as methods with a variable number of arguments. Last but not least, we learned about namespace and how to use them to organize code and avoid name collisions.

In the next chapter, we will learn about **Object-Oriented Programming (OOP)** concepts. We will explore the building blocks of OOP—encapsulation, inheritance, polymorphism, and abstraction. We will also learn about abstract classes and interfaces.

Test what you learned

1. What is a class and what is an object?

2. What is the difference between classes and structures?

3. What is a read-only field?

4. What are expression body definitions?

5. What is a default constructor and what is a static constructor?

6. What are auto-implemented properties?

7. What are indexers and how are they defined?

8. What is a static class and what can it contain?

9. What are the parameter specifiers and how do they differ?

10. What are enumerations and when are they useful?

5
Object-Oriented Programming in C#

In the previous chapter, we covered user-defined types and learned about classes, structures, and enumerations. In this chapter, we will learn about **object-oriented programming** (or **OOP** for short). A good understanding of OOP concepts is essential to write better programs using C#. OOP reduces code complexity, increases code reusability, and makes software easy to maintain and scale.

We will cover the following concepts in detail:

- Understanding OOP
- Abstraction
- Encapsulation
- Inheritance
- Polymorphism
- SOLID principles

By the end of this chapter, you will learn how to create classes and methods using OOP. Let's begin with an overview of OOP.

Understanding OOP

Object-oriented programming is a paradigm that allows us to write a program around objects. As discussed in the previous chapter, objects contain data and methods to act on that data. Each object has its own set of data and methods. If an object wants to access the data of another object, it has to access it via the methods defined in that object. An object can inherit the properties of another object using the concept of **inheritance**. Hence, we can say that object-oriented programming is organized around data and the operations that are permitted on the data.

C# is a general-purpose multi-paradigm programming language. OOP is only one of these paradigms. Other supported paradigms, such as generic and functional programming, will be discussed in later chapters.

When discussing object-oriented programming, it is important to understand the differences between classes and objects. As mentioned already, in the previous chapter, a class is a blueprint that defines data and how it is represented in memory as well as functionalities that operate on this data. On the other hand, an object is an instance of a class built and functioning according to the blueprint. It has a physical representation in memory, unlike a class that only exists in source code.

When you do object-oriented programming, you start with identifying the entities you need to operate on, how they relate to each other, and how they interact. This is a process called **data modeling**. The result of this is a set of classes that generalize the identified entities. These can vary from physical entities (people, objects, machines, and so on) to abstractions (an order, a to-do list, a connection string, and so on).

Abstraction, encapsulation, polymorphism, and inheritance are the core principles of object-oriented programming. We will explore them in detail in this chapter.

Abstraction

Abstraction is the process of describing entities and processes in simple terms by removing non-essential characteristics. A physical or abstract entity may have many characteristics but for the purpose of some application or domain, not all of them are important. By abstracting entities into simple models (that make sense for the application domain), we can build simpler and more efficient programs.

Let's consider the example of an employee. An employee is a person. A person has a name; a birthday; body characteristics, such as height, weight, hair color, and eye color; relatives and friends; likes and hobbies (such as food, books, movies, and sports); an address; properties (such as a house or apartment and cars or bikes); one or more phone numbers and email addresses; and many other things that we could fill pages listing.

Depending on the kind of application we are building, some of these are relevant and some are not. For instance, if we build a payroll system, we are interested in an employee's name, birthday, address, phone, and email, as well as hiring date, department, role, salary, and so on. If we build a social media application, we are interested in a user's name, birthday, address, relatives, friends, interests, activities, and more.

Sometimes, different levels of abstraction are required—some more general, others more particular. For instance, if we build a graphical system that can draw shapes, we might need to model a generic shape with little functionalities, such as the ability to draw itself or transform (translate and rotate) itself. We can then have two-dimensional shapes and three-dimensional shapes, each with more specific properties and functionalities based on the characteristics of these shapes.

We can build lines, ellipses, and polygons as two-dimensional shapes. A line has properties such as a start point and an end point, but an ellipse has two foci, as well as an area and a perimeter. Three-dimensional objects, such as a cube, can drop shadows. Although we are still abstracting concepts, we have moved from more general to more particular abstractions. When these abstractions are based on each other, the typical way to implement them is through inheritance.

Encapsulation

Encapsulation is defined as binding data and code that manipulates it together in a single unit. Data is privately bound within a class without direct access from the outside of the class. All objects that need to read or modify the data of an object should do it through the public methods that a class provides. This characteristic is called **data hiding** and makes code less error-prone by defining a limited number of entry points to an object's data.

Let's take a look at the `Employee` class here:

```
public class Employee
{
    private string name;
    private double salary;

    public string Name
    {
        get { return name; }
        set { name = value; }
    }
}
```

```
    public double Salary
    {
        get { return salary; }
    }

    public Employee(string name, double salary)
    {
        this.name = name;
        this.salary = salary;
    }

    public void GiveRaise(double percent)
    {
        salary *= (1.0 + percent / 100.0);
    }
}
```

An employee has two properties modeled here: name and salary. These are implemented as private class fields, which makes them accessible only from within the Employee class. Both of these values are set in the constructor. The name is exposed for reading and writing using the property called Name. The salary variable is, however, only exposed for reading, with the read-only property called Salary. To change the salary, we must call the GiveRaise() method. Of course, this is just a possible implementation. We could have used auto-implemented properties instead of fields, or maybe different other methods to modify the salary. This class can be used as follows:

```
Employee employee = new Employee("John Doe", 2500);

Console.WriteLine($"{employee.Name} earns {employee.Salary}");
employee.GiveRaise(5.5);
Console.WriteLine($"{employee.Name} earns {employee.Salary}");
```

We have created an object of the Employee class and set the values to the private fields using the constructor. The Employee class does not allow direct access to its fields. To read their values, we use the public get accessor of the public properties. To change the salary, we use the GiveRaise() method. The output of this program is as shown here:

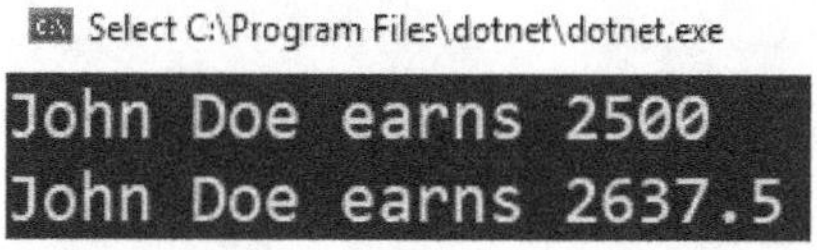

Figure 5.1 – The console output from the execution of the preceding snippet

Encapsulation allows us to hide the data inside a class from the outside world, which is why it is also known as data-hiding.

Encapsulation is important because it reduces the dependencies between different components by defining minimal public interfaces for them. It also increases code reusability and security and makes code easier to unit test.

Inheritance

Inheritance is a mechanism through which a class can inherit the properties and functionalities of another class. If we have a set of common functionalities and data shared among multiple classes, we can put them in one class known as a **parent** or **base** class. Other classes can inherit these functionalities and data of the parent class as well as extending or modifying them and adding additional functionalities and properties. A class that inherits from another class is known as a **child** or **derived** class. Inheritance, therefore, facilitates *code reusability*.

In C#, inheritance is only supported for reference types. Only types defined as classes can be derived from other types. Types that are defined as structures are value types and cannot be derived from other types. However, all types in C# are either value or reference types and are indirectly derived from the System.Object type. This relationship is implicit and does not require developers to do anything special.

There are three types of inheritance supported in C#:

- **Single inheritance**: When a class inherits from one parent class. The child class should not act as the parent class to any other class. Refer to the following diagram, where class B is inheriting for class A:

Figure 5.2 – A class diagram showing class B inheriting from class A

- **Multilevel inheritance**: This is actually an extension to the previous case, because the child is, on the other hand, a parent to another class. In the following diagram, class B is a child class to class A as well as the parent to class C:

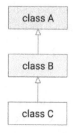

Figure 5.3 – A class diagram showing class A being the base class for class B, which in turn is the base for class C

- **Hierarchical inheritance**: A class serves as the parent class to more than one class. Refer to the following diagram. Here, the classes B and C inherit from the same parent class, A:

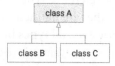

Figure 5.4 – A class diagram showing classes B and C inheriting from the base class A

Unlike other programming languages (such as C++), C# does not support multiple inheritance. This means that a class cannot be derived from more than one class.

To understand inheritance, let's consider the following example: we are building a game that must represent objects such as terrain, obstacles, people, machinery, and so on. These are various types of objects with different properties. For instance, people and machines can move and battle, obstacles can be destroyed, terrain can be crossable or not, and so on. However, all of these game objects have some common properties: they all have a position in the game and they all can be drawn on a surface (which could be a screen, memory, and so on). We can represent a base class that provides these functionalities as follows:

```
class GameUnit
{
    public Position Position { get; protected set; }

    public GameUnit(Position position)
    {
        Position = position;
    }
}
```

```
    public void Draw(Surface surface)
    {
        surface.DrawAt(GetImage(), Position);
    }

    protected virtual char GetImage() { return ' '; }
}
```

GameUnit is a class with a property called Position; the accessor get is public, but the accessor set is protected, which means it is only accessible from this class or its derived classes. The Draw() public method draws the unit on a surface at the current unit position. GetImage() is a virtual method that returns the representation on a unit (which, in our example, is a single character). In the base class, this simply returns a space, but in the derived classes, this will be implemented to return an actual character.

The Position and Surface classes seen here are implemented as follows:

```
struct Position
{
    public int X { get; private set; }
    public int Y { get; private set; }
    public Position(int x = 0, int y = 0)
    {
        X = x;
        Y = y;
    }
}

class Surface
{
    private int left;
    private int top;

    public void BeginDraw()
    {
        Console.Clear();
        left = Console.CursorLeft;
        top = Console.CursorTop;
    }

    public void DrawAt(char c, Position position)
    {
        try
        {
```

```
            Console.SetCursorPosition(left + position.X,
                                      top + position.Y);
            Console.Write(c);
        }
        catch (ArgumentOutOfRangeException e)
        {
            Console.Clear();
            Console.WriteLine(e.Message);
        }
    }
}
```

From the base class, we will now derive several other classes. To keep it simple, we will focus on terrain objects for the time being:

```
class Terrain : GameUnit
{
    public Terrain(Position position) : base(position) { }
}

class Water : Terrain
{
    public Water(Position position) : base(position) { }

    protected override char GetImage() { return '⸬'; }
}

class Hill : Terrain
{
    public Hill(Position position) : base(position) { }

    protected override char GetImage() { return '≡'; }
}
```

We have defined here a `Terrain` class, derived from `GameUnit`, which is itself a base class for all types of terrain. We don't have many things in this class, but in a real application, there would be various functionalities. `Water` and `Hill` are two classes derived from `Terrain` that override the `GetImage()` class returning a different character to represent the terrain. We can use these as follows to build a game:

```
var objects = new List<v1.GameUnit>()
{
    new v1.Water(new Position(3, 2)),
    new v1.Water(new Position(4, 2)),
```

```
        new v1.Water(new Position(5, 2)),
        new v1.Hill(new Position(3, 1)),
        new v1.Hill(new Position(5, 3)),
};

var surface = new v1.Surface();
surface.BeginDraw();

foreach (var unit in objects)
        unit.Draw(surface);
```

The output of this program is as shown in the following screenshot:

Figure 5.5 – The console output from the execution of the previous program

Virtual members

In the preceding example, we have seen a virtual method. This is a method that has an implementation in a base class but can be overridden in derived classes, which is helpful for changing implementation details. Methods are non-virtual by default. A virtual method in a base class is declared with the `virtual` keyword. An overridden implementation of a virtual method in a derived class is defined with the `override` keyword, instead of the `virtual` keyword. The method signature of the virtual and overridden methods must match.

Methods are not the only class members that can be virtual. The `virtual` keyword can be applied to properties, indexers, and events. However, the `virtual` modifier cannot be used together with `static`, `abstract`, `private`, or `override` modifiers.

A virtual member that is overridden in a derived class can be further overridden in a class derived from the derived class. This chain of virtual inheritance continues indefinitely unless explicitly stopped with the use of the `sealed` keyword, as described in a subsequent section.

The classes shown earlier can be modified to use a virtual property, called `Image` in the following code, instead of the virtual method, `GetImage()`. In this case, they would look as follows:

```csharp
class GameUnit
{
    public Position Position { get; protected set; }

    public GameUnit(Position position)
    {
        Position = position;
    }

    public void Draw(Surface surface)
    {
        surface.DrawAt(Image, Position);
    }

    protected virtual char Image => ' ';
}

class Terrain : GameUnit
{
    public Terrain(Position position) : base(position) { }
}

class Water : Terrain
{
    public Water(Position position) : base(position) { }

    protected override char Image => '⁞';
}

class Hill : Terrain
{
    public Hill(Position position) : base(position) { }

    protected override char Image => '≡';
}
```

There are cases when you want a method to be overridden in derived classes without providing an implementation in the base class. Such virtual methods are called *abstract* and will be discussed in the next section.

Abstract classes and members

The examples we have seen so far have an inconvenience because, although the GameUnit and Terrain classes are just some base classes without an actual representation in the game, we can still instantiate them. This is unfortunate because we would want to be able to only create objects of Water and Hill. Also, the GetImage() virtual method or the Image virtual property must have an implementation in the base class, which does not make much sense. We would actually only want to have an implementation in classes representing physical objects. This can be achieved using abstract classes and members.

An abstract class is declared using the abstract keyword. An abstract class cannot be instantiated, which means we cannot create the object of an abstract class. If we try to create an instance of an abstract class, it will result in a compile-time error. An abstract class is supposed to be the base class for other classes that will implement the abstractions that a class defines.

An abstract class must include at least one abstract member, which can be a method, property, indexer, or event. Abstract members are also declared using the abstract keyword. A non-abstract class that derives from an abstract class must implement all of the inherited abstract members and property accessors.

We can rewrite the game unit examples using abstract classes and members. This is shown in the following listing:

```
abstract class GameUnit
{
    public Position Position { get; protected set; }

    public GameUnit(Position position)
    {
        Position = position;
    }

    public void Draw(Surface surface)
    {
        surface.DrawAt(Image, Position);
    }

    protected abstract char Image { get; }
}

abstract class Terrain : GameUnit
{
    public Terrain(Position position) : base(position) { }
```

```
}

class Water : Terrain
{
    public Water(Position position) : base(position) { }

    protected override char Image => '::';
}

class Hill : Terrain
{
    public Hill(Position position) : base(position) { }

    protected override char Image => '≡';
}
```

In this example, the GameUnit class is declared abstract. It has an abstract property, Image, which no longer has an implementation. Terrain is derived from GameUnit but because it does not override the abstract property, it is itself an abstract class and must be declared using the abstract modifier. The Water and Hill classes are both overriding the Image property, and do so using the override keyword.

The following are a few features of an abstract class:

- An abstract class can have both abstract and non-abstract members.
- If a class contains an abstract member, then the class must be marked abstract.
- An abstract member cannot be private.
- An abstract member cannot have an implementation.
- An abstract class must provide an implementation for all of the members of all of the interfaces it implements (if any).

Similarly, an abstract method or property has the following characteristics:

- An abstract method is implicitly a virtual method.
- Members declared abstract cannot be static or virtual.
- The implementation in a derived class must specify the override keyword in the declaration of the member.

So far, we have seen how classes and members can be derived and overridden. However, it is possible to prevent this from happening. We will learn how to do so in the next section.

Sealed classes and members

If we want to restrict a class from being inherited by another class, then we declare the class as `sealed`. If we try to inherit a sealed class, it will result in a compile-time error. We use the `sealed` keyword to create a sealed class. Refer to the following example:

```
sealed class Water : Terrain
{
    public Water(Position position) : base(position) { }

    protected override char Image => ':::';
}

class Lake : Water  // ERROR: cannot derived from sealed type
{
    public Lake(Position position) : base(position) { }
}
```

The `Water` class here is declared `sealed`. An attempt to use it as a base class for another class will result in a compile-type error.

Not only can classes be declared as `sealed`, but overridden members can too. A class can stop the virtual inheritance of a member by using the `sealed` keyword in front of `override`. An attempt to override it again in a further derived class will result in a compiler error.

In the following example, the `Water` class is not sealed, but its `Image` property is. Attempting to override it in the `Lake` derived class will produce a compiler error:

```
class Water : Terrain
{
    public Water(Position position) : base(position) { }

    protected sealed override char Image => ':::';
}

class Lake : Water
{
    public Lake(Position position) : base(position) { }

    protected sealed override char Image => ':::';  // ERROR
}
```

Now that we have seen how to use sealed classes and members, let's see how to hide base class members.

Hiding base class members

In certain situations, you might want to hide an existing member of a base class with a member with the same name in the derived class, without *virtual invocation* (which is the invocation of virtual methods within the class hierarchy). This is possible by using the new keyword in front of the return type of the member in the derived class, as shown in the following example:

```
class Base
{
    public int Get() { return 42; }
}

class Derived : Base
{
    public new int Get() { return 10; }
}
```

A new member defined this way will be invoked when called through a reference to the derived type. However, if the member is invoked through a reference to the base type, the hidden base member will be called as shown here:

```
Derived d = new Derived();
Console.WriteLine(d.Get()); // prints 10

Base b = d;
Console.WriteLine(b.Get()); // prints 42
```

Unlike virtual methods, which are invoked at runtime based on the runtime type of the object used to invoke them, hidden methods are resolved at compile-time based on the compile-time type of the object used to invoke them.

A possible use for hiding members is shown in the following example, where we have a hierarchy of classes that need to support a cloning method. However, each class should return a new copy of itself and not a reference to the base class:

```
class Pet
{
    public string Name { get; private set; }

    public Pet(string name)
    { Name = name; }

    public Pet Clone() { return new Pet(Name); }
}
```

```
class Dog : Pet
{
    public string Color { get; private set; }

    public Dog(string name, string color):base(name)
    { Color = color; }

    public new Dog Clone() { return new Dog(Name, Color); }
}
```

With these defined, we can write the following code:

```
Pet pet = new Pet("Lola");
Dog dog = new Dog("Rex", "black");
Pet cpet = pet.Clone();
Dog ddog = dog.Clone();
```

Notice that this works only when we invoke the Clone() method from an object of that class, and not through a reference to the base class. Because the invocation is resolved at compile time, if you have a reference to Pet, even if the runtime type of the object is Dog, only Pet will be cloned. This is exemplified in the following sample:

```
Pet another = new Dog("Dark", "white");
Dog copy = another.Clone(); // ERROR this method returns a Pet
```

Member hiding is, in general, considered a code smell (that is, an indication of a deeper problem within the design and the code base) and should be avoided. The goals achieved through member hiding can usually be reached by better means. For instance, the cloning example shown here can be implemented by using a creational design pattern, typically the **Prototype** pattern, but possibly others such as the **Factory Method**.

So far in this chapter, we have seen how to create classes and hierarchies of classes. Another important concept in object-oriented programming is interfaces, which is the topic we will discuss next.

Interfaces

An interface contains a set of members that must be implemented by any class or struct that implements the interface. An interface defines a contract that is supported by all of the types that implement the interface. This also means that the clients using interfaces do not need to know anything about the actual implementation details, which promotes loose coupling, which helps with maintenance and testability.

Because neither multiple class inheritance nor inheritance for structures is supported in the language, interfaces provide a means to simulate them. A type, regardless of whether it is a reference type or a value type, can implement any number of interfaces.

Typically, an interface *contains only declarations* of members but *not implementations*. Beginning with C# 8, interfaces can contain default methods; this is a subject that will be covered in detail in *Chapter 15*, *New Features of C# 8*. In C#, interfaces are declared using the `interface` keyword.

The following list contains important points to consider when using interfaces:

- An interface can contain only methods, properties, indexers, and events. They cannot contain fields.

- If a type implements an interface, then it must provide an implementation for all of the members of the interface. The method signature and return type of the method of an interface cannot be altered by the type that is implementing the interface.

- When an interface defines properties or indexers, an implementation can provide extra accessors for them. For instance, if a property in an interface has only the `get` accessor, the implementation can also provide a `set` accessor.

- An interface cannot have constructors or operators.

- An interface cannot have static members.

- The interface members are implicitly defined as `public`. If you try to use an access modifier with a member of an interface, it will result in a compile-time error.

- An interface can be implemented by multiple types. A type can implement multiple interfaces.

- If a class is inheriting from another class and simultaneously implementing an interface, then the base class name must come before the name of the interface separated by a comma.

- Typically, an interface name starts with the letter `I`, such as `IEnumerable`, `IList<T>`, and so on.

To understand how interfaces work, we will consider the example with game units.

In the previous implementations, we had a class called `Surface`, which was responsible for drawing the game objects. Our implementation was printing to the console but this could be anything—the game window, memory, a bitmap, and so on. To make it possible to easily change between these and not tie the `GameUnit` class to a particular implementation of surfaces, we can define an interface that will specify the functionalities that any implementation must provide. This interface will then be used by the game unit for rendering. Such an interface can be defined as follows:

```
interface ISurface
{
    void BeginDraw();
    void EndDraw();
    void DrawAt(char c, Position position);
}
```

It contains three member functions, all implicitly `public`. This interface will then be implemented by the `Surface` class:

```
class Surface : ISurface
{
    private int left;
    private int top;

    public void BeginDraw()
    {
        Console.Clear();
        left = Console.CursorLeft;
        top = Console.CursorTop;
    }

    public void EndDraw()
    {
        Console.WriteLine();
    }

    public void DrawAt(char c, Position position)
    {
        try
        {
            Console.SetCursorPosition(left + position.X,
                                      top + position.Y);
            Console.Write(c);
```

```
        }
        catch (ArgumentOutOfRangeException e)
        {
            Console.Clear();
            Console.WriteLine(e.Message);
        }
    }
}
```

The class must implement all of the members of the interface. However, it is possible to skip that. In that case, the class must be abstract and must declare abstract members to match the interface members that it does not implement.

In the preceding example, the `Surface` class implements all three methods of the `ISurface` interface. The methods are explicitly declared as `public`. Using any other access modifier would result in a compiler error because the members are implicitly public in the interface and the class cannot lower their visibility. The `GameUnit` class will change, so that the `Draw()` method will have an `ISurface` parameter:

```
abstract class GameUnit
{
    public Position Position { get; protected set; }

    public GameUnit(Position position)
    {
        Position = position;
    }

    public void Draw(ISurface surface)
    {
        surface?.DrawAt(Image, Position);
    }

    protected abstract char Image { get; }
}
```

Let's further extend the example and consider another interface called `IMoveable` that defines a `MoveTo()` method that moves a game object to another position:

```
interface IMoveable
{
    void MoveTo(Position pos);
}
```

This interface will be implemented by all of the game objects that can be moved, such as people, machines, and so on. A class called ActionUnit acts as a base class for all such objects and implements IMoveable:

```
abstract class ActionUnit : GameUnit, IMoveable
{
    public ActionUnit(Position position) : base(position) { }

    public void MoveTo(Position pos)
    {
        Position = pos;
    }
}
```

ActionUnit is also derived from GameUnit, so the base class comes before the list of interfaces. However, since this class only acts as a base class for other classes, it does not implement the Image property and must, therefore, be abstract. A Meeple class, shown in the following listing, derives from ActionUnit:

```
class Meeple : ActionUnit
{
    public Meeple(Position position) : base(position) { }

    protected override char Image => 'M';
}
```

We can use instances of the Meeple class to extend the game we built in a previous example:

```
var objects = new List<GameUnit>()
{
    new Water(new Position(3, 2)),
    new Water(new Position(4, 2)),
    new Water(new Position(5, 2)),
    new Hill(new Position(3, 1)),
    new Hill(new Position(5, 3)),
    new Meeple(new Position(0, 0)),
    new Meeple(new Position(4, 3)),
};

ISurface surface = new Surface();
surface.BeginDraw();
```

```
foreach (var unit in objects)
    unit.Draw(surface);

surface.EndDraw();
```

The output of this program is as follows:

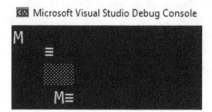

Figure 5.6 – The console output from the execution of the modified game

Now that we have learned about inheritance, it is time to look at the last pillar of OOP, which is polymorphism.

Polymorphism

The last core pillar of object-oriented programming is polymorphism. Polymorphism is a Greek word that stands for *multiple forms*. This is the ability to use one entity in multiple forms. There are two types of polymorphism:

- *Compile-time polymorphism*: When we have methods with the same name but different numbers or types of parameters, which is called method overloading.

- *Run-time polymorphism*: This has two different aspects:

  On one hand, Objects of derived classes can be seamlessly used as objects of base classes in arrays or other types of collections, method parameters, and other places.

  On the other hand, Classes can define virtual methods that can be overridden in derived classes. At runtime, the **Common Language Runtime** (**CLR**) will invoke the implementation of the virtual member corresponding to the runtime type of the object. An object's declared type and its runtime type differ when objects of derived classes are used in place of objects of base classes.

Polymorphism promotes code reuse, which can make it easier to read, test, and maintain the code. It also promotes separation of concerns, which is an important principle in object-oriented programming. Another benefit is that it helps to hide implementation details because it allows interacting with different classes through a common interface.

In the previous sections, we have seen examples of both these aspects. We have seen how to declare virtual members and how to override them, as well as how to stop the virtual inheritance with the `sealed` keyword. We have also seen examples of objects of derived classes used in arrays of base classes. Here is, again, such an example:

```
var objects = new List<GameUnit>()
{
    new Water(new Position(3, 2)),
    new Hill(new Position(3, 1)),
    new Meeple(new Position(0, 0)),
};
```

Compile-time polymorphism is represented by *method and operator overloading*. We will explore these in the following sections.

Method overloading

Method overloading allows us to declare two or more methods within the same class with the same name but different parameters. This can be either a different number of parameters or parameters of different types. The return type is not considered for overload resolution. If two methods differ only in the return type, then the compiler will issue an error. Also, the `ref`, `in`, and `out` parameter modifiers do not participate in overload resolution. That means that two methods cannot differ only in a parameter modifier, such as one method has a `ref` parameter and another one has the same parameter specified with `in` or `out` modifiers. On the other hand, a method with a parameter with no modifier can be overloaded by a method that has the same parameter specified as `ref`, `in`, or `out`.

Let's look at the following example to understand method overloading. Considering the `IMoveable` interface shown earlier, we can modify it so that it contains two methods called `MoveTo()` with different parameters:

```
interface IMoveable
{
    void MoveTo(Position pos);
    void MoveTo(int x, int y);
}

abstract class ActionUnit : GameUnit, IMoveable
{
    public ActionUnit(Position position) : base(position) { }

    public void MoveTo(Position pos)
```

```
    {
        Position = pos;
    }

    public void MoveTo(int x, int y)
    {
        Position = new Position(x, y);
    }
}
```

The `ActionUnit` class provides implementations for both of these overloads. When the overloaded method is called, the compiler finds the best match based on the type and number of supplied arguments and invokes the appropriate overload. An example is shown here:

```
Meeple m = new Meeple(new Position(3, 4));
m.MoveTo(new Position(1, 1));
m.MoveTo(2, 5);
```

The process to identify the best match for a method call is called *overload resolution*. There are many rules that define how the best match is found and listing them all is beyond the scope of this book. In very simple terms, overload resolution is performed as follows:

1. Create a set of members with the specified name.

2. Eliminate all of the members that are not accessible from the calling scope.

3. Eliminate all of the inapplicable members. An applicable member is one that has a parameter for every argument and the argument is implicitly convertible to the parameter's type.

4. If a member has a form with a variable number of arguments, then evaluate them and eliminate non-applicable forms.

5. On the remaining set, apply the rules for finding the best match. A more specific parameter is better than less specific. This means, for instance, that a derived class, which is more specific, is better than a base class. Also, a non-generic parameter is more specific than a generic parameter.

Similar to method overloading but with slightly different syntax and semantics is operator overloading, which we will look at next.

Operator overloading

Operator overloading allows us to provide user-defined functionality to an operator with respect to a particular type. A type can provide a custom implementation for an overloadable operator when one or both of the operands are of that type.

The following are a few important points to consider while implementing operator overloading:

- The `operator` keyword is used to declare an operator. Such methods must be `public` and `static`.

- The assignment operators cannot be overloaded.

- The parameters of an overloaded operator method should not use the `ref`, `in`, or `out` modifiers.

- We cannot change the operator precedence via operator overloading.

- We cannot change the number of operands required by an operator. However, an overloaded operator can ignore an operand.

The C# language has unary, binary, and ternary operators. However, only operators of the first two categories can be overloaded. Let's begin by learning how binary operators can be overloaded.

Overloading a binary operator

At least one of the arguments of a binary operator must be of type `T` or `T?`, where `T` is the type that defines the operator.

Let's consider the following type for which we want to overload operators:

```
struct Complex
{
    public double Real      { get; private set; }
    public double Imaginary { get; private set; }

    public Complex(double real = 0, double imaginary = 0)
    {
        Real = real;
        Imaginary = imaginary;
    }
}
```

This is a very simple implementation for complex numbers, with just two properties for the real and imaginary parts. We want to be able to do arithmetic operations such as addition and subtraction, as shown here:

```
var c1 = new Complex(2, 3);
var c2 = new Complex(4, 5);

var c3 = c1 + c2;
var c4 = c1 - c2;
```

To do so, we must overload the + and - binary operators as follows (the parts of the Complex structure shown previously are omitted for simplicity):

```
public struct Complex
{
    // [...] omitted members

    public static Complex operator +(Complex number1,
                                     Complex number2)
    {
        return new Complex()
        {
            Real = number1.Real + number2.Real,
            Imaginary = number2.Imaginary + number2.Imaginary
        };
    }

    public static Complex operator -(Complex number1,
                                     Complex number2)
    {
        return new Complex()
        {
            Real = number1.Real - number2.Real,
            Imaginary = number2.Imaginary - number2.Imaginary
        };
    }
}
```

We might also want to be able to do object comparison. In this case, we need to overload the ==, !=, <, >, <=, or >= operators or a combination of them:

```
if (c3 == c2) { /* do something */}
if (c1 != c4) { /* do something else */}
```

In the following listing, you can see the implementation of the == and != operators for the Complex type:

```
struct Complex
{
    // [...] omitted members

    public static bool operator ==(Complex number1,
                                   Complex number2)
    {
        return number1.Real.Equals(number2.Real) &&
               number2.Imaginary.Equals(number2.Imaginary);
    }

    public static bool operator !=(Complex number1,
      Complex number2)
    {
        return !number1.Real.Equals(number2.Real) ||
               !number2.Imaginary.Equals(number2.Imaginary);
    }

    public override bool Equals(object obj)
    {
        return Real.Equals(((Complex)obj).Real) &&
               Imaginary.Equals(((Complex)obj).Imaginary);
    }

    public override int GetHashCode()
    {
        return Real.GetHashCode() * 17 +
          Imaginary.GetHashCode();
    }
}
```

When overloading the comparison operators, you must implement them in pairs, as mentioned:

- If you overload == or !=, you must overload them both.
- If you overload < or >, you must overload them both.
- If you overload =< or >=, you must overload them both.

Moreover, when you overload == and != , you also need to override the System. Object virtual methods, Equals() and GetHashCode().

Overloading a unary operator

The single argument of a unary operator must be either T or T? where T is the type that defines the operator.

We will exemplify again using the Complex type and the increment and decrement operators. These can be implemented as follows:

```csharp
struct Complex
{
    // [...] omitted members

    public static Complex operator ++(Complex number)
    {
        return new Complex(number.Real + 1, number.Imaginary);
    }

    public static Complex operator --(Complex number)
    {
        return new Complex(number.Real - 1, number.Imaginary);
    }
}
```

In this implementation, the increment (++) operator and the decrement (--) operator alter only the real part of a complex number and return a new complex number. We can then write the following code to show how these operators can be used:

```csharp
var c = new Complex(5, 7);
Console.WriteLine(c);   // 5i + 7

c++;
Console.WriteLine(c);   // 6i + 7

++c;
Console.WriteLine(c);   // 7i + 7
```

It is important to note that when calling the increment or decrement operators, the operated object is assigned a new value. For reference types, that means a reference to a new object is assigned. As a result, the increment and decrement operators should not modify the original object and return a reference to it. Let's understand the reason by implementing the Complex type as a class:

```
public class Complex
{
    // [...] omitted members

    public static Complex operator ++(Complex number)
    {
        // WRONG implementation
        number.Real++;
        return number;
    }
}
```

This implementation is wrong because it will affect all of the references to the modified object. Consider the following example:

```
var c1 = new Complex(5, 7);
var c2 = c1;
Console.WriteLine(c1);   // 5i + 7
Console.WriteLine(c2);   // 5i + 7

c1++;
Console.WriteLine(c1);   // 6i + 7
Console.WriteLine(c2);   // 6i + 7
```

Initially, c1 and c2 are equal. We then increment the value of c1 and because of the implementation of the ++ operator in the Complex class, both c1 and c2 will have the same value. The correct implementation is as follows:

```
class Complex
{
    // [...] omitted members

    public static Complex operator ++(Complex number)
    {
        return new Complex(number.Real + 1, number.Imaginary);
    }
}
```

Although this is not a problem with value types, you should get into the habit of returning a new object from unary operators.

SOLID principles

The principles we discussed in this chapter—abstraction, encapsulation, inheritance, and polymorphism– are the pillars of object-oriented programming. However, these are not the only principles that developers employ when doing object-oriented programming. There are many other principles but some that are worth mentioning at this point are the five known by the acronym **SOLID**. These were initially introduced by Robert C. Martin in 2000, in a paper called *Design Principles and Design Patterns*. The term SOLID was later coined by Michael Feathers:

- **S** stands for the **Single responsibility principle** that states that a module or a class should have a single responsibility, where responsibility is defined as a reason to change. When a class provides functionalities that may change at different times and for different reasons, it means those functionalities do not belong together and should be separated into different classes.

- **O** stands for the **Open-close principle** that states that a module, class, or function should be opened for extensions but closed for modifications. That is, when functionalities need to change, those changes should not affect the existing implementation. Inheritance is the typical way to achieve this, as derived classes can either add more functionalities or specialize existing ones. Extension methods is another technique available in C#.

- **L** stands for the **Liskov substitution principle** that states that if S is a sub-type of T, then objects of T may be substituted with objects of S without disrupting the functionality of the program. This principle is named after Barbara Liskov, who first introduced it. To understand the principle, let's consider a system that handles shapes. We may have an ellipse class with methods to change its two foci. When implementing a circle, we might be tempted to specialize the ellipse class because, mathematically, the circle is a special ellipse with the two foci being equal. In this case, the circle has to set the two foci to the same value in both these two methods. That is something a client of these classes does not expect and therefore an ellipse may not be substituted for a circle. To avoid violating the principle, we would have to implement the circle without deriving from the ellipse. To make sure you follow this principle, you should define preconditions and post-conditions for all methods. The preconditions must hold true before the method is executed and post-conditions must hold true after its execution. When specializing a method, you can only replace its preconditions with weaker ones and post-conditions with stronger ones.

- **I** stands for the **Interface segregation principle** and says that smaller, specific interfaces are to be preferred to larger and more general ones. The reason for this is that a client may only need to implement those functionalities that it needs and nothing more. By separating responsibilities, this principle facilitates composition and decoupling.

- **D** stands for the **Dependency inversion principle** and is the last in the list. This principle states that software entities should depend on abstractions and not on implementations. High-level modules should not depend on low-level modules; instead, they should both depend on abstractions. Moreover, abstractions should not depend on concrete implementations but the other way around. Dependency on implementations introduces tight coupling, making it hard to replace components. However, dependency on high-level abstractions decouples modules and facilitates flexibility and reusability.

These five principles enable us to write code that is simpler and more understandable, which also makes it easier to maintain. At the same time, they make code more reusable and also easier to test.

Summary

In this chapter, we learned about the core concepts of object-oriented programming: abstraction, encapsulation, inheritance, and polymorphism. We learned about the language functionalities that enable them, such as inheritance, virtual members, abstract types and members, sealed types and members, interfaces, and method and operator overloading. At the end of this chapter, we briefly discussed other object-oriented principles known as SOLID.

In the next chapter, we will learn about another programming paradigm in C#—generic programming.

Test what you learned

1. What is object-oriented programming and what are its core principles?
2. What are the benefits of encapsulation?
3. What is inheritance and what types of inheritance are supported in C#?
4. What are virtual methods? What about overridden methods?
5. How do you prevent a virtual member from being overridden in a derived class?
6. What are abstract classes and what are their features?

7.   What is an interface and what kinds of members can it contain?

8.   What types of polymorphism exist?

9.   What is an overloaded method? How do you overload operators?

10. What are the SOLID principles?

Further Reading

- *Design Principles and Design Patterns by Robert C. Martin*:
  `https://web.archive.org/web/20150906155800/http://www.`
  `objectmentor.com/resources/articles/Principles_and_`
  `Patterns.pdf`

6

Generics

In the previous chapter, we learned about OOP in C#. In this chapter, we will explore the concept of generics. Generics allow us to create classes, structures, interfaces, methods, and delegates in such a manner that they will work in a type-safe environment with different data types. Generics were added as a part of the C# 2.0 release. It promotes code reusability and extensibility and is one of the most powerful features of C#.

We will learn about the following concepts in this chapter:

- Generic classes and generic inheritance
- Generic interfaces and variant generic interfaces
- Generic structures
- Generic methods
- Type constraints

By the end of this chapter, you will have gained the skills necessary to write generic types, methods, and variant generic interfaces and to use type constraints.

Understanding generics

Simply put, generics are types parametrized with other types. As we mentioned before, we can create a class, structure, interface, method, or delegate that accepts one or more data types they use as parameters. These parameters are known as **type parameters** and act as *placeholders* for the actual data types that are passed during compile time.

For example, we can create a class that models a list, which is a variable-length sequence of elements of the same type. Instead of having a different class that works with integers, doubles, strings, or any other user-defined types we might need, we can create a generic class that has a type parameter specifying the actual type of its elements. We will then specify the actual type at compile time when we instantiate the class.

Advantages of using generics include the following:

- **Generics provide reusability**: We can create a single version of the code and reuse it for different data types.

- **Generics promote type safety**: While using generics, we do not need to perform explicit typecasting. The typecasting is taken care of by the compiler.

- **Generics provide better performance**: They can avoid the need for boxing and unboxing in the case of value types. Even casting from the `object` type to a reference type is time-consuming. Therefore, by avoiding these operations, they help to improve the execution time.

Generic types and methods can be constrained so that only the types that meet requirements can be used as type parameters. Information about the actual types is used to instantiate a generic type that can be obtained at runtime using reflection.

The most common use of generics is to create collection or wrapper classes. Collections will be the subject of the next chapter.

Generic types

Both reference types and value types can be generic. We have already seen examples of generic types earlier in this book, such as `Nullable<T>` and `List<T>`.

In this section, we will learn how to create generic classes, structures, and interfaces.

Generic classes

The creation of generic classes is no different than non-generic classes. The only thing that differs is a list of type parameters and their use in the class as a placeholder for actual types. Let's look at an example of a generic class:

```
public class GenericDemo<T>
{
    public T Value { get; private set; }

    public GenericDemo(T value)
    {
        Value = value;
    }

    public override string ToString() => $"{typeof(T)} :
{Value}";
}
```

Here, we have defined a generic class, `GenericDemo`, that is accepting one type parameter, `T`. We have defined a property called `Value` of the `T` type and initialized it inside the class constructor. The constructor is accepting an argument of the `T` type. The overridden method, `ToString()`, will return a string containing the type and value of the property.

To instantiate objects of this generic class, we will proceed as follows:

```
var obj1 = new GenericDemo<int>(10);
var obj2 = new GenericDemo<string>("Hello World");
```

In this example, we are specifying the data type for the type parameter while creating the object of the generic class, `GenericDemo<T>`. Both `obj1` and `obj2` are instances of the same generic type, but their type parameter differs: one is `int` and the other is `string`. Therefore, they are not type-compatible with each other. This means if we try to assign one object to another, it will result in a compile-time error.

We can get information about the type of these objects and their generic type parameters using reflection (which we will look at in *Chapter 11, Reflection and Dynamic Programming*), as shown in the following sample:

```
var t1 = obj1.GetType();
Console.WriteLine(t1.Name);
Console.WriteLine(t1.GetGenericArguments()
                    .FirstOrDefault().Name);
var t2 = obj2.GetType();
```

```
Console.WriteLine(t2.Name);
Console.WriteLine(t2.GetGenericArguments()
                      .FirstOrDefault().Name);

Console.WriteLine(obj1);
Console.WriteLine(obj2);
```

Upon execution, we will see the output shown here:

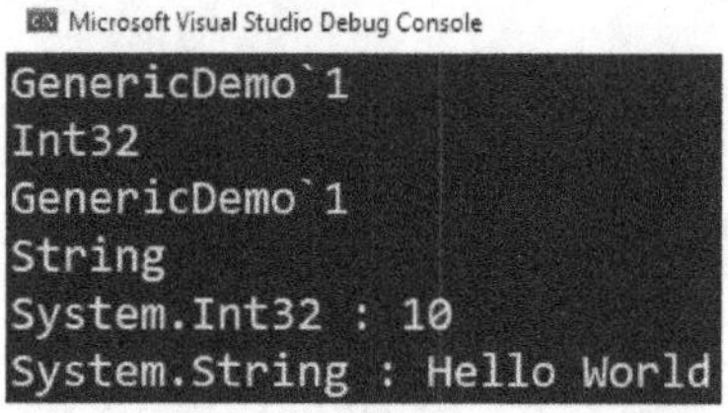

Figure 6.1 – Screenshot of the console showing the reflected content of a type

We can declare more than one type parameter for a generic type. In this case, we need to specify all of the type parameters as a comma-separated value inside the angle brackets. The following shows an example:

```
class Pair<T, U>
{
    public T Item1 { get; private set; }
    public U Item2 { get; private set; }

    public Pair(T item1, U item2)
    {
        Item1 = item1;
        Item2 = item2;
    }
}

var p1 = new Pair<int, int>(1, 2);
var p2 = new Pair<int, double>(1, 42.99);
var p3 = new Pair<string, bool>("true", true);
```

Here, Pair<T, U> is a class that requires two type parameters. We are instantiating objects p1, p2, and p3 using different combinations of types.

This class is actually very similar to the .NET class KeyValueType<TKey, TValue>, from the System.Collections.Generic namespace. In fact, there are many generic classes that the framework is providing. You should use existing types when available, rather than defining your own.

Inheritance with generic classes

A generic class can behave either as a *base class* or a *derived class*. When deriving from a generic class, the child class must specify the type parameters that are required by the base class. These type parameters can be actual types or type parameters from the derived class, which is also a generic class.

Let's understand how the inheritance of generic classes works with the example shown here:

```
public abstract class Shape<T>
{
    public abstract T Area { get; }
}
```

We have defined a generic abstract class, Shape, that contains a single and abstract property called Area that represents the area of a shape. The type of this property is also T. Consider the class definition here:

```
public class Square : Shape<int>
{
    public int Length { get; set; }

    public Square(int length)
    {
        Length = length;
    }

    public override int Area => Length * Length;
}
```

Here, we have defined a class called Square, which is inheriting from the generic abstract class Shape. We are using the int type for the type parameter. We have defined a property called Length for the Square class and initialized it in the constructor. We are overriding the Area property to calculate the area of the square. Now, consider another class definition shown here:

```
public class Circle : Shape<double>
{
    public double Radius { get; set; }

    public Circle(double radius)
    {
        Radius = radius;
    }
```

```
        public override double Area => Math.PI * Radius * Radius;
    }
```

The Circle class is also inheriting from the generic abstract class Shape<T>. The type parameter for the parent class Shape is now specified as double. The Radius property is defined to store the radius of the circle. We are again overriding the Area property to calculate the area of a circle. We can use these derived classes as follows:

```
Square objSquare = new Square(10);
Console.WriteLine($"The area of square is {objSquare.Area}");

Circle objCircle = new Circle(7.5);
Console.WriteLine($"The area of circle is {objCircle.Area}");
```

We are creating instances of Square and Circle and printing to the console the area of each shape. Upon execution, we will see the output shown here:

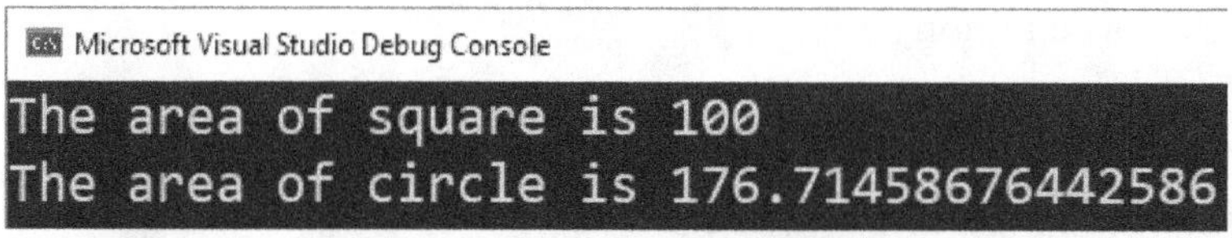

Figure 6.2 – The areas of the square and circle displayed to the console

It is important to note that although both Square and Circle derive from Shape<T>, these types cannot be treated polymorphically. One is Shape<int> and the other Shape<double>. Therefore, instances of Square and Circle cannot be put in a homogeneous container. The only possible solution is to use the object type to hold references to such instances and then perform type casts.

In this example, Shape<T> is a generic type. Shape<int> is a type that is constructed from Shape<T> by replacing the type parameter T with int. Such a type is called a **constructed type**. This is also a *closed constructed type* because all of the type parameters have been substituted. Non-generic types are all *closed types*. Generic types are *open types*. Constructed generic types can be open or closed. An open constructed type is one that has a type parameter that has not been substituted. A closed constructed type is any type that is not open.

Another important thing to remember when creating generic types is that some operators, such as arithmetic operators, cannot be used with objects of type parameters. Let's look at the following code to exemplify this case:

```
public class Square<T> : Shape<T>
{
    public T Length { get; set; }
```

```
    public Square(T length)
    {
        Length = length;
    }

    /* ERROR: Operator '*' cannot be applied to operands
    of type 'T' and 'T' */
    public override T Area => Length * Length;
}
```

The `Square` type is now a generic type. The type parameter `T` is used for the type parameter of the base class as well as the `Length` property. However, when computing the area, the use of the `*` operator generates a compiler error. That is because the compiler does not know what concrete types will be used for `T` and whether they have the `*` operator overloaded. To make sure that, under no circumstances, invalid instantiation may occur, the compiler generates an error.

It is possible to ensure that only types matching some pre-defined constraints are used at compile time to instantiate generic types or call generic methods. These are called *type constraints* and will be discussed later in this chapter in the *Type parameter constraints* section.

Now that we've seen how to create and use generic classes, let's see how to do the same with generic interfaces.

Generic interfaces

In the previous examples, the generic class `Shape<T>` does not contain anything other than an abstract property. This is not a good candidate for a class and it should rather be an interface. Generic interfaces differ from non-generic interfaces in the same way as generic classes differ from non-generic classes. The following is an example of a generic interface:

```
public interface IShape<T>
{
    public T Area { get; }
}
```

The type parameters are specified in the same manner as they are for classes or structures. This interface can be implemented as follows:

```
public class Square : IShape<int>
{
    public int Length { get; set; }

    public Square(int length)
    {
        Length = length;
    }

    public int Area => Length * Length;
}

public class Circle : IShape<double>
{
    public double Radius { get; set; }

    public Circle(double radius)
    {
        Radius = radius;
    }

    public double Area => Math.PI * Radius * Radius;
}
```

The implementation of the `Square` and `Circle` classes is only slightly different from the one seen in the previous section.

Concrete classes, such as `Square` and `Circle` here, can implement closed constructed interfaces, such as `IShape<int>` or `IShape<double>`. Generic classes can also implement a generic or closed constructed interface if the class parameter list supplies all of the type parameters required by the interface. On the other hand, generic interfaces can inherit from non-generic interfaces; however, the generic class must be contravariant.

The variance of generic interfaces will be discussed in the next section.

Variant generic interfaces

It is possible to declare type parameters in generic interfaces as *covariant* or *contravariant*:

- A *covariant* type parameter is declared with the out keyword and allows an interface method to have a return type that is more derived than the specified type parameter.

- A *contravariant* type parameter is declared with the in keyword and allows an interface method to have a parameter that is less derived than the specified type parameter.

A generic interface that has covariant or contravariant type parameters is called a **variant generic interface**. Variance is only supported with reference types.

To understand how covariance works, let's look at the System.IEnumerable<T> generic interface. This is a variant interface because its type parameter is declared covariant. The interface is defined as follows:

```
public interface IEnumerable
{
    IEnumerator GetEnumerator();
}

public interface IEnumerable<out T> : IEnumerable
{
    IEnumerator<T> GetEnumerator();
}
```

A class that implements IEnumerable<T> (and other interfaces) is List<T>. Because T is covariant, we can write the following code:

```
IEnumerable<string> names =
    new List<string> { "Marius", "Ankit", "Raffaele" };
IEnumerable<object> objects = names;
```

In this example, names is an IEnumerable<string> and objects is an IEnumerable<object>. The former does not derive from the latter, but string is derived from object, and because T is covariant, we can assign names to objects. However, this is only possible while using variant interfaces.

Classes that implement variant interfaces are not variant themselves but invariant. That means the following example, where we substitute List<T> for IEnumerable<T>, will produce a compiler error because List<string> cannot be assigned to List<object>:

```
IEnumerable<string> names =
    new List<string> { "Marius", "Ankit", "Raffaele" };
List<object> objects = names; // error
```

As mentioned earlier, variance is not supported for value types. IEnumerable<int> cannot be assigned to IEnumerable<object>:

```
IEnumerable<int> numbers = new List<int> { 1, 1, 2, 3, 5, 8 };
IEnumerable<object> objects = numbers; // error
```

In summary, a covariant type parameter in an interface must:

- Be prefixed with the out keyword
- Be only used as the return type for methods and not as a type for method parameters
- Not be used as a generic constraint for interface methods

Contravariance is the other form of variance that deals with arguments passed to interface methods. To understand how it works, let's consider a situation where we want to compare the size of various shapes, defined as follows:

```
public interface IShape
{
    public double Area { get; }
}

public class Square : IShape
{
    public double Length { get; set; }

    public Square(int length)
    {
        Length = length;
    }

    public double Area => Length * Length;
}

public class Circle : IShape
```

```
{
    public double Radius { get; set; }

    public Circle(double radius)
    {
        Radius = radius;
    }

    public double Area => Math.PI * Radius * Radius;
}
```

These are only slightly different from the types used previously because IShape is no longer generic to keep the example simple. What we want here is to be able to compare shapes. For this purpose, a series of classes are provided as follows:

```
public class ShapeComparer : IComparer<IShape>
{
    public int Compare(IShape x, IShape y)
    {
        if (x is null) return y is null ? 0 : -1;
        if (y is null) return 1;
        return x.Area.CompareTo(y.Area);
    }
}

public class SquareComparer : IComparer<Square>
{
    public int Compare(Square x, Square y)
    {
        if (x is null) return y is null ? 0 : -1;
        if (y is null) return 1;
        return x.Length.CompareTo(y.Length);
    }
}

public class CircleComparer : IComparer<Circle>
{
    public int Compare(Circle x, Circle y)
    {
        if (x is null) return y is null ? 0 : -1;
        if (y is null) return 1;
        return x.Radius.CompareTo(y.Radius);
    }
}
```

Here, `ShapeComparer` compares `IShape` objects by their area, `SquareComparer` compares squares by their length, and `CircleComparer` compares circles by their radius. All of these classes implement the `IComparer<T>` interface from the `System.Collections.Generic` namespace. This interface is defined as follows:

```
public interface IComparer<in T>
{
    int Compare(T x, T y);
}
```

This interface has a single method called `Compare()`, which takes two objects of the `T` type and returns one of the following:

- A negative number if the first is smaller than the second
- 0, if they are equal
- A positive number if the first is greater than the second

However, the key to its definition is the `in` keyword with the type parameter that makes it contravariant. Because of this, it is possible to pass `IShape` references where `Square` or `Circle` are expected. That means we can safely pass `IComparer<IShape>` where `IComparer<Square>` is required. Let's see a concrete example of that.

The following class contains a single method that checks whether a `Square` object is bigger than another. The `IsBigger()` method also takes a reference to an object implementing `IComparer<Square>`:

```
public class SquareComparison
{
    public static bool IsBigger(Square a, Square b,
                                IComparer<Square> comparer)
    {
        return comparer.Compare(a, b) >= 0;
    }
}
```

We could call this method passing both `SquareComparer` or `ShapeComparer`, and the result would be the same:

```
Square sqr1 = new Square(4);
Square sqr2 = new Square(5);

SquareComparison.IsBigger(sqr1, sqr2, new SquareComparer());
SquareComparison.IsBigger(sqr1, sqr2, new ShapeComparer());
```

Had the `IComparer<T>` interface been invariant, passing `ShapeComparer` would result in a compiler error. A compiler error is also issued, with the implementation shown here, if we try to pass `CircleComparer` because `Circle` is not a lesser derived class than `Square`; it is actually a sibling in the inheritance hierarchy.

In summary, a contravariant type parameter in an interface:

- Must be prefixed with the `in` keyword
- Must be used only for method parameters and not as a return type
- Can be used as a generic constraint for interface methods

It is possible to define an interface that is both *covariant and contravariant* as shown here:

```
interface IMultiVariant<out T, in U>
{
    T Make();
    void Take(U arg);
}
```

The `IMultiVariant<T, U>` interface shown in the preceding snippet is covariant with respect to `T` and contravariant with respect to `U`.

Generic structures

Similar to generic classes, we can also create generic structures. The syntax for a generic structure is the same as that of a generic class. The `Circle` and `Square` types used in the previous example are small and can be defined as structures instead of classes:

```
public struct Square : IShape<int>
{
    public int Length { get; set; }

    public Square(int length)
    {
        Length = length;
    }

    public int Area => Length * Length;
}

public struct Circle : IShape<double>
{
    public double Radius { get; set; }
```

```
    public Circle(double radius)
    {
        Radius = radius;
    }

    public double Area => Math.PI * Radius * Radius;
}
```

All of the rules that apply to generic classes also apply to generic structures. Because value types do not support inheritance, structures cannot derive from other generic types but can implement any number of generic or non-generic interfaces.

Generic methods

C# allows us to create generic methods that accept one or more generic type parameters. We can create a generic method inside a generic class as well as a non-generic class. Both static and non-static methods can be generic. The rules for type inference are the same for all. The type parameters must be declared after the method name and just before the parameter list, within angle brackets, just like we did for types.

Let's understand how to use generic methods with the help of the example shown here:

```
class CompareObjects
{
    public bool Compare<T>(T input1, T input2)
    {
        return input1.Equals(input2);
    }
}
```

The non-generic class `CompareObjects` contains a generic method, `Compare`, which is used to compare two objects. This method is accepting two parameters—`input1` and `input2`. We are using the `Equals()` method from the `System.Object` base class to compare the input parameters. The method will return a Boolean based on whether the inputs are equal or not. Consider the code shown here:

```
CompareObjects comps = new CompareObjects();
Console.WriteLine(comp.Compare<int>(10, 10));
Console.WriteLine(comp.Compare<double>(10.5, 10.8));
Console.WriteLine(comp.Compare<string>("a", "a"));
Console.WriteLine(comp.Compare<string>("a", "b"));
```

We are creating an object of the `CompareObjects` class and invoking the `Compare()` method for various data types. In this example, the type argument is explicitly specified. However, the compiler is able to infer that from the arguments; therefore, it can be skipped, as shown here:

```
CompareObjects comp = new CompareObjects();
Console.WriteLine(comp.Compare(10, 10));
Console.WriteLine(comp.Compare(10.5, 10.8));
Console.WriteLine(comp.Compare("a", "a"));
Console.WriteLine(comp.Compare("a", "b"));
```

If a generic method has a type parameter that is the same as a type parameter of the class, structure, or interface where it is defined, the compiler issues a warning because the method type parameter hides the type parameter of the outer type, as shown in the following code:

```
class ConflictingGenerics<T>
{
    public void DoSomething<T>(T arg) // warning
    {
    }
}
```

Generic methods, as well as generic types, support type parameter constraints to impose restrictions on types. This topic will be discussed in the next section of this chapter.

Type parameter constraints

The type parameters in a generic type or method can be replaced by any valid type. However, there are scenarios when we want to restrict the types that can be used for a type parameter. Take, for instance, the generic `Shape<T>` class or the `IShape<T>` interface we saw earlier.

The type parameter `T` was used for the type of the `Area` property. We would expect that to be either an integral type or a floating-point type. But there is no restriction and someone could use `bool`, `string`, or any other type. Of course, depending on the way the type parameter is used, that could lead to various compiler errors. However, it is useful to be able to restrict the types used to instantiate generic types or call generic methods.

For this purpose, we can apply constraints to the type parameters. The constraints are used to inform the compiler about what kind of capabilities the type parameter must have. If we do not specify a constraint, then the type parameter can be replaced by any type. Applying a constraint will limit the types that can be used as a type parameter.

Constraints are specified using the keyword `where`. C# defines the following eight types of constraints on generics:

Constraint	Description
`where T : struct`	T must be a value type.
`where T : class`	T must be a reference type.
`where T : unmanaged`	T must be an unmanaged type; it cannot be a reference type and it should not contain any reference type at any level of nesting.
`where T : new()`	T must provide a public default constructor.
`where T : <base class name>`	T must be the class or derive from the class mentioned here.
`where T : <interface name>`	T must be the interface or implement the interface mentioned here.
`where T : U`	T must derive from another generic type U.
`where T : notnull`	T must be a non-nullable type. It can be a non-nullable reference type (in C# 8) or a non-nullable value type.

A constraint should be specified after the type parameters. We can use more than one constraint by separating them with a comma. There are some rules for using these constraints:

- The `struct` constraint implies the `new()` constraint and therefore all value types must have a public parameterless constructor. These two constraints, `struct` and `new()`, cannot be used together.

- The `unmanaged` constraint implies the `struct` constraint; therefore, these two cannot be used together. It also cannot be used with the `new()` constraint.

- When using more than one constraint, the `new()` constraint must be mentioned last in the list of constraints.

- The `notnull` constraint is available as of C# 8 and must be used in a nullable context, otherwise, the compiler generates a warning. When the constraint is violated, the compiler does not generate an error but a warning.

- As of C# 7.3, `System.Enum`, `System.Delegate`, and `System.MulticastDelegate` can be used as base class constraints.

Type parameters that do not have constraints are called *unbounded*. There are several rules for unbounded type parameters:

- You cannot use the `!=` and `==` operators with these types since it is not possible to know whether the concrete type overloads them.

- They can be compared to `null`. For value types, this comparison will always yield `false`.

- They can be converted to and from `System.Object`.

- They can be converted to and from any interface type.

To understand how constraints work, let's start with the following example of a generic structure:

```
struct Point<T>
{
    public T X { get; }
    public T Y { get; }

    public Point(T x, T y)
    {
        X = x;
        Y = y;
    }
}
```

`Point<T>` is a structure that represents a point in the two-dimensional space. This class is generic because we might want to use integral values for the point coordinates or real values (floating-point values). However, we can instantiate the class using any types, such as `bool`, `string`, or `Circle`, as shown in the following example:

```
Point<int> p1 = new Point<int>(3, 4);
Point<double> p2 = new Point<double>(3.12, 4.55);
Point<bool> p3 = new Point<bool>(true, false);
Point<string> p4 = new Point<string>("alpha", "beta");
```

To restrict the instantiation of `Point<T>` to numerical types (that is integral and floating-point types), we can write constraints for the type parameter T, as shown here:

```
struct Point<T>
    where T : struct,
              IComparable, IComparable<T>,
              IConvertible,
              IEquatable<T>,
              IFormattable
{
    public T X { get; }
    public T Y { get; }

    public Point(T x, T y)
    {
        X = x;
        Y = y;
    }
}
```

We have used two types of constraints: the `struct` constraint and the interface constraint, and they are listed separated by a comma. Unfortunately, there is no constraint to define a type as numeric but these constraints are the best combination to represent one because all numerical types are value types and they all implement the five interfaces listed here. The `bool` type implements the first four but not `IFormattable`. Therefore, instantiating `Point<T>` with `bool` or `string` will now produce compiler errors.

A type or method can have more than one type parameter and each of them can have their own constraints. We can see this in the following example:

```
class RestrictedDictionary<TKey, TValue> : Dictionary<TKey,
List<TValue>>
    where TKey : System.Enum
    where TValue : class, new()
{
    public T Make<T>(TKey key) where T : TValue, new()
    {
        var value = new T();
        if (!TryGetValue(key, out List<TValue> list))
            Add(key, new List<TValue>() { value });
        else
            list.Add(value);
```

```
        return value;
    }
}
```

The `RestrictedDictionary<TKey, TValue>` class is a special dictionary that allows only enumeration types for the key type. For this, it uses the base class constraint with `System.Enum`. The type of the value must be a reference type with a public default constructor. For this, it uses the `class` and `new()` constraints. This class has a public generic method called `Make<T>()`.

The type parameter, `T`, must be either `TValue` or a type derived from `TValue` and must also have a public default constructor. This method creates a new instance of the type, `T`, adds it to the dictionary in a list associated with the specified key, and returns a reference to the newly created object.

Let's also consider the following hierarchy of shape classes. Notice that for simplicity these are kept to a minimum:

```
enum ShapeType { Sharp, Rounded };

class Shape { }
class Ellipsis  : Shape { }
class Circle    : Shape { }
class Rectangle : Shape { }
class Square    : Shape { }
```

We can use the `RestrictedDictionary` class as shown here:

```
var dictionary = new RestrictedDictionary<ShapeType, Shape>();
var c = dictionary.Make<Circle>(ShapeType.Rounded);
var e = dictionary.Make<Ellipsis>(ShapeType.Rounded);
var r = dictionary.Make<Rectangle>(ShapeType.Sharp);
var s = dictionary.Make<Square>(ShapeType.Sharp);
```

In this example, we are adding several shapes (a circle, ellipsis, rectangle, and square) to the restricted dictionary. The key type is `ShapeType` and the value type is `Shape`. The `Make()` method takes an argument of the `ShapeType` type and returns a reference to a shape object. Each type must be derived from `Shape` and have a public default constructor. Otherwise, the code would produce an error.

Summary

In this chapter, we learned about generics in C#. Generics allow us to create parameterized types in C#. Generics enhance code reusability and ensure type safety. We explored how to create generic classes and generic structs. We also implemented inheritance in a generic class.

We learned how to implement constraints on the type parameters of a generic type or method. Constraints allow us to limit the data types that can be used as a type parameter. We also learned about creating generic methods and generic interfaces.

You can use generics primarily for creating collections and wrappers. In the next chapter, we will explore the most important collections available in .NET.

Test what you learned

1. What are generics and what benefits do they provide?

2. What are type parameters?

3. How do you define a generic class? What about generic methods?

4. Can a class be derived from a generic type? What about structures?

5. What is a constructed type?

6. What is a covariant type parameter of a generic interface?

7. What is a contravariant type parameter of a generic interface?

8. What are type parameter constraints and how are they specified?

9. What does the new() type parameter constraint do?

10. What type parameter constraint was introduced in C# 8 and what does it do?

7

Collections

In the previous chapter, we learned about generic programming in C#. One of the most important applications of generics is creating generic collections. A **collection** is a group of objects. We learned how to use arrays in *Chapter 2, Data Types and Operators*. However, arrays are sequences of a fixed size and in most cases, we need to work with sequences of variable size.

The .NET frameworks provide generic classes that represent various types of collections, such as list, queue, set, map, and others. Using these classes, we can easily perform operations such as insert, update, delete, sort, and search on a collection of objects.

You will learn about the following generic collections in this chapter:

- The `List<T>` collection
- The `Stack<T>` collection
- The `Queue<T>` collection
- The `LinkedList<T>` collection
- The `Dictionary<TKey, TValue>` collection
- The `HashSet<T>` collection

By the end of this chapter, you will have a good understanding of the most important collections in .NET, what data structures they model, what the differences are between them, and when you should use them.

All the collections mentioned previously are not thread-safe. This means they cannot be used in multi-threaded scenarios when a thread might be reading while another might be writing to the same collection, without using external synchronization mechanisms. However, .NET also provides several thread-safe collections in the System. Collections.Concurrent namespace that use efficient locking or lock-free synchronization mechanisms, and, in many scenarios, provide better performance than the generic collections with external locks. In this chapter, we will also provide a walkthrough of these collections and learn about the scenarios when it's suitable to use them.

Let's start with an overview of the generic collection library by looking at the System. Collections.Generic namespace, which is where all the generic collections are located.

Introducing the System.Collections.Generic namespace

The generic collection classes that we will present in this chapter are a part of the .NET **Base Class Library (BCL)** and are all available under the System.Collections. Generic namespace. This namespace contains interfaces and classes that define generic collections and operations. All the generic collections implement a series of generic interfaces, which are also defined in this namespace. These can be broadly grouped into two categories:

- **Mutable,** which support operations for changing the content of the collection such as adding new, or removing existing elements.

- **Read-only collections,** which do not provide methods for changing the content of the collection.

The interfaces that represent mutable collections are as follows:

- IEnumerable<T>: This is the base interface for all the other interfaces and exposes an enumerator that supports iterating through the elements of a collection of T type.

- ICollection<T>: This defines methods for manipulating generic collections—Add(), Clear(), Contains(), CopyTo(), and Remove()—as well as properties, such as Count. These members should be *self-explanatory*.

- `IList<T>`: This represents a generic collection whose elements can be accessed by an *index*. It defines three methods: `IndexOf()`, which retrieves the index of an element, `Insert()`, which inserts an element at the specified index, and `RemoveAt()`, which removes the element at the specified index, in addition, it also provides an indexer for direct element access for direct element access.

- `ISet<T>`: This is the base interface that abstracts set collections. It defines methods such as `Add()`, `ExceptWith()`, `IntersetWith()`, `UnionWith()`, `IsSubsetOf()`, and `IsSupersetOf()`.

- `IDictionary<TKey, TValue>`: This is the base interface that abstracts a collection of key-value pairs. It defines the `Add()`, `ContainsKey()`, `Remove()`, and `TryGetValue()` methods, as well as an indexer and the `Keys` and `Values` properties, which return the collection of keys and values, respectively.

The relationship between these interfaces is shown in the following diagram:

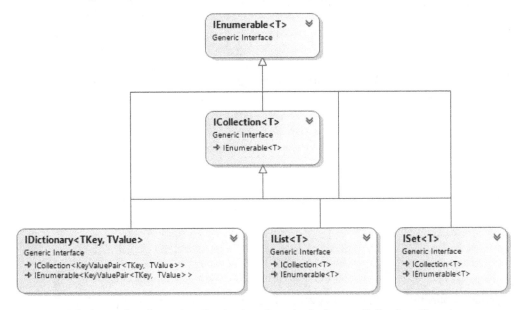

Figure 7.1 – The hierarchy of generic collection interfaces in the System.Collections.Generic namespace.

The interfaces that represent read-only collections are as follows:

- `IReadOnlyCollection<T>`: This represents a read-only generic collection of elements. It only defines one member: the `Count` property.

- `IReadOnlyList<T>`: This represents a read-only generic collection of elements that can be accessed by an index. It only defines one member: a read-only indexer.

- `IReadOnlyDictionary<TKey, TValue>`: This represents a read-only generic collection of key-value pairs. This interface defines the `ContainsKey()` and `TryGetValue()` methods, as well as the `Keys` and `Values` properties and a read-only indexer.

Again, the relationship of these interfaces is shown in the following diagram:

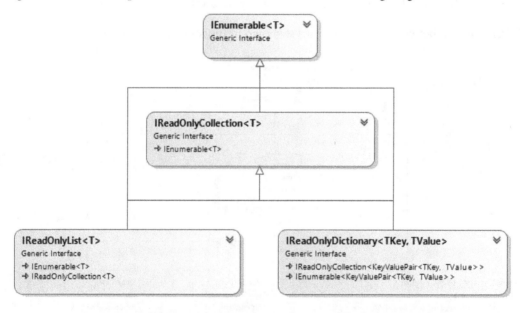

Figure 7.2 – The hierarchy of interfaces for read-only generic collections.

Each generic collection implements several of these interfaces. For instance, `List<T>` implements `IList<T>`, `ICollection<T>`, `IEnumerable<T>`, `IReadOnlyCollection<T>`, and `IReadOnlyList<T>`. The following diagram shows all the interfaces being implemented by the generic collections that we will learn about in this chapter:

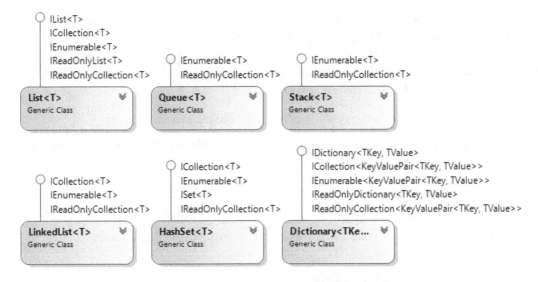

Figure 7.3 – A class diagram showing the most important generic collections
and the interfaces they implement.

The inheritance hierarchy shown in these diagrams is actually a simplification of the
actual one. All the generic collections have a non-generic equivalent. For instance,
IEnumerable<T> is the generic equivalent of IEnumerable, ICollection<T> is
the generic equivalent of ICollection, IList<T> is the generic equivalent of Ilist,
and so on. These are legacy interfaces that are implemented by legacy collections such
as ArrayList, Queue, Stack, DictionaryBase, Hashtable, and so on, all of
which are available in the System.Collections namespace. These non-generic legacy
collections are not strongly typed. Using generic collections is preferred for
several reasons:

- They offer the benefit of type safety. There is no need to derive from a base
  collection and implement type-specific members.

- They have better performance for value types because there is no boxing and
  unboxing of elements, a process that is necessary with a non-generic collection.

- Some of the generic collections provide functionalities that are not available in
  the non-generic ones, such as methods that accept delegates that can be used for
  searching or performing an action of each element.

When you need to pass collections as arguments to functions or return collections from functions, you should avoid using concrete implementations and prefer using interfaces. IEnumerable<T> is suitable when you only want to iterate through the elements, but if you need to do that multiple times, you could use IReadOnlyCollection<T>. Read-only collections should be preferred in two cases:

- When a method does not modify the collection passed as an argument

- When you return a collection if the collection is already in memory and the caller is not supposed to modify it

Ultimately, the most suitable interface varies from case to case.

In the following sections, we will introduce each of the most widely used type-safe generic collections. The non-generic collections are of little interest outside legacy code.

The List<T> collection

The List<T> generic class represents a collection of elements that can be accessed by their index. List<T> is very similar to arrays, except that the size of the collection is not fixed but variable, and it can grow or decrease as elements are added or removed. In fact, the implementation of List<T> uses an array to store the elements. When the number of elements exceeds the size of the array, a new and larger array is allocated, and the content of the previous array is copied to the new one. This means that List<T> stores the elements in contiguous memory locations. However, for value types, these locations contain the values, but for reference types, they contain references to the actual objects. Multiple references to the same object can be added to a list.

The List<T> class implements a series of generic and non-generic interfaces, as shown in the following declaration of the class:

```
public class List<T> : ICollection<T>, ICollection
                       IEnumerable<T>, IEnumerable,
                       IList<T>, IList,
                       IReadOnlyCollection<T>, IReadOnlyList<T>
{}
```

A list can be created in several ways:

- Using the default constructor, which results in an empty list with a default capacity.

- By specifying a particular capacity but no initial elements, which again leaves the list empty.

- From a collection of elements.

In the following example, `numbers` is an empty list of integers and `words` is an empty list of strings:

```
var numbers = new List<int>();
var words = new List<string>();
```

On the other hand, the following sample initializes the list with some elements. The first list will contain six integers and the second list will contain two strings:

```
var numbers = new List<int> { 1, 2, 3, 5, 7, 11 };
var words = new List<string> { "one", "two" };
```

This class supports all the typical operations that you would expect from such a collection—adding, removing, and searching elements. There are several ways to add elements to the list:

- `Add()` adds an element to the end of the list.

- `AddRange()` adds a collection of elements (in the form of an `IEnumerable<T>`) to the end of the list.

- `Insert()` inserts an element at the specified position. The position must be a valid index, within the bounds of the list; otherwise, an `ArgumentOutOfRangeException` exception is thrown.

- `InsertRange()` inserts a range of elements (in the form of an `IEnumerable<T>`) at the specified index, which must be within the bounds of the list.

All these operations may require the reallocation of the internal array that stores elements if its capacity is exceeded. `Add()` is an $O(1)$ operation if no allocation is needed and $O(n)$ when allocation is necessary.

`AddRange()` is $O(n)$ if no allocation is necessary and $O(n+k)$ if allocations are needed. `Insert()` is always an $O(n)$ operation, and `InsertRange()` is $O(n)$ if no allocation is needed and $O(n+k)$ if an allocation is necessary. In this notation, n is the number of elements in the list and k is the number of elements to add. We can see an example of these operations in the following sample:

```
var numbers = new List<int> {1, 2, 3}; // 1 2 3
numbers.Add(5);                         // 1 2 3 5
numbers.AddRange(new int[] { 7, 11 }); // 1 2 3 5 7 11
numbers.Insert(5, 1);                   // 1 2 3 5 7 1 11
```

```
numbers.Insert(5, 1);            // 1 2 3 5 7 1 1 11
numbers.InsertRange(            // 1 13 17 19 2 3 5..
    1, new int[] {13, 17, 19});  // ..7 1 1 11
```

Removing the elements is also possible in several ways using different methods:

- Remove() removes the specified element from the list.

- RemoveAt() removes the element at the specified index, which must be within the bounds of the list.

- RemoveRange() removes the specified number of elements, starting with the given index.

- RemoveAll() removes all the elements in the list that meet the requirements of the supplied predicate.

- Clear() removes all the elements in the list.

All these operations are performed in *O(n)*, where *n* is the number of elements in the list. The exception is RemoveAt(), where *n* is Count - index. The reason for this is that the elements must be moved within the internal array after one has been removed. Examples of using these functions are shown in the following snippet:

```
numbers.Remove(1);              // 13 17 19  2  3  5  7  1
                                // 1 11
numbers.RemoveRange(2, 3);      // 13 17  5  7  1  1 11
numbers.RemoveAll(e => e < 10); // 13 17 11
numbers.RemoveAt(1);            // 13 11
numbers.Clear();                // empty
```

It is possible to search for elements in the list by specifying a predicate.

> **Information box**
>
> A **predicate** is a delegate that returns a bool. They are typically used when you filter elements, such as when you search through a collection.

There are several methods that can be used to search elements:

- `Find()` returns the first element that matches the predicate or the default value of T if none is found.

- `FindLast()` returns the last element that matches the predicate or the default value of T if none is found.

- `FindAll()` returns a `List<T>` with all the elements that match the predicate or an empty list if none is found.

All these methods are performed in $O(n)$, as shown in the following code snippet:

```
var numbers = new List<int> { 1, 2, 3, 5, 7, 11 };

var a = numbers.Find(e => e < 10);        // 1
var b = numbers.FindLast(e => e < 10);    // 7
var c = numbers.FindAll(e => e < 10);     // 1 2 3 5 7
```

It is possible to search for the zero-based index of an element as well. There are several methods that allow us to do that:

- `IndexOf()` returns the index of the first element that is equal to the supplied argument.

- `LastIndexOf()` returns the last index of the searched element.

- `FindIndex()` returns the index of the first element that satisfies the supplied predicate.

- `FindLastIndex()` returns the index of the last element that satisfies the supplied predicate.

- `BinarySearch()` returns the index of the first element that satisfies the supplied element or a comparer using binary search. This function assumes that the list is already sorted; otherwise, the result is incorrect.

`BinarySearch()` is performed in $O(log\ n)$, while all the others are performed in $O(n)$. This is because they use linear search. They all return `-1` if no element that satisfies the search criteria is found. Examples are shown in the following listing:

```
var numbers = new List<int> { 1, 1, 2, 3, 5, 8, 11 };

var a = numbers.FindIndex(e => e < 10);      // 0
var b = numbers.FindLastIndex(e => e < 10); // 5
var c = numbers.IndexOf(5);                 // 4
var d = numbers.LastIndexOf(1);             // 1
var e = numbers.BinarySearch(8);            // 5
```

There are methods that allow us to modify the content of the list, such as by sorting the elements or reverting them:

- `Sort()` sorts the list according to a default or specified criteria. There are several overloads that allow us to specify either a comparison delegate or an `IComparer<T>` object, or even a sub-range of the list to sort. This operation is performed in $O(n\ log\ n)$ in most cases but $O\ (n2)$ in the worst-case scenario.

- `Reverse()` reverses the elements in the list. There is an overload that allows you to specify a sub-range to revert. This operation is performed in $O(n)$.

Examples of using these functions are shown as follows:

```
var numbers = new List<int> { 1, 5, 3, 11, 8, 1, 2 };

numbers.Sort();      // 1 1 2 3 5 8 11
numbers.Reverse();   // 11 8 5 3 2 1 1
```

There are more methods in the `List<T>` class than those shown here. However, going through all of them is beyond the scope of this book. You should look up the official documentation of the class online for a complete reference to all the members of this class.

The Stack<T> collection

A stack is a linear data structure that allows us to insert and delete items in a particular order. New items are added at the top of the stack. If we want to remove an item from the stack, we can only remove the top item. Since insertion and deletion is allowed from only one end, the item to be inserted last will be the item to be deleted first. Therefore, the stack is called a **Last in**, **First Out (LIFO)** collection.

The following diagram depicts a stack, where *push* represents adding an item to the stack and *pop* represents deleting an item from the stack:

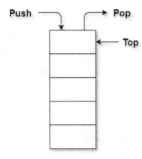

Figure 7.4 – The conceptual representation of a stack.

.NET provides the generic `Stack<T>` class for working with stacks. This class contains several constructors that allow us to create either an empty stack or a stack initialized with a collection of elements. Take a look at the following code snippet, where we are creating a stack of strings with three initial elements and an empty stack of integers:

```
var arr = new string[] { "Ankit", "Marius", "Raffaele" };
Stack<string> names = new Stack<string>(arr);
Stack<int> numbers = new Stack<int>();
```

The primary operations that are supported by the stack are as follows:

- `Push()`: Inserts an item at the top of the stack. This is an *O(1)* operation if no reallocation is necessary and *O(n)* otherwise.

- `Pop()`: Removes and returns the item from the top of the stack. This is an *O(1)* operation.

- `Peek()`: Returns an item from the top of the stack without removing it. This is an *O(1)* operation.

- `Clear()`: Removes all the elements from the stack. This is an *O(n)* operation.

Let's understand how these work with the help of the following example where, on the left, you can see the contents of the stack after each operation:

```
var numbers = new Stack<int>(new int[]{ 1, 2, 3 });// 3 2 1
numbers.Push(5);                                    // 5 3 2 1
numbers.Push(7);                                    // 7 5 3 2 1
numbers.Pop();                                      // 5 3 2 1
var n = numbers.Peek();                             // 5 3 2 1
numbers.Push(11);                                   // 11 5 3 2 1
numbers.Clear();                                    // empty
```

The Pop() and Peek() methods throw an InvalidOperationException exception if the stack is empty. In .NET Core, since version 2.0, two alternative non-throwing methods are available—TryPop() and TryPeek(). These methods return a Boolean value indicating whether a top element was found and if so, it is returned as an out argument.

The Queue<T> collection

A queue is a linear data structure where insertion and deletion of elements is performed from two different ends. A new item is added from the rear end of the queue and deletion of existing items occurs from the front. Therefore, the item to be inserted first will be the item to be deleted first. Because of this, the queue is called a **First in, First Out (FIFO)** collection. The following diagram depicts a queue, where **Enqueue** represents adding an item to the queue and **Dequeue** represents deleting an item from the queue:

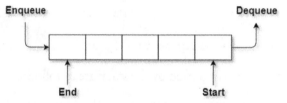

Figure 7.5 – The conceptual representation of a queue.

In .NET, the class that implements a generic queue is Queue<T>. Similarly, with Stack<T>, there are overloaded constructors that allow us to create an empty queue or a queue initialized with elements from an IEnumerable<T> collection. Take a look at the following code snippet, where we are creating a queue of strings with three initial elements and an empty queue of integers:

```
var arr = new string[] { "Ankit", "Marius", "Raffaele" };
Queue<string> names = new Queue<string>(arr);

Queue<int> numbers = new Queue<int>();
```

The primary operations that are supported for the queue are as follows:

- Enqueue(): Inserts an item at the end of the queue. This operation is *O(1)* unless the internal array needs to be reallocated, in which case it becomes an *O(n)* operation.

- Dequeue(): Removes and returns an item from the front of the queue. This is an *O(1)* operation.

- Peek(): Returns an item from the front of the queue without removing it. This is an *O(1)* operation.

- Clear(): Removes all the elements from the queue. This is an *O(n)* operation.

To understand how these methods work, let's look at the following example:

```
var numbers = new Queue<int>(new int[] { 1, 2, 3 });// 1 2 3
numbers.Enqueue(5);                                 // 1 2 3 5
numbers.Enqueue(7);                                 // 1 2 3 5 7
numbers.Dequeue();                                  // 2 3 5 7
var n = numbers.Peek();                             // 2 3 5 7
numbers.Enqueue(11);                                // 2 3 5 7 11
numbers.Clear();                                    // empty
```

The Dequeue() and Peek() methods throw an InvalidOperationException exception if the queue is empty. In .NET Core, since version 2.0, two alternatives non-throwing methods are available—TryDequeue() and TryPeek(). These methods return a Boolean value indicating whether a top element was found and if so, it is returned as an out argument.

As you can see from these examples, Stack<T> and Queue<T> have very similar implementations, although the semantics are different. Their public members are almost the same, with the difference being that the stack operations are called Push() and Pop() and the queue operations are called Enqueue() and Dequeue().

The LinkedList<T> collection

A linked list is a linear data structure that consists of a group of nodes where each node contains data as well as the address of one or more nodes. There are four types of linked list, as described here:

- **Singly Linked List**: This contains nodes that store a value and a reference to the next node in the sequence of nodes. The reference to the next node of the last node will point to null.

- **Doubly Linked List**: Here, each node contains two links – the first link points to the previous node and the next link points to the next node in the sequence. The reference to the previous node of the first node and the reference to the next node of the last node will point to null.

- **Circular Singly Linked List**: The reference to the next node of the last node will point to the first node, thus forming a circular chain.

- **Doubly Circular Linked List**: In this type of linked list, the reference to the next node of the last node will point to the first node and the reference to the previous node of the first node will point to the last node.

A conceptual representation of the doubly linked list is as follows:

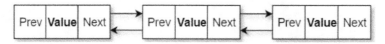

Figure 7.6 – A conceptual representation of a doubly linked-list.

Here, each node contains a value and two pointers. The **Next** pointer contains a reference to the next node in the sequence and allows easy navigation in the forward direction of the linked list. The **Prev** pointer contains a reference to the previous node in the sequence and allows us to move backward in the linked list.

.NET provides the LinkedList<T> class, which represents a doubly linked list. This class contains items of the LinkedListNode<T> type. Insertion and removal operations are performed in *O(1)* and searching is performed in *O(n)*. Nodes can be removed and reinserted either in the same linked list object or another. The list maintains an internal count, so retrieving the size of the list using the Count property is also an *O(1)* operation. The linked list does not support cycles, splitting, chaining, or anything else that can leave the list in an inconsistent state.

The LinkedListNode<T> class has the following four properties:

- List: This property will return the reference to the LinkedList<T> object to which LinkedListNode<T> belongs.

- Next: Represents the reference to the next node in the LinkedList<T> object or null if the current node is the last node.

- Previous: Represents the reference to the previous node in the LinkedList<T> object or null if the current node is the first node.

- Value: This property is of type T and represents the value contained in the node.

For value types, LinkedListNode<T> contains the actual value, whereas for reference types, it contains a reference to the object.

The class has overloaded constructors that enable us to create an empty linked list or one initialized with a sequence of elements, in the form of an `IEnumerable<T>`. Take a look at the following sample to see some examples:

```
var arr = new string[] { "Ankit", "Marius", "Raffaele" };
var words = new LinkedList<string>(arr);
var numbers = new LinkedList<int>();
```

Adding new elements to the linked list is possible in several ways using the following methods:

- `AddFirst()` adds a new node or value at the beginning of the list.

- `AddLast()` adds a new node or value at the end of the list.

- `AddAfter()` adds a new node or value in the list after the specified node.

- `AddBefore()` adds a new node or value in the list before the specified node.

We can see examples of the overload that adds a new value for each of these methods in the following sample:

```
var numbers = new LinkedList<int>();
var n2 = numbers.AddFirst(2);        // 2
var n1 = numbers.AddFirst(1);        // 1 2
var n7 = numbers.AddLast(7);         // 1 2 7
var n11 = numbers.AddLast(11);       // 1 2 7 11
var n3 = numbers.AddAfter(n2, 3);    // 1 2 3 7 11
var n5 = numbers.AddBefore(n7, 5);   // 1 2 3 5 7 11
```

Searching for elements in a linked list can be performed using one of the following methods:

- `Contains()`: This checks whether a specified value is found in the list and returns a Boolean value to indicate success or failure.

- `Find()`: This finds and returns the first node that contains the specified value.

- `FindLast()`: This finds and returns the last node that contains the specified value.

Examples of using these functions are shown here:

```
var fn1 = numbers.Find(5);
var fn2 = numbers.FindLast(5);
Console.WriteLine(fn1 == fn2);            // True

Console.WriteLine(numbers.Contains(3));   // True
Console.WriteLine(numbers.Contains(13));  // False
```

Removing elements from the list can be done in several ways using the following methods:

- `RemoveFirst()` removes the first node in the list.

- `RemoveLast()` removes the last node in the list.

- `Remove()` removes the specified node or the first occurrence of the specified value from the list.

- `Clear()` removes all the elements from the list.

You can see all these methods at work in the following listing:

```
numbers.RemoveFirst();  // 2 3 5 7 11
numbers.RemoveLast();   // 2 3 5 7
numbers.Remove(3);      // 2 5 7
numbers.Remove(n5);     // 2 7
numbers.Clear();        // empty
```

The linked list class also has several properties, including `Count`, which returns the number of elements in the list, `First`, which returns the first node, and `Last`, which returns the last node. If the list is empty, then `Count` is `0` and `First` and `Last` are both set to `null`.

The Dictionary<TKey, TValue> collection

A dictionary is a collection of key-value pairs that allows fast lookup based on a key. Adding, searching, and deleting an item are very fast operations and are performed in *O(1)*. The exception here is adding a new value if the capacity must be increased, in which case it becomes *O(n)*.

In .NET, the generic `Dictionary<TKey,TValue>` class implements a dictionary. `TKey` represents the type of the key and `TValue` represents the type of the value. The elements of the dictionary are `KeyValuePair<TKey,TValue>` objects.

`Dictionary<TKey, TValue>` has several overloaded constructors that allow us to create an empty dictionary or a dictionary filled with some initial values. The default constructor of this class will create an empty dictionary. Take a look at the following code snippet:

```
var languages = new Dictionary<int, string>();
```

Here, we are creating an empty dictionary called `languages` that has a key of the `int` type and a value of the `string` type. We can also initialize a dictionary at the time of declaration. Consider the following code snippet:

```
var languages = new Dictionary<int, string>()
{
    {1, "C#"},
    {2, "Java"},
    {3, "Python"},
    {4, "C++"}
};
```

Here, we are creating a dictionary that is initialized with four values that have the keys 1, 2, 3, and 4. This is semantically equivalent to the following initialization:

```
var languages = new Dictionary<int, string>()
{
    [1] = "C#",
    [2] = "Java",
    [3] = "Python",
    [4] = "C++"
};
```

A dictionary must contain unique keys; however, the value can be *duplicated*. Similarly, a key cannot be `null`, but a value (if it is of a reference type) can be `null`. To add, remove, or search for dictionary values, we can use the following methods:

- `Add()`: This adds a new value with the specified key to the dictionary. If the key is `null` or the key already exists in the dictionary, an exception is thrown.

- `Remove()`: This removes the value with the specified key.

- `Clear()`: This removes all the values from the dictionary.

- `ContainsKey()`: This checks if the dictionary contains the specified key and returns a Boolean value to indicate that.

- `ContainsValue()`: This checks if the dictionary contains the specified value and returns a Boolean value to indicate that. The method performs a linear search; therefore, it is an *O(n)* operation.

- `TryGetValue()`: This checks whether the dictionary contains the specified key and if so, it returns the associated value as an `out` argument. The method returns `true` if the value was successful fetched or `false` otherwise. If the key is not present, the output parameter is set to the default value of the `TValue` type (that is, `0` for numerical types, `false` for bool, and `null` for reference types).

In .NET Core 2.0 and newer, there is one additional method called `TryAdd()` that attempts to add a new value to the dictionary. The method succeeds only if the key is not already present. It returns a Boolean value to indicate success or failure.

The class also contains a set of properties, the most important of them being the following:

- `Count`: This returns the number of key-value pairs in the dictionary.

- `Keys`: This returns a collection (of the `Dictionary<TKey,TValue>.KeyCollection` type) containing all the keys in the dictionary. The order of the keys in this collection is not specified.

- `Values`: This returns a collection (of the `Dictionary<TKey,TValue>.ValueCollection` type) containing all the values in the dictionary. The order of the values in this collection is not specified but it is guaranteed to be in the same order as their associated keys in the `Keys` collection.

- `Item[]`: This is an indexer that gets or sets the value associated with the specified key. The indexer can be used to add values to the dictionary. If the key does not exist, a new key-value pair is added. If the key already exists, the value is overwritten.

Take a look at the following sample, where we are creating a dictionary and then adding key-value pairs in several ways:

```
var languages = new Dictionary<int, string>()
{
    {1, "C#"},
    {2, "Java"},
    {3, "Python"},
    {4, "C++"}
};
languages.Add(5, "JavaScript");
```

```
languages.TryAdd(5, "JavaScript");
languages[6] = "F#";
languages[5] = "TypeScript";
```

Initially, the dictionary contained the pairs [1, C#] [2, Java] [3, Python] [4, C++] and then we added [5, JavaScript] twice. However, because the second time `TryAdd()` is used, the operation will occur without any exception being thrown. We then used the indexer to add another pair, [6, F#], and also changed the value of the existing key, that is, 5, from JavaScript to TypeScript.

We can search through the dictionary with the methods mentioned earlier:

```
Console.WriteLine($"Has 5: {languages.ContainsKey(5)}");
Console.WriteLine($"Has C#: {languages.ContainsValue("C#")}");

if (languages.TryGetValue(1, out string lang))
    Console.WriteLine(lang);
else
    Console.WriteLine("Not found!");
```

We can also iterate through the elements of a dictionary using an enumerator, in which case the key-value pairs are retrieved as `KeyValuePair<TKey, TValue>` objects:

```
foreach(var kvp in languages)
{
    Console.WriteLine($"[{kvp.Key}] = {kvp.Value}");
}
```

To remove elements, we can use either `Remove()` or `Clear()`, with the latter for removing all the key-value pairs from the dictionary:

```
languages.Remove(5);
languages.Clear();
```

Another hash-based collection, which only maintains a collection of keys or unique values, is `HashSet<T>`. We will look at it in the following section.

The HashSet<T> collection

A set is a collection that contains only distinct items that can be in any order. .NET provides the `HashSet<T>` class for working with sets. This class contains methods to handle the elements of the set but also methods to model mathematical set operations such as **union** or **intersection**.

Like all the other collections, HashSet<T> contains several overloaded constructors that allow us to create either an empty set or a set filled with initial values. To declare an empty set, we use the default constructor (which is the constructor without parameters):

```
HashSet<int> numbers = new HashSet<int>();
```

But we can also initialize the set with some values, as shown in the following example:

```
HashSet<int> numbers = new HashSet<int>()
{
    1, 1, 2, 3, 5, 8, 11
};
```

To work with a set, we can use the following methods:

- Add() adds a new element to the set if the element is not already present. The function returns a Boolean value to indicate success or failure.

- Remove() removes the specified element from the set.

- RemoveWhere() removes all the elements that match the supplied predicate from the set.

- Clear() removes all the elements from the set.

- Contains() checks whether the specified element is present in the set.

We can see these methods in action in the following sample:

```
HashSet<int> numbers = new HashSet<int>() { 11, 3, 8 };
numbers.Add(1);                       // 11 3 8 1
numbers.Add(1);                       // 11 3 8 1
numbers.Add(2);                       // 11 3 8 1 2
numbers.Add(5);                       // 11 3 8 1 2 5

Console.WriteLine(numbers.Contains(1));
Console.WriteLine(numbers.Contains(7));

numbers.Remove(1);                    // 11 3 8 2 5
numbers.RemoveWhere(n => n % 2 == 0); // 11 3 5
numbers.Clear();                      // empty
```

As mentioned previously, the HashSet<T> class provides the following methods for mathematical set operations:

- UnionWith(): This performs the union of two sets. The current set object is modified by adding all the elements from the supplied set that are not present in the set.

- IntersectWith(): This performs the intersection of two sets. The current set object is modified so that it contains only the elements that are also present in the supplied set.

- ExceptWith(): This performs set subtraction. The current set object is modified by removing all the elements that are also present in the supplied set.

- SymmetricExceptWith(): This performs set symmetric difference. The current set object is modified to contain only elements that are present either in the set or in the supplied set but not in both.

Examples of using these methods are shown in the following listing:

```
HashSet<int> a = new HashSet<int>() { 1, 2, 5, 6, 9};
HashSet<int> b = new HashSet<int>() { 1, 2, 3, 4};

var s1 = new HashSet<int>(a);
s1.IntersectWith(b);                 // 1 2

var s2 = new HashSet<int>(a);
s2.UnionWith(b);                     // 1 2 5 6 9 3 4

var s3 = new HashSet<int>(a);
s3.ExceptWith(b);                    // 5 6 9

var s4 = new HashSet<int>(a);
s4.SymmetricExceptWith(b);           // 4 3 5 6 9
```

In addition to these mathematical set operations, the class also provides methods for determining set equality, overlapping, or whether a set is a subset or superset of another. Some of these methods are listed here:

- `Overlaps()` determines whether the current set and the supplied set contain any common elements. The method returns `true` if at least one common element exists or `false` otherwise.

- `IsSubsetOf()` determines if the current set is a subset of another set, which means that all its elements are also present in the other set. An empty set is a subset of any set.

- `IsSupersetOf()` determines if the current set is a superset of another set, which means that the current set contains all the elements of the other set.

Examples of using these methods are shown in the following snippet:

```
HashSet<int> a = new HashSet<int>() { 1, 2, 5, 6, 9 };
HashSet<int> b = new HashSet<int>() { 1, 2, 3, 4 };
HashSet<int> c = new HashSet<int>() { 2, 5 };

Console.WriteLine(a.Overlaps(b));      // True
Console.WriteLine(a.IsSupersetOf(c));  // True
Console.WriteLine(c.IsSubsetOf(a));    // True
```

The `HashSet<T>` class contains other methods and properties. You should check the online documentation for a complete reference of the class members.

Choosing the right collection type

So far, we have looked at the most widely used generic collection types, although the base class library provides several more. The key question that arises after looking at each of them individually is when these collections should be used. In this section, we will provide some guidelines for choosing the right collection. Let's take a look:

- `List<T>` is the default collection to use when you need to store elements contiguously and access them directly and you don't have other specific constraints. Elements of the list can be accessed directly by their index. Adding and removing elements at the end is very efficient, but doing so at the beginning or middle is costly because it involves moving at least some of the elements.

- `Stack<T>` is the typical choice when you need a sequential list with the elements typically discarded after being retrieved in a LIFO manner. Elements are added and removed from the top of the stack, both operations requiring constant time.

- `Queue<T>` is a good choice when you need a sequential list with the elements also discarded after being retrieved but in a FIFO manner. Elements are added at the end and removed from the top of the queue. Both operations are very fast.

- `LinkedList<T>` is useful when you need to add and remove many elements from the middle of the list and do it quickly. However, this comes at the expense of the ability to randomly access the elements of the list (by their index). The linked list does not store its elements contiguously and you must traverse the list from one end in order to find an element.

- `Dictionary<TKey, TValue>` should be used when you need to store values associated with a key. Inserts, deletes, and lookups are very fast – they require constant time, regardless of the size of the dictionary. The implementation uses a hash table, which means the keys are hashed and therefore the type of the key must implement `GetHashCode()` and `Equals()`. Alternatively, you need to provide an `IEqualityComparer` implementation upon the construction of the dictionary object. The elements of a dictionary are stored unordered, which prevents you from traversing the values in the dictionary in a particular order.

- `HashSet<T>` is the collection you can use when you need a list of unique values. Inserts, deletes, and lookups are very efficient. The elements are stored unordered but contiguously. A hash set is logically similar to a dictionary, where the values are also the keys, although it is a non-associative container. For this reason, the type of its elements must implement `GetHashCode()` and `Equals()`, or, alternatively, you must provide an `IEqualityComparer` implementation upon the construction of the hash set.

The following table summarizes the information from the previous list:

Collection	Order	Contiguous storage	Access type	Lookup	Add/ Remove
List<T>	User-defined	Yes	By index	O(1) – by index O(n) – by value	O(n)
Stack<T>	LIFO	Yes	Top element	O(1)	O(1)
Queue<T>	FIFO	Yes	Front element	O(1)	O(1)
LinkedList<T>	User-defined	No	No (sequential traversal)	O(n)	O(1)
Dictionary<TKey, TValue>	Unordered	Yes	By key	O(1)	O(1)
HashSet<T>	Unordered	Yes	By key	O(1)	O(1)

If performance is key for your application, then, regardless of the choice you make based on guidelines and best practices, it is important to measure to see if the chosen collection type fits your requirements. Also, keep in mind that there are more collections in the base class library than the ones discussed in this chapter. `SortedList<TKey, TValue>`, `SortedDictionary<TKey, TValue>`, and `SortedSet<T>` could also be valuable in some particular scenarios.

Using thread-safe collections

The generic collections we have seen so far are not thread-safe. This means that when they're used in multithreading scenarios, you need to protect access to these collections with external locks, which in many cases can *degrade* performance. .NET offers several thread-safe collections that use efficient locking and lock-free synchronization mechanisms to achieve thread-safety. These collections are provided in the `System.Collections.Concurrent` namespace and should be used in scenarios where more than one thread is accessing a collection concurrently. However, the actual benefit may be smaller or greater than a standard collection being protected with an external lock. A discussion about this is provided later in this section.

> **Information box**
>
> The topic of multithreading and asynchronous programming will be addressed in *Chapter 12, Multithreading and Async Programming*, where you will learn about threads and tasks, synchronization mechanisms, the await/async model, and others.
>
> Although the collections from the `System.Collections.Concurrent` namespace are thread-safe, it is not guaranteed that access to their elements through extension methods or explicit interface implementations is also thread-safe and they may require additional explicit synchronization by the caller.

The thread-safe generic collections are available and are discussed in the following subsections.

IProducerConsumerCollection<T>

This is not an actual collection, but an interface that defines methods to manipulate thread-safe collections. It provides two methods called `TryAdd()` and `TryTake()` that enable adding and removing elements to a collection in a thread-safe way and also support cancellation with a `CancellationToken` object.

In addition, it has a `ToArray()` method, which copies the element from the underlying collection to a new array, and overloads for `CopyTo()`, which copies elements of the collection to an array starting at a specified index. All implementations must make sure that all the methods of this interface are thread-safe. This interface is implemented by `ConcurrentBag<T>`, `ConcurrentStack<T>`, `ConcurrentQueue<T>`, and `BlockingCollection<T>`. You can also provide your own implementation if the standard ones do not meet your needs.

BlockingCollection<T>

This is a class that implements the producer-consumer pattern defined by the `IProducerConsumerCollection<T>` interface. It is actually a simple wrapper over the `IProducerConsumerCollection<T>` interface and does not have an internal underlying storage; instead, it must be provided with one (a collection that implements the `IProducerConsumerCollection<T>` interface). If no implementation is provided, it uses the `ConcurrentQueue<T>` class by default.

The `BlockingCollection<T>` class supports **bounding** and **blocking**. Bounding means that you can set the capacity of the collection. That means when the collection reaches its maximum capacity, any producer (a thread that adds elements to the collection) will block until a consumer (a thread that removes elements from the collection) removes an element.

On the other hand, any consumer that wants to remove an element blocks when the collection is empty until a producer adds an element to the collection. Adding and removing can be done with either `Add()` and `Take()` or the `TryAdd()` and `TryTake()` versions, which, unlike the former, support cancellation. There is also a `CompleteAdding()` method that marks the collection as complete, in which case further adding is no longer possible, and attempts to remove elements will no longer block when the collection is empty.

Let's take a look at an example to understand how this works. In the following sample code, we have a task that is producing elements to a `BlockingCollection<int>` and two tasks that are consuming from it. The collection is created as follows:

```
using var bc = new BlockingCollection<int>();
```

This uses the default constructor of the class, which will instantiate it using the
`ConcurrentQueue<int>` class as the underlying storage for the collection. The
producer task is using the blocking collection to add numbers, which in this particular
case are the first 12 elements of the Fibonacci sequence. Notice that, at the end, we are
calling `CompleteAdding()` to mark the collection as complete. Further attempts to
add would fail:

```
using var producer = Task.Run(() => {
    int a = 1, b = 1;
    bc.Add(a);
    bc.Add(b);
    for(int i = 0; i < 10; ++i)
    {
        int c = a + b;
        bc.Add(c);
        a = b;
        b = c;
    }
    bc.CompleteAdding();
});
```

The first consumer is a task that iterates indefinitely through the collection, taking one
element at a time. The call to `Take()` blocks the calling thread if the collection is empty.
However, if the collection is empty and it has been marked as complete, the operation will
throw `InvalidOperationException`:

```
using var consumer1 = Task.Run(() => {
    try
    {
        while (true)
            Console.WriteLine($"[1] {bc.Take()}");
    }
    catch (InvalidOperationException)
    {
        Console.WriteLine("[1] collection completed");
    }
    Console.WriteLine("[1] work done");
});
```

The second consumer is a task that does very similar work. However, instead of using an infinite loop, it uses a `foreach` statement. This is possible because `BlockingCollection<T>` has a method called `GetConsumingEnumerable()` that retrieves `IEnumerable<T>` that makes it possible to remove items from the collection with a `foreach` loop or `Parallel.ForEach`.

Unlike the infinite loop, the enumerator provides items until the collection is marked as completed. If the collection is empty but not marked as completed, then the operation blocks until one item becomes available. The retrieving operation can also be canceled by using a `CancellationToken` object when calling `GetConsumingEnumerable()`:

```
using var consumer2 = Task.Run(() => {
    foreach(var n in bc.GetConsumingEnumerable())
        Console.WriteLine($"[2] {n}");
    Console.WriteLine("[2] work done");
});
```

Having these three tasks, we should wait for them all to complete:

```
await Task.WhenAll(producer, consumer1, consumer2);
```

A possible output from executing this sample is as follows:

Figure 7.7 – A possible output from the execution of the preceding snippet.

Notice that the output will vary for different runs (meaning that the order of processing the elements will not be the same and from the same task).

ConcurrentQueue<T>

This is a thread-safe implementation of a queue (which is a FIFO collection). It provides three methods: Enqueue(), to add elements to the end of the collection, TryPeek(), to try to return the element at the beginning of the queue without removing it, and TryDequeue(), to try to remove and return the element at the beginning of the collection. It also provides an explicit implementation for the IProducerConsumerCollection<T> interface.

ConcurrentStack<T>

This class implements a thread-safe stack (which is a LIFO collection). It provides four methods: Push(), to add an element at the top of the stack, TryPeek(), to try to return the element at the top without removing it, TryPop(), to try to remove and return the element at the top, and TryPopRange(), to try to remove and return multiple objects from the top of the stack. In addition, it also provides an explicit implementation for the IProducerConsumerCollection<T> interface.

ConcurrentBag<T>

This class represents a thread-safe unordered collection of objects. This can be useful when you want to store objects, including duplicates, and their order is not important. The implementation is optimized for scenarios where the same thread is both the producer and consumer of the elements in the bag. Adding is done with Add() and removing is done with TryPeek() and TryTake(). You can also remove all the elements of the bag with a call to Clear(). Like the concurrent stack and queue implementation, this class also provides an explicit implementation for the IProducerConsumerCollection<T> interface.

ConcurrentDictionary<TKey, TValue>

This represents a thread-safe collection of key-value pairs. It provides methods such as TryAdd(), to try to add a new key-value pair, TryUpdate(), to try to update an existing item, AddOrUpdate(), to either add a new or update an existing item, and GetOrAdd(), to either retrieve an existing item or add a new one if the key is not found.

These operations are atomic and thread-safe with the exception of their overloads, which take delegates. These are executed outside the locks, and therefore their code is not part of the atomicity of the operation. In addition, TryGetValue() attempts to get the value of a specified key, and TryRemove() attempts to remove and return the value associated with the specified key.

Choosing the right concurrent collection type

Now that we have seen what the concurrent collections are, the important question is when these should be used, especially in relation to the non-thread-safe collections. In general, you can use them as follows:

- `BlockingCollection<T>` for when bounding and blocking scenarios are necessary.

- `ConcurrentQueue<T>` should be preferred over `Queue<T>` with an external lock when the processing time is at least 500 **floating-point operations** (**FLOPS**). Otherwise, the performance benefit can be modest or it could actually perform even worse. When the processing time per element is very small, `ConcurrentQueue<T>` performs best if one thread enqueues and another is dequeuing.

- `ConcurrentStack<T>` should be preferred over `Stack<T>` with an external lock if the same thread can either add or remove elements, in which case it is faster for both small and large processing times. However, if one thread adds and another thread removes elements, then `ConcurrentStack<T>` and `Stack<T>` with an external lock will perform relatively the same. But when the number of threads increases, `Stack<T>` might actually perform better.

- `ConcurrentDictionary<TKey, TValue>` performs better than `Dictionary<TKey, TValue>` in all scenarios where adding and updating is done concurrently from multiple threads, although if the updates are frequent but the reads are rare, the benefits are very small. If both reads and updates are frequent, then `ConcurrentDictionary<TKey, TValue>` is significantly faster. `Dictionary<TKey, TValue>` is only suitable for scenarios where all the threads perform only reads and no updates.

- `ConcurrentBag<T>` is suitable for scenarios where the same thread is both adding and consuming elements. However, in scenarios where a thread only either adds or removes, then it is slower than all the other concurrent collections.

Keep in mind that the preceding list represents only guidelines and general behavior and it might not apply in all cases. In general, when you deal with concurrency and parallelism, you need to account for the particular aspects of your scenarios. Whatever algorithms and data structures you are using, you must profile their execution to see how it performs, both in relation to a sequential implementation or other concurrent alternatives.

Summary

In this chapter, we learned about generic collections in .NET, the data structures they model, and the interfaces they implement. We looked at the most important collections in the `System.Collections.Generic` namespaces, `List<T>`, `Stack<T>`, `Queue<T>`, `LinkedList<T>`, `Dictionary<TKey, TValue>`, and `HashSet<T>`, and learned how to use them and perform operations such as adding, removing, or searching elements. In the last part of this chapter, we also looked at the `System.Collection.Concurrent` namespace and the thread-safe collections it provides. Then, we learned about the particularities of each collection and the typical scenarios where they are suitable to be used.

In the next chapter, we will explore some advanced topics such as delegates and events, tuples, regular expressions, pattern matching, and extension methods.

Test what you learned

1. Under which namespace are the generic collections present?

2. What is the base interface for all the other interfaces that define functionalities for generic collections?

3. What is the benefit of using generic collections instead of non-generic collections?

4. What is `List<T>` and how do you add and remove elements to or from it?

5. What is `Stack<T>` and how do you add and remove elements to or from it?

6. What is `Queue<T>`? What is the difference between its `Dequeue()` and `Peek()` methods?

7. What is `LinkedList<T>`? What methods can you use to add elements to the collection?

8. What is `Dictionary<K, V>` and what type are its elements?

9. What is `HashSet<T>` and how does it differ from `Dictionary<K, V>`?

10. What is `BlockingCollection<T>`? What concurrent scenarios is it suitable for?

8
Advanced Topics

In the previous chapters, we learned about the language syntax, data types, working with classes and structures, generics, collections, and other topics that have equipped you with the knowledge necessary to write at least simple C# programs. However, there's more to the language than that and in this chapter, we will explore more advanced concepts. This will include delegates, which are key for functional and asynchronous programming that we cover later in this book, as well as various forms of pattern matching including regular expressions for texts.

The topics that we will discuss are as follows:

- Delegates and events
- Anonymous types
- Tuples
- Pattern matching
- Regular expressions
- Extension methods

After completing this chapter, you will understand how to use delegates to respond to events that occur in your application, how to use tuples to handle multiple values without introducing new types, how to perform pattern matching in code with `is` and `switch` expressions as well as search and replace texts using regular expressions. Last, but not least, you will learn how to extend types without modifying their actual source code with the help of extension methods.

Let's begin this chapter by learning about delegates and events.

Delegates and events

A **callback** is a function (or more generally, any executable code) that is passed as a parameter to another function in order to be called immediately (**synchronous callbacks**) or at a later time (**asynchronous callbacks**). Operating systems (such as Windows) use callbacks extensively to allow applications to respond to events such as mouse events or key presses. Another typical example for callbacks is general purpose algorithms that use callbacks for processing elements from a collection, such as comparing them in order to sort them or filter them out.

In languages such as C and C++, a callback is simply a *function pointer* (that is, the address of a function). However, in .NET, callbacks are *strongly-typed objects* that hold not only the reference to one or more methods but also the information about their parameters and return type. In .NET and C#, callbacks are represented by delegates.

Delegates

A **delegate** is defined using the `delegate` keyword. The declaration looks like a function signature, but the compiler actually introduces a class that can hold references to methods whose signatures match the signature of the delegate. A delegate can hold references to either *static* or *instance methods*.

To better understand the way delegates are defined and used, we will consider the following example.

We have a class that represents an engine. There can be different things the engine can do but we will focus on starting and stopping this engine. When these events happen, we want to let the clients using the engine to know about this and give them the chance to do something. For simplicity, the client will only log the event to the console. In this simple model, the engine can be in any of these two states: **started** or **stopped**. We will start by declaring the delegate type called `StatusChange`:

```
public enum Status { Started, Stopped }
public delegate void StatusChange(Status status);
```

StatusChange is not a function but a *type*. We will use this for declaring a variable in the engine that will hold a reference to a callback method. The class that represents the engine is as follows:

```
public class Engine
{
    private StatusChange statusChangeHandler;

    public void RegisterStatusChangeHandler(StatusChange
handler)
    {
        statusChangeHandler = handler;
    }

    public void Start()
    {
        // start the engine
        if (statusChangeHandler != null)
            statusChangeHandler(Status.Started);
    }

    public void Stop()
    {
        // stop the engine
        if (statusChangeHandler != null)
            statusChangeHandler(Status.Stopped);
    }
}
```

There are several things to notice here:

- First, the RegisterStatusChangeHandler() method takes an argument of the delegate type (StatusChange) and assigns it to the statusChangeHandler member field.

- Second, the Start() and Stop() methods do not actually do much (for simplicity only), but you can imagine they are performing a start and a stop of the engine. However, after this, they invoke the callback, just like a regular function, passing all the necessary arguments.

- In this example, the delegate does not return any value, but a delegate can return anything. However, before invoking the callback method, a *null check* is performed. If the delegate was not assigned a reference to a method, invoking the delegate results in NullReferenceException.

The client code creates an instance of the `Engine` class, registers a handler for status changes, and then starts and stops its. The code is as follows:

```
class Program
{
    static void Main(string[] args)
    {
        Engine engine = new Engine();
        engine.RegisterStatusChangeHandler
            (OnEngineStatusChanged);

        engine.Start();
        engine.Stop();
    }

    private static void OnEngineStatusChanged(Status status)
    {
        Console.WriteLine($"Engine is now {status}");
    }
}
```

The static method, `OnEngineStatusChanged()`, is used as a callback for the engine start and stop events. Its signature matches the type of the delegate. Executing this program results in the following output:

```
Engine is now Started
Engine is now Stopped
```

An important aspect of .NET delegates is that they support *multicasting*. This means that you can actually set references to as many methods you want to be called; the delegate will then invoke them in the order they are added. Multicast delegates are represented by the `System.MulticastDelegate` class. This class has, internally, a linked list of delegates that is called an *invocation list*. This list can have any number of elements. When the multicast delegate is invoked, all of the delegates in the invocation list are called in the order they appear in the list (which is the order in which they were added). This operation is synchronous and if any error appears during the execution of the invocation list, an exception is thrown.

On the other hand, you can remove a reference to a method from the delegate when you no longer want it to be called. Both of these aspects will be exemplified in the following example where we change the `Engine` class to allow multiple callbacks to be not only registered but also unregistered:

```
public class Engine
{
    private StatusChange statusChangeHandler;

    public void RegisterStatusChangeHandler(StatusChange
handler)
    {
        statusChangeHandler += handler;
    }

    public void UnregisterStatusChangeHandler(StatusChange
handler)
    {
        statusChangeHandler -= handler;
    }

    public void Start()
    {
        statusChangeHandler?.Invoke(Status.Started);
    }

    public void Stop()
    {
        statusChangeHandler?.Invoke(Status.Stopped);
    }
}
```

Again, there are two things to notice here:

- First, the `RegisterStatusChangeHandler()` method no longer simply assigns its argument to the `statusChangeHandler` field, but actually uses the `+=` operator to add a new reference to the list the delegate is holding internally. Consequently, the `UnregisterStatusChangeHandler()` method is using the `-=` operator to remove a reference from the delegate. The `+=` and `-=` operators are overloaded for the delegate types.

- Second, the code in `Start()` and `Stop()` has slightly changed. The null-conditional operator (`?.`) is used to call the `Invoke()` method only if the object is not `null`.

On the other hand, the changes in the main program are as follows:

```
class Program
{
    static void Main(string[] args)
    {
        Engine engine = new Engine();
        engine.RegisterStatusChangeHandler
            (OnEngineStatusChanged);
        engine.RegisterStatusChangeHandler
            (OnEngineStatusChanged2);

        engine.Start();
        engine.Stop();

        engine.UnregisterStatusChangeHandler
            (OnEngineStatusChanged2);

        engine.Start();
    }

    private static void OnEngineStatusChanged(Status status)
    {
        Console.WriteLine($"Engine is now {status}");
    }

    private static void OnEngineStatusChanged2(Status status)
    {
        File.AppendAllText(@"c:\temp\engine.log",
                           $"Engine is now {status}\n");
    }
}
```

This time, we register two callbacks:

- One that records the event on the *console*.
- One that records to a *file*.

We start and stop the engine and then we unregister the callback that logs to the file on disk. Last, we start the engine again. As a result, the output on the console will be the following:

```
Engine is now Started
Engine is now Stopped
Engine is now Started
```

However, only the first two lines also appear on the file on disk, because the second callback was removed before restarting the engine.

In this second example, we used the `Invoke()` method to call the methods referred by the delegate. Where did the `Invoke()` method come from? Behind the scenes, when you declare a delegate type, the compiler generates a sealed class derived from `System.MulticastDelegate` that in turn is derived from `System.Delegate`. These are system types that you are not allowed to derive explicitly from. However, they provide all of the functionalities we have seen so far, such as the ability to add and remove methods from the delegate's invocation list.

The class created by the compiler contains three methods—`Invoke()` (used to invoke the callbacks in a *synchronous manner*), `BeginInvoke()`, and `EndInvoke()` (used to invoke the callbacks in an *asynchronous manner*). For examples of asynchronous delegates, consult additional references. You can actually check the compiler-generated code by opening the assembly in a disassembler such as **ildasm.exe** or **ILSpy**.

Events

The code we have written so far is a little too *explicit*. We had to create methods for registering and unregistering references to callback methods. That was because the delegate that held those references was private in the class. We could make it public, but then we break encapsulation and risk allowing the clients to erroneously overwrite the delegate's invocation list. To help with these aspects, .NET and C# offer *events*, which are simply syntactic sugar for the explicit code we wrote earlier for registering and unregistering callbacks. Events are introduced with the `event` keyword.

The last implementation of the engine will change to the following:

```
public class Engine
{
    public event StatusChange StatusChanged;

    public void Start()
    {
        StatusChanged?.Invoke(Status.Started);
```

```
    }

    public void Stop()
    {
        StatusChanged?.Invoke(Status.Stopped);
    }
}
```

Notice that we no longer have the methods for registering and unregistering callbacks, only an event object called StatusChanged. These are done in the client code on the event object, using the += (to add a reference to a method) and -= (to remove a reference to a method) operators. We can see the client code in the following code.

In this example, we create an Engine object and register to callbacks for the StatusChanged event—one is a reference to the OnEngineStatusChanged() method (that logs the event to a file) and the other one is a lambda expression (that logs the event to the console):

```
class Program
{
    static void Main(string[] args)
    {
        Engine engine = new Engine();
        engine.StatusChanged += OnEngineStatusChanged;
        engine.StatusChanged +=
            status => Console.WriteLine(
                        $"Engine is now {status}");

        engine.Start();
        engine.Stop();

        engine.StatusChanged -= OnEngineStatusChanged;

        engine.Start();
    }

    private static void OnEngineStatusChanged(Status status)
    {
        File.AppendAllText(@"c:\temp\engine.log",
                        $"Engine is now {status}\n");
    }
}
```

After starting and stopping the engine, we unregister the reference to
OnEngineStatusChanged() and then restart the engine. The result of executing this
program is identical to the previous one.

In all of the examples so far, the delegate type had a single argument that was the status of
the engine. However, proper implementation of the event's pattern (used throughout the
entire .NET Framework) is to have two arguments:

- The first argument is System.Object, which holds a reference to the object that
  generated the event. It is up to the client being called to use this reference or not.

- The second argument is of a type derived from System.EventArgs, which holds
  all of the event-related information.

To comply with this pattern, our implementation of Engine will change to the following:

```
public class EngineEventArgs : EventArgs
{
    public Status Status { get; private set; }

    public EngineEventArgs(Status s)
    {
        Status = s;
    }
}

public delegate void StatusChange(
        object sender, EngineEventArgs args);

public class Engine
{
    public event StatusChange StatusChanged;

    public void Start()
    {
        StatusChanged?.Invoke(this,
            new EngineEventArgs(Status. Started));
    }

    public void Stop()
    {
        StatusChanged?.Invoke(this,
            new EngineEventArgs(Status.Stopped));
    }
}
```

We will leave it as an exercise to the reader to make the necessary changes to the main program to use the new implementation of the `Engine` class.

The key takeaways about delegates and events are the following:

- Delegates allow methods to be passed as arguments to be called later, either synchronously or asynchronously.

- Delegates support multicasting, that is, the invocation of multiple callback methods.

- Static methods, instance methods, anonymous methods, and lambda expressions can be used as callbacks with delegates.

- Delegates can be generic.

- Events are syntactic sugar that help with registration and removal of callbacks.

The next topic to discuss in this chapter are anonymous types.

Anonymous types

It is sometimes necessary to construct temporary objects that hold some values, usually a subset of some larger object. To avoid creating a specific type for this purpose only, the language provides so-called *anonymous types*. These are a sort of use-and-forget types typically used in query expressions with **Language Integrated Query** (**LINQ**). This topic will be discussed in *Chapter 10, Lambdas, LINQ, and Functional Programming*.

These types are called anonymous because you do not specify a name in the source code. The name is assigned by the compiler. They consist of read-only properties only; any other member type is not allowed. The type of the read-only properties cannot be explicitly specified and is inferred by the compiler.

An anonymous type is introduced with the `new` keyword followed by a list of properties in angle-brackets (an object initializer). The following code snippet shows an example:

```
var o = new { Name = "M270 Turbo", Capacity = 1600,
Power = 75.0 };
Console.WriteLine($"{o.Name} {o.Capacity / 1000.0}1
{o.Power}kW");
```

Here, we have defined an anonymous type with three properties: `Name`, `Capacity`, and `Power`. The types of these properties are inferred by the compiler from their initialization value. In this case, they are `string` for `Name`, `int` for `Capacity`, and `double` for `Power`.

It is mandatory to specify a name for a property when it is initialized from an expression. However, if it is initialized from a field or property of another object, the name is optional. In this case, the compiler uses the same name as that of the member used to initialize it. To show an example, let's consider the following type:

```
class Engine
{
    public string Name { get; }
    public int Capacity { get; }
    public double Power { get; }

    public Engine(string name, int capacity, double power)
    {
        Name = name;
        Capacity = capacity;
        Power = power;
    }
}
```

Having this, we can write the following:

```
var e = new Engine("M270 Turbo", 1600, 75.0);
var o = new { e.Name, e.Power };
Console.WriteLine($"{o.Name} {o.Power}kW");
```

We have created an instance of the `Engine` class. From this instance, we have created another object of an anonymous type that has two properties, which the compiler calls `Name` and `Power` because they are initialized from the `Name` and `Power` properties of the `Engine` class.

Anonymous types have the following properties:

- They are implemented as sealed classes and are, therefore, reference types. The CLI does not make any difference between anonymous types and other reference types.

- They are directly derived from `System.Object` and can only be cast to `System.Object`.

- They can only contain read-only properties. No other members are allowed.

- They cannot be used as the type of a field, property, event, the return type of a method, or the type of a parameter of a method, constructor, or indexer.

- You can specify names for the read-only properties of an anonymous type. This is mandatory when initializing from an expression, but optional when initializing from a field or property. In this case, the compiler uses the name of the member for the property's name.

- The expression used to initialize a property cannot be null, an anonymous function, or a pointer type.

- The scope of an anonymous type is the method in which it is defined.

- When you declare a variable of an anonymous type, you must use `var` as a placeholder for the type name.

A similar concept of ad hoc types but with different semantics is presented by tuples, which is the topic of the next section.

Tuples

Tuples are simple types with a lightweight syntax that can typically be used when you want to return multiple values from a function without defining an explicit type or without using `out` or `ref` parameters or when you want to pass multiple values to a method as a single object.

This aspect represents the key difference between anonymous types and tuples. The former is meant for use within the scope of a single method and cannot be passed as an argument or returned from a method. The latter are intended for this exact purpose.

In C#, there are two kinds of tuples:

- **Reference tuples**, represented by the `System.Tuple` class
- **Value tuples**, represented by the `System.ValueTuple` structure

In the next subsection, we will look at both of these types.

The Tuple class

Reference tuples were introduced in .NET Framework 4.0. The generic class, `System.Tuple`, can hold up to eight values of different types. Should you need tuples with more than eight values, you will have to create nested tuples. Tuples can be instantiated in either of two ways:

- By using the *constructor* of `Tuple<T>`
- By using the *helper method*, `Tuple.Create()`

The following two lines are equivalent:

```
var engine = new Tuple<string, int, double>("M270 Turbo", 1600,
75);
var engine = Tuple.Create("M270 Turbo", 1600, 75);
```

The second line here is preferred because it is simpler as you do not have to specify the type of each value. This is because it is inferred by the compiler from the arguments.

The elements of the tuple are accessible through properties called `Item1`, `Item2`, `Item3`, `Item4`, `Item5`, `Item6`, `Item7`, and `Rest`. In the following example, we use the `Item1`, `Item2`, and `Item3` properties to print the engine name, capacity, and power to the console:

```
Console.WriteLine(
    $"{engine.Item1} {engine.Item2/1000.0}l {engine.Item3}kW");
```

Nested tuples can be used when you need more than eight elements. In this case, it makes sense to put the nested tuple as the last element. The following example creates a tuple with 10 values, the last three of them (representing various engine powers in kW) being grouped in a second, nested tuple:

```
var engine = Tuple.Create(
    "M270 DE16 LA R", 1595, 83, 73.7, 180, "gasoline", 2015,
    Tuple.Create(75, 90, 115));
Console.WriteLine($"{engine.Item1} powers: {engine.Rest.
Item1}");
```

Notice here that we used `Rest.Item1` and not simply `Rest`. The output of this program is as follows:

```
M270 DE16 LA R powers: (75, 90, 115)
```

The reason for this is that the inferred type for the variable engine is `Tuple<string, int, int, double, int, string, int, Tuple<Tuple<int, int, int>>>`. Consequently, `Rest` represents a tuple that holds a single value that is also a tuple that holds three `int` values. To access the elements of the nested tuple, you must use, for this case, `Rest.Item1.Item1`, `Rest.Item1.Item2`, and `Rest.Item1.Item3`.

To create a tuple of the type, `Tuple<string, int, int, double, int, string, int, Tuple<int, int, int>>`, you must use the explicit syntax using constructors:

```
var engine = new Tuple<string, int, int, double, int, string,
int, Tuple<int, int, int>>
    ("M270 DE16 LA R", 1595, 83, 73.7, 180, "gasoline", 2015,
    new Tuple<int, int, int>(75, 90, 115));
Console.WriteLine($"{engine.Item1} powers: {engine.Rest}");
```

`System.Tuple` is a reference type and therefore objects of this type are allocated on the heap. If many allocations of small objects occur during the execution of a program, it can impact performance.

This adds to the limitations we have seen earlier—the number of elements and the unnamed properties. To overcome these problems, C# 7.0, .NET Framework 4.7, and .NET Standard 2.0 have introduced value type tuples, which we will explore in the following section.

Value tuples

These are represented by the `System.ValueTuple` structure. If your project does not target .NET Framework 4.7 or higher or .NET Standard 2.0 or higher, you can still use `ValueTuple` by installing it as a NuGet package.

Various value tuple features have been added in the several 7.x releases of the languages. The functionalities described here are aligned with C# 8.

Apart from the value semantics, value tuples differ from the reference tuples in several important ways:

- They can hold a sequence of any number of elements, but at least two are required.
- They may have compile-time named fields.
- They have a simpler, yet richer syntax for creating, assigning, deconstructing, and comparing values.

Creating a value tuple is done using *parentheses syntax* with values specified in between. The following three declarations are equivalent:

```
ValueTuple<string, int, double> engine = ("M270 Turbo", 1600,
75.0);
(string, int, double) engine = ("M270 Turbo", 1600, 75.0);
var engine = ("M270 Turbo", 1600, 75.0);
```

In all these cases, the type of the variable engine is `ValueTuple<string, int, double>` and the tuple is said to be *unnamed*. In this case, its values are available in the public fields—`Item1`, `Item2`, and `Item3`, which are implicit names assigned by the compiler:

```
Console.WriteLine(
    $"{engine.Item1} {engine.Item2/1000.0}l {engine.Item3}kW");
```

However, when creating a value tuple, you can choose to give names to the values and therefore create synonyms for the fields, `Item1`, `Item2`, and so on. Such value tuples are called **named tuples**. You can see an example of a named tuple in the following code snippet:

```
var engine = (Name: "M270 Turbo", Capacity: 1600, Power: 75.0);
Console.WriteLine(
    $"{engine.name} {engine.capacity / 1000.0}l {engine.power}
kW");
```

These synonyms are only available at compile time because IDEs leverage the Roslyn APIs to make them available for you from the source code, but in the compiler intermediate language code, they are not available, only the unnamed fields—`Item1`, `Item2`, and so on.

The name of a field can appear on either side of the assignment; moreover, they can appear on both sides, in which case the *left name* will take *precedence* and the *right name* will be *ignored*. The following two declarations will produce a named value tuple identical to the one seen in the preceding code:

```
(string Name, int Capacity, double Power) engine =
    ("M270 Turbo", 1600, 75.0);
(string Name, int Capacity, double Power) engine =
    (name: "M270 Turbo", cap: 1600, pow: 75.0);
```

The names for the fields can also be inferred from variables used to initialize the value tuple (as for C# 7.1). In the following example, the value tuple will have fields called name, capacity (lowercase), and Item3 because the last value is a literal without an explicitly specified name:

```
var name = "M270 Turbo";
var capacity = 1600;
var engine = (name, capacity, 75);

Console.WriteLine(
    $"{engine.name} {engine.capacity / 1000.0}1 {engine.Item3}
kW");
```

Returning value tuples from a method is very simple. In the following example, the GetEngine() function returns an unnamed value type:

```
(string, int, double) GetEngine()
{
    return ("M270 Turbo", 1600, 75.0);
}
```

However, you can choose to return a named value type, in which case, you need to specify the names of the fields, as shown here:

```
(string Name, int Capacity, double Power) GetEngine2()
{
    return ("M270 Turbo", 1600, 75.0);
}
```

Beginning with C# 7.3, value tuples can be tested for *equality* and *inequality* using the ==
and != operators. These operators work by comparing, in order, each element from the
left side with each element on the right side. The comparison stops when the first pair is
not equal. However, this only happens when the shape of the tuples is the same, that is,
the number of fields and their type. The names do not participate in the test of equality or
inequality. The next example does a comparison of two value tuples:

```
var e1 = ("M270 Turbo", 1600, 75.0);
var e2 = (Name: "M270 Turbo", Capacity: 1600, Power: 75.0);
Console.WriteLine(e1 == e2);
```

Tuple equality performs a *lifted conversion* if one tuple is a nullable tuple, as well as
implicit conversions on each member of both tuples. The latter include lifted conversions,
widening conversions, or other implicit conversions. As an example, the following
tuples are equal:

```
(int, long) t1 = (1, 2);
(long, int) t2 = (1, 2);
Console.WriteLine(t1 == t2);
```

It is possible to deconstruct the value of a tuple. You can do so either by explicitly
specifying the type of the variables or using var. The following declarations are all
equivalent. In the following and last example, the use of var is combined with explicit
type names:

```
(string name, int capacity, double power) = GetEngine();
(var name, var capacity, var power) = GetEngine();
var (name, capacity, power) = GetEngine();
(var name, var capacity, double power) = GetEngine();
```

If there are values that you are not interested in, you can ignore them by using
the _ placeholder like so:

```
(var name, _, _) = GetEngine();
```

It is possible to deconstruct any .NET type provided that a method called Deconstruct
with out parameters for every value that you want to retrieve is available.

In the following example, the `Engine` class has three properties: `Name`, `Capacity`, and `Power`. The `Deconstruct()` public method takes three out arguments matching these properties. This makes it possible for objects of this type to be deconstructed using tuple syntax. The following listing shows an implementation of the `Engine` class that provides tuple deconstruction:

```
class Engine
{
    public string Name { get; }
    public int Capacity { get; }
    public double Power { get; }

    public Engine(string name, int capacity, double power)
    {
        Name = name;
        Capacity = capacity;
        Power = power;
    }

    public void Deconstruct(out string name, out int capacity,
                            out double power)
    {
        name = Name;
        capacity = Capacity;
        power = Power;
    }
}

var engine = new Engine("M270 Turbo", 1600, 75.0);
var (Name, Capacity, Power) = engine;
```

The `Deconstruct` method can be made available as an extension method, enabling you to provide deconstruction semantics even for types you did not author, provided that you only need to deconstruct values accessible through the public interface of the type. Such an example is shown here:

```
class Engine
{
    public string Name { get; }
    public int Capacity { get; }
    public double Power { get; }
```

```
    public Engine(string name, int capacity, double power)
    {
        Name = name;
        Capacity = capacity;
        Power = power;
    }
}

static class EngineExtension
{
    public static void Deconstruct(this Engine engine,
                                   out string name,
                                   out int capacity,
                                   out double power)
    {
        name = engine.Name;
        capacity = engine.Capacity;
        power = engine.Power;
    }
}
```

If you have a hierarchy of classes and you provide `Deconstruct()` methods, then you must make sure you do not introduce ambiguities, such as in cases where different overloads have the same number of arguments. It should be noted that deconstruction operators do not participate in testing equality. Therefore, the following sample will generate a compiler error:

```
var engine = new Engine("M270 Turbo", 1600, 75.0);
Console.WriteLine(engine == ("M270 Turbo", 1600, 75.0));
```

Summarizing on this topic, the support for value tuples in C# 7 makes it much easier to work with tuples in key scenarios such as holding temporary values or records from a database. This can be done without introducing new types or returning multiple values from a method without the use of `out` or `ref` parameters. With the performance benefit of value semantics and the improvements on element access based on names, as well as other key features, named values are an important improvement on the reference type tuples that we saw at the beginning of this section.

Pattern matching

Pattern matching is the process of checking whether a value has a particular shape as well as extracting information out of the value when the matching is successful. To some extent, that is what we regularly do with the `if` and `switch` statements when we check whether an object has some value and then proceed to extract information from it. However, this is a rudimentary form of pattern matching.

In C# 7, new capabilities are added to `is` and `switch` statements to enable pattern matching capabilities that drive a better separation of data and code and lead to more concise and readable code. The pattern matching capabilities are extended with new features in C# 8. You will learn about these in *Chapter 15, New Features of C# 8*.

The is expression

At runtime, the `is` operator checks that an object is compatible with a given type (the general form, `expr is type`). However, in C# 7, this was extended to include several forms of pattern matching:

- **Type pattern**, in the `expr is type varname` form, checks whether an expression can be converted to the specified type and, if so, casts it to a variable of that specified type.

- **Constant pattern**, in the `expr is constant` form, checks whether the expression evaluates to a specified constant. A particular constant is `null`, for which the pattern is `expr is null`.

- **The var pattern** is a special form of type pattern, in the `expr is var varname` form, that always succeeds and binds the value to a new local variable. A key difference from the type pattern is that `null` is always matched and the new variable is assigned `null`.

To understand how these work, we will use several classes representing vehicles:

```
class Airplane
{
    public void Fly() { }
}

class Bike
{
    public void Ride() { }
}
```

```
class Car
{
    public bool HasAutoDrive { get; }
    public void Drive() { }
    public void AutoDrive() { }
}
```

These vehicle classes are not a part of a hierarchy of classes, but they have public methods that set the vehicle in motion, according to its type. For example, the airplane flies, the bike rides, and the car drives. The next code listing shows a function that uses several forms of pattern matching:

```
void SetInMotion(object vehicle)
{
    if (vehicle is null)
        throw new ArgumentNullException(
            message: "Vehicle must not be null",
            paramName: nameof(vehicle));
    else if (vehicle is Airplane a)
        a.Fly();
    else if (vehicle is Bike b)
        b.Ride();
    else if (vehicle is Car c)
    {
        if (c.HasAutoDrive) c.AutoDrive();
        else c.Drive();
    }
    else
        throw new ArgumentException(
            message: "Unexpected vehicle type",
            paramName: nameof(vehicle));
}
```

This function sets the vehicle in motion according to its specific way of doing so. A statement like if(vehicle is Airplane a) tests whether the variable vehicle can be converted to the Airplane type, and if that is true, then it assigns it to a new variable of the Airplane type (in this example, a). This works with both value types and reference types.

The variables seen here—a, b, and c—have a local scope to the if or else statement. However, these variables are in scope and definitely assigned only when the match was successful. This prevents you from accessing the result of a pattern-matching expression when the pattern was not matched.

As well as the type pattern, a constant pattern is also used here. The `if (vehicle is null)` statement is a test to see whether the reference is actually set to the instance of an object or not; if not, an exception is thrown. However, as already mentioned, constant pattern matching can be used with anything that is a constant—a literal value, a variable declared with the const specifier, or an enumeration value. The way constant expressions are evaluated is as follows:

- If both `expr` and constant are of integral types, it basically evaluates the `expr ==` `constant` expression.

- Otherwise, it invokes the static method, `Object.Equals(expr, constant)`.

The following function shows more examples of constant pattern matching. The `IsTrue()` function converts the supplied argument to a Boolean value. The Boolean value (`true`), the integral value (`1`), the string (`"1"`), and the string (`"true"`) are converted to `true`; everything else including `null` is converted to `false`:

```
bool IsTrue(object value)
{
    if (value is null) return false;
    else if (value is 1) return true;
    else if (value is true) return true;
    else if (value is "true") return true;
    else if (value is "1") return true;
    return false;
}

Console.WriteLine(IsTrue(null));    // False
Console.WriteLine(IsTrue(0));       // False
Console.WriteLine(IsTrue(1));       // True
Console.WriteLine(IsTrue(true));    // True
Console.WriteLine(IsTrue("true"));  // True
Console.WriteLine(IsTrue("1"));     // True
Console.WriteLine(IsTrue("demo"));  // False
```

The switch expression

The more patterns you need to check, the more cumbersome it is to write these sorts of `if-else` statements. Naturally, you would want to replace them with a `switch`. Pattern matching of the same nature is supported for `switch` statements with a similar syntax.

Until C# 7.0, the `switch` statement supported constant pattern matching with integral types and strings. Since C# 7.0, the type pattern seen earlier is also supported in a `switch` statement.

The SetInMotion() function shown in the previous section can be modified as follows using a switch statement:

```
void SetInMotion(object vehicle)
{
    switch (vehicle)
    {
        case Airplane a:
            a.Fly();
            break;
        case Bike b:
            b.Ride();
            break;
        case Car c:
            if (c.HasAutoDrive) c.AutoDrive();
            else c.Drive();
            break;
        case null:
            throw new ArgumentNullException(
                message: "Vehicle must not be null",
                paramName: nameof(vehicle));
        default:
            throw new ArgumentException(
                message: "Unexpected vehicle type",
                paramName: nameof(vehicle));
    }
}
```

The switch statements that use constant pattern matching can only have one case label that matches the value of the switch expressions. Moreover, switch sections must not fall through the next section but must end with break, return, or goto. However, they can be arranged in any order without affecting the behavior of the program semantics and execution.

With type pattern matching, the rules change. The switch section can fall through the next and goto is no longer supported as a jump mechanism. The case label expressions are evaluated in the order they appear in the text and the default case is only executed if none of the case labels match the pattern. The default case can appear anywhere in switch but it is always evaluated last.

If a default case is missing and none of the existing case labels match the pattern, the execution continues after the switch statement without any code in any case label executing.

Another feature of type pattern matching with the switch expression is the support for when clauses. The following example shows another version of the SetInMotion() method that uses two case labels to match the Car type, but one of them with a condition—that the HasAutoDrive property of the Car object is set to true:

```
void SetInMotion(object vehicle)
{
    switch (vehicle)
    {
        case Airplane a:
            a.Fly();
            break;
        case Bike b:
            b.Ride();
            break;
        case Car c when c.HasAutoDrive:
            c.AutoDrive();
            break;
        case Car c:
            c.Drive();
            break;
        case null:
            throw new ArgumentNullException(
                message: "Vehicle must not be null",
                paramName: nameof(vehicle));
        default:
            throw new ArgumentException(
                message: "Unexpected vehicle type",
                paramName: nameof(vehicle));
    }
}
```

It is important to note that matching a type pattern guarantees a *non-null value*, so there is no need for further tests for null. There are special rules for matching null in the language. A null value does not match a type pattern, regardless of the type of the variable. A case label with a pattern matching for null can be added in a switch expression with a type pattern matching to specifically handle null values. Such an example is seen in the preceding implementation.

A special form of type pattern matching is using `var`. The rules are similar to `is` expressions—the type is inferred from the static type of the switch expression and a `null` value always matches. Therefore, when using the `var` pattern, you must add an explicit `null` check because the value may actually be `null`. A `var` declaration may match the same condition as the default case; in this situation, a default case, even if present, would never execute.

Let's look at the following function that executes a command received as a string argument:

```
void ExecuteCommand(string command)
{
    switch(command)
    {
        case "add":  /* add */     break;
        case "del":  /* delete */ break;
        case "exit": /* exit */    break;
        case var o when (o?.Trim().Length ?? 0) == 0:
            /* do nothing */
            break;
        default:
            /* invalid command */
            break;
    }
}
```

This function tries to match the `add`, `del`, and `exit` commands and execute them appropriately. However, if the argument is `null` or empty or has only white spaces, it will do nothing. But this is a different case than an actual command that is either not supported or not recognized. The `var` pattern match helps to differentiate between the two in a simple and elegant manner.

The following are the key takeaways for you for this topic:

- Pattern matching functionalities added in C# 7.0 are an incremental update of already existing simple pattern matching capabilities.
- The new supported patterns are the constant pattern, the type pattern, and the `var` pattern.
- Pattern matching works with `is` expressions and case blocks in `switch` statements.

- The `switch` expression pattern matching supports `where` clauses.

- The `var` pattern always matches any value including `null` and, therefore, a test for `null` is necessary.

C# 8.0 has introduced even more capabilities to the switch expression pattern matching: property patterns, tuple patterns, and positional patterns. You can learn about these in *Chapter 15, New Features on C# 8.*

Regular expressions

Another form of pattern matching is represented by regular expressions. A **regular expression** is a pattern that can be matched against a text. Although not supported directly at the language level, regular expressions are made available to .NET developers through the **Regex** class from the `System.Text.RegularExpressions` namespace. In the following pages, we will look at how you can use this class to match an input text, find parts of it, or replace portions of the text.

Regular expressions are composed of constants (that represent sets of strings) and operator symbols (that represent operations on these sets). The actual language for building regular expressions is more complex than what can be described in the scope of this chapter. If you are not familiar with regular expressions, we recommend using additional resources for learning them. You can also build and test your regular expressions using online tools such as `https://regex101.com/` or `https://regexr.com/`.

Overview

Regular expressions in .NET are built based on the Perl 5 regular expressions. As such, most of Perl 5 regular expressions are compatible with .NET regular expressions. On the other hand, the framework supports another flavor of expressions, called **ECMAScript**, which is basically another name for JavaScript (**ECMAScript** is actually an ECMA standard for scripting-languages, and JavaScript is its best-known implementation). However, when using regular expressions, you must explicitly specify this flavor instead. The implementation of the .NET regular expressions has remained the same since .NET 2.0 and is the same in .NET Core.

The following are some of the features supported by this implementation:

- Case-insensitive matching

- Right-to-left searching (for languages such as Arabic, Hebrew, or Persian that have a right-to-left writing system)

- Multi-line or single-line searching modes that change the meaning of some symbols, such as ^, $ or . (dot)

- The possibility to compile a regular expression to an assembly and to increase performance when a pattern is used to search a large number of strings

- Infinite-width look-behind that enables us to step back to any length and check in the string whether the text inside the look-behind can be matched there

- Character class subtraction that allows you to specify one character class to subtract from another character class

- Balancing groups that allow you to ensure that a subexpression is matched to an equal number of types as another one

Some of these functionalities are enabled with a flag provided as an argument to the constructor of the `Regex` class. The `RegexOptions` enumeration provides the following flags, which can be combined:

Flags	Description
None	This does nothing.
Multiline	^ and $ match at the beginning and end of any line, not just of the entire string.
Singleline	Dot (.) matches any character including \n.
RightToLeft	Search is performed from right to left.
IgnoreCase	Case-insensitive searching is enabled.
IgnorePatternWhitespace	This eliminates unescaped white spaces from the pattern and enables comments marked with #.
Compiled	The regular expression is compiled into the assembly.
CultureInvariant	This ignores cultural differences in language.
ExplicitCapture	Only valid captures are explicitly named or numbered groups of the form (?<name>...).
ECMAScript	This uses the ECMAScript-compliant engine.

Before we move to the next section to look at how to actually use regular expressions in C#, there are two more important things to mention:

- First, regular expressions have a set of special characters. One of them is \ (backslash). In combination with another literal character, this creates a new token with a special meaning. For instance, \d matches any single digit from 0 to 9. Since the backslash is also a special character in C# used for introducing character escape sequences, when you write a regular expression in a string, you need to use double backslashes, such as "(\\d+)". However, you can use verbatim strings to avoid this and keep the regular expression in its natural form. The previous example can be written as @"(\d+)".

- The other important thing to notice is that the Regex class implicitly assumes UTF-8 encoding of the string to match. That means the \w, \d, and \s tokens match any UTF-8 codepoint that is a valid character, digit, or whitespace character in any language. As an example, if you use \d+ to match any positive number of digits, you might be surprised to discover that it will match not just 0-9 but also the following characters: ٢٢١٦٧٨٦٤٥٦٨٢٦٣౨ఇ౫ఠ౧౮

  If you want to restrict matching to English digits for \d, English digits and letters and underscore for \w, and standard whitespace characters for \s, then you need to use the RegexOptions.ECMAScript option.

Let's now see how to define regular expressions and use them to figure out whether some text matches an expression.

Matching input text

The simplest functionality that regular expressions provide is checking whether an input string has a required format. This is useful for performing validation such as checking whether a string is a valid email address, IP address, date, and so on.

To understand how this works, we will validate whether an input text is a valid ISO 8061 date. For simplicity, we will only consider the form *YYYY-MM-DD*, but as an exercise, you can extend this to support other formats. The regular expression we will use for this is (\d{4})-(1[0-2]|0[1-9]|[0-9]{1})-(3[01]|[12][0-9]|0[1-9]|[1-9]{1}).

Broken down into parts, the sub-expressions are as follows:

Sub-expression	Meaning	Matches
`(\d{4})`	1st caption group	0000 ... 9999
`\d{4}`	Exactly four digits	
`(1[0-2]|0[1-9]|[1-9]{1,2})`	2nd caption group	1, 01, 2, 02, 3, 03, 4, 04, 5, 05, 6, 06, 7, 07, 8, 08, 9, 09, 10, 11, 12
`1[0-2]`	1 followed by 0, 1, or 2	10, 11, 12
`0[1-9]`	0 followed by 1, 2, ... 9	01, 02, ... 09
`[1-9]{1}`	0 to 9, exactly once	1, 2, ... 9
`(3[01]|[12][0-9]|0[1-9]|[1-9]{1})`	3rd caption group	1, 01, 2, 02, ... 9, 09, 10, 11, ... 31
`3[01]`	3 followed by 0 or 1	30, 31
`[12][0-9]`	1 or 2 followed by any digit	10, 11, ... 29
`0[1-9]`	0 followed by 1, 2, ... 9	01, 02, ... 09
`[1-9]{1}`	0 to 9, exactly once	1, 2, ... 9

The following two examples are equivalent. The `Regex` class has both static and non-static overloads for `IsMatch()`, and you can use any of the two with the same results. This is also the case for other methods, which we will see in the following sections, such as `Match()`, `Matches()`, `Replace()`, and `Split()`:

```
var pattern = @"(\d{4})-(1[0-2]|0[1-9]|[1-9]{1})-(3[01]|[12][0-9]|0[1-9]|[1-9]{1})";
var success = Regex.IsMatch("2019-12-25", pattern);

// or

var regex = new Regex(pattern);
var success = regex.IsMatch("2019-12-25");
```

If you need to match a pattern only once or a few times, then you could use the static methods as they are simpler. However, if you match the same pattern tens of thousands of times or more, using an instance of the class and calling the non-static members is potentially faster. For most common usage, this is not the case. In the following examples, we will only use the static methods.

The IsMatch() method has overloads that enable us to specify options for the regular expression and a timeout interval. This is useful when the regular expression is too complicated, or the input text is too long, and the parsing takes more than the desired amount of time. Take a look at the following example:

```
var success = Regex.IsMatch("2019-12-25",
                            pattern,
                            RegexOptions.ECMAScript,
                            TimeSpan.FromMilliseconds(1));
```

Here, we enable ECMAScript-compliant behavior of the regular expression and set a timeout value of one millisecond.

Now that we've seen how to match text, let's learn how you can search for substrings and multiple occurrences of a pattern.

Finding substrings

In the examples so far, we only checked whether the input text was of a specific pattern. But it is also possible to get information about the result. This includes, for instance, the text matched in each caption group, the entire matched value, the position in the input text, and so on. To do this, another set of overloads must be used.

The Match() methods check an input string for substrings that match a regular expression and return the first match. The Matches() methods do the same search but return all of the matches. The return type is System.Text.RegularExpressions. Match (that represents a single match) for the former and System.Text. RegularExpressions.MatchCollection (that represents a collection of matches) for the latter. Let's consider the following example:

```
var pattern =
    @"(\d{4})-(1[0-2]|0[1-9]|[1-9]{1})-(3[01]|[12][0-9]|0[1-
9]|[1-9]{1})";
var match = Regex.Match("2019-12-25", pattern);
Console.WriteLine(match.Value);
Console.WriteLine(
    $"{match.Groups[1]}.{match.Groups[2]}.{match.Groups[3]}");
```

The first value printed to the console is 2019-12-25 because that is the value of the entire match. The second is a value composed of the individual values of each capture group, but with a dot (.) as the separator. Consequently, the output text is 2019.12.25.

Capture groups may have names; the form is (?<name>...). In the following example, we call the three capture groups of the regular expression, year, month, and day:

```
var pattern =
    @"(?<year>\d{4})-(?<month>1[0-2]|0[1-9]|[1-9]{1})-
(?<day>3[01]|[12][0-9]|0[1-9]|[1-9]{1})";
var match = Regex.Match("2019-12-25", pattern);
Console.WriteLine(
    $"{match.Groups["year"]}-{match.Groups["month"]}-{match.
Groups["day"]}");
```

Should the input text have multiple substrings that match the pattern, we can get all of them using the Matches() function. In the following example, dates are provided one per line, but the last two are not valid (2019-13-21 and 2019-1-32); therefore, these are not found in the results. To parse the string, we use the multiline option, so that ^ and $ refer to the beginning and the end of each line and not to the entire string, as shown in the following example:

```
var text = "2019-05-01\n2019-5-9\n2019-12-25\n2019-13-21\n2019-
1-32";
var pattern =
    @"^(\d{4})-(1[0-2]|0[1-9]|[1-9]{1})-(3[01]|[12][0-9]|0[1-
9]|[1-9]{1})$";
var matches = Regex.Matches(
  text, pattern, RegexOptions. Multiline);
foreach(Match match in matches)
{
    Console.WriteLine(
        $"[{match.Index}..{match.Length}]={match. Value}");
}
```

The output of the program is as follows:

```
[0..10]=2019-05-01
[11..8]=2019-5-9
[20..10]=2019-12-25
```

Sometimes, we don't just want to find substrings of an input text; we also want to replace them with something else. This topic is discussed in the following section.

Replacing parts of a text

Regular expressions can also be used to replace parts of a string that match the regular expression with another string. The `Replace()` method has a set of overloads, and you can specify either a string or a so-called **match evaluator**, which is basically a function that takes a `Match` argument and returns a string. In the following example, we will use this to change the format of date from *YYYY-MM-DD* to *MM/DD/YYYY*:

```
var text = "2019-12-25";
var pattern = @"(\d{4})-(1[0-2]|0[1-9]|[1-9]{1})-(3[01]|[12]
    [0-9]|0[1-9]|[1-9]{1})";
var result = Regex.Replace(
    text, pattern,
    m => $"{m.Groups[2]}/{m.Groups[3]}/{m.Groups[1]}");
```

As a further exercise, you can write a program that converts an input date of the form 2019-12-25 to the form Dec 25, 2019.

As a conclusion to this section, regular expressions offer rich pattern matching capabilities. .NET provides the `Regex` class that represents a regular expression engine with plenty of functionalities. In this section, we have seen how to match, search, and replace texts based on a pattern. These are common operations that you will encounter in a large variety of applications. You can choose between static and instance overloads of these methods and customize the way they work with various options.

Extension methods

It is sometimes useful to add functionality to a type without changing the implementation, creating a derived type, or recompiling code in general. We can do that by creating methods in helper classes. Let's say we want to have a function that reverses the content of a string because `System.String` does not have one. Such a function can be implemented as follows:

```
static class StringExtensions
{
    public static string Reverse(string s)
    {
        var charArray = s.ToCharArray();
        Array.Reverse(charArray);
        return new string(charArray);
    }
}
```

This can be invoked as follows:

```
var text = "demo";
var rev = StringExtensions.Reverse(text);
```

The C# language allows us to define this function in a way that enables us to call it as if it was an actual member of System.String. Such functions are called **extension methods**. There are few changes to do to the Reverse() method to make it an extension method. The new implementation is shown in the following code:

```
static class StringExtensions
{
    public static string Reverse(this string s)
    {
        var charArray = s.ToCharArray();
        Array.Reverse(charArray);
        return new string(charArray);
    }
}
```

Notice that the only change to the implementation is the this keyword in front of the function parameter. With these changes, the function can be invoked as if it was part of the string class:

```
var text = "demo";
var rev = text.Reverse();
```

The following rules apply to the definition and the behavior of extension methods:

- They can extend classes, structures, and enumerations.
- They must be declared as a static method of a static, non-nested, non-generic class.
- Their first parameter is the type they add functionality to. This parameter is preceded by the this keyword.
- They can only invoke public members of the type they extend.
- They are only available when the namespace in which they are declared is brought into the current scope with a using directive.
- If an extension method (that is available in the current scope) has the same signature as an instance method of the class, the compiler will always prefer the instance member and the extension method will never be called.

The following example shows an extension method called `AllMessages()` that extends the functionality of the `System.Exception` type. This represents an exception and has a message but can also contain an inner exception. This extension method returns a string composed by concatenating all of the messages of all of the nested exceptions. The Boolean argument indicates whether the messages should be concatenated from the main exception to the most inner one or in reverse order:

```
static class ExceptionExtensions
{
    public static string AllMessages(this Exception exception,
                                     bool reverse = false)
    {
        var messages = new List<string>();
        var ex = exception;
        while(ex != null)
        {
            messages.Add(ex.Message);
            ex = ex.InnerException;
        }

        if (reverse) messages.Reverse();

        return string.Join(Environment.NewLine, messages);
    }
}
```

The extension method can be then invoked as follows:

```
var exception =
    new InvalidOperationException(
        "An invalid operation occurred",
        new NotSupportedException(
            "The operation is not supported",
            new InvalidCastException(
                "Cannot apply cast!")));

Console.WriteLine(exception.AllMessages());
Console.WriteLine(exception.AllMessages(true));
```

The most common extension methods from .NET are the LINQ standard operators that extend the `IEnumerable` and `IEnumerable<T>` types. We will explore LINQ in *Chapter 10, Lambdas, LINQ, and Functional Programming*. If you implement extension methods to extend a type you cannot change, you must keep in mind that future changes to the type may break the extension method.

Summary

In this chapter, we addressed a series of advanced language features. We started with delegates and events that implement callbacks in a strongly-typed manner. We continued anonymous types and with tuples, which are lightweight types that can hold any value and help us to avoid defining new explicit types. We then looked at pattern matching, which is the process of checking whether a value has a particular shape as well as extracting information about it. We continued with regular expressions, which are patterns with a well-defined grammar that can be matched against a text. Lastly, we learned about extension methods that make it possible to add functionality to types without changing their implementation, such as when we don't own the source code.

In the next chapter, we will discuss garbage collection and resource management.

Test what you learned

1. What are callbacks and how are these related to delegates?

2. How do you define delegates? What about events?

3. How many types of tuples exist? What are the key differences between them?

4. What are named tuples and how do you create them?

5. What is pattern matching and what statements can it be used with?

6. What are the rules for pattern matching null?

7. What class implements regular expressions and what encoding does it use by default?

8. What is the difference between the `Match()` and `Matches()` methods of this class?

9. What are extension methods and why are they helpful?

10. How do you define an extension method?

9
Resource Management

In previous chapters, we discussed and worked with value types and reference types and have also seen how they differ. We also briefly talked about how the runtime is managing the allocated memory.

In this chapter, we will get into more details of this topic and look at the language features and best practices for managing memory and resources.

The topics that will be discussed in this chapter are as follows:

- Garbage collection
- Finalizers
- The IDisposable interface
- The using statement
- Platform invoke
- Unsafe code

By the end of this chapter, you will have learned how to implement disposable types and how to dispose of objects when they are no longer needed. You will have also learned how to call native APIs and write unsafe code.

Garbage collection

The **Common Language Runtime** (**CLR**) is responsible for managing the lifetime of objects and freeing memory when it's no longer used so that new objects can be allocated within the process. It does so through a component called the **garbage collector** (**GC**), which allocates objects on the managed heap in an efficient manner and clears memory by reclaiming objects that are no longer used. The garbage collector makes developing applications easier because you do not have to worry about manually freeing memory. This is what makes applications written for .NET to be known as *managed*.

Before we discuss how all this happens, you need to understand the difference between **stack** and **heap**, as well as the differences between **types**, **objects**, and **references**.

A type (whether introduced with the `class` or `struct` keyword in C#) is a blueprint for constructing objects. It is described in the source code using language features. An object is an instantiation of a type and lives in memory. A reference is a sort of handle (basically, a storage location) that points to an object.

Now, let's discuss memory. The stack is a relatively small segment of memory allocated by the compiler that keeps track of the memory necessary for running the application. The stack has **Last In First Out** (**LIFO**) semantics and grows and shrinks as the program execution is invoking functions or returning from functions. The heap, on the other hand, is a large segment of memory that the program may use to allocate memory at runtime, and which, in .NET, is managed by the CLR.

Objects of value types may be stored in multiple locations. They are typically stored on the stack, but they can also be stored on CPU registers. Value types that are a part of a reference type are stored on the heap as part of the *enclosing object*. Objects of reference types are always stored on the heap, but references to objects are stored on the stack or CPU registers.

To understand this better, let's consider the following short program, where `Point2D` is a value type and `Engine` is a reference type:

```
class Program
{
    static void Main(string[] args)
    {
        var i = 42;
        var pt = new Point2D(1, 2); // value type
        var engine = new Engine();  // reference type
    }
}
```

Conceptually (because this is a very simplistic representation), the stack and heap will contain the following values:

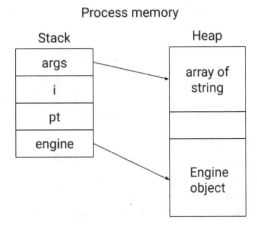

Figure 9.1 – The conceptual representation of the stack and heap content during the execution of the preceding program

The stack is managed by the compiler and, for the rest of this chapter, we will discuss the heap and how the runtime manages it. The .NET runtime divides objects into two groups:

- **Large**: These objects are those objects that are larger than 85 KB; multidimensional objects are also included in this category.
- **Small**: These objects are all other objects.

The heap is composed of several memory segments called **generations**. There are three generations of memory – **0**, **1**, and **2**:

- Generation 0 contains *small*, and usually *short-lived, objects,* such as local variables or objects instantiated for the lifetime of a function call.
- Generation 1 contains *small objects* that have survived a garbage collection of memory from generation 0.
- Generation 2 contains *long-lived small objects* that have survived a garbage collection of memory from generation 1 and large objects (which are always allocated on this segment).

When the runtime needs to allocate objects on the managed heap and there is not enough memory, it triggers a garbage collection. A garbage collection has three phases:

- First, the garbage collector builds a graph of all live objects in order to figure out what is still used and what may be deleted.

- Second, references to objects that will be compacted are updated.

- Third, the dead objects are removed, and the surviving objects are compacted. Typically, the large object heap containing large objects is not compacted because moving large chunks of data incurs performance costs.

When the garbage collection starts, all the managed threads are suspended, with the exception of the thread that started the collection. The threads are resumed when the garbage collection ends. The garbage collection's first phase starts from the so-called **application roots**, which are storage locations that contain references to objects on the heap. Application roots include references to global objects, static objects, fields, local objects, objects passed as function arguments, objects waiting to be finalized, and CPU registers that contain references to objects on the heap.

The CLR builds a graph of reachable heap objects; everything that is not reachable will be deleted. If all generation 0 objects have been evaluated, but the freed memory is not enough, the garbage collection proceeds to evaluate generation 1. If more memory is required after this, the garbage collection proceeds to evaluate generation 2.

Objects that survived the garbage collection of generation 0 are assigned to generation 1, and objects that survived from generation 1 are assigned to generation 2. However, objects that survive the garbage collection of generation 2 remain in generation 2. If the garbage collection process is finished and there is not enough memory on the large object heap (that's always part of generation 2) to allocate as requested, the CLR throws an exception of the `OutOfMemoryException` type. This does not necessarily mean there is no more memory, but that the uncompacted memory on this segment does not contain a chunk large enough for the new object.

The base class library contains a class called `System.GC` that enables us to interact with the garbage collector. However, this is seldom the case, apart from implementing the disposable pattern that we will see later in this chapter, in the *The IDisposable interface* section. Here are several members of this class:

`Collect()`	Forces the garbage collector to immediately perform a garbage collection. There are overloads that allow you to specify the generation and the collection mode.
`CollectionCount()`	Returns a value indicating the number of times the garbage collection has occurred for the specified generation.
`GetGeneration()`	Returns the generation number of a specified object.
`GetTotalMemory()`	Returns the estimated number of allocated bytes on the heap. Its Boolean parameter allows us to specify whether to wait for garbage collection to occur before returning.
`SupressFinalize()`	Requests the CLR not to invoke the finalizer of the specified object.
`WaitForPendingFinalizers()`	Suspends the current thread until all the objects that can be finalized have been finalized. This is typically called after `Collect()`.
`MaxGeneration`	Retrieves the number of generations that the system supports. The current implementations support three generations.

The following program uses the `System.GC` class to show the current generation of the `Engine` object, as well as the estimated size of the managed heap, at the time of the call:

```
class Program
{
    static void Main(string[] args)
    {
        var engine = new Engine("M270 Turbo", 1600, 75.0);
        Console.WriteLine(
          $"Generation of engine:
        {GC.GetGeneration(engine)}");
        Console.WriteLine(
          $"Estimated heap size: {GC.
        GetTotalMemory(false)}");
    }
}
```

The output of the program is as follows:

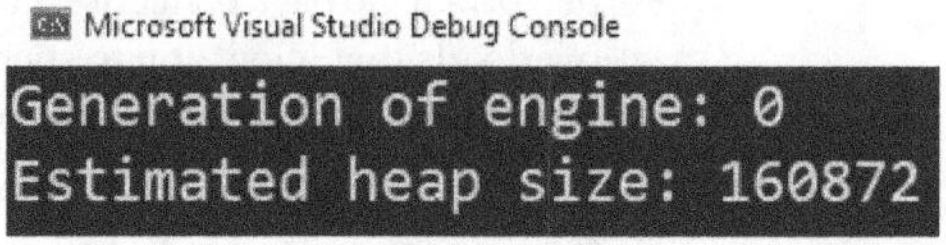
Microsoft Visual Studio Debug Console
Generation of engine: 0
Estimated heap size: 160872

Figure 9.2 – A console screenshot showing the output of the preceding program

We'll learn about finalizers in the next section.

Finalizers

The garbage collector provides the automatic disposal of managed resources. However, there are cases when you have to work with unmanaged resources such as raw file handles, windows, or other operating system resources retrieved with **Platform Invocation Services (P/Invoke)** calls, as well as COM object references in some advanced scenarios. These resources need to be explicitly released before the object is destroyed by the garbage collector; otherwise, resource leaks occur.

Every object has a special method called the **finalizer**. The `System.Object` class has a virtual and protected member called `Finalize()`, with an empty implementation. This is shown in the following code:

```
class Object
{
    protected virtual void Finalize() {}
}
```

Although this is a virtual method, you cannot actually override it directly. Instead, the C# language offers a syntax identical to the one for destructors in C++ to create a finalizer and override the `System.Object` method. However, this is only possible to implement for reference types; value types cannot have finalizers since they are not garbage collected. This is shown in the following code:

```
class ResourceWrapper
{
    // constructor
    ResourceWrapper()
    {
        // construct the object
    }
```

```
    // finalizer
    ~ResourceWrapper()
    {
        // release unmanaged resources
    }
}
```

The reason you cannot explicitly override the `Finalize()` method is that the C#
compiler will add additional code to ensure that the base class implementation is actually
called during finalization (this means the `Finalize()` method is called on all instances
in the inheritance chain). Therefore, the code shown earlier for the finalizer is replaced by
the compiler with the following:

```
class ResourceWrapper
{
    protected override void Finalize()
    {
        try
        {
            // release unmanaged resources
        }
        finally
        {
            base.Finalize();
        }
    }
}
```

Although a class may have multiple constructors, it can only have *one finalizer*. Finalizers
cannot, therefore, be overloaded or have modifiers and parameters; they also cannot be
inherited. Finalizers are not called directly, but are invoked by the garbage collector.

The way the garbage collector invokes the finalizers is as follows. When an object that has
a finalizer is created, the garbage collector adds a reference to it to an internal structure
called the *finalization queue*. When proceeding with collecting objects, the garbage
collector calls the finalizers on all the objects on the finalization queue, unless they have
been exempted from finalization with a call to `GC.SupressFinalize()`. This is also
done when the application domain is being unloaded, but only for .NET Framework; for
.NET Core, this is not the case. The invocation of the finalizers is still non-deterministic.
The exact moment of the call is undefined as well as the thread on which the invocation
occurs. Also, the finalizers of two objects, even when referring to one another, is not
guaranteed to happen in any particular order.

> **Information box**
>
> Because finalizers incur a performance loss, make sure that you do not create empty finalizers. Implement a finalizer if, and only if, your object must dispose of an unmanaged resource.

The `HandleWrapper` class shown in the following code is a wrapper for a native handler. An actual implementation may be more complex; this is shown for teaching purposes only. The raw handle may be created in native code and passed to a managed application. This class takes ownership of the handle and therefore needs to release it when the object is no longer needed. This is done with a call to the `CloseHandle()` system API using *P/Invoke*. The class defines a finalizer to do so. Let's take a look at the following code:

```
public class HandleWrapper
{
    [DllImport("kernel32.dll", SetLastError=true)]
    static extern bool CloseHandle(IntPtr hHandle);

    public IntPtr Handle { get; private set; }

    public HandleWrapper(IntPtr ptr)
    {
        Handle = ptr;
    }

    ~HandleWrapper()
    {
        if(Handle != default)
            CloseHandle(Handle);
    }
}
```

It is seldom the case when you actually need to create a finalizer. For scenarios such as the one mentioned previously, there are system wrappers available for handling unmanaged resources. You should use one of the following safe handles:

- `SafeFileHandle`: A wrapper for a file handle
- `SafeMemoryMappedFileHandle`, a wrapper for memory-mapped file handles
- `SafeMemoryMappedViewHandle`, a wrapper for a pointer to a block of unmanaged memory
- `SafeNCryptKeyHandle`, `SafeNCryptProviderHandle`, and `SafeNCryptSecretHandle`, wrappers for cryptographic handles

- `SafePipeHandle`, a wrapper for pipe handles
- `SafeRegistryHandle`, a wrapper for a handle to a registry key
- `SafeWaitHandle`, a wrapper for a wait handle

As already mentioned, finalizers are still non-deterministic. To ensure the deterministic release of resources, either managed or unmanaged, a type should provide a `Close()` method or implement the `IDisposable` interface. In this case, the finalizer could be used only to free unmanaged resources in the event the `Dispose()` method was not called.

We'll learn about the `IDisposable` interface in the next section.

The IDisposable interface

Deterministic disposal of resources can be done by implementing the `System.IDisposable` interface. This interface has a single method called `Dispose()` that can be explicitly called by users when an object is no longer used and its resources can be disposed of. However, you should only implement this interface in the following circumstances:

- The class has ownership of *unmanaged resources*
- The class has ownership of *managed resources* that are themselves disposable

The way this interface should be implemented depends on whether the class has ownership of unmanaged resources. The general pattern, when you have both managed and unmanaged resources, is as follows:

```
public class MyResource : IDisposable
{
    private bool disposed = false;

    protected virtual void Dispose(bool disposing)
    {
        if (!disposed)
        {
            if (disposing)
            {
                // dispose managed objects
            }

            // free unmanaged resources
            // set large fields to null.
```

```
                disposed = true;
        }
    }

    ~MyResource()
    {
        Dispose(false);
    }

    public void Dispose()
    {
        Dispose(true);
        GC.SuppressFinalize(this);
    }
}
```

From the `Dispose()` method of the `IDisposable` interface, we call a protected
virtual method with the same name (although it can have any name) and a parameter
specifying that the object is being destroyed. To ensure that the disposal of resources is
done only once, a Boolean field (called `disposed` here) is used. The Boolean parameter
to the overloaded `Dispose()` method indicates whether the method is being called in
a deterministic manner by the user or in a non-deterministic manner by the garbage
collector when the object is finalized.

In the former case, both managed and unmanaged resources should be
disposed of and the finalization of the object should be suppressed with a call to
`GC.SupressFinalize()`. In the latter case, only unmanaged resources must be
disposed of, because the disposal was not invoked by the user, but by the garbage collector.
The reason this function is virtual and protected is that it should be possible for derived
classes to override it, but it should not be possible to call it directly from outside the class.

Let's see how to implement this for different scenarios. For starters, we will consider the
case where the class has only disposable managed resources. In the following example,
the `Engine` class implements `IDisposable`. What it does exactly, what resources it
manages, and how it disposes of them is not important. However, the `Car` class has an
owning reference to an `Engine` object, which should be destroyed as soon as the `Car`
object is destroyed. Moreover, this should be done in a deterministic manner, when the
`Car` is no longer needed. In this case, the `IDisposable` interface must be implemented
as follows in the `Car` class:

```
public class Engine : IDisposable {}

public class Car : IDisposable
{
```

```
    private Engine engine;

    public Car(Engine e)
    {
        engine = e;
    }

    #region IDisposable Support

    private bool disposed = false;

    protected virtual void Dispose(bool disposing)
    {
        if (!disposed)
        {
            if (disposing)
            {
                engine?.Dispose();
            }

            disposed = true;
        }
    }

    public void Dispose()
    {
        Dispose(true);
    }

    #endregion
}
```

Since this class does not have a finalizer, the overloaded Dispose() method is of little use here, and the code can be further simplified. However, a derived class can override it and dispose of further resources.

In the previous section, we implemented a class called HandleWrapper that had a finalizer to close the system handle that it owned. In the following listing, you can see a modified version of this class that implements the IDisposable interface:

```
public class HandleWrapper : IDisposable
{
    [DllImport("kernel32.dll", SetLastError = true)]
    static extern bool CloseHandle(IntPtr hHandle);
```

```csharp
    public IntPtr Handle { get; private set; }

    public HandleWrapper(IntPtr ptr)
    {
        Handle = ptr;
    }

    private bool disposed = false; // To detect redundant calls

    protected virtual void Dispose(bool disposing)
    {
        if (!disposed)
        {
            if (disposing)
            {
                // nothing to dispose
            }

            if (Handle != default)
                CloseHandle(Handle);

            disposed = true;
        }
    }

    ~HandleWrapper()
    {
        Dispose(false);
    }

    public void Dispose()
    {
        Dispose(true);
        GC.SuppressFinalize(this);
    }
}
```

This class has both a `Dispose()` method (that can be called by the user) and a finalizer (called by the garbage collector in case the user did not call the `Dispose()` method). There are no managed resources to release in this example, so the Boolean parameter of the overloaded `Dispose()` method is basically unused.

The language provides us with a way to automatically dispose of objects that implement the IDisposable interface when they are no longer needed. We will learn about this in the following section.

The using statement

Before we introduce the using statement, let's see how explicit resource management is done in a proper manner. This will help you to better understand the need and workings of the using statements.

The Car class we looked at in the previous section can be used as follows:

```
Car car = null;
try
{
    car = new Car(new Engine());
    // use the car here
}
finally
{
    car?.Dispose();
}
```

A try-catch-finally block (although catch is not explicitly shown here) should be used in order to ensure proper disposal of the object when it is no longer needed. However, the C# language provides a convenient syntax for ensuring the correct disposal of an object with the using statement. This has the following form:

```
using (ResourceType resource = expression) statement
```

The compiler transforms this into the following code:

```
{
    ResourceType resource = expression;
    try {
        statement;
    }
    finally {
        resource.Dispose();
    }
}
```

The `using` statement introduces a scope for the variable defined in the statement and ensures that the object is properly disposed of before the scope is exited. The actual disposal depends on whether the resource is a value type, a nullable value type, a reference type, or a dynamic type. The call to `resource.Dispose()` earlier is actually one of the following:

```
// value types
((IDisposable)resource).Dispose();

// nullable value types or reference types
if (resource != null)
    ((IDisposable)resource).Dispose();

// dynamic
if (((IDisposable)resource) != null)
    ((IDisposable)resource).Dispose();
```

For the car example, we can use it as follows:

```
using (Car car = new Car(new Engine()))
{
    // use the car here
}
```

Multiple objects can be instantiated into the same `using` statement, as shown in the following example:

```
using (Car car1 = new Car(new Engine()),
           car2 = new Car(new Engine()))
{
    // use car1 and car2 here
}
```

On the other hand, multiple `using` statements can be chained together, as shown here, which is equivalent to the previous code:

```
using (var car1 = new Car(new Engine()))
using (var car2 = new Car(new Engine()))
{
    // use car1 and car2 here
}
```

In C# 8, the using statement can be written as follows:

```
using Car car = new Car(new Engine());
// use the car here
```

For more information about this, refer to *Chapter 15, New Features of C# 8.*

Platform invoke

Earlier in this chapter, we implemented a handle wrapper class that used a Windows API function, CloseHandle(), to delete system handles when the object was disposed of. The way a C# program can invoke Windows APIs, but also any function exported from a native **dynamic-linked library (DLL)**, is done through **Platform Invocation Services**, also known as **Platform Invoke** or **P/Invoke**.

P/Invoke locates and invokes an exported function and marshals the arguments between the managed and unmanaged boundaries. In order to be able to call a function using P/Invoke, you must know the name and signature of the function, as well as the name of the DLL from where it is exported. Then, you must create a managed definition of the unmanaged function. To understand how this works, we will look at an example of the MessageBox() function, available in user32.dll. The function signature is as follows:

```
int MessageBox(HWND hWnd, LPCTSTR lpText,
               LPCTSTR lpCaption, UINT uType);
```

We can create the following manage definition for the function:

```
static class WindowsAPI
{
    [DllImport("user32.dll")]
    public static extern int MessageBox(IntPtr hWnd,
                                        string lpText,
                                        string lpCaption,
                                        uint uType);
}
```

There are several things to notice here:

- The signature of the managed definition must match the native one, using the equivalent managed types for the parameters.

- The function must be defined as `static` and `extern`.

- The function must be decorated with `DllImportAttribute`. This attribute defines the necessary information for the runtime to call the native function.

`DllImportAttribute` requires at least the name of the DLL from which the native function is exported. You can omit the name of the entry point in the DLL, in which case the name of the managed function is used to identify it. However, you can also specify it explicitly using the `EntryPoint` property of the attribute. The other properties you can specify are as follows:

- `BestFitMapping`: A Boolean flag that indicates whether best-fit mapping is enabled. This is used when converting from Unicode to ANSI characters. Best-fit mapping enables the interop marshaler to use close-matching characters when an exact match does not exist (for instance, the copyright character is replaced with *c*).

- `CallingConvention`: The calling convention for an entry point. The default value is `Winapi`, which defaults to `StdCall`.

- `CharSet`: Specifies the marshaling behavior for string parameters. It is also used to specify the entry point name to invoke. For instance, for the message box example, Windows has two functions actually—`MessageBoxA()` and `MessageBoxW()`. The value of the `CharSet` parameter enables the runtime to choose between one or the other; more precisely, the name ending in A for `CharSet.Ansi` (which is the default for C#) and the name ending in W for `CharSet.Unicode`.

- `EntryPoint`: The entry point name or ordinal.

- `ExactSpelling`: Indicates whether the `CharSet` field determines the CLR to search the unmanaged DLL for entry-point names other than the one that has been specified.

- `PreserveSig`: A Boolean flag that indicates whether the HRESULT or `retval` values are translated directly (if `true`) or automatically converted into exceptions (if `false`). The default value is `true`.

- `SetLastError`: Indicates, if `true`, that the callee calls `SetLastError()` before returning. In this case, the CLR calls `GetLastError()` and caches the value to prevent it from being overwritten, and therefore lost, by other Windows API calls. To retrieve the value, you can call `Marshal.GetLastWin32Error()`.

- `ThrowOnUnmappableChar`: Indicates (when `true`) whether the marshaler should throw an error when converting a Unicode character into ANSI '?'. The default value is `false`.

The following table shows the data types in the Windows API and C-style functions, as well as their corresponding C# or .NET Framework types:

Windows API	C/C++	C#/.NET
VOID	void	void
HANDLE	void*	IntPtr / UIntPtr
BYTE	unsigned char	byte
SHORT	short	short
WORD	unsigned short	ushort
INT	int	int
UINT	unsigned int	uint
LONG	long	int
BOOL	long	bool / int
DWORD	unsigned long	uint32
ULONG	unsigned long	uint32
CHAR	char	char [1]
WCHAR	wchar_t	char [2]
LPSTR	char*	string / StringBuilder[1]
LPCTSTR	const char*	string / StringBuilder[1]
LPWSTR	wchar_t*	string / StringBuilder[2]
LPCWSTR	const wchar_t*	string / StringBuilder[2]
FLOAT	float	float
DOUBLE	double	double

> **Important note**
>
> [1] Decorate with `CharSet.Ansi` or use the `[MarshalAs(UnmanagedType.LPStr)]` attribute on the `string` parameter.
>
> [2] Decorate with `CharSet.Unicode` or use the `[MarshalAs(UnmanagedType.LPWStr)]` attribute on the `string` parameter.

To be able to properly call the `MessageBox()` function we defined earlier, we should also define constants for the possible arguments and return values. A snippet is shown here:

```
static class WindowsAPI
{
    public static class MessageButtons
    {
        public const int MB_OK = 0;
        public const int MB_OKCANCEL = 1;
        public const int MB_YESNOCANCEL = 3;
        public const int MB_YESNO = 4;
    }

    public static class MessageIcons
    {
        public const int MB_ICONERROR = 0x10;
        public const int MB_ICONQUESTION = 0x20;
        public const int MB_ICONWARNING = 0x30;
        public const int MB_ICONINFORMATION = 0x40;
    }

    public static class MessageResult
    {
        public const int IDOK = 1;
        public const int IDYES = 6;
        public const int IDNO = 7;
    }
}
```

With this all set, we can call the `MessageBox()` function, as follows:

```
class Program
{
    static void Main(string[] args)
    {
        var result = WindowsAPI.MessageBox(
            IntPtr.Zero,
            "Is this book helpful?",
            "Question",
            WindowsAPI.MessageButtons.MB_YESNO |
            WindowsAPI.MessageIcons.MB_ICONQUESTION);

        if(result == WindowsAPI.MessageResult.IDYES)
        {
```

```
        // time to learn more
    }
  }
}
```

Many Windows APIs require a buffer to be used to return data. For instance, the `GetUserName()` function from `advapi32.dll` returns the name of the user associated with the current thread of execution. The function signature is as follows:

```
BOOL GetUserName(LPSTR lpBuffer, LPDWORD pcbBuffer);
```

The first argument is a pointer to an array of characters, which is used to receive the name of the user, while the second is a pointer to an unsigned integer, which is used to specify the size of the buffer. The buffer needs to be large enough to receive the username. Otherwise, the function returns `false`, sets the required size in the `pcbBuffer` argument, and sets the last error to `ERROR_INSUFFICIENT_BUFFER`.

Although you could allocate a buffer large enough to hold the result (some functions impose limits on the size of the return value), you cannot always be sure. Therefore, typically, you call such a function twice:

- First, with an empty buffer to get back the actual size required for the buffer
- Then, after allocating the necessary memory, a second time with a buffer large enough to receive the result

To see how this works, we will P/Invoke the `GetUserName()` function, whose managed definition looks like this:

```
[DllImport("advapi32.dll", SetLastError = true,
          CharSet = CharSet.Unicode)]
public static extern bool GetUserName(StringBuilder lpBuffer,
                                      ref uint nSize);
```

Notice that we use `StringBuilder` for the buffer parameter. Although this can grow to any capacity, we will need to know what size to specify. Instead of specifying a random large size, we call the function twice, as shown here:

```
uint size = 0;
var result = WindowsAPI.GetUserName(null, ref size);
if(!result &&
   Marshal.GetLastWin32Error() ==
       WindowsAPI.ErrorCodes.ERROR_INSUFFICIENT_BUFFER)
{
    Console.WriteLine($"Requires buffer size: {size}");
```

```
StringBuilder buffer = new StringBuilder((int)size);
result = WindowsAPI.GetUserName(buffer, ref size);
if(result)
{
    Console.WriteLine($"User name: {buffer.ToString()}");
}
}
```

In this example, the `StringBuffer` object is created with an initial capacity, although this is not really necessary. You don't have to specify its capacity; it will grow to the required one and receive the correct result.

Let's summarize Platform Invocation Services using the following points:

- Allows calling functions exported from native DLLs.

- You must create a managed definition for a function, with the same signature and the equivalent managed types for the native ones.

- You must specify at least the function entry point and the name of the exporting DLL when defining the managed function.

There are some drawbacks when you use P/Invoke, so you should keep the following in mind:

- If you use P/Invoke to call functions from the Windows API, then your application will only work on Windows. This is not a problem if you don't intend to make it cross-platform. Otherwise, you have to avoid that altogether.

- If you need to call functions from a C++ library, you must specify the decorated names in your import declarations, which can be troublesome. If you are also authoring the C++ library, you can export functions with the `extern "C"` linkage to prevent the linker from decorating the names.

- There is a slight overhead for marshaling between the managed and unmanaged types.

- This may not be very intuitive at times; for instance, what types to use for pointers and handles.

In the last section of this chapter, we will discuss unsafe code and pointer types, which is the third category of types in C#.

Unsafe code

When we discuss the types of .NET Framework and C# language support, we refer to value types (structures) and reference types (classes). However, there is yet another type that is supported, and that is **pointer types**. If you are not familiar with the C or C++ programming languages and pointers in particular, then you should know pointers are like *references*—they are storage locations that contain the addresses of objects. A reference is basically a *safe pointer* that is managed by the CLR.

To work with pointer types, you must establish a so-called *unsafe context*. In CLR terms, this is called *unverifiable code* because the CLR cannot verify its safety. Unsafe code is not necessarily dangerous, but it's your entire responsibility to ensure that you do not introduce pointer errors or security risks.

In truth, there are very rare cases where you actually have to work with pointers in unsafe contexts in C#. There are two common scenarios when this could be the case:

- Calling functions exported from a native DLL or COM server that require pointer types as parameters. However, in most cases, you still can do this with a safe code using `System.IntPtr` and members of the `System.Runtime.InteropServices.Marshal` type.

- Optimizing particular algorithms where performance is critical.

You can define an unsafe context using the `unsafe` keyword. This can be applied to the following:

- Types (class, struct, interface, delegate), in which case the entire textual context of the type is considered unsafe:

```
unsafe struct Node
{
    public int value;
    public Node* left;
    public Node* right;
}
```

- Methods, fields, properties, events, indexers, operators, instance and static constructors, and destructors, in which case the entire textual context of the member is considered unsafe:

```
struct Node
{
    public int Value;
    public unsafe Node* Left;
```

```
        public unsafe Node* Right;
}

unsafe void Increment(int* value)
{
    *value += 1;
}
```

- A statement (block), in which case the entire textual context of the block is considered unsafe:

```
static void Main(string[] args)
{
    int value = 42;
    unsafe
    {
        int* p = &value;
        *p += 1;
    }
    Console.WriteLine(value); // prints 43
}
```

However, in order to be able to compile code that uses unsafe contexts, you must explicitly use the /unsafe compiler switch. In Visual Studio, you can check the **Allow unsafe code** option from **Project properties | Build**, under the **General** section, as shown in the following screenshot:

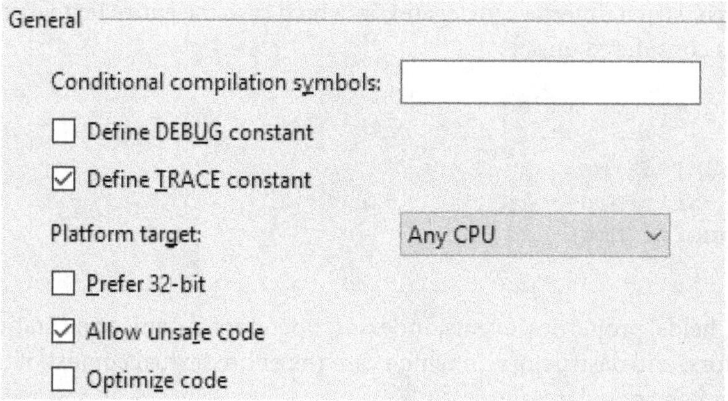

Figure 9.3 – Visual Studio's Project Properties page that allows enabling the Allow unsafe code option

Unsafe code can only be executed from another unsafe context. For instance, if you have a method that is declared as unsafe, you may only call it from an unsafe context. This is shown in the following example, where the unsafe Increment () method (introduced previously) is called from an unsafe context. An attempt to do this from a safe context results in a compiler error:

```
static void Main(string[] args)
{
    int value = 42;
    Increment(&value);        // error

    unsafe
    {
        Increment(&value); // OK
    }
}
```

If you are familiar with C or C++, you know that the pointer symbol (*) can be put either next to the type, the variable, or in between. The following are all equivalent in C/C++:

```
int* a;
int * a;
int *a;
int* a, *b; // define two variables of type pointer to int
```

However, in C#, you always put * next to the type, as in the following example:

```
int* a, b; // define two variables of type pointer to int
```

Variables can be of two types—**fixed** and **movable**. Movable variables reside in storage locations that are controlled by the garbage collector and therefore can be moved or collected. Fixed variables reside in storage locations that are unaffected by the operations of the garbage collector.

In unsafe code, you can take the address of a fixed variable using the & operator without restrictions. However, you can only do so with movable variables using a fixed statement. A fixed statement is introduced with the fixed keyword and is, in many aspects, similar to a using statement.

The following is an example of using a fixed statement:

```
class Color
{
    public byte Alpha;
    public byte Red;
    public byte Green;
    public byte Blue;

    public Color(byte a, byte r, byte g, byte b)
    {
        Alpha = a;
        Red = r;
        Green = g;
        Blue = b;
    }
}

static void SetTransparency(Color color, double value)
{
    unsafe
    {
        fixed (byte* alpha = &color.Alpha)
        {
            *alpha = (byte)(value * 255);
        }
    }
}
```

The `SetTransparency()` function changes the alpha value of a `Color` object using a pointer to the `Alpha` field. Although this is of the `byte` type, which is a value type, it resides on the managed heap because it is part of a reference type. The garbage collector may move or collect the `Color` object before the `Alpha` field is accessed. Therefore, the only possible way to retrieve its address is to use the `fixed` statement. This basically pins the managed object so that the garbage collector will not move or collect it.

Apart from `usafe` and `fixed`, there are two more keywords that can be used in unsafe contexts:

- `stackalloc`, which is used to declare a variable that allocates memory on the call stack (similar to `_alloca()` in C):

```
static unsafe void AllocArrayExample(int size)
{
    int* arr = stackalloc int[size];
```

```
        for (int i = 1; i <= size; ++i)
        arr[i] = i;
    }
```

- `sizeof`, which is used to obtain the size in bytes of a value type. For primitive types and enum types, the `sizeof` operator can actually be called in safe contexts too:

```
static void SizeOfExample()
{
    unsafe
    {
        Console.WriteLine(
            $"Pointer size: {sizeof(int*)}");
    }
}
```

Let's summarize the unsafe code by taking a look at the following key points:

- It can only be executed in unsafe contexts, introduced with the `unsafe` keyword when compiling with the `/unsafe` switch.

- Types, members, and code blocks can be unsafe contexts.

- It introduces security and stability risks that you are solely responsible for.

- There are very rare cases where you have to use it.

Summary

This chapter focused on the way the runtime (through the garbage collector) manages the lifetime of objects and resources. We learned how the garbage collector works and how to write finalizers to dispose of native resources. We have seen how to properly implement patterns for the deterministic release of objects with the `IDisposable` interface and `using` statements. We also looked at Platform Invocation Services, which enable us to make native calls from managed code, as well as writing unsafe code—which is code that the CLR cannot verify for safety.

In the next chapter of this book, we will look at a different programming paradigm, functional programming, and see what its key concepts are in C# and what they enable us to do.

Test what you learned

1. What are the stack and the heap? What is allocated on each?

2. What are the memory segments of the heap and what is allocated on each?

3. How does garbage collection work?

4. What are finalizers? What is the difference between disposing and finalizing?

5. What does the `GC.SupressFinalize()` method do?

6. What is `IDisposable` and when should it be used?

7. What is the `using` statement?

8. How do you invoke a function from a native DLL in C#?

9. What is unsafe code and what are the typical scenarios where it could be used?

10. What program elements can you declare as unsafe?

Further reading

- *Garbage Collection: Automatic Memory Management in the Microsoft .NET Framework*, Jeffrey Richter – MSDN Magazine: `https://docs.microsoft.com/en-us/archive/msdn-magazine/2000/november/garbage-collection-automatic-memory-management-in-the-microsoft-net-framework`

- *Garbage Collection: Part 2: Automatic Memory Management in the Microsoft .NET Framework*, Jeffrey Richter – MSDN Magazine: `https://docs.microsoft.com/en-us/archive/msdn-magazine/2000/december/garbage-collection-part-2-automatic-memory-management-in-the-microsoft-net-framework`

10
Lambdas, LINQ, and Functional Programming

Although C# is an object-oriented programming language at its core, it is actually a *multi-paradigm language*. So far in this book, we have discussed imperative programming, object-oriented programming, and generic programming. However, C# also supports functional programming features. Throughout *Chapter 7, Collections*, and *Chapter 8, Advanced Topics*, we have already used some of these, such as lambdas and **Language-Integrated Query (LINQ)**.

In this chapter, we'll look at these in detail from the perspective of functional programming. Learning functional programming techniques will help you to write code in a declarative manner that is often simpler and easier to understand than the equivalent imperative code.

The topics that will be covered in this chapter are as follows:

- Functional programming
- Functions as first-class citizens
- Lambda expressions
- LINQ
- More functional programming concepts

By the end of this chapter, you will be able to understand lambda expressions in detail and will be able to use them together with LINQ to query data from a variety of sources. Moreover, you will be familiarized with functional programming concepts and techniques, such as higher-order functions, closures, monads, and monoids.

Let's start this chapter with an overview of functional programming and its core principles.

Functional programming

C# is a general-purpose and multi-paradigm programming language. Yet, so far in this book, we have only covered the imperative programming paradigm, which uses statements to change the program state and is focused on describing how a program operates. In imperative programming, functions may have side effects, thus changing the program state when they execute. Alternatively, the execution of a function may depend on the program state.

The opposite paradigm is functional programming, which is concerned with describing *what* a program does and not *how* it does it. Functional programming treats computation as the evaluation of functions; it uses immutable data and avoids changing states. Functional programming is a declarative programming paradigm where expressions are used instead of statements. Functions no longer have side effects but are idempotent. This means that calling a function with the same arguments produces the same results every time.

Functional programming provides several advantages, including the following:

- The code is easier to understand and maintain because functions don't change states and only depend on the arguments they receive.
- The code is easier to test for the same reason.
- It is simpler and more efficient to implement concurrency because data is immutable and functions don't have side effects, which avoids data races.

Immutability (objects have states that do not change) and **side-effect free functions** (functions do not modify values – or states, outside their local scope) are at the core of functional programming. To understand this better, let's look at the following example. We have a struct called `Rectangle` (this could also be a class) that represents a rectangle:

```
struct Rectangle
{
    public int Left;
    public int Right;
    public int Top;
    public int Bottom;

    public int Width { get { return Right - Left; } }
    public int Height { get { return Bottom - Top; } }

    public Rectangle(int l, int t, int r, int b)
    {
        Left = l;
        Top = t;
        Right = r;
        Bottom = b;
    }
}
```

We can instantiate this type and alter its properties. For instance, if we want to inflate the width of the rectangle with 10 units, equally in each direction, we can do the following:

```
var r = new Rectangle(10, 10, 30, 20);
r.Left -= 5;
r.Right += 5;
r.Top -= 5;
r.Bottom += 5;
```

We can also write a function that we could invoke. This could be a *member function*, as follows:

```
public void Inflate(int l, int t, int r, int b)
{
    Left -= l;
    Right += r;
    Top -= t;
    Bottom += b;
}
```

```
// invoked as
r.Inflate(5, 0, 5, 0);
```

This can also be a *non-member function*, as shown in the following code. The difference between the two is only a matter of design. Writing it as an extension method is the only choice if we cannot modify the source code:

```
static void Inflate(ref Rectangle rect,
                    int l, int t, int r, int b)
{
    rect.Left -= l;
    rect.Right += r;
    rect.Top -= t;
    rect.Bottom += b;
}

// invoked as
Inflate(ref r, 5, 0, 5, 0);
```

The `Rectangle` data type is mutable because its state can be changed. The `Inflate()` method has side effects because it changes the state of a rectangle. In functional programming, `Rectangle` should be immutable. A possible implementation is shown here:

```
struct Rectangle
{
    public readonly int Left;
    public readonly int Right;
    public readonly int Top;
    public readonly int Bottom;

    public int Width { get { return Right - Left; } }
    public int Height { get { return Bottom - Top; } }

    public Rectangle(int l, int t, int r, int b)
    {
        Left = l;
        Top = t;
        Right = r;
        Bottom = b;
    }
}
```

The pure function version of the `Inflate()` method would not have side effects. Its behavior would depend solely on the arguments and the result would be the same, no matter how many times it is called with the same arguments. An example of such an implementation is as follows:

```
static Rectangle Inflate(Rectangle rect,
                         int l, int t, int r, int b)
{
    return new Rectangle(rect.Left - l, rect.Top - t,
                         rect.Right + r, rect.Bottom + b);
}
```

These can now be used as in the following example:

```
var r = new Rectangle(10, 10, 30, 20);
r = Inflate(r, 5, 0, 5, 0);
```

Functional programming stems from lambda calculus (developed by Alonzo Church), which is a framework, or mathematical system, for expressing computations based on function abstractions and applications using variable binding and substitution. Some programming languages, such as Haskell, are purely functional. Others, such as C#, support multiple paradigms and are not purely functional.

The preceding example showed a variable, r, that was initialized to a value and then changed. In pure functional programming, this is not possible. A variable, once initialized, cannot change value; instead, a new variable must be assigned. This enables expressions to be replaced with their values, a property known as **referential transparency**.

C# enables us to write code using functional programming concepts and idioms. At the core of all these are lambda expressions, which we will look at in depth shortly. Before that, we need to explore another functional programming pillar, and that is treating functions as *first-class citizens*.

Functions as first-class citizens

In *Chapter 8, Advanced Topics*, we learned about delegates and events. A delegate looks like a function but is a type that holds references to functions whose signatures match the definition of the delegate. Delegate instances can be passed as objects for function arguments. Let's look at an example where we have a delegate that takes two `int` parameters and returns an `int` value:

```
public delegate int Combine(int a, int b);
```

We then have different functions, such as Add(), which adds two integers and returns the sum, Sub(), which subtracts two integers and returns their difference, or Mul(), which multiplies two integers and returns their product. Their signature matches the delegate, so an instance of the Combine delegate can hold references to all these functions. These functions are shown as follows:

```
class Math
{
    public static int Add(int a, int b) { return a + b; }
    public static int Sub(int a, int b) { return a - b; }
    public static int Mul(int a, int b) { return a * b; }
}
```

We can write a general function that can apply one of these functions to two arguments. Such a function may look like this:

```
int Apply(int a, int b, Combine f)
{
    return f(a, b);
}
```

Invoking it is simple—we pass the arguments and a reference to the actual function that we want to invoke:

```
var s = Apply(2, 3, Math.Add);
var d = Apply(2, 3, Math.Sub);
var p = Apply(2, 3, Math.Mul);
```

For convenience, .NET defines a set of generic delegates called Func to avoid defining your own delegates all the time. These are defined in the System namespace and look like this:

```
public delegate TResult Func<out TResult>();
public delegate TResult Func<in T,out TResult>(T arg);
public delegate TResult Func<in T1,in T2,out TResult>(T1 arg1,
T2 arg2);
. . .
public delegate TResult Func<in T1,in T2,in T3,in T4,in T5,in
T6,in T7,in T8,in T9,in T10,in T11,in T12,in T13,in T14,in
T15,in T16,out TResult>(T1 arg1, T2 arg2, T3 arg3, T4 arg4, T5
arg5, T6 arg6, T7 arg7, T8 arg8, T9 arg9, T10 arg10, T11 arg11,
T12 arg12, T13 arg13, T14 arg14, T15 arg15, T16 arg16);
```

This is a set of 17 overloads that take either 0, 1, or up to 16 arguments (of potentially different types) and return a value. Using these system delegates, we can rewrite the `Apply` function as follows:

```
T Apply<T>(T a, T b, Func<T, T, T> f)
{
    return f(a, b);
}
```

This version of the function is generic so that it can be invoked with other types of arguments, not just integers. The way the function is invoked in the preceding examples does not change.

These delegates return a value, so they cannot be used for functions that don't have a return value. There is a similar set of overloads in the `System` namespace called `Action` that is defined as follows:

```
public delegate void Action();
public delegate void Action<in T>(T obj);
public delegate void Action<in T1, in T2>(T1 arg1, T2 arg2);
...
public delegate void Action<in T1, in T2, in T3, in T4, in T5, in
T6, in T7, in T8, in T9, in T10, in T11, in T12, in T13, in T14, in
T15, in T16>(T1 arg1, T2 arg2, T3 arg3, T4 arg4, T5 arg5, T6
arg6, T7 arg7, T8 arg8, T9 arg9, T10 arg10, T11 arg11, T12
arg12, T13 arg13, T14 arg14, T15 arg15, T16 arg16);
```

These delegates are very similar to the `Func` delegates we saw earlier. The only difference is that they do not return a value. There are still 17 overloads that take 0, 1, or up to 16 input arguments.

In the following example, the `Apply` function is overloaded so that it also takes a parameter of the `Action<string>` type, which is a function that has a single parameter of the `string` type and returns nothing. After applying the function, but before returning the result, this action is invoked with a string that describes the actual operation:

```
T Apply<T>(T a, T b, Func<T, T, T> f, Action<string> log)
{
    var r = f(a, b);
    log?.Invoke($"{f.Method.Name}({a},{b}) = {r}");
    return r;
}
```

We can invoke this new overload by passing `Console.WriteLine` for the last argument, which results in the operations being logged to the console:

```
var s = Apply(2, 3, Math.Add, Console.WriteLine);
var p = Apply(2, 3, Math.Mul, Console.WriteLine);
```

The `Apply` function is called a *higher-order function*. A higher-order function is a function that takes one or more functions as arguments, returns a function, or both. All the other functions are called *first-order functions*.

There are many higher-order functions that you might be using without any realization. For instance, `List<T>.Sort (Comparison<T> comparison)` is such a function. Most query predicates from LINQ (which we will explore later in this chapter in the *LINQ* section) are higher-order functions.

An example of a higher-order function is a function that returns another function, as shown in the following snippet. `ApplyReverse()` takes a function as argument and returns another function that invokes the argument function with two arguments, but in reverse order:

```
Func<T, T, T> ApplyReverse<T>(Func<T, T, T> f)
{
    return delegate(T a, T b) { return f(b, a); };
}
```

This function is invoked as follows:

```
var s = ApplyReverse<int>(Math.Add)(2, 3);
var d = ApplyReverse<int>(Math.Sub)(2, 3);
```

What we have seen so far is the possibility in C# to pass functions as arguments, return functions from functions, assign functions to variables, store them in data structures, or define anonymous functions (that is, functions without a name). It's also possible to nest functions and test references to functions for equality. A programming language that does these things is said to treat functions as first-class citizens and its functions are first-class. C# is, therefore, such a language.

Getting back to the previous examples, an alternative and simpler way of invoking the `Apply()` method is as follows:

```
var s = Apply(2, 3, (a, b) => a + b);
var d = Apply(2, 3, (a, b) => a - b);
var p = Apply(2, 3, (a, b) => a * b);
```

Here, the methods from the `Math` class have been replaced with lambda expressions such as `(a, b) => a + b`. We can even define the `Apply()` function as a lambda expression and invoke it accordingly:

```
Func<int, int, Func<int, int, int>, int> apply =
    (a, b, f) => f(a, b);


var s = apply(2, 3, (a, b) => a + b);
var d = apply(2, 3, (a, b) => a - b);
var p = apply(2, 3, (a, b) => a * b);
```

We'll look at lambda expressions in depth in the next section.

Lambda expressions

Lambda expressions are a convenient way to write anonymous functions. They are a block of code, either an expression or one or more statements, that behaves like a function and can be assigned to a delegate. As a result, a lambda expression can be passed as an argument to a function or returned from a function. They are a convenient way to write LINQ queries, pass functions to higher-order functions (including code that should be executed asynchronously by `Task.Run()`), and create expression trees.

An expression tree is a way to represent code in a tree-like data structure, with nodes as expressions (such as method calls or binary operations). These expression trees can be compiled and executed, which enables dynamic changes to be performed on executable code. Expression trees are used to implement LINQ providers for various data sources and in the DLR to provide interoperability between .NET Framework and a dynamic language.

Let's start with a simple example where we have a list of integers and we want to remove all the odd numbers from it. It can be written as follows (notice that the `IsOdd()` function can be either a class method or a local function):

```
bool IsOdd(int n) { return n % 2 == 1; }
var list = new List<int>() { 1, 2, 3, 4, 5, 6, 7, 8, 9 };
list.RemoveAll(IsOdd);
```

This code can actually be simplified with anonymous methods that allow us to pass code to a delegate without defining the separate `IsOdd()` function:

```
var list = new List<int>() { 1, 2, 3, 4, 5, 6, 7, 8, 9 };
list.RemoveAll(delegate (int n) { return n % 2 == 1; });
```

Lambda expressions allow us to simplify the code even further with a simpler syntax that the compiler transforms into something similar to the preceding code:

```
var list = new List<int>() { 1, 2, 3, 4, 5, 6, 7, 8, 9 };
list.RemoveAll(n => n % 2 == 1);
```

The lambda expression that we can see here (n => n % 2 == 1) has two parts separated by =>, which is the **lambda declaration operator**:

- The left part of the expression is the *list of parameters* (separated by a comma and enclosed in parentheses if there is more than one).

- The right part of the expression is either an *expression or a statement*. If the right part is an expression (such as in the preceding example), the lambda is called an **expression lambda**. If the right part is a statement, the lambda is called a **statement lambda**.

Statements are always enclosed in curly braces { }. Any expression lambda can actually be written as a statement lambda. Expression lambdas are a simplified version of statement lambdas. The previous example with an expression lambda can be written as follows using a statement lambda:

```
var list = new List<int>() { 1, 2, 3, 4, 5, 6, 7, 8, 9 };
list.RemoveAll(n => { return n % 2 == 1; });
```

There are several examples of lambda expressions:

Lambda	Description
() => {}	A lambda that takes no arguments and does nothing.
x => { Console.WriteLine(x); }	A lambda that takes a single argument, prints it to the console, and returns nothing.
x => x%2==1	A lambda that takes a single argument and returns a Boolean, indicating whether the argument is an odd number.
(x) => x%2==1	Same as the above.
x => {return x%2==1;}	Same as the above.
(x,y) => x+y	A lambda that takes two arguments and returns their sum.
(x,y) => {return x+y;}	Same as the above.

A lambda does not have a type of its own. Instead, its type is either the type of delegate that it is assigned to or the System.Expression type when lambdas are used to build expression trees. A lambda that does not return a value corresponds to a System.Action delegate (and can be assigned to one). A lambda that does return a value corresponds to a System.Func delegate.

When you write a lambda expression, you do not need to write the type of the parameters as these are inferred by the compiler. The rules for type inference are as follows:

- The lambda must have the same number of parameters as the delegate it is assigned to.

- Each parameter of a lambda must be implicitly converted to the corresponding parameter of the delegate it is assigned to.

- If the lambda has a return value, its type must be implicitly converted to the return type of the delegate it is assigned to.

Lambda expressions can be asynchronous. Such a lambda is preceded by the async keyword and must contain at least an await expression. The following example shows an asynchronous handler for the Click event for a button on a Windows Forms form:

```
public partial class MyForm : Form
{
    public MyForm()
    {
        InitializeComponent();

        myButton.Click += async (sender, e) =>
        {
            await ExampleMethodAsync();
        };
    }

    private async Task ExampleMethodAsync()
    {
        // a time-consuming action
        await Task.Delay(1000);
    }
}
```

In this example, MyForm is a form class and, in its constructor, we register a handler for the Click event. This is done using a lambda expression, but the lambda is asynchronous (it calls an asynchronous function) and therefore needs to be preceded with async.

Lambdas may use variables that are in the scope of the method or the type that contains the lambda expression. When a variable is used in a lambda, it is captured so that it can be used even if it goes out of scope. These variables must be definitely assigned before they are used in the lambda. In the following example, the lambda expression is capturing two variables—the value function parameter and the Data class member:

```
class Foo
{
    public int Data { get; private set; }

    public Foo(int value)
    {
        Data = value;
    }

    public void Scramble(int value, int iterations)
    {
        Func<int, int> apply = (i) => Data ^ i + value;
        for(int i = 0; i < iterations; ++i)
            Data = apply(i);
    }
}
```

Here are the rules that apply to the scope of variables in lambda expressions:

- The variables that are introduced in a lambda expression are not visible outside the lambda (for instance, in the enclosing method).

- A lambda cannot capture in, ref, or out parameters from the enclosing method.

- Variables that are captured by a lambda expression are not garbage collected, even if they would otherwise go out of scope until the delegate that the lambda is assigned to is garbage collected.

- A return statement of a lambda expression refers solely to the anonymous method that the lambda represents and does not cause the enclosing method to return.

The most common use case for lambda expressions is writing LINQ query expressions. We will look at this in the following section.

LINQ

LINQ is a set of technologies that enable developers to query a multitude of data sources in a consistent manner. Typically, you would use different languages and technologies to query different types of data, such as SQL for relational databases, and XPath for XML. SQL queries are written as strings, which makes them impossible to verify at compile time and increase the chances of having runtime errors.

LINQ defines a set of operators and a built-in language syntax for querying data. LINQ queries are strongly typed and therefore verified at compile time. LINQ also provides a framework for building your own LINQ providers, which are components that transform a query into APIs that are specific to a particular data source. The framework provides built-in support for querying objects (anything that is a collection in .NET), relational databases, and XML. Third parties have written LINQ providers for many data sources, such as web services.

LINQ enables developers to focus on what to do and be less concerned with how to do things. To better understand how this works, let's look at an example where we have an array of integers and we want to find the sum of all the odd numbers. Typically, you'd write something like the following:

```
int[] arr = { 1, 1, 3, 5, 8, 13, 21, 34};
int sum = 0;
for(int i = 0; i < arr.Length; ++i)
{
    if (arr[i] % 2 == 1)
    sum += arr[i];
}
```

With LINQ, it is possible to reduce all this verbose code to the following line:

```
int sum = arr.Where(x => x % 2 == 1).Sum();
```

Here, we are using the LINQ standard query operators, which are extension methods that operate on sequences and provide query capabilities, including filtering, projection, aggregation, sorting, and more. Many of these query operators, however, have direct support in the LINQ query syntax, which is a query language very similar to SQL. Using the query language, the solution to the problem can be written as follows:

```
int sum = (from x in arr
          where x % 2 == 1
          select x).Sum();
```

As you can see in this example, not every query operator has an equivalent in query syntax. Sum() and all the other aggregation operators do not have an equivalent. In the following sections, we will look at these two flavors of LINQ in more detail.

Standard query operators

The LINQ standard query operators are a set of extension methods that operate on sequences that implement either IEnumerable<T> or IQueryable<T>. The former exports an enumerator that enables iteration over a sequence. The latter is a LINQ-specific interface that inherits from IEnumerable<T> and provides us with the functionality to evaluate queries against a specific data source. The standard query operators are defined as extension methods to either the Enumerable or the Queryable class, depending on the type of sequence they operate on. Being extension methods, they can be called either using static method syntax or instance method syntax.

Most of the query operators may return more than one value. These methods return IEnumerable<T> or IQueryable<T>, which makes it possible to chain them together. The actual query on the data source is deferred until the enumerable object they return is iterated on. On the other hand, standard query operators that return a single value (such as Sum() or Count()) do not defer execution and execute immediately.

The following table contains the names of all the LINQ standard query operators:

Category	Methods
Sorting	OrderBy, OrderByDescending, ThenBy, ThenByDescending, Reverse
Set operations	Distinct, Except, Intersect, Union
Filtering	Where, OfType
Quantifiers	All, Any, Contains
Projection	Select, SelectMany
Partitioning	Skip, SkipWhile, Take, TakeWhile
Join operations	Join, GroupJoin
Grouping	GroupBy, ToLookup
Generation operations	Empty, DefaultIfEmpty, Range, Repeat
Equality	SequenceEqual
Element operations	ElementAt, ElementAtOrDefault, First, FirstOrDefault, Last, LastOrDefault, Single, SingleOrDefault
Aggregation	Aggregate, Average, Count, LongCount, Max, Min, Sum
Concatenation	Concat
Conversions	AsEnumerable, AsQueryable, Cast, OfType, ToArray, ToDictionary, ToList, ToLookup

There is a large number of standard query operators. Discussing every one of them is beyond the scope of this book. You should read the official documentation or additional resources to get familiar with all of them.

To familiarize ourselves more with LINQ, we will look at several examples. In the first example, we want to count the number of words in a sentence. We consider dot (.), comma (,), and space as delimiters. We split the string into parts, and then filter all those that are not empty and count them. With LINQ, this is as simple as doing the following:

```
var text = "Lorem ipsum dolor sit amet, consectetur adipiscing
elit, sed do eiusmod tempor incididunt ut labore et dolore
magna aliqua.";

var count = text.Split(new char[] { ' ', ',', '.' })
            .Where(w => !string.IsNullOrEmpty(w))
            .Count();
```

However, if we want to group all the words based on their length and print them to the console, the problem becomes a little bit more complicated. We need to create groups with the word length as the key and the word itself as the element, filter out the groups that have the length zero, and order the remaining in ascending order based on the word length:

```
var groups = text.Split(new char[] { ' ', ',', '.' })
            .GroupBy(w => w.Length, w => w.ToLower())
            .Select(g => new { Length =g.Key, Words = g })
            .Where(g => g.Length > 0)
            .OrderBy(g => g.Length);

foreach (var group in groups)
{
    Console.WriteLine($"Length={group.Length}");
    foreach (var word in group.Words)
    {
        Console.WriteLine($" {word}");
    }
}
```

While the previous query was executed when Count() was called, the execution of this query is deferred until we actually iterate over it.

The examples we've looked at so far haven't been too complicated. Using LINQ, however, you can build queries of higher complexity. To illustrate this, let's consider a system that deals with orders for customers. The system works with entities such as `Customer`, `Article`, `OrderLine`, and `Order`, which, in a very simplistic form, are shown here:

```
class Customer
{
    public long Id { get; set; }
    public string FirstName { get; set; }
    public string LastName { get; set; }
    public string Email { get; set; }
}

class Article
{
    public long Id { get; set; }
    public string EAN13 { get; set; }
    public string Name { get; set; }
    public double Price { get; set; }
}

class OrderLine
{
    public long Id { get; set; }
    public long OrderId { get; set; }
    public long ArticleId { get; set; }
    public double Quantity { get; set; }
    public double Discount { get; set; }
}

class Order
{
    public long Id { get; set; }
    public DateTime Date { get; set; }
    public long CustomerId { get; set; }
    public double Discount { get; set; }
}
```

Let's also consider that we have sequences of these types, as follows (for simplicity, only a couple of records are shown for each type, but you can find the full example in the source code that accompanies this book):

```
var articles = new List<Article>()
{
    new Article(){ Id = 1, EAN13 = "5901234123457",
                    Name = "paper", Price = 100.0},
    new Article(){ Id = 2, EAN13 = "5901234123466",
                    Name = "pen", Price = 200.0},
    /* more */
};

var customers = new List<Customer>()
{
    new Customer() { Id = 101, FirstName = "John",
            LastName = "Doe", Email = "john.doe@email.com"},
    new Customer() { Id = 102, FirstName = "Jane",
            LastName = "Doe", Email = "jane.doe@email.com"},
    /* more */
};

var orders = new List<Order>()
{
    new Order() { Id = 1001, Date = new DateTime(2020, 3, 12),
                CustomerId = customers[0].Id },
    new Order() { Id = 1002, Date = new DateTime(2020, 4, 23),
                CustomerId = customers[1].Id },
    /* more */
};

var orderlines = new List<OrderLine>()
{
    new OrderLine(){ Id = 1, OrderId=orders[0].Id,
                    ArticleId = articles[0].Id, Quantity=2},
    new OrderLine(){ Id = 2, OrderId=orders[0].Id,
                    ArticleId = articles[1].Id, Quantity=1},
    /* more */
};
```

The question we want to find the answer to is, *what are the names of all the articles that a particular customer has bought since a given day?* It can be cumbersome to write this using an imperative approach, but using LINQ, this can be expressed as follows:

```
var query =
    orders.Join(orderlines,
                o => o.Id,
                ol => ol.OrderId,
                (o, ol) => new { Order = o, Line = ol })
            .Join(customers,
                o => o.Order.CustomerId,
                c => c.Id,
                (o, c) => new { o.Order, o.Line, Customer = c})
            .Join(articles,
                o => o.Line.ArticleId,
                a => a.Id,
                (o, a) => new { o.Order, o.Line,
                                o.Customer, Article = a})
        .Where(o => o.Order.Date >= new DateTime(2020, 4, 1) &&
                o.Customer.FirstName == "John")
        .OrderBy(o => o.Article.Name)
        .Select(o => o.Article.Name);
```

In this example, we joined the orders with order lines and customers and the order lines with articles and kept only the orders made after April 1, 2020 for the customer whose first name was John. Then, we ordered them lexicographically by the article name and selected only the article name to project.

There are several `Join()` operations and the syntax may look harder to understand. Let's explain it using the following example:

```
orders.Join(orderlines,
            o => o.Id,
            ol => ol.OrderId,
            (o, ol) => new { Order = o, Line = ol })
```

Here, `orders` is called the *outer sequence*, and `orderlines` is called the *inner sequence*. The second argument of `Join()`, which is `o => o.Id`, is called the *key selector for the outer sequence*. We use this to select the orders. The third argument of `Join()`, which is `ol => ol.OrderId`, is called the *key selector of the inner sequence*. We use this to select order lines.

Basically, these two lambda expressions help matching order lines that have `OrderId` equal to an order ID. The last argument, `(o, ol) => new { Order = o, Line = ol }`, is the projection of the join operation. We are creating a new object with two properties called `Order` and `Line`.

Some standard query operators are simpler to use, while others are more complicated and may require a bit of practice to comprehend well. However, for many of them, a simpler alternative exists—the LINQ query syntax, which we will explore in the next section.

Query syntax

LINQ query syntax is basically syntactic sugar (that is, a simplified syntax designed to make things easier to write and understand) for the standard query operators. The compiler transforms queries written in query syntax into queries using the standard query operators. Query syntax is simpler and easier to read than the standard query operators, but they are semantically equivalent. However, as mentioned previously, not all the standard query operators have an equivalent in query syntax.

To see how the method syntax of the standard query operators and the query syntax compare, let's rewrite the examples from the previous section using query syntax.

First, let's look at the problem where we counted the words in a piece of text. With query syntax, the query changes to the following. Notice that `Count()` does not have an equivalent in query syntax:

```
var count = (from w in text.Split(new char[] { ' ', ',', '.' })
             where !string.IsNullOrEmpty(w)
             select w).Count();
```

The second problem, on the other hand, can be entirely written using query syntax, as shown here:

```
var groups = from w in text.Split(new char[] { ' ', ',', '.' })
             group w.ToLower() by w.Length into g
             where g.Key > 0
             orderby g.Key
             select new { Length = g.Key, Words = g };

foreach (var group in groups)
{
    Console.Write($"Length={group.Length}: ");
    Console.WriteLine(string.Join(',', group.Words));
}
```

Printing the text is a little bit different. Words are displayed on a single line, separated by a comma. To compose the text of comma-separated words, we used the `string.Join()` static method, which takes a separator and a sequence of values and joins them into a single string. The output of this program is as follows:

```
Length=2: do,ut,et
Length=3: sit,sed
Length=4: amet,elit
Length=5: lorem,ipsum,dolor,magna
Length=6: tempor,labore,dolore,aliqua
Length=7: eiusmod
Length=10: adipiscing,incididunt
Length=11: consectetur
```

The last problem that we will rewrite is the example with the customer orders. This query can be expressed very succinctly, as shown in the following code. This code resembles SQL and the `join` operations are definitely simpler to write, read, and understand:

```
var query = from o in orders
            join ol in orderlines on o.Id equals ol.OrderId
            join c in customers on o.CustomerId equals c.Id
            join a in articles on ol.ArticleId equals a.Id
            where o.Date >= new DateTime(2019, 4, 1) &&
                  c.FirstName == "John"
            orderby a.Name
            select a.Name;
```

As you can see from these examples, LINQ helps build queries in a much simpler way than using traditional imperative programming. Data sources of different natures can be queried in a consistent way with a language that looks like SQL. Queries are strongly typed and are verified at compile time, which helps to solve many potential bugs.

Now, let's take a look at some more functional programming concepts: partial function application, currying, closures, monoids, and monads.

More functional programming concepts

At the beginning of this chapter, we looked at general functional programming concepts, mainly higher-order functions and immutability. In this section, we will explore several more functional programming concepts and techniques—partial function application, currying, closures, monoids, and monads.

Partial function application

Partial function application is the process of taking a function with *N parameters* and *one argument* and returning another function with *N-1 parameters* after fixing the argument into one of the function's parameters. It is, of course, possible that the invocation is done with more than just one argument, say, *M*, in which case the returned function will have *N-M* parameters.

To understand how this works, let's start with a function that has several parameters and is returning a string (containing the value of the arguments):

```
string AsString(int a, double b, string c)
{
    return $"a={a}, b={b}, c={c}";
}
```

If we invoke this function as `AsString(42, 43.5, "44")`, the result is the string `"a=42, b=43.5, c=44"`. However, if we had a function (let's call it `Apply()`) that would bind an argument to the first parameter of this function, then we could invoke it as follows with the same result:

```
var f1 = Apply<int, double, string, string>(AsString, 42);
var result = f1(43.5, "44");
```

The implementation of such an `Apply()` function is as follows:

```
Func<T2, T3, TResult>
Apply<T1, T2, T3, TResult>(Func<T1, T2, T3, TResult> f, T1 arg)
{
    return (b, c) => f(arg, b, c);
}
```

This higher-order function takes another function and a value as parameters and returns another higher function with one parameter less. This function resolves to invoke the `f` argument function with the `arg` argument value and additional parameters.

It is also possible that we continue this process of reducing functions to another function with one less parameter until we have a function with no parameters, as follows:

```
var f1 = Apply<int, double, string, string>(AsString, 42);
var f2 = Apply(f1, 43.5);
var f3 = Apply(f2, "44");
string result = f3();
```

However, to make this possible, we need additional overloads of the `Apply()` function, with the appropriate number of arguments. For the case shown here, we need the following (in practice, if you have functions with more than three arguments, you need more overloads to account for all possible numbers of arguments):

```
Func<T2, TResult> Apply<T1, T2, TResult>(Func<T1, T2, TResult>
f, T1 arg)
{
    return b => f(arg, b);
}

Func<TResult> Apply<T1, TResult>(Func<T1, TResult> f, T1 arg)
{
    return () => f(arg);
}
```

In this example, it is important to note that the actual invocation of the `AsString()` function only happens when all the arguments are supplied; that is, the moment we invoke `f3()`.

You may be wondering when partial function application is useful. The typical case is when you invoke a function several (or many) times and some arguments are the same. In this case, there are several alternatives, including the following:

- Provide defaults for the function parameters, when you define it. However, this might not be possible for different reasons. Perhaps the defaults only make sense in some context, or maybe you do not actually own the code, so you cannot provide them.

- In the class where you invoke the function multiple times, you can write a `helper` function with fewer arguments that invoke the function with the right defaults.

Partial function application may be (in many of these cases) the simpler solution to use.

Currying

Currying is the process of taking a function with *N* arguments and decomposing it into *N* functions that take *one* argument. This technique takes its name from the mathematician and logician Haskell Curry, after whom the functional programming language **Haskell** is also named.

Currying enables working with functions that have multiple arguments in contexts where only functions with one argument could be used. An example of this is analytical techniques in mathematics that can only be applied to functions with a single argument.

Considering the `AsString()` function from the previous section, currying this function would do the following:

- Return a function, `f1`.

- When invoked with an argument, `a`, it would return a function, `f2`.

- When invoked with an argument, `b`, it would return a function, `f3`.

- When invoked with an argument, `c`, it would invoke `AsString(a, b, c)`.

These, when put in code, would look as follows:

```
var f1 = Curry<int, double, string, string>(AsString);
var f2 = f1(42);
var f3 = f2(43.5);
string result = f3("44");
```

The generic `Curry()` function seen here is similar to the `Apply()` function from the previous section. However, instead of returning a function with *N-1* arguments, it returns a function with a single argument:

```
Func<T1, Func<T2, Func<T3, TResult>>>
Curry<T1, T2, T3, TResult>(Func<T1, T2, T3, TResult> f)
{
    return a => b => c => f(a, b, c);
}
```

This function can be used to curry functions with exactly three parameters. Should you need to do that with functions that have another number of parameters, then you need appropriate overloads for it (just as in the case of `Apply()`).

You should note that you do not necessarily need to decompose the `AsString()` function three different times, as seen earlier with `f1`, `f2`, and `f3`. You can skip intermediate functions and achieve the same result by invoking the function appropriately, as shown in the following code:

```
var f = Curry<int, double, string, string>(AsString);
string result = f(42)(43.5)("44");
```

Another important concept in function programming is closures. We'll learn about closures in the next section.

Closures

Closures are defined as a technique to implement lexically scoped name-binding in a language with first-class functions. Lexical or static scoping is the setting of the scope of a variable to the block in which it was defined, so it may only be referred to by its name from within that scope.

Information box

Scopes in C# are called **static** or **lexical** and can be viewed at compile time. The opposite is *dynamic scopes*, which are only resolved at runtime, but these are not supported in C#.

As we saw earlier in this chapter, C# is a language that has first-class functions because you can assign functions to variables, pass them around, and invoke them. However, this definition of a closure is probably harder to comprehend, so we will explain it step by step using an example.

Let's consider the following example:

```
class Program
{
    static Func<int, int> Increment()
    {
        int step = 1;
        return x => x + step;
    }

    static void Main(string[] args)
    {
        var inc = Increment();
        Console.WriteLine(inc(42));
    }
}
```

Here, we have a function called `Increment()` that is returning another function that increments its argument with a value. However, that value is neither passed as an argument to the lambda nor defined as a local variable in the lambda. Instead, it is captured from the outer scope. For this reason, the step variable is called a **free variable**. When the compiler sees it in the lambda expression, it looks for the definition of the `step` variable in the scope of the lambda; if it's not found, it looks to the enclosing scope, which, in this case, is the `Increment()` function. If it wasn't there either, it would have looked further in the class scope, and so on.

What happens next is that we assign the value returned from the `Increment()` function, which is another function, to the `inc` variable and then invoke it with the value `42`. The result is that the value `43` is printed to the console.

The question is, *how does this work?* The `step` variable is actually a local function variable and should go out of scope as soon as `Increment()` is called. Yet, its value is known at the time of invoking the function returned from `Increment()`. This is because the lambda expression, `x => x + step`, is said to *close* over the free variable, `step`, thus defining a closure. Both the lambda expression and `step` are passed together (as part of the closure) so that the variable that would normally go out of scope still lives at the time the closure is invoked.

Closures are used all the time without us even realizing it. Consider the following example, where we have a list of engines and we want to search for an engine with minimum power and capacity. You would typically write something as follows using a lambda expression:

```
var list = new List<Engine>();
var minp = 75.0;
var minc = 1600;
var engine = list.Find(e => e.Power >= minp &&
                       e.Capacity >= minc);
```

But this is actually creating a closure because the lambda closes over the `minp` and `minc` free variables. Without support for closure in the language, it would be cumbersome to write code that does the same. You would basically have to write a class that is capturing the value of these variables and has a method that takes an `Engine` object and compares its properties to these values. In this case, the code could look as follows:

```
sealed class EngineFinder
{
    public EngineFinder(double minPower, int minCapacity)
    {
        this.minPower = minPower;
        this.minCapacity = minCapacity;
    }

    public double minPower;
    public int minCapacity;

    public bool IsMatch(Engine engine)
    {
        return engine.Power >= minPower &&
            engine.Capacity >= minCapacity;
```

```
        }
    }

    var engine = list.Find(new EngineFinder(minp, minc).IsMatch);
```

This is quite similar to what the compiler does when encountering a closure, but it's the kind of detail you do not have to concern yourself with.

You should also notice that the free variables that are captured by a lambda in a closure can change value. We exemplify this with the following sample where the `GetNextId()` function defines a closure that increments the value of the captured free variable, `id`, with each call:

```
Func<int> GetNextId()
{
    int id = 1;
    return () => id++;
}

var nextId = GetNextId();
Console.WriteLine(nextId()); // prints 1
Console.WriteLine(nextId()); // prints 2
Console.WriteLine(nextId()); // prints 3
```

We'll learn about monoids in the next section.

Monoids

A **monoid** is an algebraic structure with a single associative binary operation and an identity element. Any C# type that has those two elements is a monoid. Monoids are useful for defining concepts and reusing code. They help us build complex behavior out of simple components without the need to introduce new concepts in our code. Let's look at how we can create and use monoids in C#.

We could define a generic interface in C# to represent a monoid as follows:

```
interface IMonoid<T>
{
    T Combine(T a, T b);
    T Identity { get; }
}
```

The monoid ensures associativity and left and right identity so that for any values, a, b, and c, we have the following:

- `Combine((Combine(a, b), c) == Combine(a, Combine(b, c))`
- `Combine(Identify, a) == a`
- `Combine(a, Identity) == a`

Concatenating strings or a list is an example of an associative binary operation. A type that provides that function, together with an identity element (an empty string or an empty list in these cases), is a monoid. So, we can actually implement these in C# as follows:

```
struct ConcatList<T> : IMonoid<List<T>>
{
    public List<T> Identity => new List<T> { };

    public List<T> Combine(List<T> a, List<T> b)
    {
        var l = new List<T>(a);
        l.AddRange(b);
        return l;
    }
}

struct ConcatString : IMonoid<string>
{
    public string Identity => string.Empty;

    public string Combine(string a, string b)
    {
        return a + b;
    }
}
```

Both `ConcatList` and `ConcatString` are examples of monoids. The latter could be used as follows:

```
var m = new ConcatString();
var text = m.Combine("Learning", m.Combine(" ", "C# 8"));
Console.WriteLine(text);
```

This would print Learning C# 8 to the console. However, this code is a little bit cumbersome to use. We can simplify it by creating a helper class with a static method called Concat() that takes a monoid and a sequence of elements and combines them together using the monoids binary operation and its identity for the initial value:

```
static class Monoid
{
    public static T Concat<MT, T>(IEnumerable<T> seq)
        where MT : struct, IMonoid<T>
    {
        var result = default(MT).Identity;
        foreach (var e in seq)
            result = default(MT).Combine(result, e);
        return result;
    }
}
```

Having this helper class available, we can write the following simplified code:

```
var text = Monoid.Concat<ConcatString, string>(
            new[] { "Learning", " ", "C# 8"});
Console.WriteLine(text);

var list = Monoid.Concat<ConcatList<int>, List<int>>(
    new[] { new List<int>{ 1,2,3},
    new List<int> { 4, 5 },
    new List<int> { } });
Console.WriteLine(string.Join(",", list));
```

In the first part of this example, we concatenated a list of strings into a single string and printed it to the console. In the second part, we concatenated a list of lists of integers into a single list of integers, which are later also printed to the console.

In the next section, we'll take a look at monads.

Monads

This is a concept that is usually harder to explain and, perhaps, also harder to understand, although a lot of literature has been written about it. In this book, we will try to explain it in simple terms, but we recommend that you read additional resources.

In a few words, a monad is a container that encapsulates some functionality on top of the value that it wraps. We often work with monads in C# without realizing it. `Nullable<T>` is a monad that defines a special functionality that is *nullability*, which means a value may be present or not. `Task<T>` with `await` is a monad that defines a special functionality that is *asynchronicity*, which means a value can be used before it's actually computed. `IEnumerable<T>` with the LINQ query `SelectMany()` operator is also a monad.

A monad has two operations:

- One that *transforms* a value, v, into a container that wraps it (`v -> C(v)`). In functional programming, this function is called **return**.

- One that *flattens* two containers into a single container (`C(C(v)) -> C(v)`). In functional programming, this is called **bind**.

Let's look at the following example:

```
var numbers = new int[][]{ new[]{ 1, 2, 3},
                           new[]{ 4, 5 },
                           new[]{ 6, 7} };

IEnumerable<int> odds = numbers.SelectMany(
                            n => n.Where(x => x % 2 == 1));
```

Here, `numbers` is an array of arrays of integers. `SelectMany()` is used to select subsequences of odd numbers. However, this flattens the result into `IEnumerable<int>` instead of `IEnumerable<IEnumerable<int>>`. As we mentioned earlier, `IEnumerable<T>` with `SelectMany()` is a monad.

But how can you implement a monad in C#? The simplest form is as follows:

```
class Monad<T>
{
    public Monad(T value) => Value = value;

    public T Value { get; }

    public Monad<U> Bind<U>(Func<T, Monad<U>> f) => f(Value);
}
```

This is actually called the **Identity monad**. It lets you construct a container that wraps a value and, if you put a monad into a monad and bind it with the identity x => x, you will get the initial monad back:

```
var m = new Monad<int>(42);
var mm = new Monad<Monad<int>>(m);
var r = mm.Bind(x => x); // r equals m
```

Another example of how this monad can be used is shown in the following code:

```
var m = new Monad<int>(21);

var r = m.Bind(x => new Monad<int>(x * 2))
         .Bind(x => new Monad<string>($"x={x}"));

Console.WriteLine(r.Value); // prints x=42
```

In this example, m is a monad that wraps the integer value 21. We bind with a function that returns a new monad that has a value that is double the initial one. We can again bind on this monad with a function that transforms the integer into a string.

From this example, you can see that those binding operations can be chained together. This is what fluent interfaces provide—a mechanism to write code that looks like written prose by chaining methods. This can be further exemplified using the following example—given a system where a business has customers, customers place orders, and an order can contain one or more articles, you are required to find all the distinct articles bought by all the customers of a particular business.

For simplicity, let's consider the following classes:

```
class Business
{
    public IEnumerable<Customer> GetCustomers() {
      return /* … */; }
}

class Customer
{
    public IEnumerable<Order> GetOrders() { return /* … */; }
}

class Order
{
    public IEnumerable<Article> GetArticles() { return /* … */;
}
```

```
}

class Article { }
```

In a typical imperative style, you could implement the solution as follows:

```
IEnumerable<Article> GetArticlesSoldBy(Business business)
{
    var articles = new HashSet<Article>();

    foreach (var customer in business.GetCustomers())
    {
        foreach (var order in customer.GetOrders())
        {
            foreach (var article in order.GetArticles())
            {
                articles.Add(article);
            }
        }
    }

    return articles;
}
```

However, this can be simplified more by using LINQ and the IEnumerable<T> and SelectMany() monad. The functional programming style implementation could look as follows:

```
IEnumerable<Article> GetArticlesSoldBy(Business business)
{
    return business.GetCustomers()
                .SelectMany(c => c.GetOrders())
                .SelectMany(o => o.GetArticles())
                .Distinct()
                .ToList();
}
```

This uses the fluent interface pattern and the result is more concise code that is also simpler to understand.

Summary

This chapter was a departure from the imperative programming traits of C# since we explored functional programming concepts and techniques built into the language. We looked at higher-order functions, lambda expressions, partial function applications, currying, closures, monoids, and monads. We also had an introduction to LINQ with its two flavors: the method syntax and the query syntax. Most of these topics are complex and more advanced than the proposed scope of this book. Therefore, we recommend that you use other resources in order to master them.

In the next chapter, we will look at the reflection services that are available with .NET and the dynamic programming capabilities of C#.

Test what you learned

1. What are the main characteristics of functional programming? What advantages does it provide?

2. What is a higher-order function?

3. What makes functions first-class citizens in the C# language?

4. What is a lambda expression? What is the syntax for writing lambda expressions?

5. What are the rules that apply to variables' scope in lambda expressions?

6. What is LINQ? What are the standard query operators and what is the query syntax?

7. What is the difference between `Select()` and `SelectMany()`?

8. What is a partial function application and how does it differ from currying?

9. What is a monoid?

10. What is a monad?

11
Reflection and Dynamic Programming

In the previous chapter, we looked at functional programming, lambda expressions, and the features they enable, such as **Language Integrated Query (LINQ)**. This chapter is focused on reflection services and dynamic programming. You will learn what reflection is and how you can get information about types at runtime, as well as how code and resources are stored in assemblies and how these can be loaded dynamically at runtime both for reflection and code execution.

This is key for building applications that support extension in the form of add-ons or plugins. We will see what attributes are and what role they play in reflection. Another important topic that we will address in this chapter is dynamic programming and the **Dynamic Language Runtime** that enables dynamic languages to run on the **Common Language Runtime (CLR)** and to add dynamic features to statically typed languages.

The topics we will address in this chapter are the following:

- Understanding reflection
- Dynamically loading assemblies

- Understanding late binding
- Using the `dynamic` type
- Attributes

By the end of this chapter, you will have a good understanding of reflection, attributes, and their use in reflection, as well as assembly loading and code execution. On the other hand, you will also learn about the `dynamic` type and be able to interoperate with dynamic languages.

Understanding reflection

The unit of deployment in .NET is the assembly. An assembly is a file (either an executable or a dynamic-linked library) that contains **Microsoft Intermediary Language (MSIL)** code, as well as metadata about the content of the assembly and, optionally, resources. Tools such as `ildasm.exe` (**IL Disassembler**), distributed with Visual Studio; `ilspy.exe` (an open-source project); or others allow you to view the content of the assembly. The following is a screenshot of `ildasm.exe` that shows the `chapter_11_01.dll` assembly, available with the source code of this book:

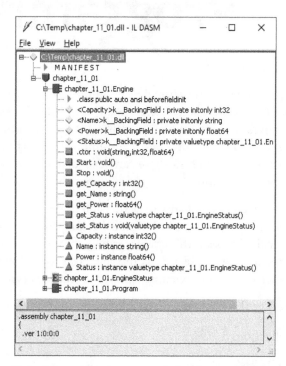

Figure 11.1 – Disassembled source code for chapter_11_01 assembly

Reflection is the process of runtime type discovery and the ability to make changes to them. This means that we can retrieve information about types, their members, and attributes at runtime. This brings several important benefits:

- The ability to load assemblies dynamically during runtime (late binding), inspect types, and execute code makes it easy to build extensible applications. An application can define functionalities through interfaces and base classes, which would then be implemented or extended in separate modules (plugins or add-ons) that could be loaded and executed at runtime based on various conditions.

- Attributes, which we will later see in this chapter, make it possible to provide meta-information about types, methods, properties, and others in a declarative way. By being able to read these attributes at runtime, a system can change their behavior. Tools, for instance, could warn that a method is used differently than intended (such as in the case of obsolete methods) or execute them in a particular way. Testing frameworks (we will look at some in the final chapter) use this functionality extensively.

- It provides the ability to execute types and members that are private or have other access levels that make them inaccessible otherwise. This is, again, very handy for testing frameworks.

- It allows modifying existing types or creating entirely new types at runtime and executing code using them.

Reflection also has some drawbacks:

- It incurs an overhead that can degrade performance. Loading, discovering, and executing code at runtime is slower and may prevent optimizations.

- It exposes the internals of types because it allows introspection on all types and members regardless of their access level.

The .NET reflection services allow you to discover, using APIs from the `System.Reflection` namespace, the same information that you can see with the tools mentioned earlier. The key to this process is the type called `System.Type`, which contains members that expose all of a type's metadata. This is done with the help of other types from the `System.Reflection` namespace, some of which are listed in the following table:

Type	Description
ConstructorInfo	It provides information about a constructor.
EventInfo	It provides information about an event.
FieldInfo	It provides information about the field.
MemberInfo	This is the base class for types that hold information about a member, such as a field, property, method, event, or constructor.
MethodInfo	It provides information about a method.
ParameterInfo	It provides information about a method parameter.
PropertyInfo	It provides information about a property.

Some of the most important members of the `System.Type` class are listed in the following table:

Member	Description
GetConstructors() GetCustomAttributes() GetEvents() GetFields() GetMembers() GetMethods() GetProperties()	Return metadata about constructors, events, fields, properties, methods, and so on. All of these methods have overloads, one without parameters that returns the public members that are declared or inherited by the current type, and one or more with parameters that search for members with the specified binding flags. All of these members return an array of one of the types listed previously (such as `PropertyInfo[]` for properties).
GetConstructor() GetEvents() GetFields() GetMembers() GetMethods() GetProperties()	These methods are similar to the previous ones, except they take the name of a member to search for and return a single object, not an array.
InvokeMember()	It allows invoking the specified member.
IsArray IsClass IsEnum IsGenericParameter IsGenericType IsInterface IsPrimitive IsSerializable IsValueType	These are some of the properties that provide information about various traits of the current type. They all have the name prefixed with `Is` and return a Boolean value.

There are several ways to retrieve an instance of `System.Type` to access type metadata at runtime; here are a few:

- Using the `GetType()` method of the `System.Object` type. Since this is the base class for all value and reference types, you can call with an instance of any type:

```
var engine = new Engine();
var type = engine.GetType();
```

- Using the `GetType()` static method from `System.Type`. There are many overloads that allow you to specify the name and various parameters:

```
var type = Type.GetType("Engine");
```

- Using the C# `typeof` operator:

```
var type = typeof(Engine);
```

Let's see how we can use reflection by looking at an actual example. We will consider the following `Engine` type, which has several properties, a constructor, and a couple of methods that change the status of the engine (started or stopped):

```
public enum EngineStatus { Stopped, Started }

public class Engine
{
    public string Name { get; }
    public int Capacity { get; }
    public double Power { get; }
    public EngineStatus Status { get; private set; }

    public Engine(string name, int capacity, double power)
    {
        Name = name;
        Capacity = capacity;
        Power = power;
        Status = EngineStatus.Stopped;
    }

    public void Start()
    {
        Status = EngineStatus.Started;
    }
```

```
      public void Stop()
      {
          Status = EngineStatus.Stopped;
      }
}
```

We will build a small program that will read metadata about the `Engine` type at runtime and print the following to the console:

- The name of the *type*
- The name of all *properties* as well as the name of their type
- The name of all *declared methods* (excluding the inherited methods)
- The name of their *return type*
- The name and type of *each parameter*

Here is the program to read and print metadata about the `Engine` type at runtime:

```
static void Main(string[] args)
{
    var type = typeof(Engine);

    Console.WriteLine(type.Name);

    var properties = type.GetProperties();
    foreach(var p in properties)
    {
        Console.WriteLine($"{p.Name} ({p.PropertyType.Name})");
    }

    var methods = type.GetMethods(BindingFlags.Public |
                                  BindingFlags.Instance |
                                  BindingFlags.DeclaredOnly);
    foreach(var m in methods)
    {
        var parameters = string.Join(
            ',',
            m.GetParameters()
             .Select(p => $"{p.ParameterType.Name} {p.Name}"));

        Console.WriteLine(
          $"{m.ReturnType.Name} {m.Name} ({parameters})");
    }
}
```

In this example, we used the `typeof` operator to retrieve an instance of the `System.Type` type to discover the metadata for the `Engine` type. To retrieve properties, we used the overload of `GetProperties()` with no parameters, which returns all of the public properties of the current type. For methods, however, we used an overload of the `GetMethod()` method, which takes as argument a bitmask comprised of one or more `BindingFlags` values.

The `BindingFlags` type is an enum with flags that control the binding and the way searching for types and methods is performed during reflection. In our example, we used `Public`, `Instance`, and `DeclareOnly` to specify public, non-static methods declared in this type only, and exclude inherited ones. The output of this program is as follows:

```
Engine
Name (String)
Capacity (Int32)
Power (Double)
Status (EngineStatus)
String get_Name ()
Int32 get_Capacity ()
Double get_Power ()
EngineStatus get_Status ()
Void Start ()
Void Stop ()
```

The `Engine` type is located in the assembly where the reflection code was executed. However, you can also reflect on types from other assemblies too, whether they are referred from the executing assembly or loaded at runtime, which is what we will look at in the next section.

Dynamically loading assemblies

The reflection services allow you to load an assembly at runtime. This is done using the `System.Reflection.Assembly` type, which provides various methods for loading assemblies.

Assemblies can be either *public* (also called *shared*) or *private*. A shared assembly is intended to be used by several applications and is usually located under the **Global Assembly Cache (GAC)**, a system repository for assemblies. A private assembly is intended to be used by a single application and is stored in the application directory or one of its sub-directories. Shared assemblies must be strongly named and enforce version constraints; these requirements are not necessary for private assemblies.

An assembly can be loaded in one of three contexts or without any:

- The *load context*, which contains assemblies loaded from the GAC, the application directory (`ApplicationBase` of the app domain), or its sub-directories of private assemblies (`PrivateBinPath` of the app domain)

- The *load-from context*, which contains assemblies loaded from paths other than the aforementioned ones that are probed by the assembly loader

- The *reflection-only context*, which contains assemblies loaded for reflection purposes only and which cannot be used to execute code

- *No context*, which is used in some particular cases such as assemblies loaded from an array of bytes

The most important methods used to load assemblies are listed in the following table:

`Load()`	This loads an assembly, identified by its `AssemblyName`, into the load context. Dependencies from the load or load-from context are automatically found, but those loaded into other contexts are not available.
`LoadFrom()`	This allows loading an assembly from a location other than GAC or your application path. Dependencies from the load context are available. However, if an assembly with the same identity is already loaded, even if loaded from a different path, the loaded assembly is returned.
`ReflectionOnlyLoad()`	This loads an assembly from GAC or the application path into the reflection context using its display name. Dependencies are not automatically loaded in this context.
`ReflectionOnlyLoadFrom()`	This loads an assembly into the reflection context using its path.

We will look at several examples of loading assemblies dynamically.

In the first example, we use `Assembly.Load()` to load an assembly called `EngineLib` from the applications directory:

```
var assembly = Assembly.Load("EngineLib");
```

Here, we only specified the name of the assembly, but we could alternatively specify the display name, which is comprised not only of the name but also the version, culture, and the public key token used to sign the assembly. For assemblies that do not have a strong name, this is `null`. The following line, where we use the display name, is equivalent to the one used previously:

```
var assembly = Assembly.Load(@"EngineLib, Version=1.0.0.0,
Culture=neutral, PublicKeyToken=null");
```

It is possible to create the display name in a type-safe way by using the `AssemblyName` class. This class has various properties and methods that allow you to build the display name. This can be done as shown here:

```
var assemblyName = new AssemblyName()
{
    Name = "EngineLib",
    Version = new Version(1,0,0,0),
    CultureInfo = null,
};

var assembly = Assembly.Load(assemblyName);
```

Public (or shared) assemblies must have a strong name. This helps to uniquely identify the assembly and therefore avoid possible conflicts. Signing is done using a public-private key; the private key is used for signing and the public key is distributed with the assembly and used to verify the signature.

Such a cryptographic pair can be generated with the `sn.exe` tool, distributed with Visual Studio; this tool can also be used for verifying a signature. For strong-name assemblies, `PublicKeyToken` must be specified or loading would fail. The following example shows how to load `WindowsBase.dll` from the GAC:

```
var assembly = Assembly.Load(@"WindowsBase, Version=4.0.0.0,
Culture=neutral, PublicKeyToken=31bf3856ad364e35");
```

The alternative to using the assembly name for loading an assembly is to use its actual path. However, in this case, you must use one of the `LoadFrom()` overloads. This is useful for cases where you must load an assembly that is neither in the GAC nor under the application's folder. An example can be an extensible system that can load plugins that may be installed in some custom directory:

```
var assembly = Assembly.LoadFrom(@"c:\learningc#8\
chapter_11_02\bin\Debug\netcoreapp2.1\EngineLib.dll");
```

The `Assembly` class has members that provide information about the assembly itself, as well as members that provide information about the types it contains. Some of the most important members are listed here:

`GetName()`	It provides the assembly display name by returning an `AssemblyName` object.
`GetCustomAttributes()`	It retrieves the attributes applied to the assembly.
`GetFiles()`	It returns an array with the files in the assembly manifest.
`GetManifestResourceNames()`	It returns an array with the names of the resources in the assembly manifest.
`GetTypes()`	It returns all of the types in the assembly.
`GetType()`	It returns a type in the assembly identified by its name.
`CreateInstance()`	It instantiates an object of the specified type.

In the following example, after loading an assembly using one of the methods shown previously, we list the assembly name and the files in the assembly manifest, as well as the names of the referenced assemblies. After that, we search for the `EngineLib.Engine` type and print the name and the type of all of its properties:

```
if (assembly != null)
{
    Console.WriteLine(
$@"Name: {assembly.GetName().FullName}
Files: {string.Join(',',
                assembly.GetFiles().Select(
                    s=>Path.GetFileName(s.Name)))}
Refs:  {string.Join(',',
                assembly.GetReferencedAssemblies().Select(
                    n=>n.Name))}");

    var type = assembly.GetType("EngineLib.Engine");

    if (type != null)
    {
        var properties = type.GetProperties();
        foreach (var p in properties)
        {
```

```
            Console.WriteLine(
                $"{p.Name} ({p.PropertyType.Name})");
        }
    }
}
```

Apart from querying for information about an assembly and its content, it is also possible to execute code from it at runtime. This is what we will look at in the next section.

Understanding late binding

When you reference an assembly at compile time, the compiler has full access to the types available in that assembly. This is called **early binding**. However, if an assembly is only loaded at runtime, the compiler has no access to the content of that assembly. This is called **late binding** and is key to building extensible applications. Using late binding, you can not only load and query assemblies but also execute code. We will see that in the following examples.

Let's imagine the `Engine` class, shown earlier, is available in an assembly called `EngineLib`. This can be loaded with either `Assembly.Load()` or `Assembly.LoadFrom()`. Once loaded, we can get information about the `Engine` type using `Assembly.GetType()` and the class methods of `Type`. However, using `Assembly.CreateInstance()`, we can instantiate an object of the class:

```
var assembly = Assembly.LoadFrom("EngineLib.dll");
if (assembly != null)
{
    var type = assembly.GetType("EngineLib.Engine");

    object engine = assembly.CreateInstance(
        "EngineLib.Engine",
        true,
        BindingFlags.CreateInstance,
        null,
        new object[] { "M270 Turbo", 1600, 75.0 },
        null,
        null);

    var pi = type.GetProperty("Status");
    if (pi != null)
        Console.WriteLine(pi.GetValue(engine));

    var mi = type.GetMethod("Start");
```

```
    if (mi != null)
        mi.Invoke(engine, null);

    if (pi != null)
        Console.WriteLine(pi.GetValue(engine));
}
```

The `Assembly.CreateInstance()` method has many parameters, but three of them are of the most importance:

- The first parameter, `string typeName`, representing the name of the assembly.

- The third parameter, `BindingFlags bindingAttr`, representing binding flags.

- The fifth parameter, `object[] args`, representing an array with the parameters used to invoke the constructor; for a default constructor, this object can be `null`.

After creating an instance of a type, we can invoke its members using instances of `PropertyInfo`, `MethodInfo`, and so on. For instance, in the previous example, we first retrieve an instance of `PropertyInfo` for the property called `Status` and then the value of the property by calling `GetValue()` and passing the engine object.

Similarly, we use `GetMethod()` to retrieve an instance of `MethodInfo` with information about the method called `Start()` and then invoke it by calling `Invoke()`. This method takes a reference to the object and an array of objects representing the arguments; since the `Start()` method has no parameters, `null` is used here.

The `Assembly.CreateInstance()` method has a lot of parameters and can be cumbersome to use. Alternatively, a simpler way to create instances of types at runtime is provided by the `System.Activator` class. It has an overloaded `CreateInstance()` method. This is actually used under the hood by `Assembly.CreateInstance()`. In its simplest form, it only takes `Type` and an array of objects representing constructor arguments and instantiates an object of that type. An example is shown here:

```
object engine = Activator.CreateInstance(
    type,
    new object[] { "M270 Turbo", 1600, 75.0 });
```

`Activator.CreateInstance()` is not only simpler to use but can provide benefits in some scenarios. For instance, it can create objects in other app domains or on another server using Remoting. On the other hand, `Assembly.CreateIntance()` will not attempt to load the assembly if it is not already loaded, while `System.Activator` will load the assembly into the current app domain.

Using late binding and invoking code in the manner shown earlier is not necessarily practical. In practice, when building an extensible system, you will probably have one or more assemblies with interfaces and common types that add-ons (or plugins, depending on how you want to call them) rely upon. You will early-bind to these base assemblies and then use late binding with the plugins.

To better understand this, we will demonstrate it with the following example. `EngineLibBase` is an assembly that defines an interface called `IEngine` and the `EngineStatus` enumeration:

```
namespace EngineLibBase
{
    public enum EngineStatus { Stopped, Started }

    public interface IEngine
    {
        EngineStatus Status { get; }
        void Start();
        void Stop();
    }
}
```

This assembly is directly referenced in the `EngineLib` assembly, which provides the `Engine` class that implements the `IEngine` interface. This is shown in the example here:

```
using EngineLibBase;

namespace EngineLib
{
    public class Engine : IEngine
    {
        public string Name { get; }
        public int Capacity { get; }
        public double Power { get; }
        public EngineStatus Status { get; private set; }
```

```
        public Engine(string name, int capacity, double power)
        {
            Name = name;
            Capacity = capacity;
            Power = power;
            Status = EngineStatus.Stopped;
        }

        public void Start()
        {
            Status = EngineStatus.Started;
        }

        public void Stop()
        {
            Status = EngineStatus.Stopped;
        }
    }
}
```

In our application, where we instantiated the Engine class, we again reference the
EngineLibBase assembly so that we can use the IEngine interface. After loading the
EngineLib assembly at runtime, we instantiate an object of the Engine class and cast it
to the IEngine interface, which makes it possible to access the members of the interface
at compile time, even though the actual instance is not known until at runtime. This is
shown in the code here:

```
var assembly = Assembly.LoadFrom("EngineLib.dll");
if (assembly != null)
{
    var type = assembly.GetType("EngineLib.Engine");
    var engine = (IEngine)Activator.CreateInstance(
        type,
        new object[] { "M270 Turbo", 1600, 75.0 });

    Console.WriteLine(engine.Status);
    engine.Start();
    Console.WriteLine(engine.Status);
}
```

As we will see further on in this chapter, this is not the only way to use late binding and execute code dynamically at runtime. The other possibility is using the DLR and the `dynamic` type. We will look at this in the following section.

Using the dynamic type

Throughout this book, we have talked about the **CLR**. .NET Framework, however, contains another component called the **Dynamic Language Runtime (DLR)**. This is another runtime environment that adds a set of services on top of the CLR to enable dynamic languages to run on the CLR and to add dynamic features to statically-typed languages. C# and Visual Basic are statically-typed languages. By contrast, languages such as JavaScript, Python, Ruby, PHP, Smalltalk, Lua, and others are dynamic languages. The key characteristic of these languages is that they identify the type of an object at runtime and not at compile time as in the case of the statically-typed languages.

The DLR provides C# (and Visual Basic) with dynamic features that enable them to interoperate with dynamic languages in a simple manner. As mentioned before, the DLR adds a set of services to the CLR. These services are as follows:

- **Expression trees** are used to present language semantics. These are the same expression trees used with LINQ but extended to include control-flow, assignments, and others.

- **Call site caching** is a service that caches information about operations and objects (such as the type of an object) so that when the same operation is performed again, it can be quickly dispatched.

- **Dynamic object interoperability** is a set of APIs intended for language implementers to model dynamic objects and operations on them. These include the following types—`IDynamicMetaObjectProvider`, `DynamicMetaObject`, `DynamicObject`, and `ExpandoObject`.

The DLR provides the infrastructure for the dynamic type, introduced in C# 4. This is a static type, meaning variables of this type are assigned the dynamic type at compile time. However, they bypass static type checking. This means that the actual type of the object is only known at runtime and the compiler cannot know and cannot enforce any checks on operations performed on objects of this type. You can actually invoke any methods with any parameters and the compiler will not check and complain; however, if the operation is not valid, an exception will be thrown at runtime.

The following code shows several examples of variables of the dynamic type. Notice that s is a string and l is List<int>. Calling l.Add() is a valid operation because List<T> contains such a method. However, calling s.Add() is invalid because the string type does not have such a method. Therefore, an exception of the RuntimeBinderException type is thrown at runtime for this call:

```
dynamic i = 42;
dynamic s = "42";
dynamic d = 42.0;
dynamic l = new List<int> { 42 };

l.Add(43); // OK

try
{
    s.Add(44); /* RuntimeBinderException:
            'string' does not contain a definition for 'Add' */
}
catch (Exception ex)
{
    Console.WriteLine(ex.Message);
}
```

The dynamic type makes it easy to consume objects whose type you do not know anything about at compile time. Consider the first example from the previous paragraph, where we loaded an assembly using reflection, instantiated an object of the Engine type and called its methods and properties. That example can be rewritten in a simpler way, as follows, using the dynamic type:

```
var assembly = Assembly.LoadFrom("EngineLib.dll");
if (assembly != null)
{
    var type = assembly.GetType("EngineLib.Engine");

    dynamic engine = Activator.CreateInstance(
        type,
```

```
            new object[] { "M270 Turbo", 1600, 75.0 });

        Console.WriteLine(engine.Status);
        engine.Start();
        Console.WriteLine(engine.Status);
}
```

An object of the `dynamic` type behaves in many cases as if it had the `object` type (except there is no compile-time checking). However, the actual source of the object's value is irrelevant. It could be a .NET object, a COM object, an HTML DOM object, an object created through reflection, such as in the previous example, and so on.

The type of the result of a dynamic operation is also `dynamic` with the exception of conversions from `dynamic` to another type and constructor calls that include arguments of the `dynamic` type. Implicit conversions from a static type to `dynamic` and the other way around are performed. This is shown in the code block here:

```
dynamic d = "42";
string s = d;
```

For static types, the compiler performs overload resolution to figure out what is the best match for a function call. Because there is no information about the `dynamic` type at compile time, the same cannot be done for methods that have at least one argument of the `dynamic` type. Instead, the overload resolution is performed at runtime.

The `dynamic` type is often used to simplify the consumption of COM objects when an interop assembly is not available. The following is an example that creates an Excel document with some dummy data:

```
dynamic excel = Activator.CreateInstance(
    Type.GetTypeFromProgID("Excel.Application.16"));
if (excel != null)
{
    excel.Visible = true;

    dynamic workBook = excel.Workbooks.Add();
    dynamic workSheet = excel.ActiveWorkbook.ActiveSheet;

    workSheet.Cells[1, 1] = "ID";
    workSheet.Cells[1, 2] = "Name";
    workSheet.Cells[2, 1] = "1";
    workSheet.Cells[2, 2] = "One";
    workSheet.Cells[3, 1] = "2";
    workSheet.Cells[3, 2] = "Two";
```

```
    workBook.SaveAs("d:\\demo.xls",
        Excel.XlFileFormat.xlWorkbookNormal,
        AccessMode : Excel.XlSaveAsAccessMode.xlExclusive);

    workBook.Close(true);
    excel.Quit();
}
```

What this code does is as follows:

- It retrieves `System.Type` for the COM object identified by the programmatic identifier, `Excel.Application.16`, and creates an instance of it.

- It sets the `Visible` property of the Excel application to `true` so that you can see the window.

- It creates a workbook and adds some data to its active worksheet.

- It saves the document on a file called `demo.xls`.

- It closes the workbook and quits the Excel application.

In the last section of this chapter, we will look at how to use attributes with reflection services.

Attributes

Attributes provide meta-information about assemblies, types, and members. This meta-information is consumed by the compiler, the CLR, or tools that use reflection services to read them. Attributes are actually types that derive from the `System.Attribute` abstract class. The .NET frameworks provide a large number of attributes, but users can define their own.

Attributes are specified in square brackets, such as in `[SerializableAttribute]`. The naming convention for attributes is that the type names are always suffixed with the word `Attribute`. The C# language provides a syntactic shortcut that allows specifying the name of the attribute without the suffix, `Attribute`, such as in `[Serializable]`. However, this is only possible as long as the type name is properly suffixed according to this convention.

We will first look at some widely used system attributes in the next section.

System attributes

.NET Framework provides hundreds of attributes in different assemblies and namespaces. Enumerating them would be not only practically impossible but would also make little sense. However, the following table lists several attributes that you will often work with; some of them we have already seen in this book:

`Serializable`	It indicates that a type can be serializable.
`Obsolete`	It indicates that a type or member is obsolete and should not be used. When using an element marked so, the compiler emits either a warning or an error (depending on the attribute properties).
`DllImport`	It indicates that a method is exported from an unmanaged DLL and provides the necessary information to invoke it.
`StructLayout`	It allows controlling the physical layout of the fields of a struct or class in memory.
`MarshalAs`	It specifies how data should be marshaled between managed and unmanaged code.
`ComVisible`	It specifies whether managed types or their members should be visible to COM.
`Guid`	It is used to supply a globally unique identifier to a type or an assembly.
`Flags`	This indicates that an enumeration is a set of flags and should be treated as a bitfield.

On the other hand, it is often necessary or useful to create your own attribute classes. In the next section, we will look at user-defined attributes.

User-defined attributes

You can create your attributes to mark program elements. What you have to do is derive from `System.Attribute` and follow the naming convention of suffixing the type with the word `Attribute`. The following is an attribute called `Description` that contains a single property, called `Text`:

```
class DescriptionAttribute : Attribute
{
    public string Text { get; private set; }

    public DescriptionAttribute(string description)
    {
        Text = description;
    }
}
```

This attribute can be used to decorate any program element. In the following example, we can see this attribute used on a class, properties, and method parameters:

```
[Description("Main component of the car")]
class Engine
{
    public string Name { get; }

    [Description("cm³")]
    public int Capacity { get; }

    [Description("kW")]
    public double Power { get; }

    public Engine([Description("The name")] string name,
                  [Description("The capacity")] int capacity,
                  [Description("The power")] double power)
    {
        Name = name;
        Capacity = capacity;
        Power = power;
    }
}
```

Attributes can have *positional* and *named* parameters:

- Positional parameters are defined by the arguments of public instance constructors. The arguments of each such constructor define a set of named parameters.

- On the other hand, every non-static public field and property that is read-write defines a named parameter.

The following sample shows the Description attribute introduced earlier, modified so that a public property called Required is available:

```
class DescriptionAttribute : Attribute
{
    public string Text { get; private set; }
    public bool Required { get; set; }
    public DescriptionAttribute(string description)
    {
        Text = description;
    }
}
```

This property can be used as a named parameter in the declaration of an attribute on a program element. This is shown in the following example:

```
[Description("Main component of the car", Required = true)]
class Engine
{
}
```

Let's learn how to use attributes in the next section.

How to use attributes?

A program element can be marked with multiple attributes. This can be done in two equivalent ways:

- The first method (which is the most widely used because it is the most descriptive and clear) is to declare each attribute separately, inside a pair of square brackets. The following example shows how this is done:

```
[Serializable]
[Description("Main component of the car")]
[ComVisible(false)]
class Engine
{
}
```

- The alternative method is to declare multiple attributes inside the same pair of square brackets, separated by a comma. The following code is equivalent to the earlier one:

```
[Serializable,
 Description("Main component of the car"),
 ComVisible(false)]
class Engine
{
}
```

Let's see how to specify an attribute's target in the next section.

Attribute targets

By default, an attribute is applied to any program element that it precedes. However, it is possible to specify the target, such as a type, a method, and so on. This is done by marking the attribute type with another attribute called `AttributeUsage`. Apart from specifying the target, this attribute allows specifying whether the newly defined attribute can be applied multiple times and whether it can be inherited.

The following modified version of `DescriptionAttribute` indicates that it can only be used on classes, structs, methods, properties, and fields. In addition, it specifies that the attribute is inherited by derived classes and that it can be used multiple times on the same element:

```
[AttributeUsage(AttributeTargets.Class|
                AttributeTargets.Struct|
                AttributeTargets.Method|
                AttributeTargets.Property|
                AttributeTargets.Field,
                AllowMultiple = true,
                Inherited = true)]
class DescriptionAttribute : Attribute
{
    public string Text { get; private set; }
    public bool Required { get; set; }

    public DescriptionAttribute(string description)
    {
        Text = description;
    }
}
```

As a result of these changes, this attribute can no longer be used for method parameters, as shown in an earlier example. That would result in a compiler error.

The attributes we've used so far target program elements, such as types and methods. But assembly-level attributes are also possible. We look at these in the next section.

Assembly attributes

There are attributes that can target an assembly and specify information about the assembly. This information can be the identity (that is, the name, version, and culture) of the assembly, manifest information, the strong name, or others. These attributes are specified using the syntax [assembly : attribute]. These attributes are usually found in the AssemblyInfo.cs file generated for every .NET Framework project. The following is an example of such attributes:

```
[assembly: AssemblyTitle("project_name")]
[assembly: AssemblyDescription("")]
[assembly: AssemblyConfiguration("")]
[assembly: AssemblyCompany("")]
[assembly: AssemblyProduct("project_name")]
[assembly: AssemblyCopyright("Copyright © 2019")]
[assembly: AssemblyTrademark("")]
[assembly: AssemblyCulture("")]
[assembly: AssemblyVersion("1.0.0.0")]
[assembly: AssemblyFileVersion("1.0.0.0")]
```

Attributes are intended for reflection services. Now that we've seen how to create and use attributes, let's see how to use them in reflection.

Attributes in reflection

Attributes have little value by themselves until somebody reflects on them and performs specific actions based on the meaning of the attributes and their values. The System.Type type as well as other types from the System.Reflection namespace have an overloaded method called GetCustomAttributes() that retrieves the attributes a particular program element is marked with. One overload takes the type of the attribute so that it only returns instances of that type; the other does not and returns all the attributes.

The following example retrieves all of the instances of the Description attribute, first from the Engine type and then from all of the properties of the type, and displays the description text in the console:

```
var e = new Engine("M270 Turbo", 1600, 75.0);
var type = e.GetType();

var attributes = type.
GetCustomAttributes(typeof(DescriptionAttribute),
                                    true);

if (attributes != null)
{
```

```
        foreach (DescriptionAttribute attr in attributes)
        {
            Console.WriteLine(attr.Text);
        }
    }
}

var properties = type.GetProperties();
foreach (var property in properties)
{
    var pattributes =
      property.GetCustomAttributes(
          typeof(DescriptionAttribute), false);
    if (attributes != null)
    {
        foreach (DescriptionAttribute attr in pattributes)
        {
            Console.WriteLine(
              $"{property.Name} [{attr.Text}]");
        }
    }
}
```

The output of this program is as follows:

```
Main component of the car
Capacity [cm3]
Power [kW]
```

Summary

In this chapter, we looked at reflection services, how to load assemblies at runtime, and querying meta-information about types. We also learned how to execute code dynamically using both system reflection on one hand and the DLR and the dynamic type on the other hand. The DLR provides dynamic features to C# and enables interoperability with dynamic languages in a simple manner. The last topic we covered in this chapter was attributes. We learned what the common system attributes are and how to create your own types as well as how to use them in reflection.

In the next chapter, we will focus on concurrency and parallelism.

Test what you learned

1. What is the unit of deployment in .NET and what does it contain?

2. What is reflection? What benefits does it provide?

3. What .NET type exposes metadata about types? How can you create an instance of this type?

4. What is the difference between public and private assemblies?

5. In .NET Framework, in what context can an assembly be loaded?

6. What is early binding? What about late binding? What benefits does the latter provide?

7. What is the Dynamic Language Runtime?

8. What is the dynamic type and what are the typical scenarios where it is used?

9. What are attributes and how do you specify them in code?

10. How do you create user-defined attributes?

12
Multithreading and Asynchronous Programming

Since the very first personal computer, we have benefitted from the constant increase of CPU power—a phenomenon that heavily influenced developers' choices of tools, languages, and application design, while historically not putting much effort into programming to take advantage of multithreading.

On the hardware side, the prediction made by Moore's law that the density of the transistors in processors should double every 2 years, thus providing more computing power, worked for some decades, but we can already observe it slowing down. Even if the CPU manufacturers started producing multi-core CPUs roughly 20 years ago, the ability to execute code concurrently was primarily used by the **operating systems (OSes)** to make executing multiple processes smoother.

This doesn't mean that code was unable to leverage the power of concurrency, but just that only a small quantity of applications fully embraced the *multithreading paradigm*. The primary reason for this is because all the code we write is executed sequentially from a single thread provided by the OS infrastructure unless we explicitly request the creation of other threads and orchestrate their execution.

This trend is mostly due to the fact that many programming languages do not provide constructs to automatically generate multithreading code. This is because it is extremely difficult to provide the semantics that fit any use case and efficiently take advantage of the concurrent processing capabilities offered by modern CPUs.

On the other hand, there are times where we don't really need to execute the application code concurrently, but we can't continue the execution because it is necessary to wait for some outstanding I/O operation. At the same time, blocking the code execution is also not acceptable and therefore a different strategy is required. This domain of problems is categorized under *asynchronous programming* and requires slightly different tools.

In this chapter, we will learn the basics of multithreading and asynchronous programming and look specifically at the following:

- What is a thread?
- Creating threads in .NET
- Understanding synchronization primitives
- The task paradigm

By the end of this chapter, you will be familiar with multithreading techniques, using primitives to synchronize code execution, tasks, continuations, and cancellation tokens. You will also understand what the potentially dangerous operations are and the basic patterns to use to avoid problems when sharing resources among multiple threads.

We will now begin familiarizing ourselves with the basic concepts needed to operate with multithreading and asynchronous programming.

What is a thread?

Every OS provides abstractions to allow multiple programs to share the same hardware resources, such as CPU, memory, and input and output devices. The process is one of those abstractions, providing a reserved virtual address space that its running code cannot escape from. This basic sandbox avoids the process code interfering with other processes, establishing the basis for a balanced ecosystem. The process has nothing to do with code execution, but primarily with memory.

The abstraction that takes care of code execution is the **thread**. Every process has at least one thread, but any process code may request the creation of more threads that will all share the same virtual address space, delimited by the owning process. Running multiple threads in a single process is roughly equivalent to a group of woodworking friends working on the same project –they need to be coordinated, paying attention to each other's progress, and taking care not to block each other's activity.

All modern OSes offer the preemptive multitasking strategy as opposed to cooperative multitasking. This means that a special component of the OS schedules the amount of time each thread can run, without needing any cooperation from the running code.

> **Tip**
>
> Earlier version of Windows, such as Windows 3.x and Windows 9x, used cooperative multitasking, meaning that any application could hang the entire operating system with a simple infinite loop. This was mostly because of CPU power and capabilities limitations. All the later operating systems, such as Windows versions starting from the very first **NT 3.1 Advanced Server** and all the Unix-like OSes, have always used preemptive multitasking, making the OS more robust and providing a better user experience.

You can see the number of threads used in each running process with either the Task Manager, Process Explorer, or Process Hacker tools. You will immediately notice that many applications, including all the .NET ones, use more than one single thread. This information doesn't tell us much about how the application is designed because modern runtimes such as the .NET CLR use background threads for internal processing, such as the **garbage collector**, the **finalization queue**, and so on.

> **Tip**
>
> In order to see the number of threads used by the running processes, open the **Task Manager** (*Ctrl + Shift + Esc*), click on the **Details** tab, and add the **Threads** column. Columns can be added by right-clicking one of the grid headers, selecting the **Select Columns** menu item, and finally checking the **Threads** voice.

The following screenshot shows a C++ console application where the user's code uses a single thread and the other three threads are created by the C++ runtime:

Name	PID	Status	CPU	Memory (a...	Threads
NativeConsole.exe	38588	Running	00	504 K	4

Figure 12.1 – The Task Manager showing NativeConsole.exe process with four threads

The namespace containing the primitives dealing with threads is `System.Threading` but later in this chapter, we will also introduce **Tasks**, which are a part of the `System.Threading.Tasks` namespace.

When a .NET application starts, the .NET runtime prepares our process, allocating memory and creating some threads, including the one that will spin the execution of our code, starting from the `Main` entry point.

The following console application accesses the current thread and prints the current thread `Id` on the screen:

```
static void Main(string[] args)
{
    Console.WriteLine($"Current Thread Id: {Thread.
CurrentThread.ManagedThreadId}");
    Console.ReadKey();
}
```

The `ManagedThreadId` property is important when diagnosing multithreading code because it correlates the execution of some code with a specific thread.

This `Id` can only be used within the running process and is different from the OS thread identifier. Should you ever require access to the native identifier, you need to use interoperability, as demonstrated in the following Windows-only snippet:

```
[DllImport("Kernel32.dll")]
private static extern int GetCurrentThreadId();
static void Main(string[] args)
{
    Console.WriteLine($"Current Thread Id: {Thread.
CurrentThread.ManagedThreadId}");
    Console.WriteLine($"Current Native Thread Id:
{GetCurrentThreadId()}");
    Console.ReadKey();
}
```

The native `Id` is the one that you can see in **Process Explorer** and the **Process Hacker** tools and is the one needed to interop with other native APIs. In the following screenshot, you can see the results printed in the console on the left, and the Process Hacker threads window on the right:

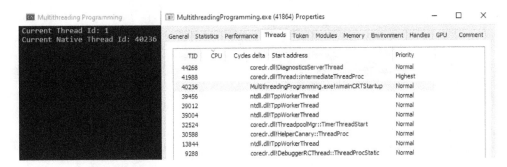

Figure 12.2 – The console application side by side with Process Hacker
showing the same native thread Id

Threads can also be created from either the OS, the .NET runtime, or some library
without our code explicitly requesting it. For example, the following class shows
a `FileSystemWatcher` class in action and prints the `ManagedThreadId` property for
each filesystem operation: the `Run` method prints the ID associated with the main thread,
while the `Wacher_Deleted` and `Watcher_Created` methods are executed from
a thread created by the OS or the infrastructure:

```
public class FileWatcher
{
    private FileSystemWatcher _watcher;
    public void Run()
    {
        var path = Path.GetFullPath(".");
        Console.WriteLine($"Observing changes in path:
{path}");
        _watcher = new FileSystemWatcher(path, "*.txt");
        _watcher.Created += Watcher_Created;
        _watcher.Deleted += Watcher_Deleted;
        Console.WriteLine($"TID: {Thread.CurrentThread.
ManagedThreadId}");
        _watcher.EnableRaisingEvents = true;
    }

    private void Watcher_Deleted(object sender,
FileSystemEventArgs e)
    {
        Console.WriteLine($"Deleted occurred in TID: {Thread.
CurrentThread.ManagedThreadId}");
    }

    private void Watcher_Created(object sender,
```

```
FileSystemEventArgs e)
    {
        Console.WriteLine($"Created occurred in TID: {Thread.
CurrentThread.ManagedThreadId}");
    }
}
```

You can experiment with this code by creating a console application and adding the
following code to the `Main` method:

```
var fw = new FileWatcher();
fw.Run();
Console.ReadKey();
```

Now, if you start creating and deleting some `.txt` files in the console folder, you will see
something like this:

```
Observing changes in path: C:\projects\Watch\bin\Debug\
netcoreapp3.1
TID: 1
Created occurred in TID: 5
Created occurred in TID: 7
Deleted occurred in TID: 5
Deleted occurred in TID: 5
```

The `TID` numbers you see will likely change every time you rerun the application: they are
neither predictable nor used in the same order.

We will now see how we can create a new thread, execute some code concurrently, and
examine the main characteristics of a thread.

Creating threads in .NET

Creating a raw thread is something that mostly makes sense only when you have a long-
running operation that depends on the CPU alone. As an example, let's say we want to
compute prime numbers, without really caring about the possible optimizations:

```
public class Primes : IEnumerable<long>
{
    public Primes(long Max = long.MaxValue)
    {
        this.Max = Max;
    }
```

```
    public long Max { get; private set; }
    IEnumerator IEnumerable.GetEnumerator() =>
((IEnumerable<long>)this).GetEnumerator();

    public IEnumerator<long> GetEnumerator()
    {
        yield return 1;
        bool bFlag;
        long start = 2;
        while (start < Max)
        {
            bFlag = false;
            var number = start;
            for (int i = 2; i < number; i++)
            {
                if (number % i == 0)
                {
                    bFlag = true;
                    break;
                }
            }

            if (!bFlag)
            {
                yield return number;
            }
            start++;
        }
    }
}
}
```

The `Primes` class implements `IEnumerable<long>` so that we can easily enumerate the prime numbers in a **foreach** statement. The `Max` argument is used to limit the resulting sequence, which is otherwise restricted by `long.MaxValue`.

Calling the preceding code is very easy to do but, as the calculation can take a very long time, it totally blocks the executing thread:

```
using System;
using System.Collections.Generic;
using System.Linq;
using System.Runtime.InteropServices;
```

```
using System.Text;
using System.Threading;
// namespace and class declaration omitted for clarity
Console.WriteLine("Start primes");
foreach (var n in new Primes(1000000))   {  /* ...  */ }
Console.WriteLine("End primes"); // the wait is too long!
```

What happens here is that the main thread is busy calculating the prime numbers. Thanks to preemptive multitasking, this thread will be interrupted by the OS scheduler to give other process' threads the opportunity to run their code. However, since our application has no other threads executing application code, we can only wait.

In any desktop application, be it a console or a GUI, the user experience is frustrating as any interaction with the mouse and keyboard is *blocked*. Even worse, the GUIs cannot even redraw the content of the screen as the only thread was stolen by the prime number's computation.

The very first step is to move the blocking code into a separate method so that we can execute it in a new and separate thread:

```
private void Worker(object param)
{
    PrintThreadInfo(Thread.CurrentThread);
    foreach (var n in new Primes(1000000))
    {
        Thread.Sleep(100);
    }
    Console.WriteLine("Computation ended!");
}
```

The Thread.Sleep method is used only to make some observations on the CPU usage. Then, Sleep tells the OS to suspend the current thread execution for the given amount of time, expressed in *milliseconds*. Generally, calling Sleep is not recommended in production code because it prevents that thread from being reused. Later in this chapter, we will discover better ways to insert delays in our code.

The `Worker` method has nothing special and it may optionally get an object parameter that can be used to initialize the local variables. Instead of invoking it directly, we just ask the infrastructure to invoke it in the context of a new thread:

```
Console.WriteLine("Start primes");
PrintThreadInfo(Thread.CurrentThread);
var t1 = new Thread(Worker);
//t1.IsBackground = true; // try with/without this line
t1.Start();
Console.WriteLine("Primes calculation is happening in
background");
```

As you can see from the preceding code, the `Thread` object is created but the thread is not started yet. We have to explicitly call the `Start` method to make it happen. This is important because the `Thread` class has other important properties that can be set only before the thread is started.

Finally, the main thread's details are printed by using the `PrintThreadInfo` method. Please note that some properties are not always available. For this reason, we have to check whether the thread is running before printing `Priority` or `IsBackground`. Since the `ThreadState` enumeration has the `Flags` attribute and the `Running` state is zero, the official documentation (`https://docs.microsoft.com/en-us/dotnet/api/system.threading.threadstate?view=netframework-4.8#remarks`) reminds us to check if the `Stopped` and `Unstarted` bits are not set:

```
private void PrintThreadInfo(Thread t)
{
    var sb = new StringBuilder();
    var state = t.ThreadState;
    sb.Append($"Id:{t.ManagedThreadId} Name:{t.Name}
State:{state} ");
    if ((state & (ThreadState.Stopped | ThreadState.Unstarted))
== 0)
    {
        sb.Append($"Priority:{t.Priority} IsBackground:{t.
IsBackground}");
    }

    Console.WriteLine(sb.ToString());
}
```

The result of the executing the preceding code is as follows:

```
Start primes
Id:1 Name: State:Running Priority:Normal IsBackground:False
Primes calculation is happening in background
Id:5 Name: State:Running Priority:Normal IsBackground:False
```

Even if this is a trivial example, we must observe a few things:

- The first is that we have no guarantees about the *output order* regarding the Primes calculation ... and Id:5 ... lines. They may appear in *reversed order*. In order to obtain a *deterministic behavior*, you need to apply a synchronization technique that we will discuss later in the *Understanding synchronization primitives* section.

- Another important consideration is the *CPU usage*. If you open **Task Manager**, under the **Performance** tab, you can set the view to show a separate graph for each logical CPU. In the following screenshot, you can see a four-core CPU that has eight logical cores (thanks to the Intel Hyper-Threading technology!). You may also want to show kernel times (shown in a darker color) because the kernel mode only executes code for the OS and drivers, while the user mode (shown in a lighter color) just executes the code we write. This distinction will allow you to immediately see which application code is being executed:

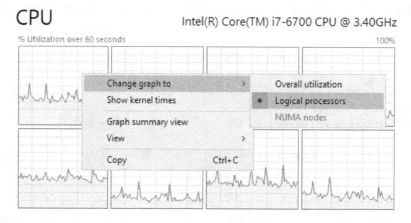

Figure 12.3 – The Task Manager showing all the logical processors

If we now execute our code without the Sleep call, we will see that one of the CPUs will show a higher amount of CPU usage as one thread keeps consuming the full amount of execution time granted by the OS. This single thread impacts the total (100%) amount of CPU time by *100% / 8 CPUs = 12.5%*. In fact, during the computation, the **Details** tab of **Task Manager** will show your process consuming roughly 12% of the CPU:

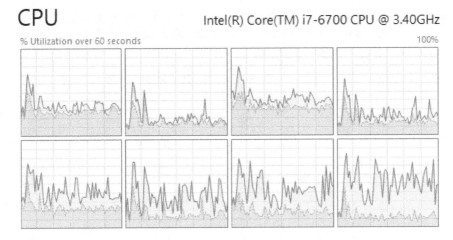

Figure 12.4 – The Task Manager showing the execution time distributed across
all the available logical CPUs

The thread computation is *distributed* across multiple logical CPUs. Every time the OS
interrupts the thread, schedules some other work of another process, and then gets back
to our thread, the thread may be executed on any other logical CPU.

Just as an experiment, you can force the execution to take place on a specific logical CPU
by adding the following code at the very beginning of the `Worker` method:

```
var threads = System.Diagnostics.Process.GetCurrentProcess().
Threads;
var processThread = threads
    .OfType<System.Diagnostics.ProcessThread>()
    .Where(pt => pt.Id == GetCurrentThreadId())
    .Single();
processThread.ProcessorAffinity = (IntPtr)2; // CPU 2
```

This code requires the following declaration inside the class:

```
[DllImport("Kernel32.dll")]
private static extern int GetCurrentThreadId();
```

Those new lines of code retrieve a list of all the `ProcessThread` objects for our process
and then filter the `ProcessThread` object whose native ID matches the one that is
doing the execution.

After setting `ProcessorAffinity`, the new execution fully loads the logical CPU 2 with our computation, as shown in the following screenshot (the light blue section of CPU 2 entirely fills the rectangle):

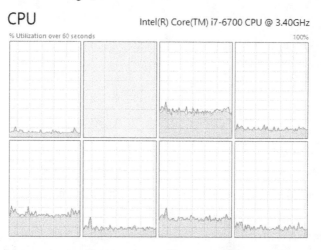

Figure 12.5 – The Task Manager showing CPU 2 fully loaded with the execution of the sample code

Immediately before starting the thread, we have the possibility to shape the thread characteristics by setting one or more of these properties:

- The `Priority` property is used from the OS scheduler to decide the slot of time the thread can run. Giving it a high priority will reduce the amount of time the thread stays suspended.

- The `Name` property is useful when debugging because you can see it in the Visual Studio Thread window.

- We briefly discussed the `ThreadState` property, which can assume many different values. One of them—`WaitSleepJoin`—represents a thread that is inside a `Wait` method or sleeping.

- The `CurrentCulture` and `CurrentUICulture` properties are read by certain APIs that are *region-dependent*. For example, when you convert a number or a date into a string (using the `ToString` method) or the `Parse` static method for the opposite conversion, the current culture settings are used.

- The `IsBackground` property specifies whether the thread should prevent the process from terminating when it is still active. When true, the process will not wait for the thread to finish its work. In our example, if you set it to true, then you can end the process by pressing any key.

You may have noticed the `Thread` class has the `Abort` method. It should never be used because it may corrupt the state of the memory or prevent the correct disposal of managed resources.

The correct way to terminate a thread is to exit normally from the method it initially started. In our case, this is the `Worker` method. A simple `return` statement is all you need.

We have seen how to create a thread manually, but there is a more convenient way to run some code in a separate thread—the `ThreadPool` class.

Using the ThreadPool class

We spent some time investigating the characteristics of threads and this was indeed very useful because the thread is the fundamental code-execution building block. Manually creating a thread is correct as long as it is executing CPU-dependent and long-running code. Anyway, since the cost of the thread is dependent on the OS, it is wiser to create an adequate amount of threads and reuse them. Their number is very dependent on the available logical CPUs and other factors, and this is the reason why it is far better to use the `ThreadPool` abstraction.

The static `ThreadPool` class provides a pool of threads that can be used to run some concurrent computation. As soon as the code terminates, the thread comes back to the pool, becoming available for a future operation without needing to be destroyed and recreated.

> **Tip**
> Be warned not to modify any property of the thread picked from `ThreadPool`. For example, if you modify `ProcessorAffinity`, this setting will continue to be valid, even if the thread is reused for different purposes. If you need to modify the thread's properties, then manual creation is still the best choice.

Running our `Worker` using the `ThreadPool` class is straightforward:

```
Console.WriteLine("Start primes");
PrintThreadInfo(Thread.CurrentThread);
ThreadPool.QueueUserWorkItem(Worker);
Console.WriteLine("Primes calculation is happening in
background");
```

Please note that the delegate parameter accepted by the `Thread` class constructor and `QueueUserWorkItem` are different, but the one taking an object parameter is compatible with both.

We have seen how to start a parallel computation, but we are still not able to orchestrate their execution. Should an algorithm be run on a different thread, we need to be aware of its termination and how to access the result.

Tip

`ThreadPool` is used from many popular libraries, including the base class library shipped with the .NET runtime. Whenever you need to access a resource requiring an I/O operation that may take a while to succeed or fail, most of the time, `ThreadPool` comes into play. Those resources include, among others, databases, filesystem objects, or anything that can be accessed through the network.

Every time you need to access a resource concurrently, be it a resource retrieved by means of an I/O operation or an instance of an object in memory, you may need to synchronize its access. In the next section, we will see how to synchronize thread execution.

Understanding synchronization primitives

Every time you write single-threaded code, any method execution occurs sequentially and requires no special action from the developer. On the other hand, when some code is executed on a separate thread, synchronization is needed to ensure that we avoid two dangerous concurrency conditions—**race** and **deadlock**. These categories of problems must be carefully avoided during design because their detection is difficult and they may occur occasionally.

A **race condition** is a situation where two or more threads access an unprotected shared resource or when the threads' executions behave differently, depending on the timing and the underlying process architecture.

A *deadlock condition* happens when two or more threads have a circular dependency on each other to access a resource.

The general recommendations when writing some code that may be executed from multiple threads are as follows:

- Avoid shared resources as much as possible. Their access must be synchronized with a lock that will affect the execution performance.

- The stack is your friend. Every time you call a method, the local stack is private, ensuring the local variables will not be shared with other callers and threads.

- Every time you need to share a resource among multiple threads, use the documentation to verify whether it is thread-safe or not. Whenever it is not thread-safe, a lock must protect the resource or the code sequence.

- Even when the shared resource is thread-safe, you must consider whether a number of statements need to be executed atomically to guarantee their reliability.

The thread library has many primitives available to protect the resources, but we will focus more on those that are more likely to be used in the asynchronous context, which is the most important topic that will be covered in this chapter.

There are two sets of synchronization primitives:

- The ones implemented in *kernel mode* by the OS

- The ones in *user mode* provided by the .NET class library

The distinction is very important because every time you transition to the kernel mode with a system call, the OS has to save the local call and stack, which will be restored right after, impacting the performance of the operation. The advantage of kernel mode primitives is the ability to give them a name and make them shared across processes, providing a powerful machine-wide synchronization mechanism.

The following example shows two threads from `ThreadPool` printing `Ping` and `Pong`. Each thread synchronizes with the other by waiting for the matching `ManualResetEventSlim`:

```
public void PingPong()
{
    bool quit = false;
    var ping = new ManualResetEventSlim(false);
    var pong = new ManualResetEventSlim(false);
    ThreadPool.QueueUserWorkItem(_ =>
    {
        Console.WriteLine($"Ping thread: {Thread.CurrentThread.
ManagedThreadId}");
        while (!quit)
```

```
        {
            pong.Wait();
            pong.Reset();
            Console.WriteLine("Ping");
            Thread.Sleep(1000);
            ping.Set();
        }
    });
    ThreadPool.QueueUserWorkItem(_ =>
    {
        Console.WriteLine($"Pong thread: {Thread.CurrentThread.
ManagedThreadId}");
        while (!quit)
        {
            ping.Wait();
            ping.Reset();
            Console.WriteLine("Pong");
            Thread.Sleep(1000);
            pong.Set();
        }
    });
    pong.Set();
    Console.ReadKey();
    quit = true;
}
```

After having created the two events, the two threads are run and print the ID of the thread they are running on. Inside those threads, each execution is suspended in the Wait method, which avoids the thread consuming any CPU power. At the end of the listing, the pong.Set method starts the game and unblocks the first thread. Since the events are *manual*, they must be reset to the unsignaled state for the next hit. At this point, a message is printed, a delay simulates some hard work and, finally, the other event is signaled, which will cause the second thread to unblock.

Alternatively, we can use the `ManualResetEvent` kernel event, whose usage is very similar. For example, in place of `Wait`, it has the `WaitOne` method. But were we to use these events in a high-performance synchronization algorithm, there would be a huge difference. The following table shows a comparison of the two synchronization primitives measured with the popular Benchmark.NET micro-benchmark library. Both tests simply call `Set()`, followed by the `Reset()` method:

Method	Mean	Error	StdDev
KernelModeEvent	1,892.11 ns	24.463 ns	22.883 ns
UserModeEvent	25.67 ns	0.320 ns	0.283 ns

There is a difference of roughly two orders of magnitude, which is not negligible at all.

Beyond the ability to use kernel events to synchronize code running in different processes, they can be used in conjunction with the powerful `WaitHandle.WaitAny` and `WaitAll` methods, as shown in the following example:

```
public void WaitMultiple()
{
    var one = new ManualResetEvent(false);
    var two = new ManualResetEvent(false);

    ThreadPool.QueueUserWorkItem(_ =>
    {
        Thread.Sleep(3000);
        one.Set();
    });
    ThreadPool.QueueUserWorkItem(_ =>
    {
        Thread.Sleep(2000);
        two.Set();
    });

    int signaled = WaitHandle.WaitAny(
        new WaitHandle[] { one, two }, 500);
    switch(signaled)
    {
        case 0:
            Console.WriteLine("One was set");
            break;
        case 1:
            Console.WriteLine("Two was set");
            break;
```

```
            case WaitHandle.WaitTimeout:
                Console.WriteLine("Time expired");
                break;
    }
}
```

You can play with the three timeouts expressed in milliseconds to see the different results. The main idea is to exit the wait as soon as any of the events or the timeout expires, whichever comes first.

> **Tip**
>
> The kernel objects of the Windows OS can be all used inside the wait primitives. For example, if you want to wait for multiple processes to exit, you can just use the `WaitHandle` primitives, shown in the preceding code block, with the process handles.

We've only just scratched the surface, but the official documentation has many samples showing various synchronization objects in action. Instead, we will continue to focus on those that are more relevant for this book, such as accessing a shared resource from multiple threads.

In the following example, we have a shared variable called `_shared`, a `ManualResetEvent` object that is used to start all the threads together, and a simple object. The `Shared` property makes use of `Thread.Sleep`, causing an explicit thread context switch on the setter. The switch is what normally happens when the OS scheduler preemptively gives control to another thread in the system. It's not a trick; it just increases the probability that the getter and the setter are not executed consecutively by each thread:

```
int _shared;
int Shared
{
    get => _shared;
    set { Thread.Sleep(1); _shared = value; }
}
ManualResetEvent evt = new ManualResetEvent(false);
object sync = new object();
```

The following method initializes the shared variable to 0 and creates 10 threads, all executing the same code in the lambda:

```
public void SharedResource()
{
    Shared = 0;
    var loop = 100;
    var threads = new List<Thread>();
    for (int i = 0; i < loop; i++)
    {
        var t = new Thread(() =>
        {
            evt.WaitOne();
            //lock (sync)
            {
                Shared++;
            }
        });
        t.Start();
        threads.Add(t);
    }

    evt.Set(); // make all threads start together
    foreach (var t in threads)
        t.Join();    // wait for the thread to finish
    Console.WriteLine($"actual:{Shared}, expected:{loop}");
}
```

All the threads start immediately and block the execution in the WaitOne event that is unblocked by the Set method. This gives more chances for many threads to execute the code in the lambda with the same timing. Finally, we call Join to wait for the end of the execution of each thread and print the results.

The synchronization problem of this code exists because the threads will read a value, increment the number in a CPU register, and write back the result in the variable. Since many threads will read the same value, the value written back to the variable is old and its real *current* value gets lost.

By uncommenting the lock statement, we instruct the compiler to surround the statements in the curly braces with a **Critical Section**, the fastest user mode synchronization object available. This results in serializing the access to that code, which has a very significant impact on the performance that is necessary and unavoidable.

The empty object instance we created at the beginning should not change; otherwise, different threads would wait for different critical sections. Please note that the lock argument can be any reference type. For example, should you need to protect a collection, you can lock it directly without the help of an external object. Anyway, in our example, Shared is a value type and must be protected with the help of a separate reference type.

If you replace the Shared property with a simple field, the problem will be less likely to occur. Also, the compiler configuration (debug versus release) will make a great difference because *inlining* and other optimizations make it even more likely that a thread context switch can't happen when accessing a field or a simple property. The physical hardware configuration and the CPU architecture are other variables that may greatly influence the outcome of these tests.

> **Tip**
> Unit testing is *not appropriate* to ensure the absence of issues such as race conditions or deadlocks. Also, be aware that virtual machines are the worst environment to test concurrent code in because the scheduler is more predictable than an OS running on the physical hardware.

We have seen how we can ensure that a number of statements are executed atomically, with no interference. But if it was just for ensuring an atomic increment of the underlying _shared field, there is a more convenient tool—the Interlocked class.

Interlocked is a static class that exposes a few useful methods to ensure the atomicity of certain operations. For example, instead of the lock statement, we could use the following code, which is much faster, even if limited to the operations exposed by Interlocked. The following code shows how to atomically increment the _shared variable:

```
Interlocked.Increment(ref _shared);
```

Among other things, we can use it for writing a variable and getting back the old value atomically (the Exchange method) or reading variables whose size is larger than the available native registers (the Read method).

We have seen why synchronization is needed and what the main tools are that we can use to protect against these concurrent access problems. But now, it is time to introduce an abstraction that will make every developer's life easier—the task paradigm.

The task paradigm

Concurrency is primarily about designing algorithms with very loosely coupled units of work, which is often not possible or extends the complexity beyond any possible benefit.

Asynchronous programming is, instead, related to the asynchronous nature of the OS and the devices, whether because they fire events or because it takes time to fulfill the requested operation. Every time the user moves the mouse, types keys on the keyboard, or retrieves some data from the internet, the OS presents data to our process in a separate thread and our code must be ready to consume it.

One of the simplest possible examples is loading a text file from disk and computing the string length, which can be different from the file length, depending on the encoding:

```
public int ReadLength(string filename)
{
    string content = File.ReadAllText(filename);
    return content.Length;
}
```

As soon as you invoke this method, the calling thread gets blocked until the OS and the library completes reading it. The operation may be lightning-fast or very slow, depending on its size and technology. The text file may be on **Network-Attached Storage (NAS)**, a local disk, a corrupted USB key, or on a remote server accessed through a **Virtual Private Network (VPN)**.

In the context of a desktop application, any blocking thread will cause an unpleasant user experience because the main thread is already responsible for redrawing the user interface and responding to the events coming from the input devices.

Server applications are no different because any blocking thread is a resource that cannot be used efficiently with other requests, preventing the application from scaling and serving other users.

For decades, the solution to this problem was to execute the long-lasting code by manually creating a separate thread, but more recently, the .NET runtimes introduced the task paradigm and the C# language introduced the `async` and `await` keywords. Since then, the whole .NET library has been revised to embrace this paradigm, providing methods that return task-based operations.

The Task Library, available in the `System.Threading.Tasks` namespace, and the language integration provide an abstraction that dramatically simplifies the management of asynchronous operations. A task represents a unit of work that performs a well-defined job. No matter whether you deal with concurrency or asynchronous events, a task defines a given job and its life cycle, going from its creation to its completion, the options for which include success, failure, or cancellation.

Tasks can be composed by defining what other tasks should be executed right after a given operation. The chained task is called **continuation** and is automatically scheduled from the libraries by means of the **Task Scheduler**.

By default, the Task Library provides a default implementation (the `TaskScheduler.Default` static property), which most developers will never need to dig into. The default implementation orchestrates the task's execution using `ThreadPool` and uses the *work-stealing* technique to redistribute the task queue over multiple threads to provide load balancing and to prevent tasks from being stalled for too long. Be aware that this default implementation is smart enough to eventually make the decision to schedule the execution of tasks directly on the main thread instead of picking one from the pool. The bravest can experiment with the creation of custom schedulers to change the scheduling strategy, but it is something not many developers really need to do.

Later, in the *Synchronization context* section, we will talk about **synchronization context**, which allows continuations to be executed in the calling thread and avoids the need to use the synchronization primitives described in the previous section.

Let's begin investigating tasks with the asynchronous version of reading a text file:

```
Task<string> content = File.ReadAllTextAsync(filename);
```

This new version of the method *immediately completes* and, instead of returning the content of the file, returns an object representing the *ongoing* operation.

Since we just initiated the operation that didn't complete yet, the steps required to manage the completion are as follows:

1. Refactor out the code following the asynchronous operation (getting the string length) in a separate method. This method is equivalent to the old-style callback that mustn't be called before the asynchronous operation has completed.

2. Monitor the ongoing task and provide a notification when it has completed or failed.

3. Once completed, retrieve the result and synchronize the execution (by means of **synchronization context**) on the main thread, or throw an exception if something has gone wrong. This step is crucial if we don't want to mess with potential race conditions.

4. Invoke the callback that we refactored out at the first point.

Of course, we don't have to manually manage all this machinery. The first interesting advantage of the Task Library is its support for continuations, which allow the developer to specify the code to be executed as soon as the task completes successfully:

```
public Task<int> ReadLengthAsync(string filename)
{
    Task<int> lengthTask = File.ReadAllTextAsync(filename)
        .ContinueWith(t => t.Result.Length);
    return lengthTask;
}
```

This new version is better than creating threads and manually writing the synchronization code, even if it can be further improved. The ContinueWith method contains the code that determines the other code to be executed as soon as the file has been successfully read.

The t variable contains the task, which is either failed or completed successfully. If it was successful, t.Result contains the string content obtained from the ReadAllTextAsync method.

Anyway, we still don't have the length; we just expressed how to retrieve the length in the *future* once the result of ReadAllTextAsync has been retrieved. This is the reason why the lengthTask variable is a Task<int>, that is, the promise of an integer.

Tasks and continuations are the building blocks that I strongly recommend experimenting with because there are times they need to be managed directly.

But the C# language also introduced two precious keywords that further simplify the code we need to write. The await keyword is used to indicate that the result of the operation and everything that comes after it is part of a continuation.

Thanks to the `await` keyword, the compiler refactors and generates new **Intermediate Language (IL)** code to provide the appropriate management of asynchronous operations and the continuation. The final code to asynchronously load the content of the file and return the string length is as follows:

```
public async Task<int> ReadLengthAsync(string filename)
{
    string content = await File.ReadAllTextAsync(filename);
    return content.Length;
}
```

The highlighted portions of code are refactored by the compiler with more than just a continuation. The compiler generates a *class* to take care of the state machine responsible for monitoring the task progress, and a method for calling the appropriate code or throwing an exception, as soon as the state of the task changes.

> **Tip**
> If you want to dig into more details on the generated code, you can use the **ILSpy** tool (`https://github.com/icsharpcode/ILSpy/releases`) and see the generated IL code.

Apparently, the compiler could get rid of the promise and let us work on the returned content, right? Not really – this code is refactored and the code we wrote is an artifact expressing our expectations rather than what normally and sequentially happens in a method.

In fact, the preceding code looks contradictory, as the `content.Length` integer will only be available in the future, but we return it directly from a method with the return type of `Task<int>`.

This is where the `async` keyword comes into play:

- The `async` keyword is a modifier that must be specified every time we want to use `await` inside a method.
- The `async` keyword informs us that the `return` statement specifies a future object or value. In our case, we return `int` but `async` informs us that it is really a `Task<int>`.
- Should an `async` method return `void`, the return type becomes the non-generic `Task`.

We now have a method that is processing the file asynchronously, but we had to change the signature from `int` to `Task<int>`.

When you write a lambda using the `await` keyword in its body, the `async` keyword is required as well. For example, let's look at the following code:

```
Func<int, int, Task<int>> adder =
    async (a, b) => await AddAsync(a, b);
```

Using `async` on a method implies that all the callers must embrace the task paradigm as well because otherwise, they could not know when the operation completes.

Synchronous implementations of asynchronous methods

We have seen how the task paradigm impacts the method signature and we know how important a method signature is. When it appears on a public API or in interfaces, it is a contract that, in most cases, we can't change. From a design perspective, it can be very valuable for anticipating the possibility of a given method being implemented with tasks, but there are cases where asynchronicity is not needed.

For those cases, the `Task` class exposes a static method allowing us to directly build a completed task with or without results. In the following example, the asynchronous method synchronously returns a completed task:

```
public Task WriteEmptyJsonObjectAsync(string filename)
{
    File.WriteAllText(filename, "{}");
    return Task.CompletedTask;
}
```

The `CompletedTask` property is created only once for the entire application domain; therefore, it is extremely lightweight and should not be any cause for concern regarding performance.

If, instead, we need to return a value, we can use the static `FromResult` method, which internally creates a new completed `Task` every time it is invoked:

```
public Task<int> AddAsync(int a, int b)
{
    return Task.FromResult(a + b);
}
```

Creating an object every time we add two numbers is definitely a performance concern because it directly impacts the amount of work the garbage collector has to do. For this reason, more recently, Microsoft introduced the `ValueTask` classes.

Occasionally asynchronous methods

The ValueTask immutable struct is a convenient wrapper around either a synchronous result or Task. This further abstraction is meant to simplify those cases where the method is required to have an asynchronous signature, but its implementation is just occasionally asynchronous.

The AddAsync method we defined with tasks in the previous section can easily be converted to use the ValueTask struct instead:

```
public ValueTask<int> AddAsync(int a, int b)
{
    return new ValueTask<int>(a + b);
}
```

The overhead of using Task is clear for a trivial sum; therefore, whenever such a method should be called in a hot path (some performance-critical code), it would certainly be a performance concern.

Anyway, there are cases where you may need to convert ValueTask into Task in order to benefit from all the utilities we will continue to discuss in the rest of this chapter. The conversion is available with the AsTask method, which returns the wrapped task, if any, or creates a fresh new Task if not.

Breaking the task chain – blocking the thread

Given a task, if you call the Wait method or access the Result getter property, they will block the thread execution until the task is either completed or canceled. The rationale behind the task paradigm is to avoid blocking threads so that they can be reused for other purposes. But blocking may also provoke very bad side effects.

Since the default source for threads in asynchronous programming is ThreadPool (should it exhaust its threads), any further request will be automatically blocked. This phenomenon is known as **thread starvation**.

The general advice is to avoid waiting and use the await keyword or the continuations to complete some work.

Manually creating a task

There are times when a library does not offer an asynchronous behavior but you don't want to keep the current thread busy for that long. In this case, you can use the `Task.Run` method, which schedules the execution of the lambda, which will most probably occur in a separate thread. The following example shows how to read the length of a file if the asynchronous `ReadAllTextAsync` method that we used previously were not available:

```
public Task<int> ReadLengthAsync(string filename)
{
    return Task.Run<int>(() =>
    {
        var content = File.ReadAllText(filename);
        return content.Length;
    });
}
```

You should always prefer the provided asynchronous version instead of using the `Run` method because the thread where this task is scheduled will block until the end of the synchronous execution.

We will now look at what the best course of action is whenever there is a very large amount of work to be done inside a task.

Long-running tasks

Even if you don't block the thread, there is still the risk of starvation whenever the asynchronous stack never awaits and becomes a long-running job, keeping the thread busy.

These cases can be treated with two different strategies:

- The first is manually *creating a thread*, which we already discussed at the beginning of this chapter. This is the best strategy when you need more control or need to modify the thread properties.

- The second possibility is *informing the task scheduler* that the task is going to run for a long time. This way, the scheduler will take a different strategy and avoid the `ThreadPool` altogether. The following code shows how to run a long-running task:

```
var t = new Task(() => Thread.Sleep(30000),
    TaskCreationOptions.LongRunning);
t.Start();
```

The essential recommendation is to try splitting the long jobs into smaller units of work that can be easily transformed into tasks.

Breaking the task chain – fire and forget

We have seen that embracing the task paradigm requires modifying the entire chain of callers. But there are times when this is not possible and also not desirable. For example, in the context of a desktop WPF application, you may have to write to a file inside a button-click event handler:

```
void Button_Click(object sender, RoutedEventArgs e) { ... }
```

We can't change its signature to return a `Task`; moreover, this would not make sense for two reasons:

- The calling library has been designed before the tasks and it would not be able to manage the task progress.

- This is one of the events designed as a **Fire-and-Forget** operation, meaning that you don't really care how long they will take or which result they are going to compute.

For these cases, you can embrace the `async`/`await` keywords while not using the returning `Task` at all:

```
async void Button_Click(object sender, RoutedEventArgs e)
{
    await File.WriteAllTextAsync("log.txt", "something");
    // ... other code
}
```

But remember, when you break the task chain, you lose the possibility to know whether the operation will ever complete or fail.

> **Information box**
>
> Every time you see `async void` in your code, you should wonder whether it could be a potential bug, or just that you really don't want to know what will happen to that task in the end. Over the years, the habit to use `async void` instead of `async Task` has been the primary source of bugs in asynchronous code.

Similarly, if you just invoke an asynchronous method without awaiting it (or using one of the ContinueWith methods), you will lose control of the invocation obtaining the same *fire-and-forget* behavior, because asynchronous methods return immediately after starting the asynchronous operation. Also, all the code following a not-awaited asynchronous operation will be executed concurrently, incurring the risk of race conditions or accessing data that is not yet available:

```
void Button_Click(object sender, RoutedEventArgs e)
{
    File.WriteAllTextAsync("log.txt", "something");
}
```

We have seen how simple it is to manage an asynchronous operation when everything completes successfully, but the code can throw exceptions and we need to catch them appropriately.

Task and exceptions

There are two kinds of exceptions that can happen when something goes wrong. The first is before any asynchronous method gets called, while the second is related to exceptions happening in the asynchronous code.

The following example shows these two cases:

```
public Task<int> CrashBeforeAsync()
{
    throw new Exception("Boom");
}
public Task<int> CrashAfterAsync()
{
    return Task.FromResult(0)
        .ContinueWith<int>(t => throw new Exception("Boom"));
}
```

In the first case, we are telling the caller that we will return a `Task<int>` but that no asynchronous operation has begun yet. This situation is exactly what happens in synchronous methods and can be caught accordingly:

```csharp
public Task<int> HandleCrashBeforeAsync()
{
    Task<int> resultTask;
    try
    {
        resultTask = CrashBeforeAsync();
    }
    catch (Exception) { throw; }
    return resultTask;
}
```

On the other hand, if the exception occurs in the continuation, the exception will not happen immediately; it will only happen as soon as the task is *consumed*:

```csharp
public async Task<int> HandleCrashAfterAsync()
{
    Task<int> resultTask = CrashAfterAsync();
    int result;
    try
    {
        result = await resultTask;
    }
    catch (Exception) { throw; }
    return result;
}
```

As soon as `resultTask` has completed as *faulted*, the exception has already happened but the compiler-generated code caught it and assigned it to the `Task.Exception` property. Since there may be multiple exceptions happening at the same time inside `Task`, the generated code encapsulates all the captured exceptions inside a single `AggregateException`. The `InnerException` and `InnerExceptions` properties in `AggregateException` contain the original exception.

Whenever you want to handle the exceptions and resolve them immediately, you may want to use the continuations instead of the `await` keyword:

```csharp
public Task<int> HandleCrashAfter2Async()
{
    Task<int> resultTask = CrashAfterAsync();
    try
```

```
    {
        return resultTask.ContinueWith<int>(t =>
        {
            if (t.IsCompletedSuccessfully) return t.Result;
            if(t.Exception.InnerException is OverflowException)
                return -1;
            throw t.Exception.InnerException;
        });
    }
    catch (Exception) { throw; }
}
```

As we mentioned previously, the exception in a *faulted* task is thrown as soon as the result gets *consumed*, which we previously mentioned in the context of using `await`. However, this can also occur in the case where the `t.Result` property is accessed.

> **Tip**
> The `Task` class exposes the `GetAwaiter` method, which returns the inner struct representing the asynchronous operation. You can get the result of the asynchronous operation with `task.GetAwaiter().GetResult()`, as well as `task.Result`, but there is a small difference. In fact, in the case of an exception, the former returns the original exception, while the latter returns an `AggregateException` containing the original exception.

Finally, it is worth mentioning that we can rewrite the `CrashAfterAsync` method with the static `Task.FromException<T>` method instead:

```
public Task<int> CrashAfterAsync() =>
    Task.FromException<int>(new Exception("Boom"));
```

Similar to what we saw with `FromResult<T>`, a new `Task` is created, but this time, its state is initialized to *faulted* and it contains the desired exception.

The preceding example is quite abstract but succinct enough to give you an idea of how to properly handle exceptions, depending on when they are thrown. There are many scenarios where this regularly happens. A real example of this duality would be an serialization exception occurring when preparing the JSON parameters or during the HTTP rest call as a result of a network failure.

In addition to transitioning to the faulted state, tasks can also be canceled, thanks to a built-in standard mechanism provided by the task paradigm.

Canceling a task

Unlike faults, cancellation is requested from the callers to interrupt the execution of one or more tasks. Cancellation can be imperative, or simply a timeout, which is very useful when a given task should not take more than a given amount of time.

From the caller's perspective, the cancellation pattern originates from the `CancellationTokenSource` class, which provides three different constructors:

- The default constructor is used when you are willing to cancel tasks by imperatively calling the `Cancel` method.

- The other constructors take either an `int` or a `TimeSpan`, which determine the maximum amount of time before a cancellation gets triggered, unless the tasks complete beforehand.

In the following example, we will experiment with canceling one of the three worker methods using a `CancellationToken` that has been obtained from a timed `CancellationTokenSource`:

```
public async Task CancellingTask()
{
    CancellationTokenSource cts2 = new
        CancellationTokenSource(TimeSpan.FromSeconds(2));
    var tok2 = cts2.Token;
    try
    {
        await WorkForever1Async(tok2);
        //await WorkForever2Async(tok2);
        //await WorkForever3Async(tok2);
        Console.WriteLine("let's continue");
    }
    catch (TaskCanceledException err)
    {
        Console.WriteLine(err.Message);
    }
}
```

The `Token` property returns a read-only struct that can be used by multiple consumers without impacting on the garbage collector or even being copied, as it is immutable.

The first consumer being examined here takes `CancellationToken` and correctly propagates it to any other method that accepts cancellations. In our example, there is just `Task.Delay`, a very convenient method used to instruct the infrastructure to trigger the continuation after 5 seconds:

```
public async Task WorkForever1Async(
    CancellationToken ct = default(CancellationToken))
{
    while (true)
    {
        await Task.Delay(5000, ct);
    }
}
```

The result of the preceding code's execution is the cancellation of the task, which is transformed into a `TaskCanceledException` by the code generated from the `await` keyword:

```
A task was canceled.
```

Another possibility is when a worker is executing only *synchronous* code and still needs to be canceled:

```
public Task WorkForever2Async(
    CancellationToken ct = default(CancellationToken))
{
    while (true)
    {
        Thread.Sleep(5000);
        if (ct.IsCancellationRequested)
            return Task.FromCanceled(ct);
    }
}
```

Please note the use of `Thread.Sleep` instead of the `Delay` method, which was necessary because we wanted a synchronous implementation.

The `Thread.Sleep` method is very different because it blocks the thread entirely and prevents the thread from being reused anywhere else, while `Task.Delay` spawns a request to call the following code as a continuation as soon as the specified amount of time has expired.

The more interesting part is testing the `IsCancellationRequested` Boolean property to allow a collaborative cancellation of the task. Being collaborative by explicitly checking that property is necessary because you may not need to interrupt the execution before having disposed of some resource, be it written on a database or anywhere else.

Once again, the result of executing the preceding method will be as follows:

```
A task was canceled.
```

The third and final case is when you don't want to throw any exception, but just to return from the execution:

```
public async Task WorkForever3Async(
    CancellationToken ct = default(CancellationToken))
{
    while (true)
    {
        await Task.Delay(5000);
        if (ct.IsCancellationRequested) return;
    }
}
```

In this case, we carefully avoided propagating `CancellationToken` to the underlying calls, because, by using `await`, it would have triggered the exception.

The execution of this final `WorkForever3Async` method does not raise any exceptions and lets the execution continue normally:

```
let's continue
```

The downside of this implementation is that the cancellation may not happen immediately. `Task.Delay` will need to complete regardless of the cancellation, which, in the worst case, can't happen before 5 seconds.

We have seen how the task paradigm makes running asynchronous operations dramatically easier, but how can we run multiple asynchronous requests at the same time? They can potentially be run in parallel to avoid useless waits.

Monitoring the progress of a task

After the user starts a long-running operation, providing feedback is very important to avoid the user becoming frustrated. This is possible when you are in control of what is happening, such as with some a time-expensive algorithm. Instead, when the long-running operation depends on a call to an external library, monitoring the progress is not possible.

The Task Library does not have specific support for monitoring progress, but the .NET library provides `IProgress<T>`, which can easily be used for this goal. This interface just provides a single member—`void Report(T value)`—which leaves total freedom on the implementation details. In the simplest cases, `T` would be an integer value representing the progress as a percentage.

For example, a load operation could be implemented as follows:

```
public async Task Load(IProgress<int> progress = null)
{
    var steps = 30;
    for (int i = 0; i < steps; i++)
    {
        await Task.Delay(300);
        progress?.Report((i + 1) * 100 / steps);
    }
}
```

The method, which in our case simulates an asynchronous operation by just calling `Task.Delay`, must have a prediction of the total number of steps that relates to 100% of the progress. After each step, the `Report` method is called to inform us about the current percentage, but ensure the code is protected from the progress being null, as the consumer may not be interested in receiving such feedback.

On the consumer side, the first thing to do is create the progress provider, which is simply a class implementing `IProgress<int>`:

```
public class ConsoleProgress : IProgress<int>
{
    void IProgress<int>.Report(int value) =>
        Console.Write($"{value}%  ");
}
```

Finally, the caller should just pass the provider instance to the `Load` method:

```
await test.Load(new ConsoleProgress());
```

As you may expect, the output is as follows:

```
3%   6%  10%  13%  16%  20%  23%  26%  30%  33%  36%  40%  43%
46%  50%  53%  56%  60%  63%  66%  70%  73%  76%  80%  83%  86%
90%  93%  96%  100%
```

The generic argument of IProgress<T> can potentially be used to pause the execution or trigger more complex logic such as pausing/resuming behavior.

Parallelizing tasks

A common programming task is retrieving some resources from the internet. For example, the essential code to download a resource via HTTP is as follows:

```
public async Task<byte[]> GetResourceAsync(string uri)
{
    using var client = new HttpClient();
    using var response = await client.GetAsync(uri);
    response.EnsureSuccessStatusCode();
    return await response.Content.ReadAsByteArrayAsync();
}
```

Thanks to EnsureSuccessStatusCode, any failure will trigger an exception, leaving the responsibility of catching it to the caller. Also, we didn't even set any header, but it's enough for our purposes.

We already know how to invoke this asynchronous method to download an image, but now the challenge is choosing the right strategy to download many of them:

- The first question is: *how can we download multiple images in parallel?* If we need to download 10 images, we don't want to sum the times needed to download each of them. Anyway, we will not enter into the discussion of how much we can scale if, let's say, you need to download millions of images. This would be out of the scope of a discussion about asynchronous machinery.

- The second question is: *do we need them all at the same time?* In this case, we can use the Task.WhenAll helper method, which takes an array of tasks and returns a single task representing the overall operation.

For these samples, we are going to use the online free service called *Lorem PicSum* (`https://picsum.photos/`). Every time you make a request to the URI you see in the code, a new and different image sized 200 x 200 will be retrieved. You can, of course, use any URI of your choice:

```
public async Task NeedAll()
{
    var uri = "https://picsum.photos/200";
    Task<byte[]>[] tasks = Enumerable.Range(0, 10)
        .Select(_ => GetResourceAsync(uri))
        .ToArray();

    Task allTask = Task.WhenAll(tasks);
    try
    {
        await allTask;
    }
    catch (Exception)
    {
        Console.WriteLine("One or more downloads failed");
    }

    foreach (var completedTask in tasks)
        Console.WriteLine(
            $"New image: {completedTask.Result.Length}");
}
```

The use of `Enumerable.Range` is a nice way to repeat an action for the given number of times. We don't really care about the generated numbers; in fact, we use the `discard` (`_`) token instead of a variable in the `Select` method.

The `Select` lambda just initiates the download operations returning the corresponding tasks that we don't await yet. Instead, we ask the `WhenAll` method to create a new `Task` that will be signaled as soon as all the tasks are completed successfully. Should any task fail, the code generated from the `await` keyword will cause an exception to be thrown.

The task obtained from the `WhenAll` method cannot be used to retrieve the results, but it guarantees that we can access the `Result` properties for all the tasks. Therefore, after awaiting `allTask`, we iterate the `tasks` array retrieving the `byte[]` array for all the downloaded images. Here is the output obtained by awaiting all the downloads at the same time:

```
New image: 6909
New image: 3846
New image: 8413
New image: 9000
New image: 7057
New image: 8565
New image: 6617
New image: 8720
New image: 4107
New image: 6763
```

In many cases, this is a good strategy because we may need all the resources before continuing. An alternative is to wait for the first download so that we can start processing it, but we still want to download them all concurrently to save time.

This alternative strategy can be pursued with the help of the `WaitAny` method. In the following example, starting the downloads is no different. We just add a `Stopwatch` class to show the time taken in milliseconds at the end of the downloads:

```
public async Task NeedAny()
{
    var sw = new Stopwatch();
    sw.Start();
    var uri = "https://picsum.photos/200";
    Task<byte[]>[] tasks = Enumerable.Range(0, 10)
        .Select(_ => GetResourceAsync(uri))
        .ToArray();

    while (tasks.Length > 0)
    {
        await Task.WhenAny(tasks);
        var elapsed = sw.ElapsedMilliseconds;
        var completed = tasks.Where(t => t.IsCompleted).
ToArray();
        foreach (var completedTask in completed)
            Console.WriteLine($"{elapsed} New image:
{completedTask.Result.Length}");
        tasks = tasks.Where(t => !t.IsCompletedSuccessfully).
```

```
ToArray();
    }
}
```

The `while` loop is used to process all the unfinished tasks. Initially, the `tasks` array contains all of them, but every time `WhenAny` completes, it means that at least one task has completed. The completed ones are immediately printed on screen, together with the milliseconds elapsed since the beginning of the operation. The other ones are reassigned to the `tasks` variable so that we can loop back and process the completed tasks until the very last one. The output of this new method is as follows:

```
368 New image: 9915
368 New image: 6032
419 New image: 6486
452 New image: 9810
471 New image: 7030
514 New image: 10009
514 New image: 10660
593 New image: 6871
658 New image: 2738
12850 New image: 6072
The last image took a lot of time to download, probably because
the online service throttles the requests. Using WhenAll, we
would have to wait about 13 seconds before getting them all.
Instead, we could start processing as soon as each image was
available.
```

Of course, you can combine these two methods together. For example, if you want to get as many downloaded images as possible in no more than 100 milliseconds, just replace the `WhenAny` line with the following one:

```
await Task.WhenAll(Task.Delay(100), Task.WhenAny(tasks));
```

In other words, we are asking to wait for any task (at least one) but not before 100 milliseconds. The `while` loop will repeat the operation, as we did previously, by consuming all the remaining tasks:

```
345 New image: 8416
345 New image: 7315
345 New image: 8237
345 New image: 6391
345 New image: 5477
457 New image: 9592
457 New image: 3922
```

```
457 New image: 8870
563 New image: 3695
```

When you test these code snippets, be sure to run them in a loop because the first run can be heavily influenced by the **Just-in-Time** compiler.

We have seen how the `Task` class provides a very powerful building block to consume asynchronous operations, but this requires libraries providing asynchronous behavior. In the next section, we will see how we can expose a manual task and trigger its completion.

Signaling tasks with the TaskCompletionSource object

Going back to the file watcher sample in the *What is a thread?* section at the beginning of this chapter, you may remember `FileSystemWatcher` exposing events and not embracing the task paradigm. You may wonder whether we write some sort of adapter to leverage the power of all the nice tools offered by the Task Library, and the answer is *yes*.

The `TaskCompletionSource` object provides an important building block that we can use to expose asynchronous behavior. It is created and used on the producer side to signal the completion of an operation, be it a success or a failure. It provides, via the `Task` property, the task object that must be used from the client to await the notification.

The following class uses `FileSystemWatcher` to monitor the filesystem in the current folder. The `Deleted` event stops the notifications and notifies the completion source about the successful deletion of a file. Similarly, the `Error` event sets the exception that will be eventually triggered on the consumer side of the `await` statement:

```
public class DeletionNotifier : IDisposable
{
    private TaskCompletionSource<FileSystemEventArgs> _tcs;
    private FileSystemWatcher _watcher;

    public DeletionNotifier()
    {
        var path = Path.GetFullPath(".");
        Console.WriteLine($"Observing changes in path: {path}");
        _watcher = new FileSystemWatcher(path, "*.txt");
        _watcher.Deleted += (s, e) =>
        {
            _watcher.EnableRaisingEvents = false;
            _tcs.SetResult(e);
        };
        _watcher.Error += (s, e) =>
        {
```

```
              _watcher.EnableRaisingEvents = false;
              _tcs.SetException(e.GetException());
          };
      }
      public Task<FileSystemEventArgs> WhenDeleted()
      {
          _tcs = new TaskCompletionSource<FileSystemEventArgs>();
          _watcher.EnableRaisingEvents = true;
          return _tcs.Task;
      }
      public void Dispose() => _watcher.Dispose();
  }
```

Every time the WhenDeleted method is called, a new completion source is created,
the file watcher is started, and the Task responsible for the notification is returned
to the client.

From the consumer perspective, this solution is awesome because it removes
any complexity:

```
  var dn = new DeletionNotifier();
  var deleted = await dn.WhenDeleted();
  Console.WriteLine($"Deleted: {deleted.Name}");
```

The downside of this solution is that only a single deletion can be detected at one time.

Also, since the code inside the Deleted event turns off the notifications, calling the
WhenDeleted method inside a loop could cause missing deletions.

But we can fix that problem! The slightly more complex solution is to buffer the events in
a thread-safe queue and change the WhenDeleted method strategy by dequeuing the
available event, if any.

The following is the revised code:

```
  public class DeletionNotifier : IDisposable
  {
      private TaskCompletionSource<FileSystemEventArgs> _tcs;
      private FileSystemWatcher _watcher;
      private ConcurrentQueue<FileSystemEventArgs> _queue;
      private Exception _error;

      public DeletionNotifier()
      {
          var path = Path.GetFullPath(".");
```

```
        Console.WriteLine($"Observing changes in path: {path}");
        _queue = new ConcurrentQueue<FileSystemEventArgs>();
        _watcher = new FileSystemWatcher(path, "*.txt");
        _watcher.Deleted += (s, e) =>
        {
          _queue.Enqueue(e);
          _tcs.TrySetResult(e);
        };
        _watcher.Error += (s, e) =>
        {
          _watcher.EnableRaisingEvents = false;
          _error = e.GetException();
          _tcs.TrySetException(_error);
        };
        _watcher.EnableRaisingEvents = true;
    }
    public Task<FileSystemEventArgs> WhenDeleted()
    {
      if (_queue.TryDequeue(out FileSystemEventArgs fsea))
        return Task.FromResult(fsea);
      if (_error != null)
        return Task.FromException<FileSystemEventArgs>(_error);

      _tcs = new TaskCompletionSource<FileSystemEventArgs>();
      return _tcs.Task;
    }

    public void Dispose() => _watcher.Dispose();
}
```

Once again, we could solve the problem with just the Task Library tools. Depending on the use case, this strategy requires recreating a new `TaskCompletionSource<T>` every time and since it is a reference type, it may affect the performance being subject to garbage collection. Should we need to reuse the same notification object, we can do so by creating a custom notification object.

In fact, the `await` keyword just needs an object implementing a method called `GetAwaiter`, returning an object that implements the `INotifyCompletion` interface. This object, in turn, must implement an `IsCompleted` property and all the required machinery miming the `TaskCompletionSource` behavior.

In the *Further reading* section, you will find an interesting article called *await anything* from the Microsoft official blog that deep dives into this topic.

Synchronization context

Depending on the application we are writing, not all threads are created equal. Desktop applications have a main thread that is the only one allowed to draw on screen and deal with graphics controls. The GUI libraries work around the concept of a queue of messages where every request is posted. The main thread is responsible for dequeueing those messages and dispatching them into the user-defined handlers that implement the desired behavior.

Every time something happens on a thread different than the UI one, a marshaling operation must occur, which will cause a message to be posted in the queue managed by the main thread. Two popular examples of marshalling messages in the UI thread are `Control.Invoke` in the context of Windows Forms applications and `Dispatcher.Invoke` for Window Presentation Foundation.

> **Information box**
>
> The very first prerelease version of WPF was multithreaded. But the code complexity required users to deal with multithreading, and the consequent possible bugs in the user's code were raising the bar too much. Even many C++ libraries, like DirectX and OpenGL, are mostly single-threaded to cut down the complexity.

On the server side, ASP.NET applications also have the context of the main thread, but there isn't just one—in fact, each user's request has its own main thread.

`SynchronizationContext` is the base class for an abstraction that defines a standard way to provide the execution of some code in the context of the *special* thread. This is no magic; in fact, the code that is being executed is defined in a lambda and posted in a queue. On the main thread, some code provided by the infrastructure dequeues the lambda and executes it in its context.

This automatic marshaling is fundamental because, after executing any asynchronous method, such as downloading an image from the internet, you want to avoid calling the `Invoke` method needed to marshal the result back into the main thread, which is required in order to update the user interface with the returned data.

Every time you await some asynchronous operation, the generated code takes care to *capture* the current `SynchronizationContext` and make sure that the continuation is executed on that specific thread. Basically, you don't need to do anything because the infrastructure already does it for you.

Are we done? Not really, because there are times where this does not happen. From what we said, the three IDs in the following example should all be the same:

```
public async Task AsyncTest1()
{
    Console.WriteLine($"Id: {Thread.CurrentThread.
ManagedThreadId}");
    await Task.Delay(100);
    Console.WriteLine($"Id: {Thread.CurrentThread.
ManagedThreadId}");
    await Task.Delay(100);
    Console.WriteLine($"Id: {Thread.CurrentThread.
ManagedThreadId}");
}
```

This is not the case because it is a console application that doesn't set, by default, any synchronization context. The reason for this is in the Microsoft documentation for the `Console` class. You will see the *Thread Safety* section, at the end of the documentation page, stating *This type is thread safe*. In other words, there is no reason to go back to the original thread.

If you instead create a new Windows Forms application and call that code in a button-click handler, you will see that the ID is always the same, thanks to `SynchronizationContext`.

It is always important to understand what happens, in terms of threading, to your asynchronous code because there are times where marshalling the result back to the main one is not desirable because marshalling has a performance impact. For example, library developers must be very careful when writing asynchronous code because they can't know if their code will be executed in the presence or absence of a synchronization context.

A clear example is when the library developer is processing chunks of data coming from the network. Every chunk is retrieved by means of an asynchronous HTTP request and the number of chunks can be very high, as in the following example:

```
public async Task AsyncLoop()
{
    Console.WriteLine($"Id: {Thread.CurrentThread.
ManagedThreadId}");
    byte[] data;
    while((data = await GetNextAsync()).Length > 0)
    {
        Console.WriteLine($"Id: {Thread.CurrentThread.
ManagedThreadId}");
```

```
        // process data
    }
}
```

Unless the processing code is going to interact with the UI (or anything related to the main thread), disabling the synchronization context is definitely a performance gain and very easy to do:

```
public async Task AsyncLoop()
{
    Console.WriteLine($"Id: {Thread.CurrentThread.
ManagedThreadId}");
    byte[] data;
    while((data = await GetNextAsync().ConfigureAwait(false)).
Length > 0)
    {
        Console.WriteLine($"Id: {Thread.CurrentThread.
ManagedThreadId}");
        // process data
    }
}
```

By applying the `ConfigureAwait` method to the asynchronous method, the result of the operation will not be posted back to the main thread, and the generated continuation will be executed on the secondary thread (whenever the asynchronous operation is scheduled on a different thread).

This modified behavior has two consequences:

- Posting the message in the main thread queue has a *performance impact.* For example, library developers may want to set `ConfigureAwait` to `false` when doing some internal work to improve the performance.

- Whenever you should decide to execute an asynchronous method synchronously using the `Wait` method or the `Result` property, you may incur a *deadlock.* This can happen because the synchronization context posts back the execution to the main thread, which is busy. While this situation should be avoided by never using `Wait` and `Result`, an alternative approach is to make the call finish its execution on the secondary thread by setting `ConfigureAwait` to `false`.

Please note that if you really want to continue the execution on the secondary thread, ensure that you apply `ConfigureAwait` to all the following calls. In fact, the first asynchronous call executed without `ConfigureAwait` will cause the execution to return to the main thread.

Since the code following `ConfigureAwait` is executed on a secondary thread, remember to manually marshal back to the main thread to avoid race conditions. For example, to update the UI, you must call the relevant *Windows Forms* or *WPF* `Invoke` method.

The task paradigm is a revolution in programming languages that could not exist without the help of the new language keyword and the compiler generation magic. This new feature had a great resonance in other languages as well. For example, ECMAScript 2017 adopted these concepts by providing both promises and async/await keyword support.

Throughout this long chapter, we learned the importance of asynchronous programming and how the Task Library makes asynchronous code intuitive and easy to write, while still not forcing us to bother too much about the implicit complexity. Beyond acquiring a general understanding of these tools, it is now important to experiment and dig into each aspect to master those techniques.

Summary

In this chapter, we discussed the most important tools that any developer can use to take advantage of the multithreading and asynchronous programming techniques.

The building blocks are the fundamental abstractions that allow code to run in a different execution context, regardless of the OS they are currently running on. Those primitives must be used with wisdom, but that doesn't limit the developer's possibilities in any way compared to native languages and libraries.

In addition to this, the task paradigm offers a natural approach when it comes to interacting with all those events whose nature is asynchronous. The `System.Threading.Tasks` namespace provides all the required abstractions to interact with asynchronous phenomena.

The library has been widely restructured and widened to support the task paradigm. And most importantly, the language offers the `async` and `await` keywords to break down the complexity and make the asynchronous world flow as if it was procedural code.

In the next chapter, we will learn about the concepts of files, file streams, and serialization.

Test what you learned

1. If you have a very CPU-intensive, long-lasting algorithm to run, which strategy out of manual thread creation, using the task library, or using the thread pool would you adopt?

2. Name a performant synchronization technique that can be used to write a file and increase an integer value in memory.

3. What method should you use to pause the execution for 100 milliseconds, and why?

4. What should you do to wait for the results produced by multiple asynchronous operations?

5. How can you create a task to await a CLR event?

6. What should you return from a method that has `Task` in the signature but does not use any asynchronous method?

7. How can you create a long-running task?

8. A button-click handler is making asynchronous access to the internet to load some data. Should you use `Control.Invoke` to update the results on screen? Why?

9. What are the reasons for evaluating the use of the `ConfigureAwait` method on a `Task`?

10. Can you update the UI directly after having used `ConfigureAwait(false)`?

Further reading

- A very powerful library that can be used to measure the performance of some code is Benchmark.NET (`https://benchmarkdotnet.org/articles/overview.html`), which is also used internally by Microsoft to make optimizations on the runtime and the core libraries.

- If you want to build your own *awaitable* object, you cannot miss this article from the Microsoft team, describing how the underlying infrastructure works: `https://devblogs.microsoft.com/pfxteam/await-anything/`.

- To dig into more details about the synchronization context and `ConfigureAwait`, you can read the following article: `https://devblogs.microsoft.com/dotnet/configureawait-faq/`.

13
Files, Streams, and Serialization

Programming is all about processing data that could come from various sources, such as local memory, disk files, or from a remote server over the network. Most data has to be persisted for either a long time or indefinitely. It has to be available between different application restarts or shared between multiple applications. Whether the storage is plain text files or various types of databases, whether they are local, from the network, or a cloud, whether the physical location is hard disk drives, solid state drives, or USB sticks, all data is preserved in a filesystem. Different platforms have different types of filesystems, but they all work with the same abstractions: paths, files, and directories.

In this chapter, we look at the functionalities that .NET provides for working with filesystems. The main topics that will be covered in this chapter are as follows:

- Overview of the `System.IO` namespace
- Working with paths
- Working with files and directories
- Working with streams
- Serializing and deserializing XML
- Serializing and deserializing JSON

By the end of this chapter, you will have learned how to create, modify, and delete files and directories. You will have also learned how to read from and write to files with different kinds of data (including binary and text). Lastly, you will have learned how to serialize objects to XML and JSON.

Let's begin by exploring the `System.IO` namespace.

Overview of the System.IO namespace

The .NET frameworks provide classes as well as other helper types such as enumerations, interfaces, and delegates that help us work with the **filesystem objects** as well as **streams**. These are grouped under the `System.IO` namespace in the Base Class Library. The complete list of types is rather long, but the following tables show the most important of these grouped into several categories.

The most important classes for working with *filesystem objects* are as follows:

Directory	A static class that exposes static methods for performing directory operations, such as creating, moving, deleting, or enumerating directories.
DirectoryInfo	This is an instance class that provides functionality equivalent to the `Directory` class.
DriveInfo	A class that models a drive and provides access to the drive information.
File	A static class that exposes static methods for creating, moving, deleting, and opening files.
FileInfo	This is an instance class that provides functionality equivalent to the `File` class.
FileSystemWatcher	A class that watches for changes to the filesystem and raises events when a directory or file that is being watched changes.
Path	This is a helper class for performing operations on strings that represent filesystem paths.

The most important classes for working with *streams* are as follows:

`BinaryReader`	This is an instance class that provides methods for reading primitive data type values from a stream with a particular encoding.
`BinaryWriter`	This is an instance class that provides methods for writing primitive data type values to a stream in a particular encoding.
`FileStream`	This represents a stream for a file with support for synchronous and asynchronous reading and writing.
`MemoryStream`	This represents a stream for a sequence of bytes that are stored in memory.
`Stream`	This is an abstract class that is the base class for all the stream classes in this namespace. It abstracts a sequence of bytes providing basic functionality of reading, writing, and seeking the stream.
`StreamReader`	This implements `TextReader` that reads from a stream with a particular encoding.
`StreamWriter`	This implements a `TextWriter` that writes to a stream with a particular encoding.
`StringReader`	This implements a `TextReader` that reads from a string.
`StringWriter`	This implements a `TextWriter` that writes to a string.
`TextReader`	An abstract class that provides synchronous and asynchronous reading operations from a sequential series of characters.
`TextWriter`	An abstract class that provides synchronous and asynchronous writing operations to a sequential series of characters.

As you can see in the previous table, the concrete classes in this list come in pairs: a reader and a writer. Typically, these are used as follows:

- `BinaryReader` and `BinaryWriter` are used to explicitly serialize and deserialize primitive data types to or from binary files.

- `StreamReader` and `StreamWriter` are used for handling character-based data, with different encodings, from text files.

- `StringReader` and `StringWriter` have similar interfaces and purposes as the previous pair, although they work on strings and string buffers and not streams.

The relationship between the classes in the previous table is shown in the following simplified class diagram:

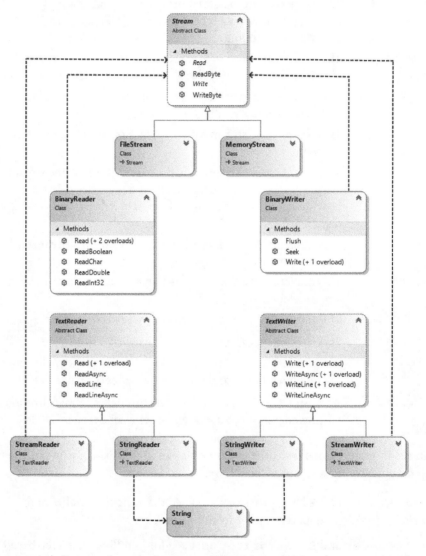

Figure 13.1 – A class diagram of stream classes as well as reader and writer classes mentioned previously

From this diagram, you can see that only `FileStream` and `MemoryStream` are actually stream classes. `BinaryReader` and `StreamReader` are adapters that read data from a stream, while `BinaryWriter` and `StreamWriter` write data to a stream. All these classes require a stream to create an instance (the stream is passed as an argument to the constructor). On the other hand, `StringReader` and `StringWriter` don't work on streams at all; instead, they read and write from a string or string buffer.

Most operations with the filesystem objects or streams throw exceptions when errors occur. The most important of these exceptions are listed here:

`DirectoryNotFoundException`	This exception is thrown when a part of a directory or file is not found.
`EndOfStreamException`	This exception is thrown when you attempt to read past the end of a stream.
`FileNotFoundException`	This exception is thrown if you attempt to access a file that does not exist.
`InvalidDataException`	This exception is thrown when a data stream is in an invalid format.
`PathTooLongException`	This exception is thrown when a path exceeds the maximum length defined by the filesystem. For instance, the maximum path length for Windows operating systems is 260 characters, although longer paths can be enabled and are supported by later versions of .NET.

In the following sections of this chapter, we will look at some of these classes in detail. For now, we will start with the `Path` class.

Working with paths

`System.IO.Path` is a static class that performs operations on strings, representing the path of a filesystem object (a file or a directory). None of the class methods verify whether the string represents the path of a valid file or directory. However, members that accept an input path verify that the path is well formed; otherwise, they throw an exception. This class can handle paths for different platforms. The format of a path such as the presence of a root element or the path separator is platform-dependent and is determined by the platform that the application is running on.

A path can be *relative* or *absolute*. An absolute path is one that fully specifies the location. On the other hand, a relative path is a partial location determined by the current location, which can be retrieved with a call to the `Directory.GetCurrentDirector()` method.

All the members of the `Path` class are static. The most important ones are listed in the following table:

`Combine()`	Combines two or more paths into a single path.
`GetDirectoryName()`	Returns the name of the directory from the specified path.
`GetFileName()`	Returns the file name and extension from the specified path.
`GetFileNameWithoutExtension()`	Returns only the file name without the extension from the specified path.
`GetFullPath()`	Returns the absolute path of the specified path or from a fully qualified base path and a relative path.
`GetPathRoot()`	Returns the root directory information from the specified path.

To see how this works, we can consider the following example, where we're using various methods of the `Path` class to print information about the `c:\Windows\System32\mmc.exe` path:

```
var path = @"c:\Windows\System32\mmc.exe";

Console.WriteLine(Path.HasExtension(path));
Console.WriteLine(Path.IsPathFullyQualified(path));
Console.WriteLine(Path.IsPathRooted(path));

Console.WriteLine(Path.GetPathRoot(path));
Console.WriteLine(Path.GetDirectoryName(path));
Console.WriteLine(Path.GetFileName(path));
Console.WriteLine(Path.GetFileNameWithoutExtension(path));
Console.WriteLine(Path.GetExtension(path));

Console.WriteLine(Path.ChangeExtension(path, ".dll"));
```

The output of this program is shown in the following screenshot:

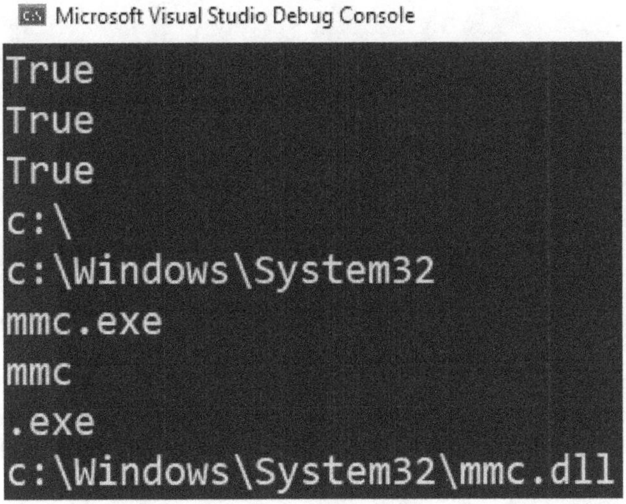

Figure 13.2 – A screenshot of executing the previous sample that prints information about a path

The Path class contains a method called Combine() and it is recommended to use it for composing a new path from two or more paths. There are four overloads of this method; these overloads take two, three, four paths, or an array of paths as input arguments. To understand how this works, we will look at the following examples, where we are concatenating two paths:

```
var path1 = Path.Combine(@"c:\temp", @"sub\data.txt");
Console.WriteLine(path1); // c:\temp\sub\data.txt

var path2 = Path.Combine(@"c:\temp\sub", @"..\", "log.txt");
Console.WriteLine(path2); // c:\temp\sub\..\log.txt
```

In the first example, the result of the concatenation is c:\temp\sub\data.txt, which properly includes a path separator between temp and sub, which was not present in any of the two input paths. In the second example, the result of the concatenation of the three paths is c:\temp\sub\..\log.txt. Notice that the path is properly composed, but not resolved to the actual path, that is, c:\temp\log.txt.

In addition to the methods listed earlier, there are several other static methods in the `Path` class, a few of them intended for working with temporary files. These are listed here:

`GetTempPath()`	Retrieves the path for the temporary folder of the current user. To determine this path, the method checks for the existence of the TMP, TEMP, and USERPROFILE environment variables and returns the first path found. If none of these is found, it returns the Windows directory.
`GetTempFileName()`	Creates a uniquely named temporary file in the temporary folder of the current user and returns its path (the one returned by the `GetTempPath()` method). This is the only method that interacts with the filesystem. The file that is created has the extension `.TMP`.
`GetRandomFile-Name()`	Returns a cryptographically strong random name that can be used for the name of a file or directory. The return value is only a name, not a full path. Unlike `GetTempFileName()`, this method does not create a file on disk. This method should be preferred over `GetTempFileName()` when security is key.

Let's look at an example of working with temporary paths:

```
var temp = Path.GetTempPath();
var name = Path.GetRandomFileName();
var path1 = Path.Combine(temp, name);
Console.WriteLine(path1);

var path2 = Path.GetTempFileName();
Console.WriteLine(path2);
File.Delete(path2);
```

As shown in the following screenshot, `path1` will contain a path such as `C:\Users\Marius\AppData\Local\Temp\w22fbbqw.y34`, although the file name (including extension) will change with each execution. Also, this path is not created on disk, unlike the second example, where the `C:\Users\Marius\AppData\Local\Temp\tmp8D5A.tmp` path is actually representing a newly created file:

Microsoft Visual Studio Debug Console

```
C:\Users\Marius\AppData\Local\Temp\w22fbbqw.y34
C:\Users\Marius\AppData\Local\Temp\tmp8D5A.tmp
```

Figure 13.3 – Screenshot of the sample demonstrating the use of the GetRandomFileName() and GetTempFileName() methods

There are two important differences between these two temporary paths—the first one uses a cryptographically strong method for generating the name, while the second uses a much simpler algorithm. On the other hand, `GetRandomFileName()` returns a name with a random extension, while `GetTempFileName()` always returns a path with a filename with the `.TMP` extension.

To verify whether a path exists and perform operations such as creating, moving, deleting, or opening a directory or file, we must use other classes from the `System.IO` namespace. We'll look at these classes in the following section.

Working with files and directories

The `System.IO` namespace contains two classes for working with directories (`Directory` and `DirectoryInfo`), and two for working with files (`File` and `FileInfo`). `Directory` and `File` are **static classes** but contain mostly the same functionality provided by the **instance classes**—`DirectoryInfo` and `FileInfo`.

The latter two are derived from the `FileSystemInfo` base abstract class, which provides members that are common for manipulating both files and directories. The most important of these members are the properties listed in the following table:

`Attributes`	This provides access to the attributes of the current file or directory.
`CreationTime,` `CreationTimeUtc`	This gets or sets the creation time of the current file or directory in local time or UTC time.
`Exists`	This indicates whether the file or directory exists on disk.
`Extension`	Returns the extension of a file, including the period (such as `.exe`).
`FullName`	Returns the fully qualified path of the file or directory.
`LastAccessTime,` `LastAccessTimeUtc`	Gets or sets the time the directory or file was last accessed in local time or UTC time.
`LastWriteTime,` `LastWriteTimeUtc`	Gets or sets the time the directory of the file was last written to, in local time or UTC time.
`Name`	Returns the name of the file or directory. For directories, if the current object represents a directory in a hierarchy, it returns the name of the last directory (such as `Sub` for `C:\Temp\Dir\Sub`).

The most important members of the `DirectoryInfo` class, excluding the ones inherited from the base class, which were listed in the preceding table, are as follows:

`Create()`, `CreateSubdirectory()`	The first method creates a directory when the parent exists. The second method creates a subdirectory and all the other subdirectories in a hierarchy up to the root, if necessary.
`Delete()`	Deletes the directory if it is empty.
`EnumerateDirectories()`, `EnumerateFiles()`	Retrieves an enumerable collection of directories or files that can be enumerated before the whole collection is returned. There are multiple overloads for various search options.
`GetDirectory()`, `GetFiles()`	Retrieves an array of non-recursive subdirectories or files of the current directory. There are multiple overloads for various search options.
`MoveTo()`	Moves a directory and its content to a new path.
`Parent`	Retrieves the parent directory of a specified subdirectory (such as `C:\Temp\Dir` for `C:\Temp\Dir\Sub`).
`Root`	Retrieves the root of a directory (such as `C:\` for `C:\Temp\Dir\Sub`).

Similarly, the most important members of the `FileInfo` class, excluding the ones inherited from the base class, are as follows:

`AppendText()`	Creates a `StreamWriter` object that appends text to the file represented by the current object.
`CopyTo()`	Copies the file represented by the current object to a new location. Overloads allow or disallow overwriting existing files.
`Create()`	Creates a new file.
`CreateText()`	Creates a `StreamWriter` object that writes text to the file represented by the current object.
`Decrypt()`	Decrypts a file if it was previously encrypted by the current account using the `Encrypt()` method.
`Delete()`	Deletes a file from disk.
`Encrypt()`	Encrypts a file so that only the same account can decrypt it.
`MoveTo()`	Moves the current file to a new location.
`Open()`	Opens a file in the specified mode. Overloads allow us to also specify file access rights and sharing options.

OpenRead()	Creates a `FileStream` object that can be used only to read content from the file.
OpenText()	Creates a `StreamReader` object using the UTF-8 encoding that can be used to read text from a file.
OpenWrite()	Creates a `FileStream` object that can be used only to write content to the file.
Replace()	Replaces the content of a specified file with the content of the file represented by the current object. This method creates a backup of the replaced file and deletes the original file.
Directory	Returns an instance of `DirectoryInfo` representing the parent directory.
DirectoryName	Returns a string representing the full path of the directory.
IsReadOnly	Determines or changes if the current file is read only.
Length	Returns the size in bytes of the current file.

Now that we have looked at the classes available for handling filesystem objects and their most important members, let's look at some examples of using them.

In the first example, we will use an instance of `DirectoryInfo` to print information about a directory (in this example, `C:\Program Files (x86)\Microsoft SDKs\ Windows\`), such as name, parent, root, creation time, and attributes, as well as the names of all its subdirectories:

```
var dir = new DirectoryInfo(@"C:\Program Files (x86)\Microsoft
SDKs\Windows\");

Console.WriteLine($"Full name : {dir.FullName}");
Console.WriteLine($"Name      : {dir.Name}");
Console.WriteLine($"Parent    : {dir.Parent}");
Console.WriteLine($"Root      : {dir.Root}");
Console.WriteLine($"Created   : {dir.CreationTime}");
Console.WriteLine($"Attribute : {dir.Attributes}");

foreach(var subdir in dir.EnumerateDirectories())
{
    Console.WriteLine(subdir.Name);
}
```

The output from executing this code is as follows (notice this will differ on each machine that executes the code):

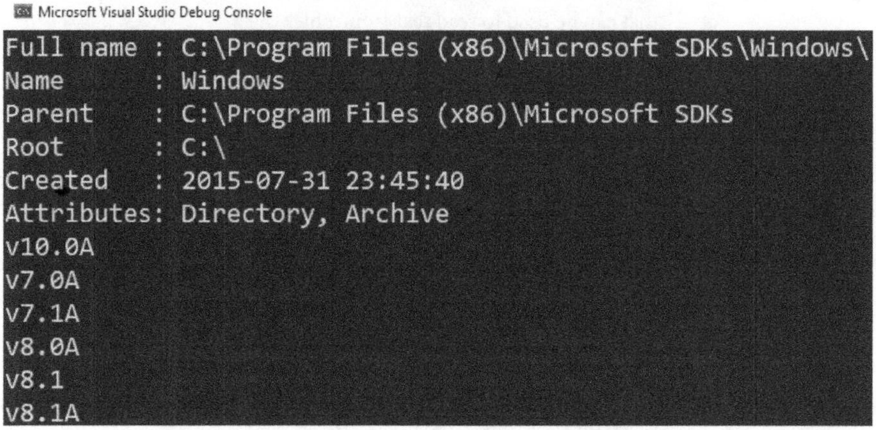

```
Microsoft Visual Studio Debug Console
Full name : C:\Program Files (x86)\Microsoft SDKs\Windows\
Name      : Windows
Parent    : C:\Program Files (x86)\Microsoft SDKs
Root      : C:\
Created   : 2015-07-31 23:45:40
Attributes: Directory, Archive
v10.0A
v7.0A
v7.1A
v8.0A
v8.1
v8.1A
```

Figure 13.4 – Screenshot of the previous sample displaying directory information

DirectoryInfo also allows us to create and delete directories, which is what we will do in the next example. First, we create the C:\Temp\Dir\Sub directory. Second, we create the subdirectory hierarchy, sub1\sub2\sub3, relative to the previously directory. Lastly, we delete the most inner directory, sub3, from the C:\Temp\Dir\Sub\sub1\ sub2 directory:

```
var dir = new DirectoryInfo(@"C:\Temp\Dir\Sub");
Console.WriteLine($"Exists: {dir.Exists}");
dir.Create();

var sub = dir.CreateSubdirectory(@"sub1\sub2\sub3");
Console.WriteLine(sub.FullName);

sub.Delete();
```

Notice that the CreateSubdirectory() method returns a DirectoryInfo instance that represents the most inner subdirectory created, which, in this case, is C:\Temp\ Dir\Sub\sub1\sub2\sub3. Therefore, when invoking Delete() on this instance, only the sub3 subdirectory is deleted.

We can write the same functionality using the `Directory` static class and its `CreateDirectory()` and `Delete()` methods, as shown in the following code:

```
var path = @"C:\Temp\Dir\Sub";
Console.WriteLine($"Exists: {Directory.Exists(path)}");
Directory.CreateDirectory(path);

var sub = Path.Combine(path, @"sub1\sub2\sub3");
Directory.CreateDirectory(sub);

Directory.Delete(sub);
Directory.Delete(path, true);
```

The first call to `Delete()` will delete the `C:\Temp\Dir\Sub\sub1\sub2\sub3` subdirectory, but only if it is empty. The second call will delete the `C:\Temp\Dir\Sub` subdirectory and all its content (files and subdirectories) in a recursive manner.

In the next example, we will list all the executable files that start with the letter T from a given directory (in this case, `C:\Program Files (x86)\Microsoft SDKs\Windows\v10.0A\bin\NETFX 4.8 Tools\`). For this, we'll use the `GetFiles()` method providing the proper filter. This method returns an array of `FileInfo` objects and we print information about the file using different properties of this class:

```
var dir = new DirectoryInfo(@"C:\Program Files (x86)\Microsoft
SDKs\Windows\v10.0A\bin\NETFX 4.8 Tools\");
foreach(var file in dir.GetFiles("t*.exe"))
{
    Console.WriteLine(
      $"{file.Name} [{file.Length}]
    [{file.Attributes}]");}
```

The output from executing this code sample could be as follows:

Figure 13.5 – A screenshot of the program listing executables that start with the letter T from a given directory

To print the information about the file, we used the `FileInfo` class, as mentioned previously. `Name`, `Length`, and `Attributes` are only some of the properties this class provides. Others include the extension and file times. An example of using them is shown in the following code snippet:

```
var file = new FileInfo(@"C:\Windows\explorer.exe");

Console.WriteLine($"Name: {file.Name}");
Console.WriteLine($"Extension: {file.Extension}");
Console.WriteLine($"Full name: {file.FullName}");
Console.WriteLine($"Length: {file.Length}");
Console.WriteLine($"Attributes: {file.Attributes}");
Console.WriteLine($"Creation: {file.CreationTime}");
Console.WriteLine($"Last access:{file.LastAccessTime}");
Console.WriteLine($"Last write: {file.LastWriteTime}");
```

Although the output will vary on each machine, it should look as follows:

```
Microsoft Visual Studio Debug Console
Name:        explorer.exe
Extension:   .exe
Full name:   C:\Windows\explorer.exe
Length:      4612520
Attributes:  Archive
Creation:    2019-10-03 22:10:06
Last access:2019-10-03 22:10:06
Last write:  2019-10-03 22:10:06
```

Figure 13.6 – Detailed file information displayed with the help of the FileInfo class

We can use what we have learned so far to create a function that writes the content of a directory recursively to the console and while doing so, also indents the names of the files and directories as it navigates deeper in the directory hierarchy. Such a function could look as follows:

```
void PrintContent(string path, string indent = null)
{
    try
    {
        foreach(var file in Directory.EnumerateFiles(path))
        {
            var fi = new FileInfo(file);
            Console.WriteLine($"{indent}{fi.Name}");
        }
```

```
        foreach(var dir in Directory.EnumerateDirectories(path))
        {
            var di = new DirectoryInfo(dir);
            Console.WriteLine($"{indent}[{di.Name}]");
            PrintContent(dir, indent + "  ");
        }
    }
    catch(Exception ex)
    {
        Console.Error.WriteLine(ex.Message);
    }
}
```

When executed with the path of the project directory as input, it prints the following output to the console (the following screenshot is a snippet of the complete output):

```
Microsoft Visual Studio Debug Console
chapter_13_01.csproj
Program.cs
[bin]
  [Debug]
    [netcoreapp3.0]
      chapter_13_01.deps.json
      chapter_13_01.dll
      chapter_13_01.exe
      chapter_13_01.pdb
      chapter_13_01.runtimeconfig.dev.json
      chapter_13_01.runtimeconfig.json
[obj]
  chapter_13_01.csproj.nuget.cache
  chapter_13_01.csproj.nuget.dgspec.json
```

Figure 13.7 – Partial output of the program that prints, recursively, the content of a specified directory

As you may have noticed, we used both GetFiles() and EnumerateFile(), as well as EnumerateDirectories(). These two sets of methods, the ones prefixed with Get and the ones prefixed with Enumerate, are similar in the sense that they return a collection of files or directories.

However, they differ in one key aspect—the `Get` methods return an array of objects, while the `Enumerate` methods return an `IEnumerable<T>` that allows clients to start iterating before all the filesystem objects are retrieved and also consume only what they want. These methods could, therefore, be a better alternative in many cases.

Most of the examples so far were focused on getting file and directory information, although we did create and delete directories. We can use the `File` and `FileInfo` classes to create and delete files. For instance, we can use `File.Create()` to create a new file or open and overwrite an existing file, as shown in the following example:

```
using (var file = new StreamWriter(
    File.Create(@"C:\Temp\Dir\demo.txt")))
{
    file.Write("This is a demo");
}
```

`File.Create()` returns a `FileStream` that, in this example, is then used to create a `StreamWriter` that allows us to write the text `This is a demo` to the file. The stream is then disposed and the file handle is properly closed.

If you are interested only in writing text or binary data, you can use static members of the `File` class, such as `WriteAllText()`, `WriteAllLines()`, or `WriteAllBytes()`. These have multiple overloads, allowing you, for instance, to specify text encoding. There are also asynchronous counterparts, `WriteAllTextAsync()`, `WriteAllLinesAsync()`, and `WriteAllBytesAsync()`. All these methods overwrite the current content of the file if it already exists. If you are interested in preserving the content and appending to its end, then you can use the `AppendAllText()` and `AppendAllLines()` methods and their asynchronous counterparts, `AppendAllTextAsync()` and `AppendAllLinesAsync()`.

The following example shows how to write and append text to an existing file using some of the methods mentioned here:

```
var path = @"C:\Temp\Dir\demo.txt";
File.WriteAllText(path, "This is a demo");
File.AppendAllText(path, "1st line");
File.AppendAllLines(path, new string[]{
    "2nd line", "3rd line"});
```

The first call, `WriteAllText()`, will write `This is a demo` to the file, overwriting any content. The second call, `AppendAllText()`, will append `1st line` without adding any new lines. The third call, `AppendAllLines()`, will write each string to the file, adding a new line after each. Therefore, after executing this code, the content of the file will be as follows:

```
This is a demo1st line2nd line
3rd line
```

Similar to writing content to a file, reading is also possible using the `File` class and its `ReadAllText()`, `ReadAllLines()`, and `ReadAllBytes()` methods. As with the write methods, there are also asynchronous versions, `ReadAllTextAsync()`, `ReadAllLinesAsync()`, and `ReadAllBytesAsync()`. An example of using some of these methods is shown in the following code:

```
var path = @"C:\Temp\Dir\demo.txt";
string text = File.ReadAllText(path);
string[] lines = File.ReadAllLines(path);
```

After executing this code, the `text` variable will contain the entire text read from the file. On the other hand, `lines` will be an array with two elements, the first being `This is a demo1st line2nd line` and the second being `3rd line`.

Plain text is not the only kind of data we would usually write to a file, and files are not the only storage systems for data. Sometimes, we might be interested in reading and writing from and to pipes, networks, local memory, or others. To handle all of this, .NET provides *streams*, which is the topic of the next section.

Working with streams

A **stream** is a sequence of bytes that can be stored locally in memory, in a file, a pipe, remotely on the network, or other conceivable sources. .NET abstracts this concept with a class called `Stream`, which provides support for reading from and writing to a stream. On the other hand, the streams are conceptually grouped into three categories:

- **Backing store**: These are streams that represent the source or the destination of a sequence of bytes. They are an endpoint for input or output data such as a file or network. Backing store streams work at the byte level. .NET provides classes such as `FileStream`, `MemoryStream`, and `NetworkStream` to implement backing stores.

- **Decorators**: These are streams that read or write data from or to another stream, transforming it in some way. Like backing stores, they work with bytes. Decorators can be chained together. .NET provides decorator streams such as `BufferedStream`, `CryptoStream`, `DeflateStream`, and `GZipStream`.

- **Adapters**: They are not actually streams but wrappers that help us work with sources of data at a higher level than bytes. They allow us to read/write primitive types (`bool`, `int`, `double`, etc.), text, XML data, and so on. Adaptors provided by .NET include `BinaryReader` and `BinaryWriter`, `StreamReader` and `StreamWriter`, and `XmlReader` and `XmlWriter`.

The following diagram shows, conceptually, the stream architecture:

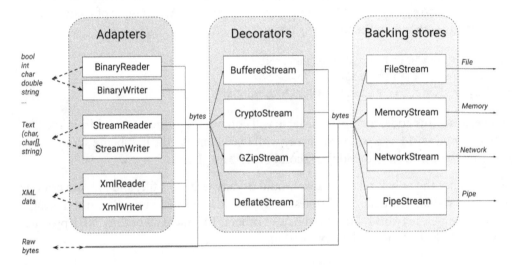

Figure 13.8 – A conceptual diagram of the stream's architecture

Discussing all the stream classes pictured in the preceding diagram is beyond the scope of this book. However, in this section, we will focus on the `BinaryReader`/`BinaryWriter` and `StreamReader`/`StreamWriter` adapters, as well as the `FileStream` and `MemoryStream` backing store streams.

Overview of the stream classes

As I mentioned earlier, the base class for all stream classes is the `System.IO.Stream` class. This is an abstract class that provides methods and properties for reading and writing from and to a stream. Many of these are abstract and are implemented in derived classes. The following are the most important methods of the class:

Close()	Closes the current stream and releases the source (such as a filehandle). This method is called when you dispose of the stream. You should prefer using deterministic disposal rather than calling this method explicitly.
CopyTo() / CopyToAsync()	Reads the bytes from the current stream and writes them to another stream.
Dispose()	Releases all resources used by this stream object, including the source stream.
Flush() / FlushAsync()	Writes the buffered data to the underlying backing store and clears all buffers.
Read() / ReadAsync()	Reads a sequence of bytes from the current stream object.
ReadByte()	Reads one byte from the current stream object.
Seek()	Sets the position of the current stream.
Write() / WriteAsync()	Writes a sequence of bytes to the current stream object.
WriteByte()	Writes one byte to the current stream object.

Some of the operations listed have asynchronous companions, which are suffixed with the word Async (such as ReadAsync() or WriteAsync()). The read and write operations advance the pointer that indicates the position in the current stream with the number of bytes read or written.

The Stream class also provides several useful properties that are listed in the following table:

CanRead	Indicates if the current stream supports reading.
CanSeek	Indicates if the current stream supports seeking.
CanTimeout	Indicates if the current stream can time out.
CanWrite	Indicates if the current stream supports writing.
Length	Retrieves the length of the stream (that is the number of bytes).
Position	Gets or sets the position within the current stream.
ReadTimeout	Gets or sets the number of milliseconds the stream will attempt to read before timing out.
WriteTimeout	Gets or sets the number of milliseconds the stream will attempt to write before timing out.

The class that represents a backing store stream for a file is called `FileStream`. This class is derived from the abstract `Stream` class and implements the abstract members. It supports both synchronous and asynchronous operations and can be used for opening, reading, writing, and closing not only disk files but other operating system objects, such as pipes and the standard input and output. The asynchronous methods are useful for performing time-consuming operations without blocking the main thread.

The `FileStream` class supports random access to a file. The `Seek()` method allows us to move the position of the current pointer for reading/writing within the stream. When changing the position, you must specify a byte offset and a seek origin. The byte offset is relative to the seek origin, which can be the beginning, the current position, or the end of the stream.

The class provides many constructors for creating an instance of the class. You can supply a file handle (either as an `IntPtr` or a `SafeFileHandle`) or a file path, as well as a file mode (which determines how the file should be opened), file access (which determines how the file should be accessed – for reading, writing, or both), and file share (which determines how other file streams can access the same file) in various combinations. Listing all these constructors is impractical here but we will see several examples throughout this chapter.

The class that represents a backing store for memory is called `MemoryStream` and is also derived from `Stream`. Most of the members of this class are implementations of the abstract members of the base class. However, the class features several constructors that allow us to create either a **resizable stream** (initially empty or with a specified capacity) or a **non-resizable stream** from an array of bytes. Memory streams created from an array of bytes cannot be expanded or shrunk and can be writeable or read-only.

Working with file streams

The `FileStream` class allows us to read and write a sequence of bytes from/to a file. It operates with raw data such as `byte[]`, `Span<byte>`, or `Memory<byte>`. We can obtain a `FileStream` object using static methods of the `File` class or non-static methods of the `FileInfo` class:

`Create()`	Opens a file stream for the specified path, either creating the file or overwriting an existing one.
`Open()`	Opens a file stream for the specified path with options such as file mode, access, and sharing.
`OpenRead()`	Opens a file stream for the specified path for reading.
`OpenWrite()`	Opens a file stream for the specified path for writing.

We can see how this works using the following example, where we write four bytes to the file located at C:\Temp\data.raw and then we read the entire content of the file and print it to the console:

```
var path = @"C:\Temp\data.raw";
var data = new byte[] { 0xBA, 0xAD, 0xF0, 0x0D};
using(FileStream wr = File.Create(path))
{
    wr.Write(data, 0, data.Length);
}

using(FileStream rd = File.OpenRead(path))
{
    var buffer = new byte[rd.Length];
    rd.Read(buffer, 0, buffer.Length);

    Console.WriteLine(
        string.Join(" ", buffer.Select(
                    e => $"{e:X02}")));
}
```

In the first part, we use File.Create() to open a file for writing. If the file does not exist, then it is created. If the file exists, then its content will be overwritten. The FileStream.Write() method is used to write the content of the byte array to the file. The stream will be flushed to the file and the file handle will be closed when the FileStream object is disposed of at the end of the using statement.

In the second part, we use File.OpenRead() to open the file that was previously written, but this time for reading. We allocate an array large enough to receive the entire content of the file and use FileStream.Read() to read its content. The output of this code is as follows:

Figure 13.9 – The content of created binary file displayed to the console

Handling raw data can be cumbersome. For this reason, .NET provides stream adapters that allow us to handle higher-level data. The first pair of adapters is BinaryReader and BinaryWriter, which provide support for reading and writing primitive types and strings in binary format. An example of using these two is shown here:

```
var path = @"C:\Temp\data.bin";
using (var wr = new BinaryWriter(File.Create(path)))
{
    wr.Write(true);
    wr.Write('x');
    wr.Write(42);
    wr.Write(19.99);
    wr.Write(49.99M);
    wr.Write("text");
}

using(var rd = new BinaryReader(File.OpenRead(path)))
{
    Console.WriteLine(rd.ReadBoolean()); // True
    Console.WriteLine(rd.ReadChar());    // x
    Console.WriteLine(rd.ReadInt32());   // 42
    Console.WriteLine(rd.ReadDouble());  // 19.99
    Console.WriteLine(rd.ReadDecimal()); // 49.99
    Console.WriteLine(rd.ReadString());  // text
}
```

We first open a file with File.Create() that returns FileStream. This stream is used as an argument for the constructor of the BinaryWriter stream adapter. The Write() method is overloaded for all the primitive types (char, bool, sbyte, byte, short, ushort, int, uint, long, ulong, float, double, and decimal), as well as for byte[], char[], and string.

Secondly, we reopen the same file, but for reading using File.OpenRead(). The FileStream object returned by this method is used as an argument to the constructor of the BinaryReader stream adapter. This class has a set of reading methods, one for each primitive type, such as ReadBoolean(), ReadChar(), ReadInt16(), ReadInt32(), ReadDouble(), and ReadDecimal(), as well as methods for reading a byte[] – ReadBytes(), a char[] - ReadChars(), and strings—ReadString(). You can see some of these methods used in the previous example.

By default, both BinaryReader and BinaryWriter handle strings using the *UTF-8 encoding*. However, they both have overloaded constructors that allow us to specify another encoding using the System.Text.Encoding class.

Although these two adapters can be used for processing strings, using them for reading and writing text files can be cumbersome because of a lack of support for features such as line handling. To handle text files, the StreamReader and StreamWriter adapters should be used. By default, they process text as UTF-8 encoded, but their constructors allow us to specify a different encoding. In the following example, we write text to a file and then read it back and print it to the console:

```
var path = @"C:\Temp\data.txt";
using(StreamWriter wr = File.CreateText(path))
{
    wr.WriteLine("1st line");
    wr.WriteLine("2nd line");
}

using(StreamReader rd = File.OpenText(path))
{
    while(!rd.EndOfStream)
        Console.WriteLine(rd.ReadLine());
}
```

The File.CreateText() method opens a file for writing (either creating or overwriting it) and returns an instance of the StreamWriter class that uses UTF-8 encoding. The WriteLine() method writes a string to the file and then adds a new line. There are overloaded versions of WriteLine() but also overloaded Write() methods that can write a char, char[], or string without adding a new line after.

In the second part, we use the File.OpenText() method to open the previously written text file for reading. This returns a StreamReader object that reads UTF-8 text. The ReadLine() method is used to read the content line by line in a loop until the end of the stream. The EndOfStream property is used to check whether the current stream position reached the end of the stream.

Instead of using the File.OpenText() method, we could use File.Open(), which allows us to specify the opening mode, file access, and sharing. We could rewrite the reading part shown earlier as follows:

```
using(var rd = new StreamReader(
  File.Open(path, FileMode.Open,
        FileAccess.Read,
        FileShare.Read)))
{
    while (!rd.EndOfStream)
        Console.WriteLine(rd.ReadLine());
}
```

Sometimes, we need a stream to handle temporary data. Using files can be cumbersome and also adds unnecessary overhead to the I/O operations. For this purpose, memory streams are the most suitable.

Working with memory streams

A **memory stream** is a backing store for local memory. Such a stream is useful for operations when we need temporary storage for transforming data. Examples can include XML serialization or data compression and decompression. We will look at these two operations in the upcoming code.

The static `Serializer<T>` class shown in the following code contains two methods—`Serialize()` and `Deserialize()`. The former takes a `T` object, uses `XmlSerializer` to generate an XML representation of it, and returns the XML data as a string. The latter takes a string containing XML data and uses `XmlSerializer` to read it and create a new object of type `T` from it. Here is the code:

```
public static class Serializer<T>
{
    static readonly XmlSerializer _serializer =
        new XmlSerializer(typeof(T));
    static readonly Encoding _encoding = Encoding.UTF8;

    public static string Serialize(T value)
    {
        using (var ms = new MemoryStream())
        {
            _serializer.Serialize(ms, value);
            return _encoding.GetString(ms.ToArray());
        }
    }

    public static T Deserialize(string value)
    {
        using (var ms = new MemoryStream(
            _encoding.GetBytes(value)))
        {
            return (T)_serializer.Deserialize(ms);
        }
    }
}
```

The memory stream created in the `Serialize()` method is resizable. It is initially empty and grows as needed. However, the one created in the `Deserialize()` method is non-resizable because it is initialized from an array of bytes. This stream is used for read-only purposes.

The `MemoryStream` class implements the `IDisposable` interface because it derives from `Stream`, which implements `IDisposable`. However, `MemoryStream` has no resources to dispose of and, therefore, the `Dispose()` method does nothing. Calling it explicitly has no effect on the stream. Therefore, it is not necessary to wrap a memory stream variable in a `using` statement, as we did in the previous example.

Let's consider the following implementation of an `Employee` class:

```
public class Employee
{
    public int EmployeeId { get; set; }
    public string FirstName { get; set; }
    public string LastName { get; set; }

    public override string ToString() =>
        $"[{EmployeeId}] {LastName}, {FirstName}";
}
```

We can serialize and deserialize instances of this class as follows:

```
var employee = new Employee
{
    EmployeeId = 42,
    FirstName = "John",
    LastName = "Doe"
};

var text = Serializer<Employee>.Serialize(employee);
var result = Serializer<Employee>.Deserialize(text);

Console.WriteLine(employee);
Console.WriteLine(text);
Console.WriteLine(result);
```

The result of executing this code is shown in the following screenshot:

```
Microsoft Visual Studio Debug Console                                    —    □    ×
<?xml version="1.0"?>
<Employee xmlns:xsi="http://www.w3.org/2001/XMLSchema-instance"
 xmlns:xsd="http://www.w3.org/2001/XMLSchema">
  <EmployeeId>42</EmployeeId>
  <FirstName>John</FirstName>
  <LastName>Doe</LastName>
</Employee>
[42] Doe, John
```

Figure 13.10 – An XML-serialized Employee object displayed to the console

The other example we mentioned when a memory stream is handy is in the *compression and decompression of data*. The GZipStream class from the System. IO.Compression namespace is a stream decorator that supports compression and decompression of streams using the GZip data format specification. A MemoryStream object is used as a backing store for the GZipStream decorator. The static Compression class shown here provides two methods that compress and decompress an array of bytes:

```
public static class Compression
{
    public static byte[] Compress(byte[] data)
    {
        if (data == null) return null;
        if (data.Length == 0) return new byte[] { };

        using var ms = new MemoryStream();
        using var gzips =
            new GZipStream(ms,
        CompressionMode.Compress);
        gzips.Write(data, 0, data.Length);
        gzips.Close();
        return ms.ToArray();
    }

    public static byte[] Decompress(byte[] data)
    {
        if (data == null) return null;
        if (data.Length == 0) return new byte[] { };
```

```
    using var source = new MemoryStream(data);
    using var gzips =
        new GZipStream(source,
    CompressionMode.Decompress);
    using var target = new MemoryStream(data.Length * 2);
    gzips.CopyTo(target);
    return target.ToArray();
    }
}
```

We can use this helper class to compress a string to an array of bytes and then decompress it back to a string. Such an example is shown in the following code:

```
var text = "Lorem ipsum dolor sit amet, consectetur adipiscing
elit, sed do eiusmod tempor incididunt ut labore et dolore
magna aliqua.";
var data = Encoding.UTF8.GetBytes(text);
var compressed = Compression.Compress(data);
var decompressed = Compression.Decompress(compressed);
var result = Encoding.UTF8.GetString(decompressed);

Console.WriteLine($"Text size: {text.Length}");
Console.WriteLine($"Compressed: {compressed.Length}");
Console.WriteLine($"Decompressed: {decompressed.Length}");
Console.WriteLine(result);
if (text == result)
    Console.WriteLine("Decompression successful!");
```

The output from executing this sample code is shown in the following screenshot:

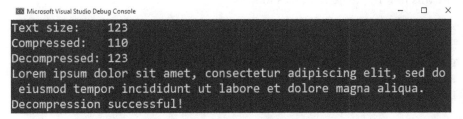

Figure 13.11 – A screenshot with the result of compressing and decompressing a text

In this section, we have seen how to simply serialize and deserialize XML. We will elaborate on this topic in the next section.

Serializing and deserializing XML

In the previous section, we have seen how we can use the `XmlSerializer` class, from the `System.Xml.Serialization` namespace, to serialize and deserialize data. This class is handy for serializing objects to XML and deserializing XML to objects. Although, in the previous example, we used a memory stream to serialize, it actually works with any stream; moreover, it also works with the `TextWriter` and `XmlWriter` adapters.

The following sample shows a modified `Serializer<T>` class, where we specify the path of a file where the XML document is to be written to or read from:

```
public static class Serializer<T>
{
    static readonly XmlSerializer _serializer =
        new XmlSerializer(typeof(T));

    public static void Serialize(T value, string path)
    {
        using var ms = File.CreateText(path);
        _serializer.Serialize(ms, value);
    }

    public static T Deserialize(string path)
    {
        using var ms = File.OpenText(path);
        return (T)_serializer.Deserialize(ms);
    }
}
```

We can use this new implementation as follows:

```
var employee = new Employee
{
    EmployeeId = 42,
    FirstName = "John",
    LastName = "Doe"
};

var path = Path.Combine(Path.GetTempPath(), "employee1.xml");
Serializer<Employee>.Serialize(employee, path);
var result = Serializer<Employee>.Deserialize(path);
```

The result of XML serialization using this code is a document with the following content:

```xml
<?xml version="1.0" encoding="utf-8"?>
<Employee xmlns:xsi="http://www.w3.org/2001/XMLSchema-instance"
xmlns:xsd="http://www.w3.org/2001/XMLSchema">
  <EmployeeId>42</EmployeeId>
  <FirstName>John</FirstName>
  <LastName>Doe</LastName>
</Employee>
```

XmlSerializer works by serializing all the public properties and fields of a type to XML. It uses some default settings such as types becoming nodes and properties and fields becoming elements. The name of a type, property, or field becomes the name of the node or element and the value of a field or property its text. It also adds default namespaces (which you can see in the preceding code). However, it is possible to control the way serialization is performed using attributes on types and members. Such an example is shown in the following code:

```csharp
[XmlType("employee")]
public class Employee
{
    [XmlAttribute("id")]
    public int EmployeeId { get; set; }

    [XmlElement(ElementName = "firstName")]
    public string FirstName { get; set; }

    [XmlElement(ElementName = "lastName")]
    public string LastName { get; set; }

    public override string ToString() =>
        $"[{EmployeeId}] {LastName}, {FirstName}";
}
```

Serializing an instance of this Employee class implementation would produce an XML document such as the following:

```xml
<?xml version="1.0" encoding="utf-8"?>
<employee xmlns:xsi="http://www.w3.org/2001/XMLSchema-instance"
xmlns:xsd="http://www.w3.org/2001/XMLSchema" id="42">
  <firstName>John</firstName>
  <lastName>Doe</lastName>
</employee>
```

We have used several attributes here, XmlType, XmlAttribute, and XmlElement, but the list is long. The following table lists the most important XML attributes and what they do. These attributes are available in the System.Xml.Serialization namespace:

Type	Applies to	Description
XmlArrayAttribute	Public field or property, parameter, return value that returns an array	The members of the arrays are serialized as members of an XML array.
XmlAttributeAttribute	Public field or property, parameter, return value	The member is serialized as an XML attribute.
XmlElementAttribute	Public field or property, parameter, return value	The member is serialized as an XML element.
XmlEnumAttribute	Public field that is an enumeration	The member is serialized as the element name of an enumeration.
XmlIgnoreAttribute	Public field or property	The member is ignored during XML serialization.
XmlRootAttribute	Public class, struct, enum, interface	The type is serialized as the XML root element.
XmlTextAttribute	Public field or property	The member is serialized as XML text.
XmlTypeAttribute	Public class, struct, enum, interface	Specifies the name and namespace of the XML type.

The way the XmlSerializer class works is that, at runtime, it generates serialization code for each type in a temporary serialization assembly every time the application runs. In some cases, this can be a performance issue that can be avoided by generating these assemblies in advance. The **XML Serializer Generator Tool** (Sgen.exe) can be used to generate these assemblies. If your assembly that contains serialization code is called MyAssembly.dll, the generated serializing assembly will be called MyAssembly.XmlSerializer.dll. This tool is deployed as part of the Windows SDK.

You can also generate an XML schema (an XSD document) from classes or classes from an existing XML schema using the **XML Schema Definition Tool** (xsd.exe). This tool is distributed as part of the Windows SDK or with Visual Studio.

A possible issue with `XmlSerializer` is that it serializes a single .NET object to an XML document (of course, the object can be complex and contain other objects and arrays of objects). If you have two separate objects that you want to write to the same document, it does not work properly. Let's imagine that we also have the following class, representing a department in a company:

```
public class Department
{
    [XmlAttribute]
    public int Id { get; set; }

    public string Name { get; set; }
}
```

We might want to write an XML document containing an employee and a department. Using `XmlSerializer` will not work properly. This is shown in the following example:

```
public static class Serializer<T>
{
    static readonly XmlSerializer _serializer =
        new XmlSerializer(typeof(T));

    public static void Serialize(T value, StreamWriter stream)
    {
        _serializer.Serialize(stream, value);
    }

    public static T Deserialize(StreamReader stream)
    {
        return (T)_serializer.Deserialize(stream);
    }
}
```

We could try to use the following code for serializing an employee and a department to the same XML document:

```
var employee = new Employee
{
    EmployeeId = 42,
    FirstName = "John",
    LastName = "Doe"
};
```

```
var department = new Department
{
    Id = 102,
    Name = "IT"
};

var path = Path.Combine(Path.GetTempPath(), "employee.xml");
using (var wr = File.CreateText(path))
{
    Serializer<Employee>.Serialize(employee, wr);
    wr.WriteLine();
    Serializer<Department>.Serialize(department, wr);
}
```

The XML document that is generated to the disk file will have the content shown in the following code. This is not valid XML because it has multiple document declarations and does not have a single root element:

```xml
<?xml version="1.0" encoding="utf-8"?>
<employee xmlns:xsi="http://www.w3.org/2001/XMLSchema-instance"
xmlns:xsd="http://www.w3.org/2001/XMLSchema" id="42">
    <firstName>John</firstName>
    <lastName>Doe</lastName>
</employee>
<?xml version="1.0" encoding="utf-8"?>
<Department xmlns:xsi="http://www.w3.org/2001/XMLSchema-
instance" xmlns:xsd="http://www.w3.org/2001/XMLSchema"
Id="102">
    <Name>IT</Name>
</Department>
```

To make it work, we'd have to create an additional type that would contain an employee and a department, and we would have to serialize an instance of this type. This extra object will be serialized as the root element of the XML document. We will demonstrate this with the following example (notice that we have an extra property called Version here):

```csharp
public class Data
{
    [XmlAttribute]
    public int Version { get; set; }
    public Employee Employee { get; set; }
    public Department Department { get; set; }
}
```

```
var data = new Data()
{
    Version = 1,
    Employee = new Employee {
        EmployeeId = 42,
        FirstName = "John",
        LastName = "Doe"
    },
    Department = new Department {
        Id = 102,
        Name = "IT"
    }
};

var path = Path.Combine(Path.GetTempPath(), "employee.xml");
using (var wr = File.CreateText(path))
{
    Serializer<Data>.Serialize(data, wr);
}
```

This time, the output is a well-formed XML document that is listed in the following code:

```
<?xml version="1.0" encoding="utf-8"?>
<Data xmlns:xsi="http://www.w3.org/2001/XMLSchema-instance"
xmlns:xsd="http://www.w3.org/2001/XMLSchema" Version="1">
  <Employee id="42">
    <firstName>John</firstName>
    <lastName>Doe</lastName>
  </Employee>
  <Department Id="102">
    <Name>IT</Name>
  </Department>
</Data>
```

To allow further control for reading and writing XML, the .NET base class library contains two classes called XmlReader and XmlWriter that provide a fast, non-cached, forward-only way to read or generate XML data from or to a stream or file.

The XmlWriter class can be used to write XML data to a stream, file, text reader, or string. It provides features such as the following:

- Validating characters and XML names
- Verifying that an XML document is well-formed

- Support for CLR types so that you don't need to manually convert everything to a string

- Base64 and BaseHex encoding for binary data to be written in the XML document

The `XmlWriter` class contains many methods; some of these methods are listed in the following table. Although this list only includes the synchronous method, all of them have asynchronous companions such as `WriteElementStringAsync()` for `WriteElementString()`:

`WriteStartDocument()`	Writes the XML declaration with version 1.0.
`WriteEndDocument()`	Closes any open element or attribute.
`WriteDocType()`	Writes a DOCTYPE declaration with the specified name and attributes.
`WriteComment()`	Writes a `<!-- .. -->` comment with the specified text.
`WriteValue()`	Overloaded method for writing built-in types to the output.
`WriteCData()`	Writes a `<![CDATA[...]]>` block with the specified text.
`WriteBase64()`	Encodes binary data as Base64 and writes the resulting text.
`WriteBinHex()`	Encodes binary data as BinHex and writes the resulting text.
`WriteStartElement()`	Writes the start of the element tag with the specified name.
`WriteEndElement()`	Writes the end of the element tag opened with a call to `WriteStartElement()`.
`WriteElementString()`	Writes an element with the specified name and string value.
`WriteNode()`	Copies an element from `XmlReader` or `XPathNavigator` to the output.
`WriteStartAttribute()`	Writes the start of an attribute with the specified name.
`WriteEndAttribute()`	Writes the end of the attribute opened with a call to `WriteStartAttribute()`.
`WriteAttributeString()`	Writes an attribute with the specified name and string value.

While using `XmlWriter`, it is possible to specify various settings such as encoding, indentation, how attributes should be written (on a new or the same line), omitting the XML declaration, and others. These settings are controlled using an instance of the `XmlWriterSettings` class.

The following listing shows an example of using `XmlWriter` to create an XML document that contains an employee and a department as a part of a root element called `Data`. In fact, the result is the same as from the previous example, except that no namespaces are created:

```
var employee = new Employee
{
    EmployeeId = 42,
    FirstName = "John",
    LastName = "Doe"
};

var department = new Department
{
    Id = 102,
    Name = "IT"
};

var path = Path.Combine(Path.GetTempPath(), "employee.xml");

var settings = new XmlWriterSettings
{
    Encoding = Encoding.UTF8,
    Indent = true
};

var namespaces = new XmlSerializerNamespaces();
namespaces.Add(string.Empty, string.Empty);

using (var wr = XmlWriter.Create(path, settings))
{
    wr.WriteStartDocument();
    wr.WriteStartElement("Data");
    wr.WriteStartAttribute("Version");
    wr.WriteValue(1);
    wr.WriteEndAttribute();

    var employeeSerializer =
      new XmlSerializer(typeof(Employee));
```

```
    employeeSerializer.Serialize(wr, employee, namespaces);

    var depSerializer = new XmlSerializer(typeof(Department));
    depSerializer.Serialize(wr, department, namespaces);

    wr.WriteEndElement();
    wr.WriteEndDocument();
}
```

In this example, we have used the following components:

- An instance of `XmlWriterSettings` to set encoding to UTF-8 and enable indentation of the output.

- `XmlWriter.Create()` to create an instance of an implementation of the `XmlWriter` class.

- Various methods of the `XmlWriter` class to write XML data.

- An instance of `XmlSerializerNamespaces` to control the generated namespaces. In this example, we added an empty scheme and namespace, which results in no namespaces written to the XML document.

- Instances of the `XmlSerializer` class to simplify the serialization of the `Employee` and `Department` objects to the XML document. This is possible because the `Serialize()` method can take an `XmlWriter` as a destination for the XML document it generates.

The companion class for `XmlWriter` is `XmlReader`. This class allows us to move through XML data and read its content but in a forward-only manner, which means you cannot go back from a given point. The `XmlReader` class is an abstract one, just like `XmlWriter`, and there are concrete implementations such as `XmlTextReader`, `XmlNodeReader`, or `XmlValidatingReader`.

However, for most scenarios, you should use `XmlReadern`. To create an instance of it, use the static `XmlReader.Create()` method. The class contains a long list of methods and properties, a few of them listed in the following table. Just like in the case of `XmlWriter`, `XmlReader` has both synchronous and asynchronous methods. Only some from the first category are listed here:

`Create()`	The overloaded method that creates a new instance of an implementation of `XmlReader`.
`MoveToAttribute()`	Moves the reading position to the specified attribute (by index, name, or local name and namespace URI).
`MoveToContent()`	Moves the reading position to the next content node or the end of the stream.
`Read()`	Reads the next node from the stream.
`ReadContentAs...()`	This is a set of methods such as `ReadContentAsBase64()`, `ReadContentAsInt()`, `ReadContentAsDouble()`, and so on that reads the text content at the current position as the indicated data type (Base64 text, `int`, `double`, and so on).
`ReadElementContentAs...()`	Similar to the previous set of methods, except that it reads the current element and returns its value as the specified type (Base64, `int`, `double`, and so on).
`ReadInnerXml()`	Reads all the content of the current node, including the markup.
`ReadOuterXml()`	Reads all the content of the current node and all its children, including the markup.
`ReadSubtree()`	Returns an instance of `XmlReader` that can be used to read the content of the current node and all its children.
`ReadToDescendant()`	Reads to the next descendant specified with a qualified name or namespace URI and local name.
`ReadToFollowing()`	Reads until it finds an element with the specified qualified name or namespace URI and a local name.
`ReadNoNextSibling()`	Reads to the next sibling with the specified qualified name or namespace URI and a local name.
`Skip()`	Skips the children of the current node.
`AttributeCount`	Returns the number of attributes of the current node.

EOF	Indicates whether the reading position is at the end of the stream.
HasAttributes	Indicates whether the current node has any attributes.
HasValue	Indicates whether the current node has a value.
LocalName	Gets the local name of the current node (for instance, widget for <local:widget />).
Name	Gets the qualified name of the current node (for instance, local:widget for <local:widget />).
NodeType	Gets the type of the current node.
Prefix	Gets the prefix, if any of the current node (for instance, local for <local:widget />).
Value	Gets the text value of the current node.
ValueType	Gets the CLR type of the current node.

When creating an instance of XmlReader, you can specify a set of features that you want to enable, such as schemas that should be used to perform validation, ignoring comments or white spaces, validation of type assignment, and others. The XmlReaderSettings class is used for this purpose.

In the following example, we use XmlReader to read the content of the XML document written earlier and display a representation of its content to the console:

```csharp
var rdsettings = new XmlReaderSettings()
{
    IgnoreComments = true,
    IgnoreWhitespace = true
};

using (var rd = XmlReader.Create(path, rdsettings))
{
    string indent = string.Empty;
    while(rd.Read())
    {
        switch(rd.NodeType)
        {
            case XmlNodeType.Element:
                Console.Write(
                    $"{indent}{{ {rd.Name} : ");
                indent = indent + " ";
```

```
            while (rd.MoveToNextAttribute())
            {
                Console.WriteLine();
                Console.WriteLine($"{indent}{{{rd.
Name}:{rd.Value}}}");
            }
            break;
        case XmlNodeType.Text:
            Console.Write(rd.Value);
            break;
        case XmlNodeType.EndElement:
            indent = indent.Remove(0, 2);
            Console.WriteLine($"{indent}}}");
            break;
        default:
            Console.WriteLine($"[{rd.Name} {rd.Value}]");
            break;
        }
    }
}
```

The output of executing this code is as follows:

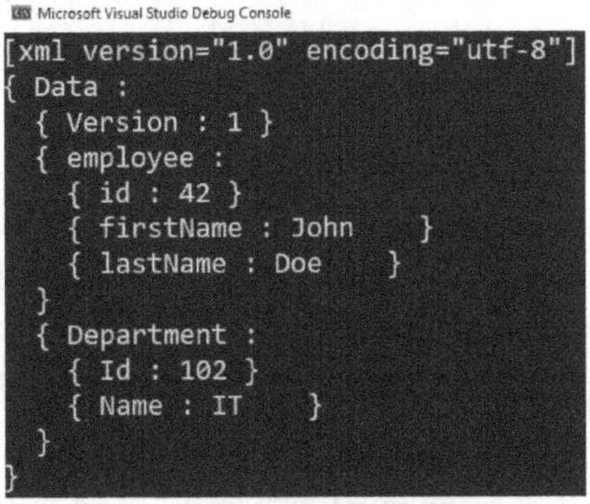

Figure 13.12 – A screenshot with the content of the XML document read from disk and displayed on the console

Here are several key points from this sample:

- We created an instance of XmlReaderSettings to tell XmlReader to ignore comments and white spaces.

- We used XmlReader.Create() to create a new instance of an implementation of XmlReader that reads XML data from a file with the specified path..

- The Read() method is used in a loop to read the XML document node by node.

- We use properties such as NodeType, Name, and Value to check the type of each node, its name, and its value.

There are many details concerning handling XML data with XmlReader and XmlWriter, as well as serialization using XmlSerializer. Discussing all these here would take too much time. We recommend that you use additional resources, such as the official documentation, to learn more about these classes.

Now that we have seen how to handle XML data, let's look at JSON.

Serializing and deserializing JSON

In recent times, **JavaScript Object Notation (JSON)** has become the de facto standard for data serialization, not only for web and mobile but also for desktop. .NET did not provide a proper library for serializing and deserializing JSON; therefore, developers have resorted to third-party libraries. One of these libraries is **Json.NET** (also known as **Newtonsoft. Json**, after its creator, Newton-King). This has become the preferred library for most .NET developers and a dependency of ASP.NET Core. However, with the release of .NET Core 3.0, Microsoft is providing its own JSON serializer, known as **System.Text.Json**, after the namespace where it is available. In this last part of this chapter, we will look at these two libraries and see some of their capabilities and how they compare to each other.

Using Json.NET

Json.NET is currently the most widely used .NET library for JSON serialization and deserialization. It's a high-performance, easy-to-use, open source library, available as a NuGet package called **Newtonsoft.Json**. This is, in fact, by far, the most downloaded package on NuGet. Some of the features it provides are listed here:

- Simple APIs for most common serialization and deserialization scenarios with JsonConvert, which is a wrapper over JsonSerializer.

- More fine-grained control over the serialization/deserialization process with JsonSerializer. This class can write text to or read text from a stream, directly via JsonTextWriter and JsonTextReader.

- The possibility to create, modify, parse, and query JSON using JObject, JArray, and JValue.

- The possibility to convert between XML and JSON.

- The possibility to query JSON with JSON Path, an XPath-like query language.

- Validation of JSON with JSON Schema.

- Support for **Binary JSON (BSON)** via `BsonReader` and `BsonWriter`. This is a binary-encoded serialization of JSON-like documents.

In this section, we will explore several common serialization and deserialization scenarios using Json.NET. For this purpose, we will use the following implementation of an `Employee` class:

```
public enum EmployeeStatus { Active, Inactive }

public class Employee
{
    public int EmployeeId { get; set; }
    public string FirstName { get; set; }
    public string LastName { get; set; }
    public DateTime? HireDate { get; set; }
    public List<string> Telephones { get; set; }
    public bool IsOnLeave { get; set; }

    [JsonConverter(typeof(StringEnumConverter))]
    public EmployeeStatus Status { get; set; }

    [JsonIgnore]
    public DateTime LastModified { get; set; }

    public override string ToString() =>
        $"[{EmployeeId}] {LastName}, {FirstName}";
}
```

Although the library is rich in functionalities, covering them all here is beyond the scope of this book. We recommend reading the online documentation for Json.NET that's available at `https://www.newtonsoft.com/json`.

Getting a string that contains the JSON serialization of an `Employee` object is straightforward, as shown in the following example:

```
var employee = new Employee
{
    EmployeeId = 42,
    FirstName = "John",
    LastName = "Doe"
};

var text = JsonConvert.SerializeObject(employee);
```

By default, JsonConvert.SerializeObject() will produce minified JSON, which does not contain indentation and white spaces. The result of the preceding code is the following JSON:

```
{"EmployeeId":42,"FirstName":"John","LastName":"Doe",
"HireDate":null,"Telephones":null,"IsOnLeave":false,
"Status":"Active"}
```

Although this is suitable for transferring data over a network, such as when communicating with a web service, because the size is smaller, it's harder to read by a human. If you want the JSON document to be readable, you should use indentation. This can be specified by providing formatting options, available with the Formatting enumeration. An example of this is shown here:

```
var text = JsonConvert.SerializeObject(
    employee, Formatting.Indented);
```

This time, the result is the following:

```
{
    "EmployeeId": 42,
    "FirstName": "John",
    "LastName": "Doe",
    "HireDate": null,
    "Telephones": null,
    "IsOnLeave": false,
    "Status": "Active"
}
```

Indentation is not the only serialization option we can specify. In fact, there are many options you can set using the JsonSerializerSettings class, which can be provided as an argument to the SerializeObject() method. For instance, we might want to skip serializing properties or fields of reference, or nullable types that are set to null. Examples include HireDate and Telephones, which are of the DateTime? and List<string> types, respectively. This can be done as follows:

```
var text = JsonConvert.SerializeObject(
    employee,
    Formatting.Indented,
    new JsonSerializerSettings()
    {
        NullValueHandling = NullValueHandling.Ignore,
    });
```

The result of serializing the `employee` object we used in the previous examples is shown in the following listing. You will notice that `HireDate` and `Telephones` are no longer present in the resulting JSON:

```
{
  "EmployeeId": 42,
  "FirstName": "John",
  "LastName": "Doe",
  "IsOnLeave": false,
  "Status": "Active"
}
```

Another option that can be specified for serialization controls how default values are handled. `DefaultValueHandling` is an enumeration that specifies how members with default values should be serialized or deserialized. By specifying `Ignore`, you enable the serializer to skip from the output the members whose value is the same as their type's default value (`0` for numeric types, `false` for `bool`, and `null` for reference and nullable types). The default value that is ignored can actually be changed with the use of an attribute, called `DefaultValueAttribute`, being specified on the member. Let's consider the following example:

```
var text = JsonConvert.SerializeObject(
    employee,
    Formatting.Indented,
    new JsonSerializerSettings()
    {
        NullValueHandling = NullValueHandling.Ignore,
        DefaultValueHandling = DefaultValueHandling.Ignore
    });
```

This time, the resulting JSON is even simpler, as shown in the following listing. This is because the `IsOnLeave` and `Status` properties are set to their default value, which is `false` and `EmployeeStatus.Active`, respectively:

```
{
  "EmployeeId": 42,
  "FirstName": "John",
  "LastName": "Doe"
}
```

We mentioned earlier the attribute called `DefaultValueAttribute`. You may have noticed a couple of other attributes, `JsonIgnoreAttribute` and `JsonConverterAttribute`, being used in the declaration of the `Employee` class. The serialization can be controlled with attributes, and the library supports both standard .NET serialization attributes (such as `SerializableAttribute`, `DataContractAttribute`, `DataMemberAttribute`, and `NonSerializedAttributes`) and built-in Json.NET attributes. When both are present, the built-in Json.NET attributes take precedence over the others. The built-in Json.NET attributes are shown in the following table:

Name	Target	Description
JsonObjectAttribute	Class, struct, interface	Specifies how the type should be serialized.
JsonArrayAttribute	Class, interface	Specifies that a type representing a collection should be serialized as a JSON array.
JsonDictionaryAttribute	Class, interface	Specifies that a class representing a dictionary of key-value pairs should be serialized as a JSON object.
JsonPropertyAttribute	Property, field, parameter	Specifies how a member should be serialized as a JSON property.
JsonConverterAttribute	Class, struct, enum, interface, property, field, parameter	Specifies how JsonConverter should be used to serialize the type or member.
JsonExtensionDataAttribute	Property, field representing a collection	Tells the serializer to deserialize properties of a JSON document that do not have matching members in the destination object to the collection field or property decorated with this attribute.
JsonConstructorAttribute	Constructor	Tells the serializer that this constructor should be used to create an instance of the class during deserialization.
JsonIgnoreAttribute	Property, field	Excludes the member from the serialization.

Of these attributes, we have used `JsonIgnoreAttribute` to indicate that the `LastModified` property of the `Employee` class should not be serialized and `JsonConverterAttribute` to indicate that the `Status` property should be serialized using the `StringEnumConverter` class. The result is that this property will be serialized as a string (with the values `Active` or `Inactive`) and not as a number (with the values `0` or `1`).

The `JsonConvert.SerializeObject()` method returns a string. It is possible to serialize and deserialize using streams, such as a file or a memory stream. To do so, however, we must use the `JsonSerializer` class. This class has overloaded methods called `Serialize()` and `Deserialize()`, as well as a series of properties that allow us to customize the serialization. The following example shows how we can use the class to serialize the employee object we used so far to a text file on disk:

```
var path = Path.Combine(Path.GetTempPath() + "employee.json");
var serializer = new JsonSerializer()
{
    Formatting = Formatting.Indented,
    NullValueHandling = NullValueHandling.Ignore,
    DefaultValueHandling = DefaultValueHandling.Ignore
};

using (var sw = File.CreateText(path))
using (var jw = new JsonTextWriter(sw))
{
    serializer.Serialize(jw, employee);
}
```

We specified that we want to use indentation and skip the members that are `null` or have a value that is the type's default value. The result of serialization is a text file with the following content:

```
{
    "EmployeeId": 42,
    "FirstName": "John",
    "LastName": "Doe"
}
```

The opposite process of deserialization is also straightforward. Using `JsonSerializer`, we can read from the text file we created earlier. For this purpose, we use `JsonTextReader`, which is a companion class for `JsonTextWriter`:

```
using (var sr = File.OpenText(path))
using (var jr = new JsonTextReader(sr))
{
    var result = serializer.Deserialize<Employee>(jr);

    Console.WriteLine(result);
}
```

Deserialization from a string is also possible and straightforward using the `JsonConvert` class. The overloaded `DeserializeObject()` method is used for this purpose, as shown here:

```
var json = @"{
    ""EmployeeId"": 42,
    ""FirstName"": ""John"",
    ""LastName"": ""Doe""
}";

var result = JsonConvert.DeserializeObject<Employee>(json);
```

Although widely used, the Json.NET library has some drawbacks:

- The .NET `string` type uses UTF-16 encoding, yet most network protocols, including HTTP, use UTF-8. Json.NET converts between these two, which affects performance.

- As a third-party library, and not a component of the Base Class Library (or the Foundation Class Library), you may have projects with dependencies on different versions. ASP.NET Core used Json.NET as a dependency, which sometimes leads to version conflicts.

- It does not leverage new .NET types such as `Span<T>`, which are designed to increase performance in some scenarios, such as when parsing text.

To overcome these issues, Microsoft has provided its own implementation of a JSON serializer, which we will look at in the following section.

Using System.Text.Json

This is the new JSON serializer shipped with .NET Core. It replaces Json.NET in ASP. NET Core, for which an integration package is now available. If you are targeting .NET Framework or .NET Standard, you can still use **System.Text.Json**, which is available as a NuGet package, also called **System.Text.Json**.

The new serializer performs better than Json.NET mainly for two reasons: it uses `Span<T>` and UTF-8 natively (therefore avoiding transcoding between UTF-8 and UTF-16). According to Microsoft, this serializer offers speed-ups of 1.3x to 5x over Json. NET, depending on the scenario.

However, the APIs were inspired by Json.NET and the transition from Json.NET is seamless for simple scenarios, like the ones we saw in the previous section of this chapter. The following example shows how we can serialize an `Employee` object into a `string`:

```
var employee = new Employee
{
    EmployeeId = 42,
    FirstName = "John",
    LastName = "Doe"
};

var text = JsonSerializer.Serialize(employee);
```

This looks very similar to Json.NET and it also produces minified JSON, which you can see in the following code:

```
{"EmployeeId":42,"FirstName":"John","LastName":"Doe",
"HireDate":null,"Telephones":null,"IsOnLeave":false,
"Status":"Active"}
```

However, serialization can be customized by providing various options, such as indentation, handling of null values, naming policy, trailing commas, ignoring read-only properties, and others. Such options are provided with the `JsonSerializerOptions` class. An example with indentation and skipping null values is shown here:

```
var text = JsonSerializer.Serialize(
    employee,
    new JsonSerializerOptions()
    {
        WriteIndented = true,
        IgnoreNullValues = true
    });
```

The output, in this case, is as follows:

```
{
    "EmployeeId": 42,
    "FirstName": "John",
    "LastName": "Doe",
    "IsOnLeave": false,
    "Status": "Active"
}
```

The implementation of the Employee class used in these examples is almost identical to the one from the previous section. Let's take a look at the following code and try to spot the difference:

```csharp
public class Employee
{
    public int EmployeeId { get; set; }
    public string FirstName { get; set; }
    public string LastName { get; set; }
    public DateTime? HireDate { get; set; }
    public List<string> Telephones { get; set; }
    public bool IsOnLeave { get; set; }

    [JsonConverter(typeof(JsonStringEnumConverter))]
    public EmployeeStatus Status { get; set; }

    [JsonIgnore]
    public DateTime LastModified { get; set; }

    public override string ToString() =>
        $"[{EmployeeId}] {LastName}, {FirstName}";
}
```

We again used the JsonIgnoreAttribute and JsonConverterAttribute attributes to specify that the LastModified property should be skipped and that the Status property should be serialized as a string and not a number. The only difference is the type of converter that we used here, which is called JsonStringEnumConverter (while with Json.NET it was called StringEnumConverter). However, these are not the **Json.NET** attributes, but attributes of **System.Text.Json** that are available, along with others, in the System.Text.Json.Serialization namespace. These attributes are listed in the following table:

Type	Target	Description
JsonConverterAttribute	Class, struct, enum, property	Specifies what converter to use to serialize the value of the type or member.
JsonExtensionDataAttribute	Property	Specifies that all the properties in the JSON document that do not have a matching member in the deserialized object should be added to the dictionary marked with this attribute during deserialization and written during serialization.
JsonIgnoreAttribute	Property	Specifies that a member should be skipped during serialization and deserialization.
JsonPropertyNameAttribute	Property	Indicates the name of the property in the JSON document.

From this table, we can see that the **System.Text.Json** serializer does not support serializing and deserializing fields, which is something Json.NET does. If this is something that you need, you must either change the field to a property, provide a property for the field, or resort to a serializer that supports fields.

If you want more control over what is written or read, you can use the Utf8JsonWriter and Utf8JsonReader classes. These provide high-performance APIs for forward-only, no-cached, writing, or read-only reading of UTF-8 encoded JSON text. In the following example, we will use Utf8JsonWriter to write a JSON document to a file on disk containing an employee:

```
var path = Path.Combine(Path.GetTempPath() + "employee.json");
var options = new JsonWriterOptions()
{
    Indented = true
};

using (var sw = File.CreateText(path))
using (var jw = new Utf8JsonWriter(sw.BaseStream, options))
{
    jw.WriteStartObject();
    jw.WriteNumber("EmployeeId", 42);
```

```
    jw.WriteString("FirstName", "John");
    jw.WriteString("LastName", "Doe");
    jw.WriteBoolean("IsOnLeave", false);
    jw.WriteString("Status", EmployeeStatus.Active.ToString());
    jw.WriteEndObject();
}
```

The result of executing this code is a text file with the following content:

```
{
  "EmployeeId": 42,
  "FirstName": "John",
  "LastName": "Doe",
  "IsOnLeave": false,
  "Status": "Active"
}
```

To read the JSON document generated here, we can use Utf8JsonReader. However, this reader does not work with streams but with views of raw data in the form of ReadOnlySpan<byte> or ReadOnlySequence<byte>. This reader allows us to read the data token by token and process it accordingly. An example is shown in the following snippet:

```
byte[] data = Encoding.UTF8.GetBytes(text);
Utf8JsonReader reader = new Utf8JsonReader(data, true,
                                           default);

while (reader.Read())
{
    switch (reader.TokenType)
    {
        case JsonTokenType.PropertyName:
            Console.Write($@"""{reader.GetString()}"" : ");
            break;
        case JsonTokenType.String:
            Console.WriteLine($"{reader.GetString()},");
            break;
        case JsonTokenType.Number:
            Console.WriteLine($"{reader.GetInt32()},");
            break;
        case JsonTokenType.False:
        case JsonTokenType.True:
            Console.WriteLine($"{reader.GetBoolean()},");
            break;
```

```
      }
   }
}
```

The output of executing this code is as follows:

```
"EmployeeId" : 42,
"FirstName" : John,
"LastName" : Doe,
"IsOnLeave" : False,
"Status" : Active,
```

The **System.Text.Json** serializer is more complex than what the examples here may show. We recommend that you read the online documentation to better familiarize yourself with its APIs.

Json.NET and **System.Text.Json** are not the only JSON serializers for .NET, nor the most performant. If JSON performance is key for your application, you might want to use either **Utf8Json** (available at `https://github.com/neuecc/Utf8Json`) or **Jil** (available at `https://github.com/kevin-montrose/Jil`), which outperform both serializers that we looked at in this chapter.

Summary

We started this chapter with an overview of the `System.IO` namespace and looked at the capabilities it provides for working with the filesystem. We then learned about handling paths and filesystem objects. We saw how we can create, edit, move, delete, or enumerate files and directories.

We have also seen how to read and write data from and to disk files with the help of streams. We looked at different kinds of streams and learned about writing and reading to and from file and memory streams using different stream adapters.

In the last part of this chapter, we looked at data serialization and learned how to serialize and deserialize XML and JSON. For the latter, we explored the Json.NET serializer, which is the most popular .NET library for JSON, and `System.Text.Json`, the new .NET library for JSON.

In the next chapter, we will address a different topic called error handling. You will learn about error codes and exceptions and what best practices for handling errors are.

Test what you learned

1. What are the most important classes in the `System.IO` namespace for working with filesystem objects?

2. What is the recommended method for concatenating paths?

3. How can you retrieve the path for the temporary folder of the current user?

4. What is the difference between the `File` and `FileInfo` classes? What about the difference between `Directory` and `DirectoryInfo`?

5. What methods can you use to create directories? What about enumerating directories?

6. What are the three categories of streams in .NET?

7. What is the base class for the stream classes in .NET and what functionalities does it provide?

8. What encoding do `BinaryReader` and `BinaryWriter` assume by default for strings? How can this be changed?

9. How do you serialize objects of the `T` type to XML?

10. What is the JSON serializer shipped with .NET Core and how do you use it to serialize objects of a `T` type?

14
Error Handling

Historically, managing runtime errors has always been a hard problem to solve because of their complex and different natures, spanning from hardware failures to business logic errors.

Some of these errors, such as *division by zero* and *null dereferencing*, are generated by the CPU itself as an exception, while others are generated at the software level and propagated either as an exception or as an error code, depending on the runtime and programming language.

The .NET platform has been designed to manage an error condition through an exception strategy, which has the big advantage of dramatically simplifying the handling code. This means that any property or method may throw an exception and communicate the error condition through exception objects.

Throwing exceptions raises an important question—*is the exception part of the contract between the library implementor and its consumer, or is it, rather, an implementation detail?*

In this chapter, we will start analyzing the language syntax needed to participate in the exception model either from a producer or consumer perspective. However, we will also need to go beyond the syntax, analyzing the implications for the developer seeking to debug the causes and the design problems related to both the error-throwing and error-handling sides. The following three sections of this chapter will cover these topics:

- Errors

- Exceptions

- Debugging and monitoring exceptions

At the end of this chapter, you will be able to catch exceptions from existing libraries, understand whether a method should return a failure code or throw an exception, and create custom exception types whenever it makes sense to.

Errors

In software development, the two strategies used to manage errors are **error codes** and **exception handling**. The error code model relies exclusively on returning a number whose value represents either success or any possible error. Historically, there has never been a convergence in the way error codes are structured. For example, the **Win32** subsystem error codes and the **Component Object Model** (**COM**) define two different sets of error codes in the `winerror.h` file, even if they are both parts of the Windows operating system. In other words, error codes are not part of a standard and they need to be translated when the call traverses a boundary, such as a different operating system or runtime environment.

Another important aspect of error codes is that they are part of the method declaration. For example, it feels very natural defining the division method as follows:

```
double Div(double a, double b) { ... }
```

But if the denominator is 0, we should communicate the invalid parameter error to the caller. Adopting error codes has a direct impact on the method signature, which in this case would be the following:

```
int Div(double a, double b, out double result) { ... }
```

This last signature (which returns an error code of type integer) is not as neat as any library user would expect. Also, the calling code has the responsibility of determining whether the operation was successful or not, which opens up multiple issues.

The first problem is the complexity of the code checking for the error code, as in this example:

```
var api = new SomeApi();
if (api.Begin() == 0)
{
    if (api.DoWork() == 0)
    {
        api.End();
    }
}
```

Assuming that 0 is the success code, the code inside each block must be indented, creating an annoying and confusing triangle as large as the number of called methods. Even by reversing the logic and checking the failure condition, the situation does not improve because of the number of if statements that must be in place to avoid nasty bugs.

The preceding code also shows a common situation where the api.End() method returns an apparently useless error code as it *ends* the sequence of calls while it could be required to handle it. This problem arises because the error codes leave the caller the responsibility to decide on the importance of the error severity. One of the advantages of the exceptions model is that it instead gives this power to the called method, which can *enforce* the severity of the error. This definitely makes more sense, as the severity is likely to be implementation-specific.

The preceding code also hides a potential performance issue due to the characteristic of modern CPUs providing a feature known as **branch prediction**, which is a sort of guess made by the CPU when pre-loading the instructions following a jump. Depending on many factors, the CPU may pre-load *one* path, making the others run slower because their code was not prefetched.

Finally, as far as the type member properties are designed in all modern languages, they don't fit with the error codes because there is no syntax allowing the caller to be made aware of the error and so using an exception is the only way to communicate the problem.

For all these reasons, when the .NET runtime was initially designed, the team decided to embrace the exception paradigm, which treats any error condition as *out-of-band information* and not a part of the method signature.

Exceptions

Exceptions are a mechanism provided by the runtime to make the execution suddenly interrupt and jump to the code handling the error. Since the handler may have been declared by any caller in the calling path, the runtime takes care of restoring the stack and any other outstanding `finally` block, which we will examine in the *The finally block* section of this chapter.

The calling code may want to handle the exception and if it does, it may decide to resume normal execution or just let the exception continue to the other handlers (if any). Whenever no handling code is provided by the application, the runtime catches the error condition and does the only reasonable thing—it terminates the application.

This brings us back to the original question that we asked in the introduction—*is the exception part of the contract between the library implementor and its consumer, or is it rather an implementation detail?*

Since the implementor communicates an anomaly to its callers through exceptions, it looks like the exception is a part of the contract. At least this has been the conclusion of other languages' implementors, including Java and C++, which gave the ability to specify the list of possible exceptions generated in the method. Anyway, the most recent C++ standards deprecated and later removed the exception specification in the declaration, leaving just the ability to specify whether a method may throw an exception or not.

The .NET platform decided not to tie exceptions to the method signature because it is considered an implementation detail. In fact, multiple implementations of the same interface or base class may use different technologies throwing different exceptions. For example, when you create a proxy to an object, you may require different types of exceptions to be thrown in addition to the ones declared in the proxied object.

Since exceptions are not a part of the signature, the .NET platform defines a base class called `System.Exception` for all the possible exceptions. This type is effectively part of the contract bounding the consumers (the callers) to the producers (the called methods).

The .NET runtime is, of course, the subject hooking the exception and taking care of executing the matching handler. For this reason, the exceptions are only valid in the .NET context and every time you cross the boundary, either with a **Platform Invocation Services (P/Invoke)** call, COM interoperability, or a call to a web service, the exception object must be appropriately converted because it would not make any sense outside the .NET runtime. In order to ease the errors that cross the boundaries with Win32 and COM, the .NET base class library defines `Win32Exception` and `COMException`, derived from `Exception`.

Apparently, the exception model is the universal panacea for managing errors, but there's still a very important aspect to consider—the *performance aspect*.

The whole process of capturing the exception, unwinding the stack, calling the relevant `finally` block, and the execution of other necessary infrastructural code takes time. From this perspective, there is no doubt the error codes are far more performant, but this is payback for all the advantages we already mentioned.

When we talk about performance, it must be measured, which in turn depends on whether the given performance-impacting code is run often or not. In other words, if the use of exceptions is *exceptional*, it will not affect the overall performance. For example, the `System.IO.File.Exists` method returns a Boolean telling us whether the file exists on the filesystem. However, this does not throw an exception because not finding a file is not an exceptional case and throwing an exception could severely hit performance when called repeatedly.

Let's now get our hands on the code by examining the statements needed to handle exceptions. As you go through the following sections, you will notice that we briefly introduced some of these concepts in *Chapter 3*, *Control Statements and Exceptions*, when we talked about exception handling. In this chapter, we will cover these topics in more depth.

Catching exceptions

As a general rule, it is always better to avoid errors before an exception gets thrown. For example, validating input parameters from the presentation layer is your best chance.

Before trying to open and read a file, you may want to check for its existence:

```
if (!File.Exists(filename)) return null;
var content = File.ReadAllText(filename);
```

But this check does not protect the code from other possible errors because the filename may contain a forward slash (/), which is forbidden in both Windows and Linux operating systems. It would not make sense to try sanitizing the filename because other errors may happen while accessing the filesystem, such as a wrong path or damaged media.

Whenever the error occurs and cannot be easily prevented, the code must be protected with the proposition offered by the C# language: the `try` and `catch` block statements.

The following snippet demonstrates how to protect `File.ReadAllText` from any possible error:

```
try
{
    var content = File.ReadAllText(filename);
    return content.Length;
}
catch (Exception) { /* ... */ }

return 0;
```

The `try` block surrounds the code we want to protect. Therefore, any exception thrown by `File.ReadAllText` would cause the execution to immediately stop (`content.Length` would not be executed) and jump to the matching catch handler.

The `catch` block must immediately follow a `try` block and specify the code that must be executed only in case the exception being thrown matches the type specified inside the round brackets.

The preceding example is able to catch any error in the `catch` block since `Exception` is the *base class for the hierarchy* of all the exceptions. But this is not necessarily a good thing because you may want to recover from specific exceptions while leaving the responsibility for other failures to the caller.

> **Information box**
>
> Most of the problems related to the filename can be avoided by adding a check with `File.Exists`, but we omitted it on purpose in order to have a wider choice of possible exceptions in our sample.

The preceding snippet may fail with providing different values for the filename. For example, if `filename` is null, `ArgumentNullException` is thrown from the `File.ReadAllText` method. If instead `filename` is /, then it gets interpreted as an access to the root drive, which requires administrative privileges and so the exception would be `System.UnauthorizedAccessException`. When the value is //, then `System.IO.IOException` is thrown because the path is invalid.

Since it can be useful for making different decisions depending on the exception types, the C# syntax provides the ability to specify multiple `catch` blocks, as in the following example:

```
try
{
    if (validateExistence && !File.Exists(filename)) return 0;
    var content = File.ReadAllText(filename);
    return content.Length;
}
catch (ArgumentNullException) { /* ... */ }
catch (IOException) { /* ... */ }
catch (UnauthorizedAccessException) { /* ... */ }
catch (Exception) { /* ... */ }
```

The official .NET class library documentation contains an *Exceptions* section for any member that can throw an exception. If you use Visual Studio and hover over an API with your mouse cursor, you will see a tooltip showing a list of all the possible exceptions. The following screenshot shows the tooltip for the `File.ReadAllText` method:

```
try
{
    var content = File.ReadAllText(filename);
    return content.Length;
}                              ⊚  string File.ReadAllText(string path) (+ 1 overload)
                               Opens a text file, reads all the text in the file, and then closes the file.
catch (ArgumentNullException   Exceptions:
catch (IOException) { /* ...      ArgumentException
catch (UnauthorizedAccessExc     ArgumentNullException
                                 PathTooLongException
catch (Exception) { /* ... *     DirectoryNotFoundException
                                 IOException
return 0;                         UnauthorizedAccessException
                                 FileNotFoundException
                                 NotSupportedException
                                 System.Security.SecurityException
```

Figure 14.1 – A tooltip showing the exceptions for the File.ReadAllText method

Let's now imagine that `filename` specifies a nonexistent file: what is going to happen in this code? According to the tooltip exception list, we can easily guess that a `FileNotFoundException` exception will be thrown. The class hierarchy for this exception is `IOException`, `SystemException`, and of course `Exception`, respectively.

There are two catch blocks satisfying the match—IOException and Exception—but the first wins because the catch block order is very important. If you try to reverse the order of those blocks, you will get a compilation error and get feedback in the editor because this would result in unreachable catch blocks. The following example shows the red squiggle generated by the Visual Studio editor when a catch(Exception) is specified as the first one:

```csharp
try
{
    if (validateExistence && !File.Exists(filename)) return 0;
    var content = File.ReadAllText(filename);
    return content.Length;
}
catch (Exception) { /* ... */ }
catch (ArgumentNullException) { /* ... */ }
catch (IOException) { /* ... */ }
catch (UnauthorizedAccessException) { /* ... */ }

return 0;
```

Figure 14.2 – The editor complains when catch (Exception) is the first exception used

The error emitted by the compiler is CS0160:

```
error CS0160: A previous catch clause already catches all
exceptions of this or of a super type ('Exception')
```

The examples we have seen show how to catch an exception in the same method. But the power of the exception model is its ability to walk back through the call chain to find the most appropriate handler.

In the following example, we have two different methods where we appropriately handled ArgumentNullException:

```csharp
public string ReadTextFile(string filename)
{
    try
    {
        var content = File.ReadAllText(filename);
        return content;
    }
    catch (ArgumentNullException) { /* ... */ }
    return null;
}
public void WriteTextFile(string filename, string content)
{
    try
    {
```

```
        File.WriteAllText(filename, content);
    }
    catch (ArgumentNullException) { /* ... */ }
}
```

Even if the `try..catch` blocks are already declared in these two methods, whenever `IOException` occurs, those handlers are not invoked. The runtime instead starts looking for a compatible handler in the caller chain. This process, entirely managed by the .NET runtime, is called **stack unwinding** and consists of jumping away from the call to the first compatible handler in the callers, whose return address is retrieved from the stack.

In the following example, the `try..catch` blocks intercept `IOException`, which could be thrown by the `ReadAllText` or `WriteAllText` APIs used by the `ReadTextFile` and `WriteTextFile` methods:

```
public void CopyReversedTextFile(string source, string target)
{
    try
    {
        var content = ReadTextFile(source);
        content = content.Replace("\r\n", "\r");
        WriteTextFile(target, content);
    }
    catch (IOException) { /*...*/ }
}
```

Regardless of how deep the call stack is, the `try..catch` blocks will protect this code from any case of `IOException`.

Through all the preceding examples, we have learned how to distinguish the exception type, but the `catch` block receives an object of that type providing contextual information about the nature of the exception. Let's now take a look at the exception objects.

The exception objects

In addition to the exception type, the catch block syntax may specify the name of the variable, referencing the caught exception. The following example shows a method for computing the length of the content string for all the specified files:

```
int[] GetFileLengths(params string[] filenames)
{
    try
    {
        var sizes = new int[filenames.Length];
        int i = 0;
        foreach(var filename in filenames)
        {
            var content = File.ReadAllText(filename);
            sizes[i++] = content.Length;  // may differ from
file size
        }
        return sizes;
    }
    catch (FileNotFoundException err)
    {
        Debug.WriteLine($"Cannot find {err.FileName}");
        return null;
    }
}
```

Every time we open a file without previously using File.Exists to avoid the exception, we may receive FileNotFoundException. This object is a specialization of IOException and exposes a Filename property, providing the filename that can't be found. I cannot even remember the number of times I wished to get such feedback from faulty applications!

> **Information box**
>
> We will see in more detail the base exception members in the *Debugging and monitoring* section, but you can already start investigating the properties exposed by the multitude of exceptions thrown in the base class library.

The following code shows another interesting example while catching
`ArgumentException`—an exception occurring when the argument fails the validation
from the method that is using it:

```
private void CopyFrom(string source)
{
    try
    {
        var target = CreateFilename(source);
        File.Copy(source, target);
    }
    catch (ArgumentException err)
    {
        Debug.WriteLine($"The parameter {err.ParamName} is
invalid");
        return;
    }
}
```

The `catch` block intercepts the fault for both the `source` and `target` parameters. Any
error related to the `source` parameter validation should bounce back to the caller, while
the `target` parameter is computed locally.

How can we just catch the ones we are interested in? The answer lies in a language feature
that was introduced in C# 6.

Conditional catch

The `catch` block may optionally specify a `when` clause to restrict the scope of
the handler.

The following example is very similar to the previous one, but it restricts the `catch` block
to just hook `ArgumentException`, whose `ParamName` is `"destFileName"`, which is
the name of the second parameter of the `File.Copy` method:

```
private void CopyFrom(string source)
{
    try
    {
        var target = CreateFilename(source);
        File.Copy(source, target);
    }
    catch (ArgumentException err) when (err.ParamName ==
"destFileName")
```

```
    {
        Debug.WriteLine($"The parameter {err.ParamName} is
invalid");
        return;
    }
}
```

The when clause accepts any valid Boolean expression and should not necessarily use the exception object specified in the `catch` block.

Please note that in this example, we have used the `"destFileName"` string to specify the second argument of `File.Copy`. If you use Visual Studio, you can see the argument names by positioning the caret over the desired parameter and using the shortcut *Ctrl + Shift + spacebar*, which shows the following suggestion window:

Figure 14.3 – The suggestion window shown by the editor

It is now time to jump to the producer side to see how we can throw an exception.

Throwing exceptions

When we use an API that already provides the required parameter's validation, you may decide not to validate the parameter and eventually throw an exception. In the following example, we open a log file, giving its name specified by `logName`:

```
private string ReadLog(string logName)
{
    return File.ReadAllText(logName);
}
```

The decision to validate `logName` for a null or empty string does not provide any value because the called method already provides a validation that takes into consideration more cases, such as invalid paths or nonexistent files.

But the `logName` parameter may express different semantics, specifying the name of the log rather than the filename to write on disk (if any). The solution for reconciling the two possible meanings is to add the `".log"` extension if it is not already there:

```
private string ReadLog(string logName)
{
    var filename = "App-" + (logName.EndsWith(".log") ? logName
: logName + ".log");
    return File.ReadAllText(filename);
}
```

This makes more sense, but `logName` can be `null`, causing a `NullReferenceException` exception on the highlighted code, which would make troubleshooting harder.

To overcome this problem, we can add the `null` parameter validation:

```
private string ReadLog(string logName)
{
    if(logName == null) throw new
ArgumentNullException(nameof(logName));
    var filename = "App-" + (logName.EndsWith(".log") ? logName
: logName + ".log");
    return File.ReadAllText(filename);
}
```

The `throw` statement accepts any object derived from an exception and immediately interrupts the execution of the method. The runtime hooks the exception and dispatches it to the appropriate handler, as we have already investigated in the previous sections.

> **Tip**
>
> Please note the use of `nameof(logName)` to specify the name of the offending argument. We used this parameter in the previous section while catching the exceptions from the `File.Copy` method. Make sure to never specify the name of the argument as a literal. Using `nameof()` guarantees that the name is always *valid* and avoids problems during refactoring.

The `throw` statement is very simple but please remember to use it only for exceptional cases; otherwise, you may incur performance problems. In the following example, we compare two loops using the popular `Benchmark.NET` micro-benchmark library. The one in the `LoopNop` method executes code that never throws while the other one inside `LoopEx` throws at each iteration:

```
public int Loop { get; } = 1000;

[Benchmark]
public void LoopNop()
{
    for (var i = 0; i < Loop; i++)
    {
        try { Nop(i); }
        catch (Exception) { }
    }
}
[MethodImpl(MethodImplOptions.NoOptimization |
MethodImplOptions.NoInlining)]
private void Nop(int i) { }
```

The `LoopNop` method just loops over the `Nop` empty method 1,000 times. The `Nop` method is marked as `NoInlining` to avoid any compiler optimization in removing the call.

The second method performs the same loop 1,000 times, but calls the `Crash` method, which just throws at each iteration:

```
[Benchmark]
public void LoopEx()
{
    for (var i = 0; i < Loop; i++)
    {
        try { Crash(i); }
        catch (Exception) { }
    }
}


[MethodImpl(MethodImplOptions.NoOptimization |
MethodImplOptions.NoInlining)]
private void Crash(int i) =>
    throw new InvalidOperationException();
```

The Crash method creates a new exception every time, which is a realistic usage of the exception object. But even when reusing the same object every time, the performance hit of the exception model is huge.

The outcome of the benchmark is to get an idea about the *orders of magnitude* affecting the use of exceptions, which in our example is four orders.

The following output shows the outcome of the benchmark:

Method	Mean	Error	Allocated
LoopNop	2.284 us	0.0444 us	-
LoopEx	25,365.467 us	486.2660 us	320000 B

This benchmark just demonstrated that throwing exceptions must be only used for exceptional cases and should not raise any doubts on the validity of the exception model.

We have seen some of the exception types provided in the base class library. Now, we will take a look at the most common exceptions and when to use them.

Common exception types

The exceptions available in the base class library express the semantics for the most popular categories of faults. Among all the exceptions provided in the base class library, it is worth mentioning the ones that are most often used by developers. Throughout this chapter, we have already seen other popular exceptions, such as NullReferenceException, but they are generally only thrown by the runtime:

- ArgumentNullException: This is generally used at the beginning of a method when validating the method parameters. Since reference types may assume the null value, it is used to inform the caller that null is not an acceptable value for the method.

- ArgumentException: This is another exception used at the beginning of a method. Its meaning is wider and is thrown when the parameter value is not valid.

- InvalidOperationException: This is commonly used to reject the method invocation every time the state of the object is not valid for the action requested.

- FormatException: This is used by the class library to signal a badly formatted string. It can also be used in user code that is parsing text for any other purpose.

- IndexOutOfRangeException: This is used every time a parameter points outside of the expected range of a container, such as an array or a collection.

- `NotImplementedException`: This is used to inform the caller that no implementation is available for the called method. For example, when you ask Visual Studio to implement an interface inside the class body, the code generator generates the properties and methods throwing this exception.

- `TypeLoadException`: You may rarely need to throw this exception. It usually occurs when a type cannot be loaded in memory. It is common whenever an exception occurs inside a static constructor and, unless you happen to remember this note, you may have a hard time diagnosing it.

An exhaustive list of all the exceptions of the base class library can be found in the `Exception` class documentation (`https://docs.microsoft.com/en-us/dotnet/api/system.exception?view=netcore-3.1`).

When deciding to throw an exception, it is very important to use one that fully expresses the semantics of the error. Every time you cannot find an appropriate class in .NET, it is more appropriate to define a custom exception type.

Creating a custom exception type

Defining an exception type is as easy as writing a simple class; the only requirement is inheriting from an exception type such as `Exception`.

The following code declares a custom exception used to express a failure in the data layer of the application:

```
public class DataLayerException : Exception
{
    public DataLayerException(string queryKeyword = null)
        : base()
    {
        this.QueryKeyword = queryKeyword;
    }

    public DataLayerException(string message, string
queryKeyword = null)
        : base(message)
    {
        this.QueryKeyword = queryKeyword;
    }

    public DataLayerException(string message, Exception
innerException, string queryKeyword = null)
        : base(message, innerException)
```

```
    {
        this.QueryKeyword = queryKeyword;
    }

    public string QueryKeyword { get; private set; }
}
```

The preceding custom exception class defines three constructors because they are meant to provide a homogeneous experience when the developer constructs them:

- The default constructor might exist whenever you don't need to build an exception with additional parameters. In our case, we allow the building of the exception object with a null QueryKeyword by default.

- The constructor taking the message parameter is important in expressing any human information that may simplify the diagnostics. The message should provide diagnostic information only and is never intended to be shown to the end user.

- The constructor taking the inner exception is valuable in providing additional information about the underlying exception, if any, that caused the current error situation.

Once the new custom exception is defined, it can be used in conjunction with the throw statement. In the following example, we see some hypothetical code making a query to a repository and converting the underlying error condition into our custom exception:

```
public IList<string> GetCustomerNames(string queryKeyword)
{
    var repository = new Repository();
    try
    {
        return repository.GetCustomerNames(queryKeyword);
    }
    catch (Exception err)
    {
        throw new DataLayerException($"Error on repository
{repository.RepositoryName}", err, queryKeyword);
    }
}
```

The exception being caught is passed to the constructor as an argument in order to preserve the original cause of the error, while still throwing the custom exception that better represents the nature of the error.

Throwing inside the `catch` block brings to light an architectural issue on the semantics of the error. In the previous example, we can't recover the error, but we still want to catch it because the repository being queried may be very different depending on the installation of our application. For example, if the repository is a database, the inner exception would be related to *SQL Server*, while if it was the filesystem, it would be `IOException`.

If we want the higher levels of the application to be able to treat the error appropriately and give them a chance to recover the error, we need to abstract the underlying error and provide a business-logic exception such as the `DataLayerException` that we defined.

> **Information box**
>
> .NET Framework originally defined `ApplicationException` as the base class for all the custom exceptions. Since there was no enforcing, the base class library itself never adopted this best practice widely. For this reason, the current best practice is deriving all the custom exceptions from `Exception`, as you can read in the official documentation:
>
> https://docs.microsoft.com/en-us/dotnet/api/
> system.applicationexception?view=netcore-3.1

The ability to throw from inside the `catch` block is not limited to custom exceptions.

Rethrowing an exception

We have just seen how to throw a new exception within a `catch` block, but there is an important shortcut that rethrows the same exception.

The `catch` block is typically used to try to recover the error or just to log it. In both cases, we may want to let the exception continue as if it were not caught at all. The C# language provides a simple use of the `throw` statement for this case, as we can see in the following example:

```csharp
public string ReadAllText(string filename)
{
    try
    {
        return File.ReadAllText(filename);
    }
    catch (Exception err)
```

```
    {
        Log(err.ToString());
        throw;
    }
}
```

The `throw` statement is not followed by any parameter, but it is the equivalent of specifying the same exception received in the `catch` block:

```
catch (Exception err)
{
    Log(err.ToString());
    throw err;
}
}
```

Unless the `err` reference is changed to point to a different object, the two statements are equivalent and have the big advantage of preserving the original stack that caused the error. Anyway, we are still able to add more information to that exception object (the `HelpLink` property is a typical example).

If we throw a different exception object, the original stack is not a part of the exception being thrown, and this is the reason why `innerException` exists.

In certain cases, you may want to save the exception captured by the `catch` block and rethrow it later. By simply throwing the captured exception, the captured stack would be different and less useful. If you need to preserve the stack where the exception was initially captured, you can use the `ExceptionDispatchInfo` class, which provides two simple methods. The `Capture` static method takes an exception and returns an instance of `ExceptionDispatchInfo` that includes all the stack information at the moment of the `Capture` call. You can save this object and later throw the exception along with the original stack information using its `Throw` method. This pattern is shown in the following sample:

```
public void Foo()
{
    ExceptionDispatchInfo exceptionDispatchInfo = null;
    try
    {
        ExecuteFunctionThatThrows();
    }
    catch(Exception ex)
    {
        exceptionDispatchInfo = ExceptionDispatchInfo.
```

```
Capture(ex);
    }

    // do something you cannot do in the catch block

    // rethrow
    if (exceptionDispatchInfo != null)
        exceptionDispatchInfo.Throw();
}
```

Here, we are calling a method that throws an exception, which is then caught in the
catch clause. We store a reference to this exception captured with a call to the static
ExceptionDispatchInfo.Capture method, which helps preserve the call stack.
At the end of the method, we rethrow the exception with a call to the Throw method of
ExceptionDispatchInfo.

The finally block

The finally block is the last C# statement related to *exception management*. It is
extremely important because it allows expression of the portion of code that must be
invoked after the try block, regardless of whether an exception has occurred or not.

Over the previous sections, we have seen how the execution of code behaves depending
on whether an exception occurs or not. The execution of the code inside a try block may
be interrupted by an outstanding exception skipping portions of that code. As soon as an
error occurs, we have the guarantee that a matching catch block will be executed, giving
it the opportunity to write the problem to the log and maybe execute some recovery logic.

The finally block can be specified even without any catch block, meaning that
any exception will be bounced back to the call chain, but the code specified inside the
finally block will be executed in any case right after the try block.

The following example shows three methods whose calls are *nested*. The first method, M1,
calls M2, which calls M3, which calls Crash, which finally throws an exception, as shown
in the following code:

```
private void M1()
{
    try { M2(); }
    catch (Exception) { Debug.WriteLine("catch in M1"); }
    finally { Debug.WriteLine("finally in M1"); }
}
private void M2()
{
```

```
    try { M3(); }
    catch (Exception) { Debug.WriteLine("catch in M2"); }
    finally { Debug.WriteLine("finally in M2"); }
}
private void M3()
{
    try { Crash(); }
    finally { Debug.WriteLine("finally in M3"); }
}
private void Crash() => throw new Exception("Boom");
```

When we invoke M1 and the call chain reaches Crash, there is no catch block in M3 to handle the exception, but its finally block is invoked *before* leaving the method. At this point, the runtime bounces back to the M2 caller, which catches the exception but also invokes its finally code. Lastly, as the exception has been handled, M2 naturally returns the control to M1 and its finally code is executed as well, as in the following output:

```
finally in M3
catch in M2
finally in M2
finally in M1
```

You can repeat this experiment by adding extra-verbose logging to the try blocks if you wish, but the point here is that the finally block is *always executed* right *before leaving* the method.

Another common use for the try..finally combo is to ensure that a resource has been correctly disposed, and C# has made of this pattern a keyword, which is the using statement. The following example shows two equivalent snippets. The IL code generated by the C# compiler is substantially the same, as you can test for yourself using the ILSpy tool by decompiling in IL language:

```
void FinallyBlock()
{
    Resource res = new Resource();
    try
    {
        Console.WriteLine();
    }
    finally
    {
        res?.Dispose();
    }
}
```

```
void UsingStatement()
{
    using(var res = new Resource())
    {
        Console.WriteLine();
    }
}
```

Of course, the `using` statement limits its usage to objects implementing the `IDisposable` interface, but it generates the same pattern. This is a topic that we looked at in depth in *Chapter 9, Resource Management*.

Now that we have seen all the aspects of exceptions, both from a consumer and producer perspective, we will discuss the diagnostic investigation of problems related to exceptions.

Debugging and monitoring exceptions

Debugging exceptions is a bit different compared to debugging normal code because the natural flow gets interrupted and handled by the runtime. Unless you put a breakpoint on the code that handles the exception, there is a risk of not understanding where exactly the problem started. This can happen when an exception is caught and not re-thrown or if the method does not re-throw within the `catch` block.

This may seem like an important downside of the exception model, but the .NET runtime provides all the necessary support to overcome this issue. In fact, the runtime has built-in support for the debuggers, providing valuable hooks to the debugger willing to intercept the exceptions.

From a debugger perspective, you have two possibilities, or *chances*, to intercept any exception being thrown:

- **First-chance exceptions** represent the exceptions at a very early stage, as soon as they are thrown and before jumping to their handlers, if any. The advantage of intercepting an exception (in a first-chance state) is that we can identify precisely which code has caused an exception. Conversely, the intercepted exception may be legitimate and handled correctly. In other words, the debugger will stop any exception occurring, even those that are not causing any trouble. By default, the debugger never stops when a first-chance exception occurs, but it prints a trace in the debugger output window.

- **Second-chance** or **unhandled exceptions** are the fatal ones. These mean that the .NET runtime did not find any suitable handler to manage them and calls the debugger before forcibly closing the application that is crashing. The debugger always stops when a second-chance exception occurs, which always represents a bug condition. Second-chance exceptions are printed in the output window and presented in the exception dialog as unhandled exceptions.

With the default settings, the Visual Studio debugger will break, showing the last line of code that could run before crashing the application. This code is not necessarily responsible for crashing the application; therefore, you may need to modify those settings to get a better understanding of the cause.

Debugging second-chance exceptions

When the exception being thrown is available in our source code, the default settings of the debugger are sufficient to understand the cause of the problem, as the following example shows:

```
public void TestMethod1() => Crash1();
private void Crash1() => throw new Exception("This will make
the app crash");
```

The Visual Studio debugger will stop at the highlighted code showing the infamous exception dialog:

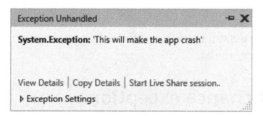

Figure 14.4 – The dialog showing the exception type, message, and links to get more information

Additional information is also provided in the output window:

```
Exception thrown: 'System.Exception' in ExceptionDiagnostics.
dll
An unhandled exception of type 'System.Exception' occurred in
ExceptionDiagnostics.dll
This will make the app crash
```

The Visual Studio debugger keeps improving the diagnostic output version after version. In many cases, it is able to print a message that fully represents the origin of the problem. In the following example code, the exception is caused by a `null` reference:

```
public void TestMethod2() => Crash2(null);
private void Crash2(string str) => Console.WriteLine(str.
Length);
```

The dialog shows an **str was null** message, which tells us precisely what happened:

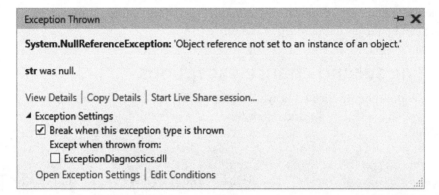

Figure 14.5 – The exception dialog showing the details seen before the variable is null

Similarly, the output window shows a similar message:

```
**str** was null.
```

Now that we have seen the default behavior of the debugger, let's take into consideration a scenario that's a bit more complex.

Debugging first-chance exceptions

In this chapter, we have underlined the value of trying to recover from an exception or rethrowing a different exception in order to give the calling code better semantics. There are cases where this adds some difficulty in debugging, as in the following code:

```
public void TestMethod3()
{
    try
    {
        Crash1();
    }
    catch (Exception) { }
}
```

Since the `catch` block does not rethrow, the exception is simply swallowed and so the debugger will not break at all. But this situation may reveal the real cause of the issue. *How can we ask the debugger to stop at this exception?*

The answer lies in the exception window of Visual Studio (or other debuggers exposing the same feature). From the **Debug | Window | Exception Settings** menu, Visual Studio will show the following window:

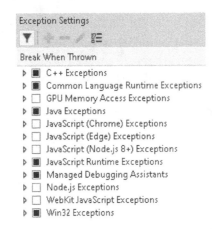

Figure 14.6 – The Exception Settings window

The relevant exceptions for the .NET runtime are those under the **Common Language Runtime Exceptions** item:

Figure 14.7 – A portion of the Exception Settings window showing the selectable exceptions

Most of those exceptions are unchecked, meaning that, as we already said, the debugger will *not* stop at a first-chance exception unless that checkbox is selected.

For example, if we want to break on the `throw` statement of the last example, we just select `System.Exception` from the list.

> **Tip**
>
> Please note that every exception in this list only includes the exact type and not the hierarchy of the derived types. In other words, `System.Exception` will not hook the whole hierarchy.

By scrolling through the list, you may notice that `System.NullReferenceException` and others are checked by default as those exceptions are reasonably considered bugs that should always be avoided by validating the arguments in the code.

Since the list of exceptions is very long, the **Common Language Runtime Exceptions** root item is a three-state toggle that selects either all items, none, or resets to the default settings.

AppDomain exception events

The first- and second-chance exceptions can also be monitored, but not intercepted, thanks to two events provided by the `AppDomain` object. You can subscribe to those events by using the following code in your application:

```
AppDomain.CurrentDomain.FirstChanceException += CurrentDomain_
FirstChanceException;
AppDomain.CurrentDomain.UnhandledException += CurrentDomain_
UnhandledException;
// ...
private static void CurrentDomain_FirstChanceException(object
sender,     System.Runtime.ExceptionServices.
FirstChanceExceptionEventArgs e)
{
    Console.WriteLine($"First-Chance. {e.Exception.Message}");
}

private static void CurrentDomain_UnhandledException(object
sender, UnhandledExceptionEventArgs e)
{
    var ex = (Exception)e.ExceptionObject;
    Console.WriteLine($"Unhandled Exception. IsTerminating:
{e.IsTerminating} - {ex.Message}");
}
```

Most of the time, you will not want to monitor the first-chance exceptions as they may not cause any trouble to the application. Anyway, it can be useful to get rid of them any time you believe they might cause performance issues due to legitimately handled exceptions.

The second-chance (unhandled) exceptions are useful for providing a log for any exceptions that could not be caught or that were unexpected. Beyond that, in a desktop-application context, the typical use case is showing a custom crash dialog box.

> **Tip**
>
> Please be aware that .NET Core always has a single app domain while .NET Framework may have more than one, which is often true in ASP.NET applications when **Internet Information Services (IIS)** recycles the host process.

We have seen how we can get detailed information about the exception to happen during a debugging session and what the best options are to log them. We will now see the kind of debugging information provided in the exception object that can be used after the application has crashed.

Logging exceptions

After creating the exception object, the runtime enriches its state in order to provide the most detailed diagnostic information that can be used to identify the fault. Regardless of the way you get access to the exception object, either from the `catch` block or the `AppDomain` events, there is additional information that you can access.

We already discussed the `InnerException` property, which recursively provides access to all the inner exceptions of the chain. The following example shows how to iterate the whole chain:

```
private static void Dump(Exception err)
{
    var current = err;
    while (current != null)
    {
        Console.WriteLine(current.InnerException?.Message);
        current = current.InnerException;
    }
}
```

Accessing the inner exceptions to create a dump is not really needed when creating a log because the `ToString` method of the exception object provides the dump of the whole chain even if it is very verbose.

The `ToString` method prints the `StackTrace` string property provided by the runtime to capture the whole method chain where the exception happened.

Since `StackTrace` is a string assembled from the runtime, the exception object also provides the `TargetSite` property of the `MethodBase` type, which is the reflection object representing the faulting method. This object exposes, among others, the `Name` property with the method name.

Finally, the `GetBaseException` method returns the first exception that originally generated the fault, provided that any re-throw statement preserves the inner exception or specifies no argument, as we have already discussed in the *Rethrowing an exception* section. If you instead need to know whether there has been an exception that has been swallowed by some handler, you will need to hook the first-chance exceptions event.

There are more advanced debugging techniques that you may want to investigate using the links provided in the *Further reading* section. They include the creation of a dump, which is a binary file containing the memory of the application process at the moment of the crash. The dump can be investigated with the debugging tools at a later moment. Another powerful and very advanced tool is the **Son Of Strike** (**SOS**) plugin that is available either from the WinDbg debugger (Windows only) or the `dotnet-dump analyze` .NET Core tool.

These are low-level tools, typically used in so-called **post-mortem debugging**. They allow us to create a snapshot of the memory used by the faulty application and later examine its state. The power of SOS and `dotnet-dump` is to provide .NET-specific information in addition to the standard elements offered by the native debuggers.

For example, with these tools, you may get information on the current stack state for each thread, the most recent exception data, how each object in memory is referenced or references other objects, the memory used by each object, and other information related to the application metadata and the .NET runtime.

Summary

In this chapter, we first understood why .NET embraced the exception model, in contrast to the error codes used by many other technologies.

The exception model has demonstrated that it is very powerful, providing an efficient and clean way to report errors to the call chain. It avoids polluting the code with additional parameters and error-checking conditionals, which may cause a loss of efficiency in certain cases. We also verified with a benchmark that the exception model must only be used for exceptional cases because otherwise, it may severely affect the application's performance.

We have also seen in detail the syntax of the `try`, `catch`, and `finally` statements that allow us to intercept and handle the exceptions and provide a deterministic disposal of any outstanding resource.

Finally, we examined the diagnostics and logging options, which are extremely useful in providing all the necessary information to fix the bugs.

In the next chapter, we will be learning about the new features of C# 8, which enhance the language by giving us more expressivity and power in terms of performance and robustness.

Test what you learned

1. Which `block` statement can be used to surround some code that may potentially throw an exception?

2. What is the typical task inside any `catch` block?

3. When specifying multiple `catch` blocks, what order should be respected and why?

4. Should we specify the exception variable name in the `catch` statement? Why?

5. You just caught an exception in a `catch` block. Why should you want to rethrow it?

6. What is the role of the `finally` block?

7. Can you specify a `finally` block without a `catch` block?

8. What are first-chance exceptions?

9. How can you break the Visual Studio debugger into a first-chance exception?

10. When would you want to hook the `UnhandledException` event of the AppDomain?

Further reading

- **The dotnet-dump tool (only for .NET Core)**: https://docs.microsoft.com/en-us/dotnet/core/diagnostics/dotnet-dump

- **The WinDbg debugger**: https://docs.microsoft.com/en-us/windows-hardware/drivers/debugger/debugger-download-tools

- **Using the SOS debugging extension in WinDbg (only for .NET Framework)**: https://docs.microsoft.com/en-us/windows-hardware/drivers/debugger/debugging-managed-code

15
New Features
of C# 8

C# is a mature programming language, but it is still evolving to satisfy new requirements coming from emergent software architectures. The main focus of most of the four language versions of C# 7 is on providing the tools for impressive performance when using value types.

With the latest version, C# 8 introduces many new important features focusing on four main areas: making code more compact and easier to read, along with performance, robustness, and expressivity. The fundamental change in C# 8 is that it is the first release of the language without official support in .NET Framework because some of its features require the .NET Core runtime enhancements.

In this chapter, we will go through the following new language features:

- Nullable reference types
- Default implementation of interface members
- Ranges and indices
- Pattern matching
- The using declaration
- Asynchronous Dispose

- Disposable patterns in structs and ref structs

- Asynchronous streams

- Read-only struct members

- Null coalescing assignment

- Static local functions

- Better interpolated verbatim strings

- Using stackalloc in nested expressions

- Unmanaged constructed types

By the end of this chapter, you will understand the use cases for using each of these features and be able to progressively adopt them in your listings. As always, the more you put these features into practice, the sooner you will master them.

We will now start with a language feature that has the great ambition of reducing one of the primary causes of crashes in .NET-based applications—`NullReferenceException`.

Nullable reference types

In the previous chapter, we learned that the type system in C# is split into **reference types** and **value types**. Value types are allocated on the stack and subject to memory copies every time they are assigned to a new variable. On the other hand, reference types are allocated on the heap, which is managed by the garbage collector. Every time we allocate a new reference type, we receive a reference acting as a key to identify the allocated memory back from the garbage collector.

The reference is essentially a pointer that can assume the special null value, which is the simplest, and therefore most popular, way to indicate the absence of a value. Remember, instead of using the null value, another solution is to adopt the special case architectural pattern, which, in its simplest form, is an instance of that object with a Boolean field indicating whether the object is valid, which is how `Nullable<T>` works. In many other cases, developers don't really need to use null values, the validation of which requires a remarkable amount of code that will affect runtime performance as well.

The problem with the null reference is that the compiler can't argue about potential problems because it is syntactically correct, but dereferencing it at runtime will lead to a `NullReferenceException`, which is the first cause for application crashes in the .NET world.

Let's consider for a moment a simple class with two constructors, where only the second one initializes the _name field:

```
public class SomeClass
{
    private string _name;
    public SomeClass() { }
    public SomeClass(string name) { _name = name; }
    public int NameLength
    {
        get { return _name.Length; }
    }
}
```

When the first constructor is used, the NameLength property will cause a NullReferenceException.

In terms of tests, this is the code that highlights the following two cases:

```
Assert.ThrowsException<NullReferenceException>(() => new
SomeClass().NameLength);
Assert.IsTrue(new SomeClass("Raf").NameLength >= 0);
```

The fundamental problem is that our code behavior depends on the values assumed at runtime, and obviously, the compiler cannot know if we will ever initialize the _name field after calling the default constructor.

Information box

The null reference is a concept invented by Sir Tony Hoare in 1965. However, in 2009, he regretted his invention, calling it *my billion-dollar mistake* (https://en.wikipedia.org/wiki/Tony_Hoare). As nulls cannot be easily removed from a framework, nullable reference types aim to resolve the problem using a code analysis approach.

This concept is widespread in most programming languages, including all the ones in the .NET ecosystem. This means that any effort to remove the null concept from the framework would be a huge breaking change, potentially destroying current applications. What can the compiler do to resolve this problem? The answer is to undertake *static code analysis*, a technique used to understand the runtime behavior of the source code without running it.

> **Information box**
>
> In 2011, Microsoft started working on a revolutionary project called **Roslyn**, which became the official and current C# compiler in all the .NET SDKs a few years later. The innovation of the Roslyn compiler (whose NuGet package is officially named `Microsoft.CodeAnalysis`) is the ability to expose the APIs for all the processing normally done by the compilers.
>
> Traditionally, compilers are black boxes, but Roslyn makes it possible to programmatically parse the source code, get the syntax and semantic trees, use visitors to retrieve or rewrite specific nodes, and analyze the semantics of the source code.

You may have already seen static code analysis at work in Visual Studio when the yellow light bulb or the squiggles underneath some code suggest some refactoring or a potential issue in the editor. These abilities can be further extended by writing custom analyzers, distributed as Visual Studio extensions or in NuGet packages.

Since static code analysis can't know the value assumed by a reference at runtime, it just examines all the possible usage paths and tries to tell if one of those may dereference (using the dot or the square brackets) a null reference. But the analysis can suggest two different strategies, depending on whether it is desirable or not for the reference to assume the null value:

- We may want to prevent a reference from ever assuming the null value. In this case, the analyzer would suggest initializing at declaration or construction time and on any other following assignments.

- We may need the reference to assume the null value. In this other case, the analyzer will verify that there is adequate null-checking code (an `if` statement or similar) to avoid any possible path that could dereference a null.

The choice between these two strategies is the developer's choice, who is called to provide additional information so that the compiler knows which feedback it should provide.

The C# 8 nullable reference types feature ships the advanced static code analysis feature supporting both strategies, thanks to the ability to annotate the references to inform the compiler about the intended reference usage. For this purpose, the C# syntax has been extended to provide the ability to decorate the reference types as potentially nullable. Under this new rule, the string field declared in the previous sample class assumes that the reference cannot be null and must be initialized at construction time:

```
private string _name;  // must be initialized at construction
time
```

When developers wants to give a hint to the compiler on the _name reference to potentially be null, they must declare it with a question mark decoration:

```
private string? _name;
```

Using the question mark character as a decorator is not new; it was introduced in C# 2 to shorten the Nullable<T> declaration to T? and consisted of wrapping a *value type* into a structure using a Boolean field to know whether a value type is set to null.

The question mark decoration for reference types is new in C# 8 and its meaning is similar, but no wrapper is involved. Instead, this decoration is just a way to inform the code analysis about the intended use of the reference.

By default, the code analysis is turned *off* because the existing applications always assumed that any reference could be null, and enabling it by default on the existing code would result in a large number of squiggles and compiler messages all over the code.

> **Note**
> When a reference is decorated with the question mark and the nullable reference types feature is not yet enabled, Visual Studio will squiggle the question mark in green, advising that the question mark functionality isn't in effect, as the feature is not active.

In addition to the question mark, C# adds the **forgiving operator**, represented by an *exclamation mark*, which is used to inform the code analysis to *forgive* a statement for that specific case. Using the forgiving operator is rare because it means the analysis has failed to recognize a case where the developer themselves knows the reference cannot be null. A realistic example of its usage is when some unsafe/native code changes the memory values pointed by a reference without any evidence in the managed code. In other very edge cases, the pure managed code can be so complex that the compiler fails to recognize it. I would personally opt to simplify the code instead of using the forgiving operator.

Remember that the *question mark* is used while declaring the *reference*, while the *exclamation mark* is used when *dereferencing* it. The following example shows a statement that will not be analyzed from the static code analysis and will not provide any feedback because the developer is making a strong promise that the reference will never be null:

```
var len = _name!.Length;
```

It is worth repeating that it should be used only in extremely rare cases.

Enabling the nullable reference type feature

There are multiple options to enable this feature; the reason to do so is to be able to progressively adapt the feature on existing code without being blocked or receiving a huge amount of messages. Every time you start with a new project, you may want to fully enable this feature to avoid excessive annoyance by opening the Visual Studio solution explorer, double-clicking the project node, and editing the `.csproj` file. Alternatively, you can right-click the project node and select **Edit Project File** from the context menu.

By adding the nullable XML tag, the feature will be enabled for the entire project, which is the best option when starting a new project:

```
<PropertyGroup>
  <TargetFramework>netcoreapp3.0</TargetFramework>
  <Nullable>enable</Nullable>
</PropertyGroup>
```

You can do the same on an existing project, but the amount of feedback provided by the compiler may be excessive, distracting the developer. For this reason, the C# compiler provides four new pragma directives, making it possible to enable and disable the feature for selected portions of the code. Interestingly, the restore pragma restores the previously defined setting to allow nesting of the pragma directives:

```
#nullable enable
public class SomeClass
{
    private string? _name;
    public SomeClass() { }
    public SomeClass(string name) { _name = name; }
    public int NameLength
    {
        // you should see a green squiggle below _name
        get { return _name.Length; }
    }
}
#nullable restore
```

The range of possible settings for this feature enables some other nuances, depending on whether you want to be able to use the decorations (question and exclamation marks) and/or get the warnings on code that may potentially cause a `NullReferenceException`:

- **Enabling both the warnings and annotations**: This is done by just enabling the feature, as we mentioned previously. Under this rule, the code can be annotated with the question mark to hint to the compiler about the intended usage of the references. The code editor will show any potential problem and the compiler will generate warnings for those issues:

```
Csproj: <Nullable>enable</Nullable>
Code: #nullable enable
```

- **Disabling both the warnings and annotations**: This is the default setting, but can be used to explicitly disable the `Nullable` feature either on the whole project or on selected portions of the code:

```
Csproj: <Nullable>disable</Nullable>
Code: #nullable disable
```

- **Enabling only the annotations but not the compiler warnings**: When you are adopting this feature in existing projects, it can be very useful to start annotating the code without receiving any warning in the IDE or in the compiler output. It's worth remembering that many companies enforce gated check-ins, rejecting any code producing warnings. In this case, it can be useful to enable the annotations project-wide, and enable the warnings file by file, to progressively migrate the code:

```
Csproj: <Nullable>annotations</Nullable>
Code: #nullable enable annotations
```

- **Enabling only the warnings but not the annotations in the editor**: When the warnings are enabled, the IDE will start generating green squiggles on potentially dangerous dereferencing code and on question mark decorators, as the annotations are not enabled. This setting is useful when you adopt this feature on existing projects and are not willing to enable decorators (for example, because the code is required to be compiled with older compilers). In this situation, you get very useful suggestions in the IDE and in the compiler output about the code that could cause the `NullReferenceException`:

```
Csproj: <Nullable>warnings</Nullable>
Code: #nullable enable warnings
```

- **Restoring the previous settings in the code (only in code files)**: When using pragmas, it is always better to mark the end of a given region using a restore pragma, instead of an enable/disable, to make nested regions behave correctly:

```
#nullable restore annotations
#nullable restore warnings
```

- **Selectively disabling the settings (only in code files)**: The final setting is the one used to selectively disable either the annotations or the warnings in a given region of code. It is useful when you want to apply inverse logic, that is, enabling the feature for the whole project and disabling only selected portions of code:

```
#nullable disable annotations
#nullable disable warnings
```

This fine-grained ability to control the nullable reference types feature is very important when adopting this feature in existing projects. Outside that, you may find it simpler to just enable it project-wide.

Working with nullable reference types

Once enabled, the code analysis provides feedback in the code editor, which differs depending on whether the reference has been decorated with the question mark. The developer may choose not to decorate the variable, implying that the reference should never assume the null value. In this case, the declaration looks very familiar:

```
private string _name;
```

Here, the code analysis will squiggle the constructor code that is responsible for not initializing the string that, in the absence of the question mark, cannot be null. The remedies, in this case, are straightforward: you can either initialize the _name variable to an empty string or remove the default constructor, forcing all the callers to provide a non-nullable string at the creation of the object.

The other strategy is to declare the _name variable as nullable:

```
private string? _name;
```

The code analysis will show the green squiggle when dereferencing the Length property. In this case, the solution is to explicitly check for _name being null and return an appropriate value (or throw an exception). This is a possible implementation for the property:

```
public int NameLength2
{
    get
    {
        if (_name == null) return 0; else return _name.Length;
    }
}
```

The following is an alternative and more elegant implementation of the same code:

```
public int NameLength2 => _name?.Length ?? 0;
```

Annotating code is simple as it resembles the strategy already used with the nullable types, but with the arrays, the decoration is slightly more complex since there are two possible reference types in the game: the array itself and the items held in the array.

An array of strings can be declared as follows:

```
private string[]?  _names; // array can be null
private string?[]  _names; // items in the array can be null
private string?[]? _names; // both the array and its items can
                           // be null
private string[]   _names; // neither of the two can be null
```

But remember, the more question marks we use, the more checks for null we need to do. Let's consider this simple class:

```
public class OtherClass
{
    private string?[]? _names;
    public OtherClass() { }
    public int Count => _names?.Length ?? 0;
    public string GetItemLength(int index)
    {
        if (_names == null) return string.Empty;
        var name = _names[index];
        if (name == null) return string.Empty;
        return name;
    }
}
```

The `Count` property is short only because we used a modern compact syntax, but it still contains a null check. `GetItemLength` returns the length of the *n*th item held in the array, and since both the arrays and the items could be null, two different null checks are required.

If you are thinking to just return `string?` as the return type of the `GetItemLength` method, this solution will make the implementation code a bit shorter but all the callers will be forced to check for nulls, requiring even more code changes.

Migrating existing code to nullable reference types

Every project has its own characteristics, but from my personal experience, I've managed to identify a couple of best practices when migrating existing projects to this powerful feature.

The first suggestion is to start enabling this feature from the project at the bottom of the dependency tree. In the project context, you may want to enable the analysis using pragma directives, starting from the most frequently used code files, such as helpers, extension methods, and so on.

The second suggestion is to try avoiding the question mark: every time you decorate the reference with the question mark, the code analysis will require you to write some code to provide proof that a null dereferencing cannot occur, incrementing the amount of boilerplate code, which can affect the performance of the hot paths.

Lastly, when you compile a library using this feature, the compiler will apply two hidden attributes to leave a track in the metadata about the nullability of the references used publicly in your code. Every time some code referencing your library is compiled, the compiler will know whether the library methods accept nullable references or not, assuming a not-nullable reference parameter only if the attribute specifically advertises that. It is therefore a best practice to use this feature on public libraries so that others can benefit from this metadata.

The nullable reference types are very useful to decrease the amount of `NullReferenceException` exceptions at runtime, which is the primary cause for an application to crash.

While this feature is optional, it is very convenient to use pragma directives to progressively apply the small changes required for the code to be null-proof. This is a typical task that any team should add to its technical debts to improve code quality. In addition to that, library authors embracing this feature automatically provide the nullability metadata in their libraries, making the whole chain of references more stable.

Default implementation of interface members

We have already learned that interfaces are used to define a contract that every implementing type must fulfill. Every interface member defines a portion of the contract by specifying a name and its signature (input and output parameters). The implementation (or body) of the defined members are then provided by the concrete types implementing the interface.

With the *default implementation of interface members*, C# 8 widens the interface type syntax to include the following features:

- Interfaces can now define bodies for *methods*, *properties*, *indexers*, and *events*.
- Interfaces may declare *static members*, including *static constructors* and *nested types*.
- They may explicitly specify visibility modifiers, such as *private*, *protected*, *internal*, and *public* (which continues to be the default).
- They may also specify other modifiers, such as *virtual*, *abstract*, *sealed*, *extern*, and *partial*.

The syntax for this new feature is straightforward, as it is as simple as adding an implementation to a member:

```
public interface ICalc
{
    int Add(int x, int y) => x + y;
    int Mul(int x, int y) => x * y;
}
```

At first sight, adding implementations to the member of the interface looks contradictory. In fact, the preceding example demonstrates the syntax well, but it is certainly not a good design strategy. You may wonder what could be a good use case for defining a default implementation on interface members. The first reason is *interface versioning*, which has been traditionally very hard to manage.

Interface versioning

As an example, let's start from a classic interface, `IWelcome`, declaring two simple properties and a `Person` class to implement it:

```
public interface IWelcome
{
    string FirstName { get; }
    string LastName { get; }
}
```

```
public class Person : IWelcome
{
    public Person(string firstName, string lastName)
    {
        this.FirstName = firstName;
        this.LastName = lastName;
    }
    public string FirstName { get; }
    public string LastName { get; }
}
```

It is now possible to add a new method with a default implementation:

```
public interface IWelcome
{
    string FirstName { get; }
    string LastName { get; }
    string Greet() => $"Welcome {FirstName}";
}
```

The implementing class does not need to be updated. It can even reside in a different assembly without having any impact on the interface change.

Since the implementation is provided by the interface and the class does not provide an implementation for the Greet method, it is still not accessible from a Person reference. In other words, the following declaration is not legal:

```
var p = new Person("John", "Doe");
p.Greet(); // Wrong, Greet() is not available in Person
```

In order to invoke the default implementation, we need an IWelcome reference:

```
IWelcome p = new Person("John", "Doe");
Assert.AreEqual("Welcome John", p.Greet()); // valid code
```

The impact of this feature on a long-established interface is extremely important: for example, the List<T> class exposes the AddRange method, which is unfortunately not available in the IList<T> interface. After almost 20 years of applications relying on that interface, any change would be a huge breaking change.

What are the changes that could make sense on an interface? Removal of a member can be avoided by discouraging its usage via ObsoleteAttribute and maybe, a few versions later, it will start throwing NotImplementedException, without ever needing to remove that member from the interface.

Changing a member is always a bad practice because interfaces are contracts; usually, the need for a change can be modeled by a new member with a different name and signature.

Adding a new member is, therefore, the only true challenge because it breaks binary compatibility and forces a requirement change to every interface implementer. If the interface is very popular, for example, `IList<T>`, it is nearly impossible to add new members as it would break everybody's code.

Traditionally, the interface versioning problem has been solved by creating a new interface that extends the previous one, but this solution isn't that practical, since the adoption of the new interface requires the implementers to replace the old interface with the new one in their object inheritance declaration and, of course, implement the new members.

The default implementation in C# 8 does not behave the same way as a normal class implementation, as it defines the *baseline* implementation for that hierarchy. Let's suppose you have a hierarchy of interfaces and a class defined as follows:

```
public interface IDog // defined in Assembly1
{
    string Name { get; }
    string Noise => "barks";
}
public interface ILabrador : IDog // defined in Assembly1
{
    int RetrieverAbility { get; }
}
public class Labrador : ILabrador // defined in Assembly2
{
    public Labrador(string name)
    {
        this.Name = name;
    }
    public string Name { get; }
    public int RetrieverAbility { get; set; }
}
```

In the current situation, the following assert is true:

```
IDog archie = new Labrador("Archie");
Assert.AreEqual("barks", archie.Noise);
```

Now, fix the ILabrador default implementation and modify the interface, as follows:

```
public interface ILabrador : IDog
{
    int RetrieverAbility { get; }
    string IDog.Noise => "woofs"; // Version 2
}
```

It is worth noting that the Noise method must be redefined by specifying the full path: IDog.Noise. The reason for this is because .NET allows multiple inheritances with interfaces; therefore, in a more complex inheritance structure, there could be more than a single path leading to the Noise method.

The syntax, therefore, requires specifying the full path to overcome this potential ambiguity. If the compiler finds any ambiguity that cannot be resolved by just specifying the full path, it will generate an explicit error.

The default implementation of ILabrador redefines the baseline implementation of Noise in IDog. This means that, even if we are using an IDog reference, the change in ILabrador will affect the result, as follows:

```
IDog archie = new Labrador("Archie");
Assert.AreEqual("woofs", archie.Noise);
```

Furthermore, you may have noticed in the comments of the preceding sample that the interfaces and the class lie in two different assemblies. If the first assembly containing ILabrador is recompiled with the new member and the second assembly is instead untouched, you will still see Noise being updated to woofs. This means that patching the first assembly will cause all the applications to benefit from the update, even without recompiling the whole code.

Interface reabstraction

The ability to redefine the default implementation from a derived interface is fundamental to understanding reabstraction. The principle is the same, but the deriving interface may decide to *erase* the default interface implementation, marking the member as abstract.

Going on with the previous example, we could define the following interface:

```
public interface IYellowLabrador : ILabrador
{
    abstract string IDog.Noise { get; }
}
```

But this time, the implementers of the new interface are required to implement the `Noise` method as well:

```
public class YellowLabrador : IYellowLabrador
{
    public YellowLabrador(string name)
    {
        this.Name = name;
    }
    public string Name { get; }
    public int RetrieverAbility { get; set; }
    public string Noise { get; set; }
}
```

This capability is useful because the default implementation was written to provide the best possible implementation that can be commonly used by all the types in the hierarchy. But there is a possibility that a branch of those types does not fit well with that implementation and you want to erase it at the interface level to avoid any misbehavior.

Interfaces as traits

Treating the concept of trait composition in detail would require an entire chapter, but it is worth noting that C# 8 has only just opened the door to traits, leaving future versions of the language with the opportunity to fill the gaps, as you can read in the design notes of the C# language public repository.

Trait composition is a concept that's well known in other languages such as C++. It involves the ability to define a set of members for determining a well-known behavior. The goal is defining different types (traits) with the goal to give any class the ability to compose its own behavior by just inheriting the traits.

Before this release of the language, we used to create static helper classes to define a set of reusable behaviors. In C# 8, we can define those members inside the interfaces so that they can be reused by just inheriting the interfaces. The choice of interfaces is very convenient because .NET supports multiple inheritances only on interfaces, allowing multiple traits to be inherited in a new class.

If you are going to experiment with traits, try to model them without thinking about the classical interface usage; rather, look at them for their intrinsic ability to open to multiple inheritances and thus compose a set of methods.

Traits are usually very useful when the availability of the behaviors you need to compose is very dependent on each class that you are going to define. In terms of design, this would translate into either a very long list of interfaces, each one defining a single behavior, or a single interface with many objects implementing part of its methods by throwing NotImplementedException.

Let's try to look at a very simple example where you want to expose an alphabet transliteration service to your application. There are multiple ways to achieve this: either with the Windows native APIs, a NuGet library, or a cloud service. We could be tempted to define a single interface with a long list of methods supporting all the possible permutations from one alphabet to another, but it would not be very practical because each of those libraries or services supports only a part of all the possible transliterations. This would result in many implementations throwing NotImplementedException.

Another approach would be to define one interface for each possible transliteration, but the class implementing these interfaces would need to redirect the member implementation to some external helper class that calls the appropriate library.

The traits solution looks a bit simpler because it just models what we can do. For example, here, there are two possible transliteration interfaces:

```
public interface ICyrillicToLatin
{
  public string Convert(string input)
  {
    return Transliteration.CyrillicToLatin(input, Language.
Russian);
  }
}
public interface ILatinToCyrillic
{
  public string Convert(string input)
  {
    return Transliteration.LatinToCyrillic(input, Language.
Russian);
  }
}
```

They are still interfaces, but the class that needs the common implementation can add the interface to the inheritance list, without anything else:

```
class CompositeTransliterator : ICyrillicToLatin,
ILatinToCyrillic
{
  // ...
}
```

Finally, in order to make the consumer's life easier, the class could expose a switch expression using pattern matching to invoke the try transliteration to/from a given alphabet and return the computed result:

```
public string TransliterateCyrillic(string input)
{
    string result;
    return this switch
    {
        ICyrillicToLatin c when (result = c.Convert(input)) !=
input => result,
        ILatinToCyrillic l when (result = l.Convert(input)) !=
input => result,
        _ => throw new NotImplementedException("N/A"),
    };
}
```

This code tries to transliterate the text with all the available services, and if one of them is implemented by the class, a conversion is tried. As soon as the phrase can be converted (that is, the conversion result is different from the input), it is returned to the caller.

Default interface implementations in interfaces are a valuable feature for all pragmatists. Java and Swift are examples of programming languages that already support this feature. If you are a library developer needing to port your code across multiple languages, it will make your life easier and avoiding re-architecting portions of code to overcome its absence in previous versions of the language.

As always, the recommendation is to use the default implementation with wisdom. It would not be useful if the use case already fit well with the previous tools and patterns.

A fun edge case of the default implementation is that you can now define the entry point of your application with the following code:

```
interface IProgram
{
    static void Main() => Console.WriteLine("Hello, world");
}
```

The default interface members are a controversial feature leveraging the intrinsic capability of the .NET interfaces to support multiple inheritance. The pragmatist should appreciate the practical use cases justifying this little revolution, while the others can just continue using the interfaces as they always did before.

We can now move on to the next feature, which should help in avoiding some headaches and `IndexOutOfRangeException` exceptions when slicing arrays and lists.

Ranges and indices

Another convenient functionality introduced in C# 8 is the new syntax to identify single elements or ranges inside a sequence. The language already offers the ability to get or set elements in an array using the square brackets and a numeric index, but this concept has been extended by adding two operators to identify an item from the end of a sequence and to extract a range between two indices.

In addition to the aforementioned operators, the base class library now offers two new system types, `System.Index` and `System.Range`, which we will immediately see in action. Let's consider an array of strings containing six country names:

```
var countries = new[] { "Italy", "Romania", "Switzerland",
"Germany", "France", "England" };
var length = countries.Length;
```

We already know how to use the numeric indexer to get a reference to the first item:

```
Assert.IsTrue(countries[0] == "Italy");
```

The new `System.Index` type is just a convenient wrapper for the numeric index that can be directly used on the arrays:

```
var italyIndex = new Index(0);
Assert.IsTrue(countries[0] == countries[italyIndex]);
```

The interesting part is when we need to address the item starting from the end of the sequence:

```
// first item from the end is length - 1
Assert.IsTrue(countries[length - 1] == "England");
var englandIndex = new Index(1, true);
Assert.IsTrue(countries[length - 1] ==
countries[englandIndex]);
```

The new ^ operator provides us with a succinct and effective way to get the last item:

```
Assert.IsTrue(countries[^1] == countries[englandIndex]);
```

It is very important to note that, while zero is the first index when counting from the beginning, it points to one item beyond the total length when counting from the end. This means that the [^0] expression will always throw IndexOutOfRangeException:

```
Assert.ThrowsException<IndexOutOfRangeException>(() =>
countries[^0]);
```

When it comes to ranges, the value of the new syntax is more evident, since it is a brand new concept that never existed before in the language or in the base class library. The new .. operator delimits two indices that are used to identify a range. The delimiters on the left and the right of the operator can be also omitted whenever the items at the boundaries should be skipped.

The following example shows three ways to specify all the items in an array:

```
var countries = new[] { "Italy", "Romania", "Switzerland",
"Germany", "France", "England" };
var expected = countries.ToArray();
var all1 = countries[..];
var all2 = countries[0..^0];
var allRange = new Range(0, new Index(0, true));
var all3 = countries[allRange];
Assert.IsTrue(expected.SequenceEqual(all1));
Assert.IsTrue(expected.SequenceEqual(all2));
Assert.IsTrue(expected.SequenceEqual(all3));
```

The expected variable just gets a clone of the countries array and the convenient SequenceEqual Linq extension method returns true when the items in the two sequences are identical and are ordered the same. The previous example is not very useful, but highlights the semantics at the boundaries: the *left* boundary is always *inclusive*, while the *right* boundary is always *exclusive*.

The following example is more realistic and shows three different ways to specify a range that just skips the first item of the sequence:

```
var countries = new[] { "Italy", "Romania", "Switzerland",
"Germany", "France", "England" };
var expected = new[] { "Romania", "Switzerland", "Germany",
"France", "England" };
var skipFirst1 = countries[1..];
var skipFirst2 = countries[1..^0];
var skipFirstRange = new Range(1, new Index(0, true));
var skipFirst3 = countries[skipFirstRange];
Assert.IsTrue(expected.SequenceEqual(skipFirst1));
Assert.IsTrue(expected.SequenceEqual(skipFirst2));
Assert.IsTrue(expected.SequenceEqual(skipFirst3));
```

Similarly, the following example shows how to skip the last item in the sequence:

```
var countries = new[] { "Italy", "Romania", "Switzerland",
"Germany", "France", "England" };
var expected = new[] { "Italy", "Romania", "Switzerland",
"Germany", "France" };
var skipLast1 = countries[..^1];
var skipLast2 = countries[0..^1];
var skipLastRange = new Range(0, new Index(1, true));
var skipLast3 = countries[skipLastRange];
Assert.IsTrue(expected.SequenceEqual(skipLast1));
Assert.IsTrue(expected.SequenceEqual(skipLast2));
Assert.IsTrue(expected.SequenceEqual(skipLast3));
```

Putting everything together is straightforward, and the following example shows how to skip both the first and the last element of the sequence:

```
var countries = new[] { "Italy", "Romania", "Switzerland",
"Germany", "France", "England" };
var expected = new[] { "Romania", "Switzerland", "Germany",
"France" };
var skipFirstAndLast1 = countries[1..^1];
var skipFirstAndLastRange = new Range(1, new Index(1, true));
var skipFirstAndLast2 = countries[skipFirstAndLastRange];
Assert.IsTrue(expected.SequenceEqual(skipFirstAndLast1));
Assert.IsTrue(expected.SequenceEqual(skipFirstAndLast2));
```

The range syntax to specify the starting and the ending indices can start counting from the start or the end. In the following example, the sliced array will return just the second and the third element, both counted from the beginning:

```
var countries = new[] { "Italy", "Romania", "Switzerland",
"Germany", "France", "England" };
var expected = new[] { "Romania", "Switzerland" };
var skipSecondAndThird1 = countries[1..3];
var skipSecondAndThirdRange = new Range(1, 3);
var skipSecondAndThird2 = countries[skipSecondAndThirdRange];
Assert.IsTrue(expected.SequenceEqual(skipSecondAndThird1));
Assert.IsTrue(expected.SequenceEqual(skipSecondAndThird2));
```

Of course, the same is valid when counting from the end, which is the goal of the following example:

```
var countries = new[] { "Italy", "Romania", "Switzerland",
"Germany", "France", "England" };
var expected = new[] { "Germany", "France" };
var fromEnd1 = countries[^3..^1];
var fromEndRange = new Range(new Index(3, true), new Index(1,
true));
var fromEnd2 = countries[fromEndRange];
Assert.IsTrue(expected.SequenceEqual(fromEnd1));
Assert.IsTrue(expected.SequenceEqual(fromEnd2));
```

This syntax is very simple, but you may have noticed that we only made use of arrays, which, as well as strings, are treated as special by C#. In fact, if we try to use this same syntax with a List<T>, it won't work, since there are no members that know what Index and Range are:

```
var countries = new MyList<string>(new[] { "Italy", "Romania",
"Switzerland", "Germany", "France", "England" });
var expected = new[] { "Romania", "Switzerland", "Germany",
"France" };
MyList<string> sliced = countries[1..^1];
Assert.IsTrue(expected.SequenceEqual(sliced));
```

The question now is, how can we make the following test pass? There are three different ways to make it compile and work. The first one is straightforward and consists of providing an indexer that takes a System.Range as a parameter:

```
public class MyList<T> : List<T>
{
  public MyList() { }
  public MyList(IEnumerable<T> items) : base(items) { }
  public MyList<T> this[Range range]
  {
    get
    {
      (var from, var count) = range.GetOffsetAndLength(this.
Count);
      return new MyList<T>(this.GetRange(from, count));
    }
  }
}
```

The List<T> base class provides the indexer taking an integer, while MyList<T> adds an overload taking a Range type, which is used from C# 8 as an alias of the .. syntax. In the new indexer, we use Range.GetOffsetAndLength, a very convenient method that returns a tuple with the initial index and the length of the sequence to slice. Finally, the List<T>.GetRange base method provides the sliced sequence used to create the new MyList<T> collection.

Another possible solution to make the previous test pass is to take advantage of the special Slice method with which the C# 8 compiler searches *by pattern*. In the absence of the indexer that we wrote before, if the compiler finds a method called Slice that takes two integers, it *remaps* the range syntax to a call to the Slice method. As a result, the following code is neater and simpler to read:

```
public class MyList<T> : List<T>
{
    public MyList() { }
    public MyList(IEnumerable<T> items) : base(items) { }
    public MyList<T> Slice(int offset, int count)
    {
        return new MyList<T>(this.GetRange(offset, count));
    }
}
```

Please note that any call with a range syntax such as countries[1..^1] will invoke the Slice method.

This solution is nice but can't solve the problem of the popular List<T> class, a class that can be found almost everywhere in the code, especially because the Linq extension method known as ToList() returns an IList<T>. Writing a Slice extension method will not work because the compiler looks for Slice among the instance methods, while extension methods are static.

The solution is to write an extension method taking a Range, as shown in the following example. This time, the countries reference is any collection inheriting ICollection<T> and supports slicing with the nice syntax of countries.Slice(1..^1):

```
public static class CollectionExtensions
{
    public static IEnumerable<T> Slice<T>(this ICollection<T>
items, Range range)
    {
        (var offset, var count) = range.
GetOffsetAndLength(items.Count);
        return items.Skip(offset).Take(count);
    }
}
```

In all the previous examples, we explicitly created Index and Range using their constructors, but I would recommend taking some time to explore the convenient static factories provided by the Index and Range classes, such as Range.All() or Index.FromEnd().

Ranges and indices provide powerful and expressive operators and types to simplify the selection of single or multiple items in a sequence. The main purpose is to make the code more readable and less prone to errors without impacting the performance.

The most important advice on ranges to remember is that boundaries are inclusive only on the left side of the range.

Pattern matching

Pattern matching was introduced in C# 7, but version 8 of the language specification widens its usage by smoothing the syntax and making it more compact and readable. This chapter will avoid repeating the features already seen in the previous versions and just focus on the new concepts.

The popular switch statement has evolved in C# to become an *expression* with a very fluent syntax. For example, suppose you are reading the console keys in an application using the Console.ReadKey method to get the colors matching the R, G, and B characters:

```
public Color ToColor(ConsoleKey key)
{
    return key switch
    {
        ConsoleKey.R => Color.Red,
        ConsoleKey.G => Color.Green,
        ConsoleKey.B => Color.Blue,
        _ => throw new ArgumentException($"Invalid
{nameof(key)}"),
    };
}
```

Or, if you prefer an even more compact version, we could write this as follows:

```
public Color ToColor(ConsoleKey key) => key switch
    {
        ConsoleKey.R => Color.Red,
        ConsoleKey.G => Color.Green,
        ConsoleKey.B => Color.Blue,
        _ => throw new ArgumentException($"Invalid
{nameof(key)}"),
    };
```

The switch expression is not semantically changed from the previous innovations of C# 7 pattern matching; rather, it has become simpler and more compact with some important things to highlight:

- As an expression, the switch statement must return a value (the Color enumeration in our sample).

- The discard character (_) replaces the default keyword in the classical switch statement.

- The subexpressions mapping the keys to the colors are evaluated in order, where the first match wins and exits.

Things can get even more interesting when using the switch expression to match types, as shown in the following example:

```
string GetString(object o) => o switch
    {
        string s    => $"string '{s}'",
        int i       => $"integer {i:d4}",
        double d    => $"double {d:n}",
        Derived d   => $"Derived: {d.Other}",
        Base b      => $"Base: {b.Name}",
        null        =>  "null",
        _           => $"Fallback: {o}",
    };
```

This method takes an unknown object as input and returns a string that is formatted differently depending on its runtime type, which must match with the exact type. For example, GetString((Int16)1) will not match nor return the string Fallback: 1. Another failed matching is GetString(10.6m) because the literal is a decimal and the returned string will be Fallback: 10.6.

Before C# 7, testing the type identity on value or reference types was pretty cumbersome because it required a second step to either cast the value type to the desired type or a null-check conditional operation for the reference types. Thanks to C# 7, we learned to use is pattern matching, which is perfect when checking a single type.

With the new C# 8 syntax, the resulting code is more succinct and less error-prone, with a number of advantages:

- Not having to care about null references in every case, which has the positive effect of being a better candidate for the method to be inlined by the **Just-in-time Compiler (JIT)**, resulting in better performance.

- The evaluation respects the order, which is very useful when testing type hierarchies. In our example, it is fundamental to evaluate the Derived class before Base, because otherwise the switch expression would always match Base.

- Explicitly capturing the nulls in *null case* captures avoids any conditional expression.

The switch expression is very powerful, but the improvements to pattern matching are not over yet.

Recursive pattern matching

Pattern matching has been extended to allow drilling down into object properties and tuples. The syntax at the base of this improvement consists of the ability to specify an expression between curly braces after a pattern:

```
var weekDays = Enum.GetNames(typeof(DayOfWeek));
var expected = new[] { "Sunday", "Monday", "Friday", };
var six = weekDays
    .Where(w => w is string { Length: 6 })
    .ToArray();
Assert.IsTrue(six.SequenceEqual(expected));
```

The expression inside the curly braces can only specify properties and must make use of constant literals. This allows us to match the type and, at the same time, evaluate its properties possibly recurring over subexpressions.

The true power comes into play when we need to evaluate objects structured in a graph, like in the following two **Plain Old CLR Objects (POCO)** classes that are referenced through the Customer property of the Order class:

```
public class Order
{
    public Guid Id { get; set; }
    public bool IsMadeOnWeb { get; set; }
    public Customer Customer { get; set; }
    public decimal Quantity { get; set; }
}

public class Customer
{
    public Guid Id { get; set; }
    public string Name { get; set; }
    public string Country { get; set; }
}
```

Now, let's suppose we're working on an e-commerce application where the discount depends on the order properties:

```
public decimal GetDiscount(Order order) => order switch
{
    var o when o.Quantity > 100 => 7.5m,
    { IsMadeOnWeb: true } => 5.0m,
    { Customer: { Country: "Italy" } } => 2.0m,
    _ => 0,
};
```

Here, the first subexpression reassigns the reference to the o variable whose Quantity property, thanks to the when clause, is then evaluated. If o.Quantity > 100 is satisfied, a 7.5% discount is returned.

In the second case, when Order.IsMadeOnWeb is true, a good 5% discount is returned. The third case evaluates the property obtained by navigating Order.Customer. Country, returning a 2% discount just because the order originates from Italy. Finally, the discard character represents the fallback to zero discount.

The syntax with the properties is great, but things get a bit more complicated when it comes to tuples because you may want to match a single tuple item, as well as multiple ones, and their position is also fundamental.

Let's consider, for example, a simple Point struct with, not surprisingly, two integer properties of X and Y:

```
struct Point
{
    public Point(int x, int y)
    {
        X = x;
        Y = y;
    }
    public int X { get; set; }
    public int Y { get; set; }
}
```

How can we write a method that returns whether the point lies on the horizontal or vertical axis? The condition is satisfied if either X or Y is zero; therefore, a possible approach is doing the following:

```
bool IsOnAxis(Point p) => (p.X, p.Y) switch
{
    (0, _) => true,
    (_, 0) => true,
    (_, _) => false,
};
```

Traditionally, we would write this method with one if using an or operator, but the more the parameters come into play, the more unreadable the code becomes. An interesting point of the previous example is that we built a tuple on the fly and evaluated it inside the switch expression, matching the parameters by their position and discarding (with the _ character) the ones that were not relevant to the evaluation.

Things get even more interesting when writing the special Deconstruct method in the Point structure, as it simplifies the tuple's creation:

```
public struct Point
{
    public Point(int x, int y)
    {
        X = x;
        Y = y;
    }
    public int X { get; set; }
    public int Y { get; set; }
    public void Deconstruct(out int x, out int y)
    {
        x = X;
        y = Y;
    }
}

public bool IsOnAnyAxis(Point p) => p switch
{
    (0, _) => true,
    (_, 0) => true,
    _ => false,
};
```

When using tuples in a switch expression, there is space for getting more power by evaluating its values using the when clause.

In the following example, we use the when clause to identify the diagonal positions in addition to the axis. For this purpose, we define the SpecialPosition enumerator and use the switch expression together with the when clause to match the diagonals:

```
enum SpecialPosition
{
    None,
    Origin,
    XAxis,
    YAxis,
    MainDiagonal,
    AntiDiagonal,
}

SpecialPosition GetSpecialPosition(Point p) => p switch
{
    (0, 0) => SpecialPosition.Origin,
    (0, _) => SpecialPosition.YAxis,
    (_, 0) => SpecialPosition.XAxis,
    var (x, y) when x ==  y => SpecialPosition.MainDiagonal,
    var (x, y) when x == -y => SpecialPosition.AntiDiagonal,
    _ => SpecialPosition.None,
};
```

Pattern matching gained a lot of power over the last two versions of the language and now allows the developer to focus on the important parts of the code without being distracted by the boilerplate code required by the previous language rules.

The switch expression is specifically suited for all those expressions whose outcome can be derived from multiple choices, should the evaluation need to dig into an object graph or evaluate tuples. The powerful discard character allows partial evaluations, avoiding code that is often complex and prone to errors.

The using declaration

The using declaration is a very convenient syntax equivalent to the try/finally block and provides a deterministic call to the Dispose method. This declaration can be used on all the objects implementing the IDisposable interface:

```
class DisposableClass : IDisposable
{
    public void Dispose() => Console.WriteLine("Dispose!");
}
```

We already know that the using declaration deterministically invokes the Dispose method as soon as its closing curly brace is encountered:

```
void SomeMethod()
{
    using (var x = new DisposableClass())
    {
        //...

    }       // Dispose is called
}
```

Every time multiple disposable objects need to be used in the same scope, the nested using declarations are nested, causing an annoying triangle-shaped code alignment:

```
using (var x = new Disposable1())
{
    using (var y = new Disposable2())
    {
        using (var z = new Disposable3())
        {
            //...
        }
    }
}
```

This annoyance can be finally removed if it is fine for the Dispose method to be called at the end of the current block (the closed curly brace), no matter whether the block is a statement (such as a for/if/...) or the current method.

The new syntax in C# 8 allows us to entirely remove the curly braces from the `using` declarations, transforming the previous example into the following:

```
void SomeMethod()
{
    using (var x = new Disposable1());
    using (var y = new Disposable2());
    using (var z = new Disposable3());
    //...
} // Dispose methods are called
```

The first curly brace closing the current block will automatically trigger the three `Dispose` methods in the inverse order of declaration. But there is more to cover about `Dispose`; in fact, this compact syntax is also valid for the `async using` declaration, which will be covered in the next section.

Asynchronous Dispose

After the advent of Tasks in .NET, most of the libraries managing I/O operations progressively moved to an asynchronous behavior. For example, the `System.Net.Websocket` class members embrace the Task-based programming strategy, providing a better developer experience and more efficient behavior.

Every time a developer needs to write a C# client to access some service based on the WebSocket protocol, they typically write a wrapper class exposing specialized *send* methods and implementing the dispose pattern to invoke the `Websocket.CloseAsync` method. We also know that any asynchronous method should return a `Task`, but the Dispose method has been defined as void far before the `Task` era, and therefore doesn't fit well in the `Task` chain.

The Websocket example is very realistic as I had this exact problem some time ago, where blocking the current thread to wait for the CloseAsync to finish inside the Dispose caused a deadlock.

Starting from C# 8 and .NET Core 3.0, we now have two important tools:

- The `IAsyncDisposable` interface defined in .NET Core 3, returning a lightweight `ValueTask` type
- The `await using` construct leveraging the new `AsyncDisposable` interface

Let's see how to use those in code:

```
public class AsyncDisposableClass : IAsyncDisposable
{
    public ValueTask DisposeAsync()
    {
        Console.WriteLine("Dispose called");
        return new ValueTask();
    }
}

private async Task SomeMethodAsync()
{
    await using (var x = new AsyncDisposableClass())
    {
        // ...
    }
}
```

It is worth remembering that the `await using` declaration benefits from succinct, single-line syntax, as we discussed previously:

```
private async Task SomeMethodAsync()
{
    await using (var x = new AsyncDisposableClass());
}
```

If you are a library author exposing a disposable type, you can implement either one of the two, or even both the `IDisposable` and `IAsyncDisposable` interfaces.

Disposable patterns in structs and ref structs

Over time, C# introduced some *pattern-based* constructs to resolve issues deriving from rules that could not be applied in every circumstance. This happens, for example, with the `foreach` statement not requiring an object to implement the `IEnumerable<>` interface, instead just relying on the presence of the `GetEnumerator` method, and similarly the object returned by `GetEnumerator` not needing to implement `IEnumerator` but just exposing the required members instead.

This change was driven by the recent introduction of the `ref structs`, which are important for diminishing the pressure on the garbage collector as they are guaranteed to live only on the stack but do not allow the implementation of interfaces.

The pattern-based approach has now been extended to the `Dispose` and `DisposeAsync` methods under certain conditions that we are going to discuss now.

Starting from C# 8, developers can define `Dispose` or `DisposeAsync` without implementing `IDisposable` or `IAsyncDisposable`. Implementing the `Dispose` method by pattern has been *limited* to `ref struct` types because extending it to any other type could eventually cause a breaking change for types already defining a `Dispose` method without declaring `IDisposable` in the inheritance list.

The following definition is a valid implementation of the `Dispose` and `DisposeAsync` methods:

```
ref struct MyRefStruct
{
    public void Dispose() => Debug.WriteLine("Dispose");
    public ValueTask DisposeAsync()
    {
        Debug.WriteLine("DisposeAsync");
        return default(ValueTask);
    }
}
```

The `Dispose` method can be used as usual:

```
public void TestMethod1()
{
    using var s1 = new MyRefStruct();
}
```

But this other declaration is not allowed because we cannot use `ref` inside an asynchronous method:

```
public async Task TestMethod2()
{
    //await using var s2 = new MyRefStruct(); // Error!
}
```

The workaround is to expand the `await using` declaration with a full `try/finally`:

```
public Task TestMethod3()
{
    var s2 = new MyRefStruct();
    Task result;
    try { /*...*/ }
    finally
```

```
    {
        result = s2.DisposeAsync().AsTask();
    }
    return result;
}
```

This code is certainly not very nice to read, but we should consider that declaring the asynchronous version of `Dispose` (in a type whose life cycle is limited to the stack) is probably not a great idea.

While the `Dispose` by pattern has been precautionarily limited to `ref structs`, the `DisposeAsync` by pattern has no restrictions, so it is perfectly legal to declare `DisposeAsync` in an old-fashioned class and use it with the `await using` statement.

Asynchronous streams

Asynchronous streams are the final missing piece in the task story that began several years ago when the `Task` class, `async`, and `await` were first introduced. An example of an unresolved use case is the processing of data chunks coming from the internet while they are being downloaded. The basic point here is that we don't want to await the entire stream of data, but instead take a single chunk at a time, processing it and then awaiting the next one. This processing can therefore happen while the other pieces of data are still downloading and the unused thread time can be spent to serve other users as well, incrementing the total scalability of the application.

Before digging into the new C# feature, let's rapidly review how an enumerable is made in the synchronous world. The following examples show an enumerable sequence that can be used inside a `foreach` statement; you may notice that the enumerated type is an integer instead of the hypothetical byte array composing the chunks downloaded from the internet, but this is not really relevant.

The simplest possible implementation leverages the C# iterator, which is implemented through the `yield` keyword:

```
static IEnumerable<int> SyncIterator()
{
    foreach (var item in Enumerable.Range(0, 10))
    {
        Thread.Sleep(500);
        yield return item;
    }
}
```

Its main consumer is, of course, a `foreach` statement:

```
foreach (var item in SyncIterator())
{
    // ...
}
```

Under the hood, the compiler generates the code, exposing an `IEnumerable<T>` whose responsibility is to provide the enumerator, a class made of the `Current`, `Reset`, and `MoveNext` members unrolling the sequence. The relevant part of this code is `Thread.Sleep` inside the `MoveNext` method, which simulates a slow iteration.

The following code is equivalent, but implements the `IEnumerable` and `IEnumerator` interfaces manually:

```
public class SyncSequence : IEnumerable<int>
{
    private int[] _data = Enumerable.Range(0, 10).ToArray();
    public IEnumerator<int> GetEnumerator() => new
SyncSequenceEnumerator<int>(_data);
    IEnumerator IEnumerable.GetEnumerator() => new
SyncSequenceEnumerator<int>(_data);
    private class SyncSequenceEnumerator<T> : IEnumerator<T>,
IEnumerator, IDisposable
    {
        private T[] _sequence;
        private int _index;
        public SyncSequenceEnumerator(T[] sequence)
        {
            _sequence = sequence;
            _index = -1;
        }
        object IEnumerator.Current => _sequence[_index];
        public T Current => _sequence[_index];
        public void Dispose() { }
        public void Reset() => _index = -1;
        public bool MoveNext()
        {
            Thread.Sleep(500);
            _index++;
            if (_sequence.Length <= _index) return false;
            return true;
        }
    }
}
```

Once again, the `foreach` statement can easily consume the sequence, sharing the problem of the blocked thread caused by `Thread.Sleep`, which in real life would be an ongoing I/O operation inside the network stack of the operating system:

```
foreach (var item in new SyncSequence())
{
    // ...
}
```

In order to resolve this problem, C# 8 introduced the very convenient `await foreach`, which is used to iterate an asynchronous enumeration, which in turn requires two new interfaces: `IAsyncEnumerable<T>` and `IAsyncEnumerator<T>`.

The simplest possible producer and consumer for the new asynchronous streams are very similar to the previous ones:

```
async IAsyncEnumerable<int> AsyncIterator()
{
    foreach (var item in Enumerable.Range(0, 10))
    {
        await Task.Delay(500);
        yield return item;
    }
}

await foreach (var item in AsyncIterator())
{
    // ...
}
```

Should we need to implement those two interfaces (manually), it would not be much different than the synchronous implementation where, not surprisingly, we have to implement the asynchronous version of `MoveNext` called `MoveNextAsync`:

```
public class AsyncSequence : IAsyncEnumerable<int>
{
    private int[] _data = Enumerable.Range(0, 10).ToArray();
    public IAsyncEnumerator<int>
GetAsyncEnumerator(CancellationToken cancellationToken =
default)
    {
        return new MyAsyncEnumerator<int>(_data);
    }

    private class MyAsyncEnumerator<T> : IAsyncEnumerator<T>
```

```
{
    private T[] _sequence;
    private int _index;
    public MyAsyncEnumerator(T[] sequence)
    {
        _sequence = sequence;
        _index = -1;
    }
    public T Current => _sequence[_index];
    public ValueTask DisposeAsync() => default(ValueTask);
    public async ValueTask<bool> MoveNextAsync()
    {
        await Task.Delay(500);
        _index++;
        if (_sequence.Length <= _index) return false;
        return true;
    }
}
}
```

In the same way that `IEnumerator<T>` derives from `IDisposable<T>`, the `IAsyncEnumerator<T>` interface derives from `IAsyncDisposable<T>`, which we already discussed.

`MoveNextAsync` and `Current` are the only other members required by the `IAsyncEnumerator<T>` interface, whose methods return the *lightweight* `ValueTask` type already seen in `DisposeAsync`.

Note

At the time of writing, the only class in the base class library implementing `IAsyncEnumerable<T>` is `System.Threading.Channel`, so in order to fully leverage the power of the asynchronous streams, you should adopt an external library or implement those two interfaces by yourself, which is pretty straightforward.

The code consuming the new asynchronous sequence is structurally the same:

```
await foreach (var item in new AsyncSequence())
{
    // ...
}
```

For the sake of completeness, the consuming code is equivalent to the following:

```
var sequence = new AsyncSequence();
IAsyncEnumerator<int> enumerator = sequence.
GetAsyncEnumerator();

try
{
    while (await enumerator.MoveNextAsync())
    {
        // some code using enumerator.Current
    }
}
finally { await enumerator.DisposeAsync(); }
```

The static `TaskAsyncEnumerableExtensions` class contains some extension methods that allow the configuration of `IAsyncEnumerable` objects, as you would expect from any other `Task` object.

The first extension method is `ConfigureAwait`, which we already examined in *Chapter 12, Multithreading and Asynchronous Programming*. The other is `WithCancellation`, which takes a `CancellationToken` value that can be used to cancel the ongoing task.

Asynchronous streams are very powerful as they simplify the developer code while making it more powerful. On the producer side, implementing the required interfaces (`IAsyncEnumerable` and `IAsyncEnumerator`) is very simple, and on the consumer side, it is easy to enumerate the sequence asynchronously thanks to the new `async foreach`.

One drawback is that the current library ecosystem is not compatible with the new interfaces. For this reason, the community already wrote a new set of Linq-style extension methods providing the same *look and feel* of the ones baked into the base class library.

It is also important to use the right tool for every use case. In other words, there is no need to transform everything into something asynchronous just because the language has been extended. This is just an important tool that every developer can use whenever it makes sense.

Readonly struct members

Following the introduction of the `readonly` struct in C# 7, it is now possible to specify the `readonly` modifier singularly on its members. This feature has been added for all those cases where the struct type cannot be entirely marked as read-only, but when only one or more members can guarantee not to modify the state of the instance.

The main reason why I love this feature is because expressing the intents explicitly is a best practice in terms of maintenance and usability.

It is also important from a performance perspective because the `readonly` struct provides a sort of *hint* to the compiler, which can apply better optimizations. The modifier can be applied on fields, properties, and methods to guarantee it does not mutate the struct instance, but does not give any guarantee on the referenced objects.

When dealing with properties, the modifier can be applied on the property or on just one of the accessors:

```
public readonly int Num0
{
    get => _i;
    set { } // not useful but valid
}

public readonly int Num1
{
    get => _i;
    //set => _i = value; // not valid
}

public int Num2
{
    readonly get => _i;
    set => _i = value; // ok
}

public int Num3
{
    get => ++_i;       // strongly discouraged but it works
    readonly set { } // does not make sense but it works
}
```

For example, let's define a `Vector` `struct` exposing two methods returning the vector length where only one of the two is marked as `readonly`:

```csharp
public struct Vector
{
    public float x;
    public float y;
    private readonly float SquaredRo => (x * x) + (y * y);
    public readonly float GetLengthRo() => MathF.
Sqrt(SquaredRo);
    public float GetLength() => MathF.Sqrt(SquaredRo);
}
```

Since value types such as `Vector` are subject to be copied when they are passed as parameters, a common solution is to apply the `in` modifier (which means a `readonly` `ref`), as in the following example:

```csharp
public static float SomeMethod(in Vector vector)
{
    // a local copy is done because GetLength is not readonly
    return vector.GetLength();
}
```

Unfortunately, the `in` modifier cannot give any guarantees about the immutability of the other data addressed by the reference. Therefore, as soon as the compiler sees the `GetLength` method being invoked, it has to assume a potential change to the vector instance, causing a defensive hidden local copy of `Vector`, regardless of the fact that it has been passed by the reference.

If instead we replace the call to `GetLength` with the read-only `GetLengthRo` method, the compiler understands there is no risk in modifying the `Vector` content and can avoid generating the local copy, providing better performance to the application:

```csharp
public static float ReadonlyBehavior(in Vector vector)
{
    // no local copy is done because GetLengthRo is readonly
    return vector.GetLengthRo();
}
```

It is worth saying that the compiler is smart enough to provide some automatic optimizations. For example, automatically generated property getters are already marked as read-only, but remember to apply the `readonly` modifier to all the other members not mutating the instance state, providing an important hint to the compiler and obtaining the best possible optimizations in change.

> **Note**
> Version after version, the compiler improves its capability to detect potential
> side effects such as local copies. You can verify the generated IL code by
> yourself using a decompiler such as `ildasm` or the `ILSpy` tools, but be
> warned that these optimizations are subject to changes over time.

If you mark a method as read-only, even if it is modifying the state of its instance, the
compiler will generate either an error or a warning, depending on the situation:

- The compiler will complain with a `CS1604` error if the `readonly` method tries to
  modify any field of the struct.

- The compiler will generate a `CS8656` warning every time the code accesses
  a not read-only property getter to advise about the generation of the code
  needed to create a defensive hidden local copy of the struct, as stated in the
  message description.

In the CS8656 warning message, the compiler advises that it is going to generate a copy of
`'this'` to avoid mutating the current instance:

```
"Call to a non readonly member '...' from a 'readonly' member
results in an implicit copy of 'this'".
```

There is one important side effect regarding the ability of the compiler to recognize
undesired situations. It cannot detect any attempt to modify the changes to a referenced
object, as demonstrated by the following code:

```csharp
struct Undetected
{
    private IDictionary<string, object> _bag;
    public Undetected(IDictionary<string, object> bag)
    {
        _bag = bag;
    }
    public readonly string Description
    {
        get => (string)_bag["Description"];
        set => _bag["Description"] = value;
    }
}
```

While we apparently don't see any drawbacks in not applying the `readonly` modifier on struct members that are not modifying the state of the value type, be very careful, because it can make a big difference to the performance of hot paths.

Null coalescing assignment

The null coalescing operator, `??`, has been extended in C# 8 to support assignment. A popular usage for the null coalescing operator involves the parameter checks at the beginning of a method, like in the following example:

```
class Person
{
    public Person(string firstName, string lastName, int age)
    {
        this.FirstName = firstName ?? throw new
ArgumentNullException(nameof(firstName));
        this.LastName = lastName ?? throw new
ArgumentNullException(nameof(lastName));
        this.Age = age;
    }
    public string FirstName { get; set; }
    public string LastName { get; set; }
    public int Age { get; set; }
}
```

The new assignment allows us to reassign the reference whenever it is null, as demonstrated by the following example:

```
void Accumulate(ref List<string> list, params string[] words)
{
    list ??= new List<string>();
    list.AddRange(words);
}
```

The parameter list can initially be null and in this case, it will be reassigned to a new instance, but the following times, the assignment will not occur anymore:

```
List<string> x = null;
Accumulate(ref x, "one", "two");
Accumulate(ref x, "three");
Assert.IsTrue(x.Count == 3);
```

The null coalescing assignment doesn't look very important, but its ability to execute the rightmost expression is a big value that you should not underestimate.

Static local functions

Local functions have been introduced to make the code more readable by constraining the visibility of a certain piece of code to a single method:

```
void PrintName(Person person)
{
    var p = person ?? throw new
ArgumentNullException(nameof(person));
    Console.WriteLine(Obfuscated());
    string Obfuscated()
    {
        if (p.Age < 18) return $"{p.FirstName[0]}.
{p.LastName[0]}.";
        return $"{p.FirstName} {p.LastName}";
    }
}
```

In this example, the Obfuscated method can only be used by PrintName and has the advantage of being able to ignore any parameter check, because the context where the p captured parameter is used does not allow its value to be null. This can deliver performance advantages in complex scenarios, but its ability to capture the local variables (including this) can be confusing.

With C# 8, it is now possible to avoid any capturing by marking the local function as static:

```
private void PrintName(Person person)
{
    var p = person ?? throw new
ArgumentNullException(nameof(person));
    Console.WriteLine(Obfuscated(p));
    static string Obfuscated(Person p)
    {
        if (p.Age < 18) return $"{p.FirstName[0]}.
{p.LastName[0]}.";
        return $"{p.FirstName} {p.LastName}";
    }
}
```

This new version of the method enforces its ability to self-describe while still having the advantage of ignoring any parameter-checking due to the known context. It is worth noting that capturing is usually not an issue in terms of performance, but can severely impact readability because C# allows automatic capturing by default, in contrast to other languages such as C++ lambdas.

Better interpolated verbatim strings

We have already learned that string literals supports some *variants* to avoid escaping characters:

```
string s1 = "c:\\temp";
string s2 = @"c:\temp";
Assert.AreEqual(s1, s2);
```

They can also be used to improve formatting, thanks to interpolation:

```
var s3 = $"The path for {folder} is c:\\{folder}";
```

Since the introduction of interpolated strings, we have always been able to mix the two formatting styles:

```
var s4 = $@"The path for {folder} is c:\{folder}";
Assert.AreEqual(s3, s4);
```

But inverting the $ and @ characters was not possible before C# 8:

```
var s5 = @$"The path for {folder} is c:\{folder}";
Assert.AreEqual(s3, s5);
```

With this small improvement, you don't have to bother about the order of the prefixes.

Using stackalloc in nested expressions

With C# 7, we started using Span<T>, ReadOnlySpan<T>, and Memory<T> because they are `ref struct` instances that are guaranteed to be allocated on the stack, and therefore won't affect the garbage collector. Thanks to Span, it was also possible to avoid declaring the `stackalloc` statements that are directly assigned to Span or ReadOnlySpan as unsafe:

```
Span<int> nums = stackalloc int[10];
```

Starting from C# 8, the compiler widens the use of `stackalloc` to any expression expecting `Span` or `ReadOnlySpan`. In the following example, the test trims the `input` string from three special characters, obtaining the string specified in the `expected` variable:

```
string input = " this string can be trimmed \r\n";
var expected = "this string can be trimmed";
ReadOnlySpan<char> trimmedSpan = input.AsSpan()
    .Trim(stackalloc[] { ' ', '\r', '\n' });
string result = trimmedSpan.ToString();
Assert.AreEqual(expected, result);
```

The operations performed by the preceding example are as follows:

- The `AsSpan` extension method converts the string into `ReadOnlySpan<char>`.

- The `Trim` extension method narrows the boundaries of `ReadOnlySpan<char>` to the characters specified with the `stackalloc` array. This `Trim` method does not require any allocation.

- Finally, the `ToString` method is called to create a new string from `ReadOnlySpan<char>`.

The advantage of this code is that, beyond the new `int []` expression, which is used to verify the test, and the `ToString` method, which is used to create the result, no other heap allocations are performed.

Unmanaged constructed types

Before digging into this new C# feature, it is necessary to understand the subject by analyzing the definitions of **unmanaged** and **constructed types** cited by the language specifications:

- A type is called `constructed` if it is generic and the type parameter is already defined. For example, `List<string>` is a constructed type while `List<T>` is not.

- A type is called `unmanaged` when it can be used in an unsafe context. This is true for many built-in basic types. The official documentation includes the list of these types: `sbyte`, `byte`, `short`, `ushort`, `int`, `uint`, `long`, `ulong`, `char`, `float`, `double`, `decimal`, `bool`, `enums`, `pointers`, and `struct`.

An example of an unmanaged constructed type that it was not possible to declare before C# 8 is as follows:

```
struct Header<T>
{
    T Word1;
    T Word2;
    T Word3;
}
```

The two main advantages of allowing generic structs to be unmanaged are as follows:

- They can be allocated on the stack using `stackalloc`.

- We can use those types with pointers and unsafe code to interoperate with native code. This is useful when dealing with native chunks whose fields could, for example, be either 32 or 64 bits:

```
Span<Header<int>> records1 = stackalloc Header<int>[10];
Span<Header<long>> records2 = stackalloc Header<long>[10];
```

With this feature, the language specifications are going in the direction of easing the native interoperability without incurring the performance hits that, in the past, required the use of the C or C++ languages.

Summary

There is no doubt that the new C# 8 features mark an important milestone in terms of code robustness and clarity. It is not unusual for a language to become (version after version) more complex and difficult to read, but C# introduced features such as pattern matching and ranges that allow any developer to express their intent with more concise and unambiguous code.

While it is controversial, the default interface members introduced the Traits paradigm to the .NET world and addressed problems such as interface versioning, which caused developers to struggle for years.

We learned about a key feature, that is, built-in nullable reference static code analysis, which allows us to progressively review the code and dramatically cut down the number of errors due to dereferencing null references.

This was not the end of tuning the language for productivity, as we continued through the C#7 performance journey with asynchronous streams, read-only struct members, and the updates to `stackalloc` and unmanaged constructed types, all of which combine to make C# a compelling competitor among the native languages while still enforcing code safety.

Other smaller features such as the succinct `using` declaration, asynchronous `Dispose`, the disposable pattern, static local functions, the fix on the interpolated string, and null-coalescing assignment are very simple to remember and deliver practical advantages.

New language features are not just additional tools in the developer's Swiss Army knife, but a big opportunity to improve the code base. If we go back in time and think of generic types introduced in C# 2.0, they boosted the productivity and performance by orders of magnitude. Later on, the language introduced LINQ queries, lambda expressions, and extension methods, thereby bringing more expressivity and opening up new design strategies that were much harder before then. The entire history of programming languages, not only C#, is characterized by improvements targeting the requirements of modern development. Nowadays, application development is clearly oriented toward shorter development life cycles by adopting the **Continuous Integration/Continuous Delivery (CI/CD)** pipeline, which brings with it strong requirements regarding code quality and productivity. By considering this broader view, there is no doubt that staying up to date on the latest language features is mandatory for any developer.

In the next chapter, we will learn how .NET Core 3 can transform language formalism into running code, both on Windows and on Linux. We will go through creating a library that can be consumed from any .NET runtime flavor; consuming packages, which is the real richness of this ecosystem; and finally, publishing the application, turning all of our work into great value for the end user.

Test what you learned

1. How can you minimize the amount of `NullReferenceException` exceptions in your code?

2. What is the best syntax to use to read the last item in an array?

3. When using `switch` expressions, what keyword is equivalent to using the discard character (_)?

4. How can you await an asynchronous call closing a file in the `Dispose` method?

5. When assigning the `orders` variable in the following statement, is the method call invoked on every execution?

```
var orders ??= GetOrders();
```

6. Is defining a sequence as `IAsyncEnumerable` mandatory for it to be iterated with the new `async foreach` statement?

Further reading

If you want to follow the evolution of C#, you can examine the proposals and the conversations around the next release of the language on GitHub at `https://github.com/dotnet/csharplang`.

16

C# in Action with .NET Core 3

The C# programming language is the medium that we use to turn ideas into runnable code. At compile time, the whole set of rules, grammar, constraints, and semantics get transformed into the **Intermediate Language**—a high-level assembly language used to instruct the **Common Language Runtime (CLR)**, which in turn provides the necessary services to run the code.

In order to execute some code, native languages such as C, C++, and Rust require a thin runtime library to interact with the **operating system (OS)** and execute abstractions such as *program loading*, *constructors*, and *deconstructors*. On the other hand, higher-level languages such as C# and Java need a more complex runtime engine to provide other fundamental services such as *garbage collection*, *just-in-time compilation*, and *exception management*.

When .NET Framework was first created, the CLR was designed to run exclusively on Windows, but later, many other runtimes (implementing the same ECMA specifications) emerged, playing an important role in the market. For example, the Mono runtime was the first community-driven project to run on the Linux platform, and the Microsoft Silverlight project had brief success running inside the browsers of all the major platforms. Other runtimes, such as .NET Micro Framework for running on microcontrollers, .NET Compact Framework for targeting the embedded Windows CE OS, and other more recent flavors of the runtime running on Windows Phone and the Universal Windows Platform are good examples of the variety of the .NET implementations that have the ability to run the same set of instructions we still use today.

Each of those runtimes was built upon a number of requirements dictated by the historical context of the time, with no exceptions. At its birth, about 20 years ago, .NET Framework was designed to satisfy the growing Windows-based personal computer ecosystem, whose power grew over time in terms of CPU power, memory, and storage. Over the years, most of those runtimes successfully shifted toward more constrained hardware specifications, still offering roughly the same set of features. For example, even if modern mobile phones have very powerful microprocessors, code efficiency is still vital to preserve the battery life of those devices, a requirement that was not relevant when .NET Framework was initially designed.

Although the .NET specifications used by those runtimes are still the same, there are differences that make every developer's life hard when trying to design an application that is able to run on multiple runtimes, especially when a requirement is for it to be able to run cross-platform and/or cross-device.

The .NET Core 3 runtime was born to resolve those issues, by offering a new runtime that satisfies all the modern requirements. In this chapter, we are going to examine the factors related to the runtime when developing a C# application:

- Using the .NET **command-line interface (CLI)**
- Developing on Linux distributions
- What .NET Standard is and how can it help the application design
- Consuming NuGet packages
- Migrating an application designed with .NET Framework
- Publishing an application

By the end of this chapter, you will be more familiar with the .NET Core tools that allow you to compile and publish your application so that you can design a library to share the code with other applications running on .NET Core or other runtime flavors. Also, where you already have an application based on .NET Framework, you will learn the main steps to migrate it to fully leverage the .NET Core runtime.

Using the .NET command-line interface (CLI)

The **command-line interface (CLI)** is a new but strategic tool in the .NET ecosystem, enabling a modern developmental approach that can be used the same way across all platforms. At first sight, defining a tool based on the old console as "modern" might look strange, but in the world of modern development, the ability to script the build process to embrace the **Continuous Integration** and **Continuous Delivery/Deployment** (CI/CD) strategy is fundamental to provide faster and higher quality development life cycles.

After installing the .NET Core SDK (see `https://dotnet.microsoft.com/`), the .NET CLI is available through the Linux Terminal or Windows Command Prompt. A good alternative on Windows is the new **Windows Terminal** application, which can be downloaded through the Windows Store and provides a great replacement for the traditional Command Prompt, as well as the **PowerShell** terminal.

The .NET CLI has a rich list of commands, enabling a complete set of operations for the entire development life cycle. Detailed and contextual help for every command is obtained by adding the `--help` string as the last argument. The most relevant commands are as follows:

- `dotnet new`: The `new` command creates a folder for a new application project or solution, based on a long list of predefined templates that can be easily installed in addition to the default ones. Typing this command alone will just list all the available templates.

- `dotnet restore`: The `restore` command restores the referenced libraries from the NuGet server (outside the default `nuget.org` internet packages repository, the user can create a `nuget.config` file to specify other locations such as GitHub, or even a local folder).

- `dotnet run`: The `run` command builds, restores, and runs the project in a single shot.

- `dotnet test`: The `test` command runs the test for the specified project.

- `dotnet publish`: The `publish` command creates the deployable binaries, as we will discuss in the *Publishing an application* section.

In addition to these commands, the .NET CLI can be used to invoke other tools. Some of them are preinstalled. For example, `dotnet dev-certs` is a tool that's used to manage the HTTPS certificates on the local machine. Another example of the preinstalled tools on offer is `dotnet watch`, which observes the changes made to the source files in a project and automatically reruns the application every time any change occurs.

The `dotnet tool` command is the gateway to extend the CLI capability because it allows us to download and install additional tools through the configured NuGet servers. At the time of writing, there is still no way to filter the packages containing .NET tools on `https://nuget.org`; therefore, your best option is reading the suggestions from articles or other users.

When creating a new project (using the CLI), you may want to decide the runtime version first. The `dotnet --info` command returns a list of all the installed runtimes and SDKs. By default, the CLI uses the more recently installed **SDK**, but you may change the version for a specific directory tree by creating a special file called `global.json`. The settings in this file will affect all the operations done by the .NET CLI (which is also used by Visual Studio) for all the folders under the one containing the file:

```
C:\Projects>dotnet new globaljson
The template "global.json file" was created successfully.
```

Now, you can edit the file with your favorite editor and change the SDK version to one of the values listed previously:

```
{
    "sdk": {
        "version": "3.0.100"
    }
}
```

Be careful to choose the **SDK** version, and not the runtime version, when picking the number from the list obtained with the `info` parameter.

This process is useful to keep an application tied to a specific SDK instead of automatically inheriting the latest one installed. That being said, it is now time to create a new empty solution, which is a codeless container for one or more projects. Creating a solution is optional, but is very useful when you need to create multiple cross-referenced projects:

```
C:\Projects>dotnet new sln -o HelloSolution
The template "Solution File" was created successfully.
```

It's now time to create a new console project under the solution folder. The solution name can be omitted from the `sln add` command since there is only one solution in the folder:

```
cd HelloSolution
dotnet new console -o Hello
dotnet sln add Hello
```

Finally, we can build and run the project:

```
cd Hello
C:\Projects\HelloSolution\Hello>dotnet run
Hello World!
```

Alternatively, we can use the `watch` command to rerun the project every time any file is changed:

```
C:\Projects\HelloSolution\Hello>dotnet watch run
watch : Started
Hello World!
watch : Exited
watch : Waiting for a file to change before restarting
dotnet...
watch : Started
Hello Raf!
watch : Exited
watch : Waiting for a file to change before restarting
dotnet...
```

As soon as the first `Waiting for a file to change before restarting dotnet...` message was printed on the console, I modified and saved the `Program.cs` file using the Visual Studio Code editor. The changes on that file triggered the build process automatically, and the binary files were created as usual in the `bin` folder, whose tree structure has been slightly changed from .NET Framework.

There is still the `Debug` or `Release` folder, which in turn contains a new subfolder with the name of the framework; in this case, `netcoreapp3.0`. The new project system is multi-target capable and can generate different binaries depending on the framework, runtime, and bitness specified in the project file. The contents of that folder are as follows:

- `Hello.dll`. This is the assembly containing the `IL` code that was generated by the compiler.

- `Hello.exe`: The `.exe` file is a host application that bootstraps your application. Later, we will talk about publishing/deploying an application with more options.

- `Hello.pdb`: The `.pdb` file contains the symbols that allow the debugger to cross-reference the `IL` code to the source files, and the symbol (that is, variable, method, or class) names to the actual code.

- `Hello.deps.json`: This file contains the full dependency tree in JSON format. It is used to retrieve the libraries needed during compilation and it is a very effective way to discover undesired dependencies or problems when mixing different versions of the same assembly.

- `Hello.runtimeconfig.json` and `Hello.runtimeconfig.dev.json`: These are used by the runtime to know which shared runtime should be used to run the application. The `.dev` file contains configurations that are used in addition to the base file when the environment specifies that the application should be run in a development environment.

We just created a very basic application, but those steps are all that is required to create a complex application made of several libraries and using other, more complex templates. An interesting fact is that the same steps can be executed on the *Linux Terminal* to obtain the same results.

Developing on Linux distributions

The requirements revolution felt by developers did not stop with the mobile market and is still ongoing today. For example, the need to run across multiple OSes is more important than ever since the cloud era began. Many applications started moving from on-premises to cloud architectures, from virtual machines to containers, and from service-oriented architectures to microservices. This shift is so big that even the Microsoft CEO proudly celebrated the prevalence of Linux OSes on Azure, which is a clear sign of the importance of being able to create cross-platform applications.

There is no doubt that the ability of .NET Core to run on different OSes, devices, and CPU architectures is vital, but it comes with an awesome level of abstraction that minimizes the efforts of the developers, hiding most of the differences. For example, the Linux panorama offers a multitude of distributions, but you don't need to worry, as the abstraction doesn't affect the application's performance.

The lesson learned from the IT industry is that the technologies currently driving the growth of the cloud are not the final destination, but just a transition. At the time of writing, a technology called **Web Assembly System Interface (WASI)** is being standardized as a powerful abstraction to sandbox small units of code, providing a security isolation that can be used to run not only web applications (already available in every browser through **WebAssembly**) but also cloud or even classic standalone applications.

We still don't know if WASI will be successful, but there is no doubt that a modern runtime must be ready to ride the wave, and this implies embracing the agility to rapidly evolve and mutate as soon as new requirements knock at the door.

Preparing the development box

There are multiple options when it comes to creating a development environment on Linux. The first is to install Linux on the physical machine itself, which gives benefits in terms of performance throughout the whole development life cycle. The choice of the primary OS is very subjective and, while Windows and macOS currently offer a better desktop experience, the choice mostly depends on the application ecosystem that you need.

Another well-tested scenario is developing inside a virtual machine. In this case, you can use *Windows Hyper-V* or *Parallels Desktop* on Mac. If you don't have a distribution of choice, I strongly suggest you start installing Ubuntu desktop.

On Windows, you will find it very useful to use the integrated Linux support called **Windows Subsystem for Linux (WSL)**, which can be installed as an additional Windows 10 component. The current mature release, at the time of writing, is **WSL 1**, which runs a Linux distribution over the Windows kernel. In this solution, the Linux system calls are automatically remapped to the Windows kernel mode implementations.

While the distribution installed in this configuration is a fully genuine Linux distribution, some of its system calls cannot be translated and others, such as filesystem operations, are slower because their translation is not trivial. With **WSL 1**, most of the .NET Core code will run flawlessly; therefore, it is a good option for quickly switching between the Windows desktop and a true Linux environment.

The future of WSL is already available in the latest Windows preview and will soon be released in full. In this configuration, the full Linux kernel is installed on Windows and coexists with the Windows kernel, removing any of the previous limitations and providing near-native speed. As soon as it becomes fully available, I strongly recommend this development environment.

Once you prepare the Linux machine, you have three options:

- Install the .NET Core **SDK** because you want to manage the developer life cycle from within Linux.

- Install the .NET Core runtime because you just want to run the application and/or its tests on Linux to verify the cross-platform development is working as expected.

- Don't install either of the two, because you want to test the application as a self-contained deployment. We will investigate this option later in the *Publishing an application* section.

The prerequisites and packages needed for the SDK or the runtimes are continuously subject to change; therefore, it is better to refer to the official download page at `https://dot.net`. Once installed, the **SDK** should be able to run `dotnet --info` from a Terminal and show the following information:

```
The runtime and sdk versions listed by this command may be
different from the ones on Windows. You should consider the
opportunity to create a global.json outside the sources
repository in order to avoid mismatches when cloning a
repository on different operating systems.
```

If you decided to use the virtual machine or WSL, you should now install the **SSH daemon** so that you can communicate from the host machine to Linux. You should refer to the Linux distribution-specific instructions, but generally, the **openssh** package is the most popular choice:

```
sudo apt-get install openssh-server
(eventually configure the configuration file /etc/ssh/sshd_
config)
systemctl start ssh
```

Now, the Linux machine can be contacted either via the hostname (if it is automatically registered to your DNS) or the IP address. You can obtain these two pieces of information by typing the following:

- `ip address`
- `hostname`

There is a variety of free **SSH** and **SCP** clients on Windows, such as PuTTY, WinSCP, or Bitvise SSH Client, that support both protocols. The first option is used to obtain a remote terminal on Windows while the second option is used to transfer files between the two machines. You can also verify the connection by just using the `ssh` command-line tool in Windows:

```
ssh username@machinenameORipaddress
```

If it doesn't work because of a configuration problem, the typical troubleshooting path is to restore the default permissions on the configuration file:

```
Install-Module -Force OpenSSHUtils -Scope AllUsers
Repair-UserSshConfigPermission ~/.ssh/config
Get-ChildItem ~\.ssh\* -Include "id_rsa","id_dsa" -ErrorAction
SilentlyContinue | % {
    Repair-UserKeyPermission -FilePath $_.FullName @
psBoundParameters
}
```

There are, of course, many optional tools for Linux, but it is worth mentioning a few of them here:

- **Net-tools**: This is a package containing many network-related tools to diagnose the network protocols such as *arp*, *hostname*, *netstat*, and *route*. Some distributions already include them; otherwise, you can install by using your favorite package manager, such as **apt-get** on Ubuntu.

- **LLDB**: This is a Linux-native debugger. Microsoft provides the SOS extension for LLDB containing the same set of commands as the more popular SOS for WinDbg. This extension provides a lot of .NET-specific commands to diagnose leaks, walk the objects graph, investigate exceptions, and they can also be used on crash dumps.

- **Build-essential**: This is a package containing many developer tools, including the C/C++ compiler and related libraries to develop native code. This is useful if you wish to create native code to be invoked using **PInvoke** calls from .NET.

- **Editor and Visual Studio Code**: This is probably the best choice on Linux and macOS. Its capabilities can be expanded with the *Extensions* published in the Visual Studio Code marketplace (`https://marketplace.visualstudio.com/vscode`). Two interesting Visual Studio Code extensions using the `ssh` tool under the hood are *Remote – SSH* and *Remote – WSL*. The SSH extension allows us to develop on the remote Linux machine via SSH, whereas the WSL one allows us to develop on the local WSL subsystem.

You can just follow the most updated extension's instructions to configure the remote machine (exhaustive documentation can be found at the installation link in the *Further reading* section at the end of this chapter). Once installed, by hitting *F1*, you can access the Visual Studio Code commands. Then, type Remote-SSH, click **Add New SSH Host**, and finally repeat and pick **Connect to Host**:

Figure 16.1 – Connecting to a remote host via SSH from Visual Studio Code

This first connection will remotely install the required tools on Linux to enable the **Remote Development** scenario, which is where all the compilation and run tasks are done remotely, instead of on the machine where you type the code.

Even if you can just deploy the binaries and run them remotely, this configuration is very useful to test code that is demonstrating anomalies when running on Linux. In Visual Studio Code, you can open the Terminal window using the **View | Terminal** menu. The integrated Terminal window can be used to create the solution and projects and watch the sources to rerun the application automatically in the same way we previously did.

Writing cross-platform aware code

The abstractions provided by .NET Core let you forget many of the peculiarities that exist and work differently from one OS to another, but there are still things that must be considered carefully when developing the code. Most of these apparently insignificant details should become a best practice of the developer in order to avoid problems when running the application on different systems.

Filesystem casing

The most common mistake is not to consider the filesystem casing. On Linux, the files and folder names are *case-sensitive*; therefore, it is not unusual to discover problems due to a path containing the wrong casing for a file or a folder name.

Home directory

The structure of the user profiles is different in Windows and Linux, and even more importantly, the home directory when running the application with sudo (admin) privileges is different than the current logged-in user.

Path separators

We all know that Linux and Windows use the forward slash and the backslash characters to separate the files and folders, respectively. This is why the `System.IO.Path` class exposes the available separators through a few properties. Even better, avoid using the separators at all. For example, to compose a folder, the following statement should be preferred:

```
Path.Combine("..", "..", "..", "..", "Test",
    "bin", "Debug", "netcoreapp3.0", "test.exe");
```

Finally, to transform a relative into a full path, use the `Path.GetFullPath` method.

End-of-line separators

When dealing with text files, the end-of-line separator in Windows is `\r\n` (0x0D, 0x0A), while on Linux, we just use `\r` (0x0D). As for the `Path` class, the separator can be retrieved at runtime with `Environment.NewLine`, but most of the time, you can forget the difference by letting the `System.IO.TextReader.ReadLine` and `System.IO.TextWriter.WriteLine` abstractions take care of that.

Digital certificates

While Windows has a standard central repository for digital certificates, Linux does not, and it is up to the developer to decide whether to rely only on the certificate file or a distribution-specific solution. When you need to store a certificate, including the private key, it must be protected, because the private key is a secret that must never be disclosed. Providing the appropriate restrictions to defend those certificates is up to the developer.

Platform-specific APIs

Every platform-specific API such as the **Windows Registry** should, of course, be avoided, even if the API is available as a part of the **.NET Standard** contract, because it is likely to fail at runtime with a `NotImplementedException`. On Windows, the registry has historically been used to store per-user or even global settings related to the application. Linux has no equivalent; therefore, in modern development, it is better to get rid of the registry entirely. Another popular API is **Windows Management Instrumentation (WMI)**, which is only available on Windows and has no equivalent on Linux.

Security

Everything related to Windows accounts is, again, only available on Windows. The easiest way to modify the filesystem security flags on Linux is to spawn a new process running the standard `chmod` command-line tool with the appropriate arguments.

Environment variables

A very powerful and common denominator among all the platforms is the availability of the environment variables. Windows developers generally don't use them very often, while they are quite popular on Linux. For example, ASP.NET Core uses them to switch configurations between development, staging, and production, but can also be used to retrieve the standard variables, such as HOME on Linux and HOMEPATH on Windows, both of which represent the root folder for the current user's profile.

Gaps you may discover only at runtime

There are times where you may need to detect at runtime the OS or the CPU architecture that the code is running on. For this purpose, the `System.Runtime.InteropServices.RuntimeInformation` class provides a lot of interesting information:

- The `OSDescription` property returns a string describing the OS the application is running on.

- The `OSArchitecture` property returns a string with the OS architecture. For example, the *X64* value stands for the Intel 64-bit architecture.

- The `FrameworkDescription` property returns a string describing the current framework, such as *.NET Core 3.0.1*. The short string *3.0.1* is instead available through the `Environment.Version` property.

- The `ProcessArchitecture` property returns the processor architecture. This distinction exists because Windows can create 32-bit processes on its 64-bit flavor.

- The `GetRuntimeDirectory` method returns the full path, pointing to the runtime used by the application.

- Finally, the `RuntimeInformation.IsOSPlatform` method returns a Boolean that can be used to execute platform-specific code:

```
if (RuntimeInformation.IsOSPlatform(OSPlatform.Linux))
    Console.WriteLine("Linux!");
else if (RuntimeInformation.IsOSPlatform(OSPlatform.Windows))
    Console.WriteLine("Windows!");
else if (RuntimeInformation.IsOSPlatform(OSPlatform.OSX))
```

```
    Console.WriteLine("MacOS!");
else if (RuntimeInformation.IsOSPlatform(OSPlatform.FreeBSD))
    Console.WriteLine("FreeBSD!");
else
    Console.WriteLine("Unknown :(");
```

You should always evaluate whether to use this technique to adopt platform-specific decisions, or to create a NuGet package containing one DLL for each platform. This latter solution is more maintainable but is not discussed in this book.

What .NET Standard is and how can it help the application design

While .NET Core is the best candidate for running your code almost everywhere, it is also true that we currently may need to run our code on different runtimes, such as .NET Framework for existing Windows applications, Xamarin for developing mobile applications, and Blazor for running code in the WebAssembly sandbox or on other older runtimes.

The first attempt to share compiled libraries across multiple runtimes was done with the **portable class library**, where the developer could only use the APIs that were available in all the selected runtimes. The resulting intersection was impractical because restricting the number of available APIs to just the common APIs was way too limiting. .NET Standard initiative was born to resolve this issue by creating versioned sets of API definitions for a number of well-known APIs. In order to be .NET Standard-compliant, any runtime must guarantee to implement that complete set of APIs. Think of .NET Standard as a sort of giant interface holding all the included APIs. Furthermore, every new version of .NET Standard adds new APIs to the previous ones.

> **Tip**
> Even if an API is a part of a .NET Standard contract, it can be implemented on certain platforms by throwing NotImplementedException. This solution was allowed to ease the migration of old applications to .NET Standard and must be taken into consideration when using a .NET Standard library.

.NET Standard version 1.0 defined a very small set of APIs to satisfy almost all the available runtimes of the past, such as **Silverlight** and **Windows Phone 8**. Version after version, the number of defined APIs has grown larger, excluding older runtimes but also offering more APIs overall to developers. For example, version 1.5 offered a good compromise in terms of the number of APIs because it supported the very popular .NET Framework 4.6.2. In the .NET Standard repository on GitHub (`https://github.com/dotnet/standard/tree/master/docs/versions`), you can find the complete list of the versions and supported API sets.

At the time of writing, you should care about the .NET Standard versions only as a library author. If you look at the very popular `Newtonsoft.Json` package on NuGet, you will see that it complies to .NET Standard 1.0. This makes very sense because it allows the library to be used by almost the entire .NET ecosystem. The simple rule is that library developers should support the lowest possible version.

From the application developer's perspective, the problem is different because you may want to use the highest possible number in order to have the largest number of APIs available. If your target is to develop applications just for .NET Framework and .NET Core (which is very common when migrating to a new runtime), your choice will be version 2.0 because this is the last version of the .NET Standard contract supported from .NET Framework.

At the time of writing, the most recent version of .NET Standard is 2.1, which includes APIs such as `Span<T>`, and many new method overloads that take `Span<T>` instead of arrays, thereby providing better performance results.

Creating a .NET Standard library

Creating a .NET Standard library is straightforward. In Visual Studio, there is a specific template, whereas from the command line, the following command creates a .NET Standard library whose version is 2.0 by default. You can list the other choices by appending `--help` onto the end of the following command, or you can stay with `netstandard2.0` and create the library project:

```
C:\Projects\HelloSolution>dotnet new classlib -o MyLibrary
```

Once created, the library can be added to the previous solution with this command:

```
dotnet sln add MyLibrary
```

Finally, you can add the `MyLibrary` reference to the `Hello` project with this other command:

```
C:\Projects\HelloSolution>dotnet add Hello reference MyLibrary
Reference `..\MyLibrary\MyLibrary.csproj` added to the project.
```

The generated assembly is a class library that can be referenced from all the projects targeting the runtimes and supporting that .NET Standard version.

Deciding between the .NET Standard and .NET Core libraries

Every time you need to share some code across multiple runtimes, the best option is to try to fit it, whenever possible, into a .NET Standard library.

We already said that library authors should target the lowest possible version number, but of course, if you are the only library consumer, you may decide to adopt .NET Standard 2.0 to share codes, for example, between .NET Framework, .NET Core Mono 5.4, and Unity 2018.1.

Every time your library is going to be exclusively consumed by a .NET Core application, you may want to create a .NET Core class library instead as it does not limit the API set that you can use in your application:

```
C:\Projects\HelloSolution>dotnet new classlib -f netcoreapp3.0
-o NetCoreLibrary
C:\Projects\HelloSolution>dotnet add Hello reference
NetCoreLibrary
```

In the previous example, a new .NET Core class library (`NetCoreLibrary`) has been created and added to the reference of the `Hello` project.

Consuming NuGet packages

Packages play a very important role in modern application development because they define a self-contained unit of code that can be used as a brick to build larger applications.

This same definition was used in the past for libraries composed by a single `.dll` file, but modern development often requires more files to make a unit of code that's properly self-contained. The simplest example is when a package contains the library as well as its dependencies, but another, more complex, example is writing a library needing platform invocation calls to native APIs.

Native interoperability can also be written in a single library by using the aforementioned `RuntimeInformation` class, but it is generally better for both performance and maintenance to split the code into one library for each OS and CPU architecture. The advantage of packaging the platform-dependent libraries is that it lets the .NET Core build tools copy the relevant library in the output folder at publishing time. Beyond the interoperability with native code, there are other cases, such as providing different implementations depending on the runtime (for example, .NET Core, .NET Framework, Mono, and so on).

Adding packages to a project

There are multiple ways to add a package reference to a project; it mostly depends on your IDE of choice. Visual Studio offers full visual support by opening the **Solution Explorer** (this is the window showing the solution and projects hierarchy), expanding a project tree, right-clicking the **Dependencies** node, and picking the **Manage NuGet Packages** menu item. The following is a typical NuGet window, listing the packages available from **nuget. org** that can be added to your project:

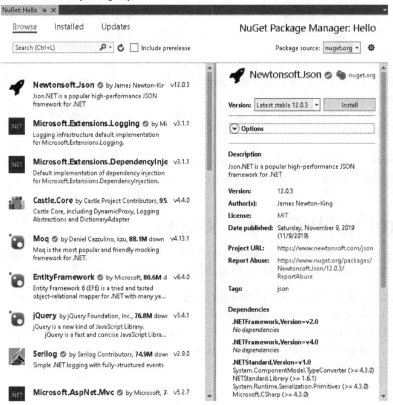

Figure 16.2 – The NuGet Package Manager Window

The NuGet window allows you to add, remove, or update to a different version of the project packages:

- On the right, the **Package source** combo box shows the list of websites or local folders providing packages. The list can be configured by clicking on the nearby gear icon.

- On the left, the **Browse** tab shows all the packages available from the selected source. You can decide to search the list and filter for not-yet-stable packages (previews) by clicking the **Include prerelease** checkbox. Search filtering can be improved using special prefixes such as **id**, **packageid**, **version**, **title**, **tags**, **author**, **description**, **summary**, and **owner**. For example, the Microsoft packages are listed by searching for `author:microsoft`.

- The **Installed** tab only shows the packages that are already installed in the project.

- The **Updates** tab shows the installed packages for which a new version is available from the selected source.

- Once you've selected a package on the right-hand side of the tab, you select the desired version and it will proceed to install, uninstall, or update, depending on the tab you started from.

When a solution is composed of multiple projects, it is important to be consistent in the version packages. For this reason, Visual Studio offers the ability to **Manage NuGet Packages for Solution**, a menu item available by right-clicking the **Solution** node. This window is similar, but has an additional tab called **Consolidate**, showing the packages that are installed with different versions in multiple projects. Ideally, this tab shouldn't show any packages:

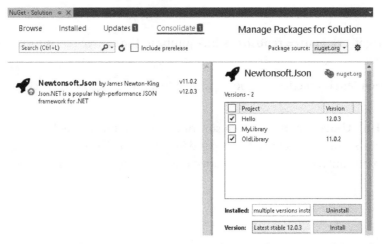

Figure 16.3 – The NuGet Package Manager for the Solution, Consolidate tab

An alternative way to search for packages is going straight to the source. In the following screenshot, you can see the `http://nuget.org` website, which is the primary repository of .NET packages:

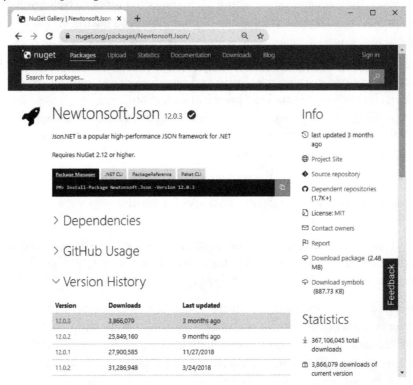

Figure 16.4 – Searching on the NuGet gallery website

This web page shows important details for each package you select:

- On the right, the **Source repository** link jumps to the source repository whenever it is available.

- The **Dependencies** section can be expanded to show which other packages it relies on.

- The **GitHub Usage** section acts as a sort of reputation for the package, showing how many open source projects took a dependency from it. The more a package is used by the community, the higher the chance that it is supported and reliable.

In the upper part of the page, the package section shows different ways to add the package to your project:

- **Package Manager** shows the manual command you can execute from the window with the same name in Visual Studio.

- **.NET CLI** shows the .NET CLI command.

- **PackageReference** shows the XML tag to copy the package into the .csproj directly.

- **Paket CLI** is an alternative CLI tool to the .NET CLI.

Adding a package via the CLI is straightforward because nuget.org already provides us with the exact command string to type into the console Terminal. Remember to enter the project folder first, and then type the command. For example, the following is the command to add a reference to the Newtonsoft.Json package from the command line:

```
dotnet add package Newtonsoft.Json --version 12.0.3
```

Regardless of the OS, if you are using Visual Studio Code, it provides the handy Terminal window from which you can type any .NET CLI command.

Another frequently used method to add a package reference is to directly edit the .csproj file. With .NET Core, the project file structure was drastically simplified, getting rid of all the past tags and also offering the ability, within Visual Studio, to edit and update the file without closing or unloading the project.

The following is the relevant portion of a .csproj file where you can add the PackageReference tag by hand:

```
<Project Sdk="Microsoft.NET.Sdk">
  ...
  <ItemGroup>
    ...
  </ItemGroup>

  <ItemGroup>
    <PackageReference Include="Newtonsoft.Json"
Version="12.0.3" />
  </ItemGroup>
</Project>
```

As you can see, the ItemGroup element can be repeated multiple times and each of them may contain multiple PackageReference tags.

Migrating from .NET Framework to .NET Core

I believe the most important new feature of the .NET Core runtime is its ability to be deployed side by side with any other .NET Core version, guaranteeing that any future release will not affect older runtimes or libraries and, consequently, applications. The primary reason that prevented Microsoft from modernizing and improving the performance of .NET Framework was the shared nature of the .NET runtime and base class libraries. Because of that, the smallest change to those libraries could potentially cause unacceptable breaking changes to the hundreds of millions of installations already deployed.

The obvious consequence of the new side-by-side deployment strategy in .NET Core is the total absence of the **Global Assembly Cache (GAC)**, which provided a central repository to which a system or user library could be deployed. The runtime is now completely isolated from the rest of the system, a decision that enabled the ability to deploy the application in a so-called **self-contained deployment** where all the required code, including the runtime and the system library, together with the application code, are copied into a single folder. We will dig into the deployment options later in the *Publishing an application* section.

Among all the available runtimes, .NET Framework has always been the touchstone and, at the time of writing, is still a valid ecosystem that will be supported for a very long time by Microsoft since it is redistributed with the Windows client and server OSes. Though, as wise developers, we can't ignore the fact that with the release of .NET Core 3, Microsoft made two important statements:

- .NET Framework 4.8 will be the *last version* of this runtime and libraries.
- .NET 5 will be the new *short name* for .NET Core to be released at the end of 2020.

There is no doubt that .NET Core 3 demarcates a turning point in the history of the .NET runtime as it provides all the workloads that were previously supported by .NET Framework. Starting from .NET Core 3, you can now create server and Windows desktop applications, leverage the power of machine learning, or develop cloud applications. This is also a strong piece of advice for all relevant developers who are invited to create all-new applications using .NET Core, because it offers the latest state-of-the-art technology in terms of runtime, libraries, compilers, and tools.

Analyzing your architecture

Before starting any migration step, it is important to verify whether the technologies, frameworks, and third-party libraries are available on .NET Core.

The old .NET Framework base class library has been ported entirely, as have the great majority of the most popular NuGet packages authored by Microsoft and other third parties, giving all of us a very high chance of finding updated versions compatible with .NET Core. If those dependencies are available as .NET Standard 2.0 or a lower version (remember that .NET Standard 2.1 is not supported by .NET Framework), then they are good to go. But as we have seen previously, the NuGet package can contain multiple libraries targeting different runtimes, so it is important to verify the compatibility of the library on the vendor's page.

If your projects rely heavily on Windows because they need Windows APIs, you may want to take a look at the **Windows Compatibility Pack NuGet** package, which contains about 20,000 APIs.

> **Information box**
> Even if a library is only .NET Framework-compatible, in most cases, it can be referenced by .NET Core thanks to a *shim mechanism* that makes this possible. In this case, Visual Studio shows a yellow triangle indicating a warning in the build log. The potential incompatibilities should be tested carefully to verify the correctness of the application.

Although .NET Core supports the vast majority of the past workloads, some of them are not available and others have been rewritten, making the migration process a bit harder, but giving other advantages in return.

Migrating ASP.NET Web Forms applications

This technology is very old and considered obsolete, because the web of today has evolved with very different paradigms in comparison to the web technologies of the past. The best route to migrate this code is using the **Blazor template**, which allows us to run C# code inside the browser thanks to the *WebAssembly* support, which is now available in any modern browser. While this solution is not a real port, but a rewrite, it allows us to stay on C# for both the server and most of the client code.

Windows Communication Foundation (WCF)

On .NET Core, support for the **Windows Communication Foundation (WCF)** is available only for the client side, which means just consuming the WCF services. Nowadays, there are more performant and simpler technologies available, such as **gRPC** (requiring HTTP2) and **REST** (Web API). For those who still need to create SOAP-based web services, a community-driven open source project called **CoreWCF** is available on GitHub. Before you start migrating your old code using this library, you should verify that all of the WCF options used in your projects are also available on CoreWCF.

At the time of writing, neither .NET Core nor CoreWCF support the **WS-*** standards at all.

Windows Workflow Foundation

Workflow Foundation has not been ported, but another open source project called **CoreWF** is available on GitHub. As we mentioned previously for WCF, you should verify the full availability of the features used in your projects first.

Entity Framework

Entity Framework 6 (EF6) is also available on .NET Core and you should not have any issue in migrating this project, but it is worth mentioning that this technology is considered *feature complete* by Microsoft, which is now only developing **Entity Framework Core (EF Core)**. Depending on how your repository access is structured, including the model graph and the providers used in your project, you may want to consider migrating your access code to EF Core. In this case, be aware that, in .NET Core 3, many-to-many relationships are supported but require the intermediate entity class to be described in the model. The APIs in EF Core are very different but, on the other hand, they offer a lot of new functionalities. The roadmap for .NET 5 (which is the new name for .NET Core) includes a lot of new features that you may want to consider.

For all the aforementioned reasons, you may find it easier to first migrate using EF6 and only later migrate to EF Core. This decision is very project dependent.

ASP.NET MVC

The ASP.NET MVC framework has been entirely rewritten on ASP.NET Core, but it still offers the same key functionalities. Unless you deeply customize and extend the infrastructure, the migration is definitely straightforward, but still requires some small rewriting of code because of the namespace and type changes.

Code Access Security APIs

All of the **Code Access Security (CAS)** APIs have been removed from .NET Core because the only trustable boundary is the one offered natively by the process hosting the code. If you are still using CAS, it is highly recommended to get rid of it, regardless of your .NET Core migration.

AppDomains and Remoting APIs

With .NET Core, there is always a single AppDomain per process. For this reason, you will see that most of the AppDomain APIs are gone and not available. If you have used AppDomains to isolate and unload certain assemblies, you should look at `AssemblyLoadContext`, a new API in .NET Core 3 that allows you to address this problem in a powerful way without requiring remoting communication, which has been removed from .NET Core as well.

Preparing the migration process

A common step to pursue when starting the migration process from .NET Framework to .NET Core is updating .NET Framework to at least version 4.7.2.

Version 4.7.2 is a special version, as it was the first release to fully support the .NET Standard binary contract, avoiding the requirement of external NuGet packages needed to fill the gaps. This step shouldn't cause any issues and you can continue to deploy the current projects with this latest version of .NET Framework with no fear. Depending on the complexity of the solution, you may want to work on the migration while still running production code on .NET Framework until everything is fully tested.

At this point, the analysis should focus on external dependencies such as NuGet packages from third parties that you don't have control over. Once you have identified the newer packages, update them so that your .NET Framework solution can run on the newer versions. You still have a deployable solution that starts off with a few pieces that are compatible with .NET Core, even if you didn't change any lines of code.

The Portability Analyzer Tool

The **API Port tool** is available on GitHub at `https://github.com/microsoft/dotnet-apiport` and provides us with the ability to create a detailed report of a .NET application that lists all the APIs used and whether they are available on other platforms. The tool is available both as a Visual Studio extension or via the CLI so that you can automate the process as desired. The ultimate report provided by the tool is an Excel spreadsheet containing a cross-reference of all the APIs that allows you to plan the migration without getting any undesirable surprises during the process.

Migrating the libraries

We can finally start updating the library projects in the solution. It is important to have a clear view of the dependency tree of the entire solution and packages. If the project is very large, you may want to leverage the power of external tools such as the popular **NDepend**. On the dependency tree, you should identify the libraries at the bottom of the tree that have no other dependencies on external packages—they are the best starting point.

In most cases, migrating a library with no dependencies (or a library depends on a package that can run on both frameworks) is straightforward. There is no automated support, so you should create a new **.NET Standard 2.0** project.

> **Tip**
> At the time of writing, the `https://github.com/dotnet/try-convert/releases` repository contains the preview of a tool that is able to convert projects into .NET Core. As the name `try-convert` suggests, it cannot handle all types of project, but can still be used as a starting point for the migration.

Migrating to the new `.csproj` project structure can be done in one of two ways:

- Creating a new project and moving the source files over it
- Modifying the `.csproj` file of the old project

The first strategy is simpler, but it has the downside of changing the project name, which also implies changing the default for the namespace name and the assembly name. These can be renamed by making the following changes to the `.csproj` file:

```
<PropertyGroup>
   ...
  <AssemblyName>MyLibrary2</AssemblyName>
 <RootNamespace>MyLibrary2</RootNamespace>
</PropertyGroup>
```

Remember that creating a new project also implies fixing the references of all the dependent projects.

The second strategy consists of replacing the contents of the `.csproj` file, which requires you to have tested the changes prior to this on a separate project. When migrating the package references, be advised that new .NET Core projects ignore the `packages.config` file and require all the references to be specified in the `PackageReference` tags, as mentioned earlier in the *Consuming NuGet packages* section.

Finding the missing APIs

During the migration, you might discover some missing APIs. For this specific case, Microsoft created the `https://apisof.net/` website, which has classified more than 700,000 APIs among those available through the base class library and NuGet. Thanks to its search capability, you can search for any class, method, property, or event and discover its usage and which platform and version supports it.

Migrating the tests

Once you've migrated the lower-level dependent libraries, it is a good idea to create the test projects so that any migrated code gets tested on both frameworks. The test projects themselves shouldn't really be migrated, as you may want to test the code on both frameworks. For this reason, you may want to share the test code in a **Shared Project** (a template available from the following screen in Visual Studio), which is a special project that doesn't produce any binary:

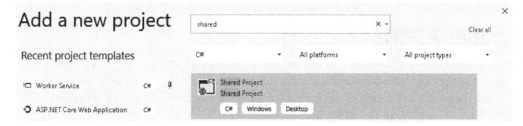

Figure 16.5 – The Add a new project Visual Studio dialog box

All the projects referencing a Shared Project inherit its source code, as it was included directly. All the major test frameworks (xUnit, NUnit, and MSTest) have been ported to .NET Core, but there may be a few differences in the supported test APIs; therefore, any infrastructural code using the test API should be verified first.

Lastly, if the test code uses AppDomains to unload certain assemblies, remember to rewrite it using the more powerful `AssemblyLoadContext` API. The migration should now continue by iterating over the porting libraries and their tests until all the infrastructure has been migrated and is working on both frameworks.

Migrating the desktop projects

The WPF and Windows Forms workloads are available on .NET Core 3 and their migration should be straightforward. At the time of writing, the Windows Forms designer is available as a preview, but you can still share the designer code in the Shared Project mentioned previously to continue using the .NET Framework designer.

On .NET Core 3.1, some of the Windows Forms controls have been removed, but they can be replaced with newer ones exhibiting the same functionalities:

Old control	Replacement
MenuItem	Toolstrip
Menu	ToolStripDropDown or ToolStripDropDownMenu
MenuItem	ToolStripMenuItem
ContextMenu	ContextMenuStrip
Toolbar	ToolStrip
DataGrid	DataGridView

Another missing feature is **ClickOnce**, a deployment system that is widely used inside many companies. Microsoft's suggestion is to migrate the deployment package to the newer **MSIX** technology.

Migrating ASP.NET projects

Migrating ASP.NET MVC projects is the only workload that requires more manual work and code changes, but also brings many clear advantages from the newly rewritten ASP. NET Core framework in terms of performance and simplification, such as the unified `Controller` hierarchy of the **MVC** and **WebAPI** worlds.

> **Tip**
>
> Before starting, I strongly suggest being familiar with the *ASP.NET Core MVC* framework, with particular focus on dependency injection, identity, authorization, configuration, and logging, the details of which go far beyond the scope of this book.

To migrate a ASP.NET web project, it is always better to start from a new ASP.NET Core MVC template instead of tweaking the old `.csproj`, since the code won't run as-is and will always require some changes.

Any code related to the ASP.NET infrastructure is the first you may want to migrate. For example, Global.asax generally contains the initialization code, while **HTTP Modules** and **Handlers** are infrastructural code meant to intercept the requests and responses. The general rules for migrating this code are as follows:

- Static structures or global helpers should be converted into a **Dependency Injection (DI)** singleton service.

- Any code that is meant to intercept, read, or modify the HTTP requests and responses should become middleware and be configured in the Startup class.

- Identify any code outside of the Controller logic, determine its life cycle, and make it available through **DI**. Every time you need to explicitly request an instance of these services out of your Controller constructor, consider creating a factory instead and provide the factory through **DI** to the Controller.

With the old MVC framework, most of the infrastructure customization was needed to provide external services to the controller. This is not required anymore because **DI** allows controllers to require any service at any time.

A second key step is determining the identity framework infrastructure requirement. The new template provides a lot of enhancements, as well as basic support for legal *GDPR requirements*. In most cases, it is better to start from the new infrastructure and migrate the database, instead of just porting the old code. On NuGet, you will find support for many providers, starting from OAuth generic ones to social identity providers, OpenID specification providers, and many others. It is also possible to leverage the popular open source project **Identity Server**, an identity provider that is now part of the .NET Foundation.

The authorization framework has changed as well and brings two important key features. The first is being claim-based. This presents a lot of advantages in comparison to the old role-based security (which has several limitations). Claims can also be used as roles whenever your checks are just Booleans, but they allow more complex logic structured as Policies inside ASP.NET Core, which is definitely worth adopting.

Once all the infrastructure has been ported or converted, the application logic can finally be moved to the new controllers. As we mentioned previously, there is now a single Controller base class that is used for both MVC and Web API controllers. Matching a controller from a request is done via the routing mechanism. In ASP.NET Core, the routing is configured through attributes in your Controller class.

Every controller may expose one or more `Actions` that can be tagged with the attributes defining the HTTP verbs they are restricted to, such as `HttpGet` and `HttpPost`. Actions related to the HTTP `GET` verb do not take any input parameters, while other verbs such as `POST` and `PUT` can benefit from the *model-binding* feature, which automatically maps the values passed by the requests to the input parameters. You can find more information about model binding in the official documentation at `https://docs.microsoft.com/en-us/aspnet/core/mvc/models/model-binding`.

The response of the HTTP roundtrip depends, of course, on its HTTP verb. The typical return types for actions are as follows:

- An object representing the response value to return to the HTTP client. It will be serialized by the infrastructure according to the types specified by the client in the accept header.

- A `Task<T>`, where `T` is the response value specified in the preceding. Tasks should be used whenever the content retrieval requires some "slow" access, such as accessing the filesystem or a database.

- An object implementing `IActionResult`, such as `OkResult` and `NotFoundResult` created by the homonymous method name in the `ControllerBase` class, which is the base class for any Controller. They are used to give full control over the status code and the response headers. The full list of ready-to-use `IActionResult` types is defined in the `Microsoft.AspNetCore.MVC` namespace. Some of these objects have a constructor that take the object to return, such as `OkObjectResult`, which returns an object as content and sets the HTTP status code to 200.

- An object implementing `Task<IActionResult>`, which is the asynchronous version of the previous case.

- The last case is returning `void`, which lets the infrastructure return the default response with no content at all.

Once the code has been migrated, you have to consider the hosting environment. The web server for ASP.NET Core applications is called **Kestrel**, so every setting previously written in the `web.config` file should be revised either in the new `appsettings.json` configuration file or directly in the code for Kestrel configurations in the `Program.cs` file.

Be advised that using IIS is still possible, but this can only be used as a reverse proxy and requires the use of the official ASP.NET Core IIS Module, which forwards all the HTTP traffic to and from the Kestrel web server.

This solution brings an excellent, improved, and cross-platform solution to ASP.NET Core, but if you still want to host the project on IIS, it is definitely possible by installing the official **ASP.NET Core IIS Module** on the hosting server. The module will forward all the HTTP requests and responses to the Kestrel web server, so most of the settings in IIS can be safely ignored.

Summing up the migration steps

Planning a migration is certainly not always easy, but there is a clear path that can be applied to any group of projects. Some of the following steps may be harder or easier, depending on the technology they were implemented on, while some others are pretty straightforward and only require practicing in advance, but the number of available APIs make the process far easier starting from .NET Core version 3. The rough steps to migrate an application are as follows:

1. Ensure you are using the technologies available in .NET Core. You may want to consider a replacement when they are not but analyze the implications on the application architecture carefully.

2. Once you've decided to start the migration, upgrade all of your projects to the latest .NET Framework as a very first step.

3. Ensure all the third-party dependencies are available as .NET Standard and migrate your current .NET Framework projects to use them.

4. Analyze your projects using the Portability Analyzer Tool or verify the availability of the APIs at `https://apisof.net/`.

5. Every time you migrate a single .NET Framework library project to .NET Standard, the application can be potentially merged back on the main branch and be deployed in production.

6. Migrate the projects by navigating the dependency tree from the ones with no dependencies, going all the way up to the applications referencing the ones that have already been migrated.

At first glance, migration can look a bit scary, but there are many advantages that you will appreciate as soon as the application starts running on.NET Core. Among them, the deployment offers new, exciting, and powerful features, which we are going to discuss in the next section.

Publishing an application

The last essential step for making an application usable outside the developer machine is **publishing**. There are two kinds of deployment: framework-dependent and self-contained.

Framework-dependent deployment (FDD) creates a folder with all the required binaries needed to run the application on any computer with the same OS and the .NET runtime installed. FDD deployment has several advantages:

- It lowers the size of the deployment folder.

- It makes the security updates easy to install by an IT manager instead of the need to redeploy them.

- When deploying in Docker containers, you can start from pre-built images already containing the .NET runtime for the version you need.

The other publishing option is **self-contained deployment (SCD)**, which creates/copies all the required files to run the application, including the runtime and all the base class libraries. The main advantage of SCD is that it gets rid of any requirements on the hosting target, enabling scenarios where you can run the application just by copying the folder.

> **Tip**
> On Linux, some basic libraries may be needed on certain distributions that are very constrained. On the `https://dot.net`, you can find updated information about those requirements.

On the other hand, the self-contained deployment scenario also has some drawbacks:

- The application must be published for a specific OS and CPU architecture.

- You should promptly respond to security bulletins every time the .NET Core runtime gets any security update. In this case, after applying the updates to the developer machine, you will have to rebuild and redeploy the application.

- The total deployment size is much larger.

Starting from .NET Core 2.2, the FDD produces automatically executable files instead of just `.dll` files for the main projects, while in the past, FDD applications needed to be run through the `dotnet run` command. Now, they are created as executables and also known as **Framework Dependent Executables (FDE)**, which is the default when publishing an application using the .NET Core 3 **SDK**.

Publishing as an FDD

If you want to keep the deployment size compact, just make sure your version of choice for the .NET Core runtime is installed on the target machine and that you publish the application as an **FDD**. Publishing an application as an **FDD** from the command line is straightforward; first, you enter the project folder and then type the following command:

```
C:\Projects\HelloSolution\Hello>dotnet publish -c Release
```

The CLI will build and publish the project, also printing the path of the publishing folder on the screen:

```
Hello -> C:\Projects\HelloSolution\Hello\bin\Release\
netcoreapp3.0\publish\
```

The target folder can be changed by appending the -o argument to the previous command:

```
C:\Projects\HelloSolution\Hello>dotnet publish -c Release -o
myfolder
```

In this case, the output folder will be as follows:

```
Hello -> C:\Projects\HelloSolution\Hello\myfolder\
```

The publishing command can also specify the requested runtime accepting a **Runtime Identifier (RID)** (https://docs.microsoft.com/en-us/dotnet/core/rid-catalog). For example, publishing the application for Linux on the 64-bit architecture is done with the following command:

```
dotnet publish -c Release -r linux-x64 --no-self-contained
```

Unless you also specify the output folder, this will reflect the specified RID:

```
Hello -> C:\Projects\HelloSolution\Hello\bin\Release\
netcoreapp3.0\linux-x64\publish\
```

The --no-self-contained argument is needed because, by default, the application is published as self-contained if a runtime identifier is specified.

Publishing as an SCD

Using SCD means getting rid of any installed runtime dependencies. For this reason, when you decide to publish as an SCD, you also have to specify the runtime identifier (the target OS and CPU architecture) so that all the required runtime dependencies are published together with the application.

Publishing as an SCD just requires adding the `--self-contained` and `-r` option followed by the runtime identifier. The shorter version is just specifying the `-r` option as, by default, this turns on the self-contained options as well. For example, publishing a self-contained application for the 64-bit version of Windows is done with the following command:

```
dotnet publish -c Release -r win-x64
```

The output folder, in this case, will be as follows, as specified by the output messages of the command line:

```
  Hello -> C:\Projects\HelloSolution\Hello\bin\Release\
netcoreapp3.0\win-x64\publish\
```

Whether you'll depend on the runtime installation or not is just one of the options when publishing. Now, we will examine other interesting possibilities.

Understanding other publishing options

Starting from .NET Core 3, it is possible to specify a number of interesting options when publishing. These options can be either specified on the command line or even forced inside the `.csproj` file, making them the default for the project inside the `PropertyGroup` tag.

Single-file publishing

Publishing as a single file is a very convenient feature that creates a single file for all of the project files. Having a single executable enables the possibility of moving the application easily through a USB key or as a download. The only files that cannot be embedded in the executable are the configuration files and the web static files (for example, HTML).

The following is the command line that's used to publish the application as a single file. Single-file publishing is compatible with FDD; in this case, you can append `--no-self-contained` to the command line:

```
dotnet publish -r win-x64 -o folder -p:PublishSingleFile=true
```

Alternatively, you can turn on the single-file publishing option in the .csproj file:

```
<PublishSingleFile>true</PublishSingleFile>
<RuntimeIdentifier>win-x64</RuntimeIdentifier>
```

You will immediately notice the size of the binary as particularly large because it contains all the dependent code, even the portions of the assemblies that you didn't need. What if we can get rid of all the unused methods, properties, or classes from inside our references? The solution comes from **IL trimming**.

IL trimming

Trimming is the ability to remove all the unused code from the deployment binary. This feature comes from the **Mono IL Linker** code base. This setting requires the deployment to be self-contained, which, in turn, requires the runtime identifier to be specified.

The **PublishTrimmed** factory can be turned on when publishing on the command line:

```
dotnet publish -c Release -r win-x64 -p:PublishTrimmed=true
```

Otherwise, it can be specified in the **csproj** file:

```
<PublishTrimmed>true</PublishTrimmed>
```

When heavily using reflection, the trimmer loses the ability to understand which libraries and members are needed. For example, if you dynamically compose the member name, the trimmer can't know the members to keep or discard. In this case, there are other two options, `TrimmerRootAssembly` and `TrimmerRootDescription`, that can be used to specify the code that should not be trimmed away.

Ahead-of-Time (AOT) compilation

AOT compilation allows us to precompile the application by generating almost all the native CPU assembly code on the developer machine. If you have never heard of the **ngen** tool in .NET Framework, it was used to generate the native assembly code on the target machine, making the application bootstrap performance much faster, as the **Just-in-Time (JIT)** compiler was no longer needed. The AOT compiler has the same goal but uses a different strategy: in fact, the compilation is done on the developer machine and because of this, the quality of the generated code is lower. This is because the compiler cannot make assumptions on the CPU that will run the code.

In order to balance the lower-quality code, .NET Core 3 enables **TieredCompilation** by default. Whenever an application method is called more than 30 times, it is considered "hot" and scheduled on a remote thread to be recompiled from the **JIT compiler**, thereby providing better performance.

The **AOT** compilation can be enabled when publishing from the command line, as follows:

```
dotnet publish -c Release -r win-x64 -p:PublishReadyToRun=true
```

Alternatively, you can modify the `.csproj` file to make this setting persistent:

```
<PublishReadyToRun>true</PublishReadyToRun>
```

The AOT compilation provides a better startup, but also requires specifying the runtime identifier, which means compiling for a specific OS and CPU architecture. This setting wipes out the advantage of IL code being deployed on multiple platforms.

Quick JIT

Every time you are worried about the need to pre-generate the native compilation but still need to provide a fast application bootstrap, you can enable **QuickJIT**, a faster **JIT** compiler that has the downside of producing less performant code. Once again, the tiered compilation balances the code-quality disadvantages and recompiles the code as soon it qualifies as a hot path.

Enabling Quick JIT from the command line is no different than the other options:

```
dotnet publish -c Release -p:TieredCompilationQuickJit=true
```

Enabling Quick JIT in the **csproj** file is similar as well:

```
<TieredCompilationQuickJit>false</TieredCompilationQuickJit>
```

It is important to observe that the calls to external libraries cannot be compiled in native code by the AOT compiler as the libraries may be replaced with newer versions in the target machine, invalidating the generated code. Every time some code cannot be compiled as native, it will be compiled with the **JIT** on the target machine. For this reason, it totally makes sense to enable **AOT** and **QuickJIT** together.

> **Tip**
> The **ngen** compiler of .NET Framework is able to generate the assembly code for all the IL in the assemblies, but as soon as any dependent assembly is replaced, all the native code is invalidated, requiring the JIT to compile all the code.

Whether your application needs to be self-contained, single-file, or precompiled, there is a multitude of deployment options that .NET Core offers to make your application shine in every scenario, and you can now pick the one you prefer.

Summary

In this chapter, we went through all the fundamental steps to follow in order to build a new application using the .NET Core runtime, which is accompanied by an increased number of APIs. We started by looking at the new powerful command line that offers all the commands that can be used to control the development life cycle of the application. The command-line extensibility removes any limitations, allowing anyone to add local and global tools to the ecosystem.

We have also seen how the command-line commands are exactly the same when developing on Linux OSes, which can be used as a developer box directly or through Windows, as you please. In fact, the Visual Studio Code remote extensions let you develop and debug the code on a Linux machine from Windows.

But we also saw that .NET Core 3 is not a one-way trip, because .NET Standard libraries allow us to share code with all the recent runtimes, making it easier to reuse the code. In addition to that, the very rich ecosystem of NuGet packages makes consuming libraries straightforward.

Adopting the new runtime is not that hard: some applications can be migrated by just converting the project file, while others require more coding, but the resulting application will benefit from the new ecosystem.

In the last section, we examined the complete set of possibilities when publishing an application, which is the culmination of the application development process. At this point, you are able to transform ideas and algorithms into a running application, possibly running on the most popular OSes.

In the next chapter, we will talk about unit testing, a practice that is extremely important for guaranteeing code quality across time and providing proof that future development iterations will not introduce breaking changes or regressions.

Test what you learned

1. After installing five different SDKs, how can you tell the CLI to use a specific version for an entire solution?

2. How can you concatenate some paths so that they work correctly on both Windows and Linux?

3. How can you share some code among three different applications based on .NET Framework, .NET Core 3, and Xamarin?

4. What is the fastest method for a new library project to add the exact same references to an existing one?

5. When migrating a complex solution, where should we start?

6. What deployment options guarantee faster application startup time?

Further reading

The Visual Studio Code extensions to compile and debug a project on a remote Linux or WSL session, can be found at the following links:

- `https://marketplace.visualstudio.com/items?itemName=ms-vscode-remote.remote-ssh`

- `https://marketplace.visualstudio.com/items?itemName=ms-vscode-remote.remote-wsl`

The ability to create NuGet packages containing multiple binaries, each of them targeting a different CPU architecture or framework version is described at the following link: `https://docs.microsoft.com/en-us/nuget/create-packages/supporting-multiple-target-frameworks`.

17
Unit Testing

Throughout this book, you have learned all you need to know to be able to program using the C# language—from statements to classes, from generics to functional programming, from reflection to concurrency, and many others. We also covered many topics related to .NET Framework and .NET Core, including collections, regular expressions, files and streams, resource management, and **Language Integrated Query** (**LINQ**).

However, a key aspect of programming is making sure that code behaves as intended. Code that is not properly tested is prone to unexpected bugs. There are various types and levels of testing, but the one typically performed by developers while developing is *unit testing*. This is the topic covered in this final chapter of this book. In this chapter, you will learn what unit testing is and what are the built-in tools available to write unit tests for C#. Then, we will look in detail at how we can leverage these tools to unit test our C# code.

In this chapter, we will focus on the following topics:

- What is unit testing?
- What are Microsoft tools for unit testing?
- Creating a C# unit testing project
- Writing unit tests
- Writing data-driven unit tests

Let's start with an overview of unit testing.

What is unit testing?

Unit testing is a type of software testing where individual units of code are tested to validate whether they are working as they were designed. Unit testing is the first level of software testing, the others being integration testing, system testing, and acceptance testing. A discussion of these types of testing is beyond the scope of this book. Unit testing is typically performed by software developers.

Performing unit testing has important benefits:

- It helps to identify and fix bugs earlier in the development cycle, thereby helping to save time and money.

- It helps developers to better understand the code and allows them to make quick changes to the code base.

- It helps with code reuse by requiring it to be more modular to test it better.

- It can act as project documentation.

- It helps to speed up development because the effort of identifying bugs using various methods of manual testing done by developers is greater than the time spent writing unit tests.

- It simplifies debugging because when tests fail, only the latest changes need to be looked at and debugged.

The unit of testing may differ. It can be a *function* (as it typically is in imperative programming) or a *class* (in object-oriented programming). Units are tested individually and in isolation from other units. This requires that units are designed to be loosely coupled but also employs the use of substitutes such as stubs, mocks, and fakes. Although the definition of these concepts may vary, stubs are functions that stand in as replacements for other functions, simulating their behavior. Examples could include stubs for functions that retrieve data from a web service or temporary substitutes for functionalities that will be added at a later time. Mocks are objects that simulate the behavior of other objects, usually complex, that are impractical to use for a unit test. The term **fake** may refer either to a *stub* or a *mock* and is used to indicate an entity that is not real.

Apart from using substitutes, unit testing often requires the use of test harnesses. A test harness is an automated testing framework that allows testing to be automated by supporting the creation of tests, executing the tests, and generating reports.

The measure of how much of the code base is covered by unit tests is called **code coverage**. Code coverage offers an indication of the degree a code base has been tested by providing a quantitative measure. Code coverage helps us to identify the parts of a program that are not well covered by test cases and allows us to create more tests to increase coverage.

What are Microsoft tools for unit testing?

If you are working with Visual Studio, several tools help you to write unit tests for your C# code. These tools include the following:

- **Test Explorer**: This is a component of the IDE that allows you to view the unit tests, run them, and see their results. The **Test Explorer** does not work solely with MSTest (Microsoft's testing unit framework). It has an extensible API that allows developing adapters for third-party frameworks. Some of the frameworks that provide adapters for **Test Explorer** are **NUnit** and **xUnit**.

- **Microsoft unit test framework for managed code or MSTest**: This is installed with Visual Studio but is also available as a NuGet package. There is also a unit testing framework for native code with similar functionalities.

- **Code coverage tools**: They allow you to determine the amount of code that unit tests are covering.

- **Microsoft Fakes isolation framework**: This allows you to create substitutes for classes and methods. Currently, this only works for .NET Framework and with Visual Studio Enterprise. At this time, .NET standard projects are not supported.

The experience of working with the Microsoft testing framework for .NET Framework and .NET Core is a bit different at the time of writing this book because there are no unit testing templates for .NET Core test projects. This means that you need to manually create test classes and methods and decorate them with the proper attributes, as we will see shortly.

Creating a C# unit testing project

In this section, we will look together at how you can create a unit testing project in Visual Studio 2019. When you open the **File | New Project** menu, you can choose between various testing projects:

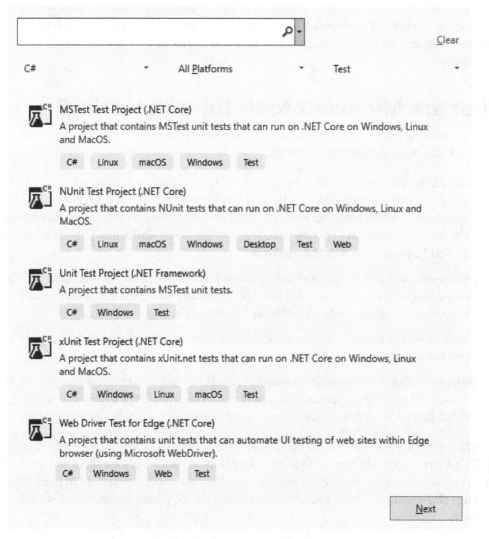

Figure 17.1 - Visual Studio 2019 unit testing project templates

If you need to test a .NET Framework project, then you select **Unit Test Project (.NET Framework)**.

A project is created for you with a single unit testing file with the
following content:

```csharp
using System;
using Microsoft.VisualStudio.TestTools.UnitTesting;

namespace UnitTestDemo
{
    [TestClass]
    public class UnitTest1
    {
        [TestMethod]
        public void TestMethod1()
        {
        }
    }
}
```

Here, UnitTest1 is a class containing test methods. This class is marked with the
TestClassAttribute attribute. Another attribute, TestMethodAttribute, is
used to mark the TestMethod1() method. These attributes are used by the testing
framework to identify classes and methods that contain tests. These are then shown in
Test Explorer, where you can run or debug them and view their results, as you can see in
the following screenshot:

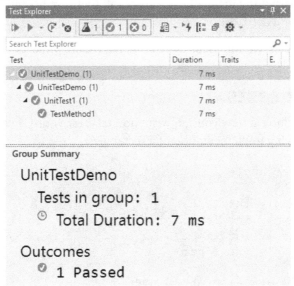

Figure 17.2 - Test Explorer in Visual Studio showing the result of executing the empty unit test created
from the selected template

You can add more unit testing classes either by hand or by using the test templates available in Visual Studio, as shown in the following screenshot:

Figure 17.3 - The Add New Item dialog in Visual Studio with a selection of unit test items

If you are testing a .NET Core project, then you should select the template called **MSTest Test Project (.NET Core)** when creating the test project (refer to the screenshot at the beginning of this section). The result is a project with a single file and the same content shown earlier. However, adding more unit testing items is not possible using the wizards, and you must create everything manually. At this point, there are no item templates available for MSTest for .NET Core.

For the rest of this chapter, we will focus on testing .NET Core projects.

Writing unit tests

In this section, we will look at how you can write unit tests for your C# code. To do so, we will consider the following implementation of a rectangle:

```
public struct Rectangle
{
    public readonly int Left;
    public readonly int Top;
    public readonly int Right;
    public readonly int Bottom;

    public int Width => Right - Left;
    public int Height => Bottom - Top;
    public int Area => Width * Height;
```

```
    public Rectangle(int left, int top, int right, int bottom)
    {
        Left = left;
        Top = top;
        Right = right;
        Bottom = bottom;
    }

    public static Rectangle Empty => new Rectangle(0, 0, 0, 0);
}
```

This implementation should be straightforward and not require further explanations. This is a simple class that does not offer too many functionalities concerning rectangles. We can provide more in the form of extension methods. The following listing shows extensions for increasing and decreasing the size of a rectangle, as well as checking whether two rectangles intersect, and determining the resulting rectangle of their intersection:

```
public static class RectangleExtensions
{
    public static Rectangle Inflate(this Rectangle r,
                                    int left, int top,
                                    int right, int bottom) =>
        new Rectangle(r.Left + left, r.Top + top,
                      r.Right + right, r.Bottom + bottom);

    public static Rectangle Deflate(this Rectangle r,
                                    int left, int top,
                                    int right, int bottom) =>
        new Rectangle(r.Left - left, r.Top - top,
                      r.Right - right, r.Bottom - bottom);

    public static Rectangle Interset(
      this Rectangle a, Rectangle b)
    {
        int l = Math.Max(a.Left, b.Left);
        int r = Math.Min(a.Right, b.Right);
        int t = Math.Max(a.Top, b.Top);
        int bt = Math.Min(a.Bottom, b.Bottom);

        if (r >= l && bt >= t)
            return new Rectangle(l, t, r, bt);
```

```
        return Rectangle.Empty;
    }

    public static bool IntersectsWith(
        this Rectangle a, Rectangle b) =>
        ((b.Left < a.Right) && (a.Left < b.Right)) &&
        ((b.Top < a.Bottom) && (a.Top < b.Bottom));
}
```

We will start by testing the Rectangle structure and to do so, we will have to create a unit testing project as described in the previous section. After the project is created, we can edit the generated stub with the following code:

```
[TestClass]
public class RectangleTests
{
    [TestMethod]
    public void TestEmpty()
    {
        var rectangle = Rectangle.Empty;
        Assert.AreEqual(0, rectangle.Left);
        Assert.AreEqual(0, rectangle.Top);
        Assert.AreEqual(0, rectangle.Right);
        Assert.AreEqual(0, rectangle.Bottom);
    }

    [TestMethod]
    public void TestConstructor()
    {
        var rectangle = new Rectangle(1, 2, 3, 4);
        Assert.AreEqual(1, rectangle.Left);
        Assert.AreEqual(2, rectangle.Top);
        Assert.AreEqual(3, rectangle.Right);
        Assert.AreEqual(4, rectangle.Bottom);
    }

    [TestMethod]
    public void TestProperties()
    {
      var rectangle = new Rectangle(1, 2, 3, 4);
      Assert.AreEqual(2, rectangle.Width, "With must be 2");
      Assert.AreEqual(2, rectangle.Height, "Height must be 2");
      Assert.AreEqual(4, rectangle.Area, "Area must be 4");
    }
```

```
[TestMethod]
public void TestPropertiesMore()
{
    var rectangle = new Rectangle(1, 2, -3, -4);
    Assert.IsTrue(rectangle.Width < 0,
                  "Width should be negative");
    Assert.IsFalse(rectangle.Height > 0,
                   "Height should be negative");
}
}
```

In this listing, we have a test class, called `RectangleTests`, that contains several testing methods:

- `TestEmpty()`

- `TestConstructor()`

- `TestProperties()`

- `TestPropertiesMore()`

Each of these methods tests some part of the `Rectangle` class. To do so, we are using the `Assert` class from `Microsoft.VisualStudio.TestTools.UnitTesting`. This class contains a collection of static methods that help us to perform tests. When a test fails, an exception is thrown and the execution of the test method stops and continues with the next testing method.

In the following screenshot, we can see the results of executing the test methods we wrote earlier. You can see that all of the tests have executed successfully:

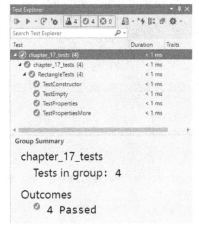

Figure 17.4 - Test Explorer showing successful execution of the test methods written earlier

When a test fails, it will be shown with a red bullet and you can check in the **Test Explorer** window the reason for the failure. For instance, suppose we change the TestProperties() method to have the following incorrect test:

```
Assert.AreEqual(6, rectangle.Area, "Area must be 6");
```

This will make the TestProperties() test method fail, as you can see in the following screenshot:

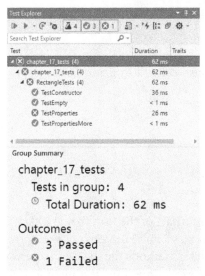

Figure 17.5 - Test Explorer showing the execution of test methods with the TestProperties() method having failed

The reason for the failure is detailed in the **Test Detail Summary** pane, as shown in the following screenshot. This pane is displayed when you click on a failed test:

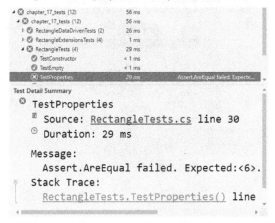

Figure 17.6 - Test Detail Summary pane of Test Explorer showing details regarding the failed test

From the report in this pane, we can see that `Assert.AreEqual()` at line 30 in `RectangleTests.cs` failed because the expected result was 6, but the actual value was 4. We also got the message that we supplied to the `Assert.AreEqual()` method. The entire text message from the previous screenshot is as follows:

```
TestProperties
    Source: RectangleTests.cs line 30
    Duration: 29 ms

  Message:
    Assert.AreEqual failed. Expected:<6>. Actual:<4>. Area must
be 6
    Stack Trace:
      RectangleTests.TestProperties() line 35
```

In the test code written so far, we have used several asserting methods—`AreEqual()`, `IsTrue()`, and `IsFalse()`. These, however, are not the only assertion methods available; there is a long list of them. Some of the most frequently used assertion methods are shown in the following table:

AreEqual()	Tests whether an object equals an expected one and throws an exception if they are not equal
AreNotEqual()	The opposite method that tests whether an object is not equal to a supplied one and throws an exception if they are
AreSame()	Tests whether the specified references refer to the same object and throws an exception if they don't
AreNotSame()	The opposite method that tests whether the specified references point to different objects and throws an exception if they represent the same object
IsFalse()	Tests whether the specified condition is false and throws an exception otherwise
IsTrue()	Tests whether the specified condition is true and throws an exception otherwise
IsNull()	Tests whether the specified object is null and throws an exception otherwise
IsNotNull()	Tests whether the specified object is not null and throws an exception if it is
IsInstanceOfType()	Tests whether the specified object is an instance of the expected type and throws an exception if the expected type is not in the inheritance hierarchy of the object
IsNotInstanceOfType()	The opposite method that tests whether the specified object is not an instance of the specified type and throws an exception if the specified type is in the inheritance hierarchy of the object
ThrowsException<T>()	Tests whether the code specified by a supplied delegate throws an exception of the type T

All of the methods listed in this table are actually overloaded methods. You can get the complete reference by checking the documentation available online.

Analyzing code coverage

When we created the `Rectangle` class, we also created several extension methods for it, so we should be writing more unit tests to cover these two. We could put these tests into another test class. Although the source code accompanying this book contains more unit tests, for brevity, we only list some of them here:

```
[TestClass]
public class RectangleExtensionsTests
{
    [TestMethod]
    public void TestInflate()
    {
        var rectangle1 = Rectangle.Empty.Inflate(1, 2, 3, 4);
        Assert.AreEqual(1, rectangle1.Left);
        Assert.AreEqual(2, rectangle1.Top);
        Assert.AreEqual(3, rectangle1.Right);
        Assert.AreEqual(4, rectangle1.Bottom);
    }

    [TestMethod]
    public void TestDeflate()
    {
        var rectangle1 = Rectangle.Empty.Deflate(1, 2, 3, 4);
        Assert.AreEqual(-1, rectangle1.Left);
        Assert.AreEqual(-2, rectangle1.Top);
        Assert.AreEqual(-3, rectangle1.Right);
        Assert.AreEqual(-4, rectangle1.Bottom);
    }

    [TestMethod]
    public void TestIntersectsWith()
    {
        var rectangle = new Rectangle(1, 2, 10, 12);
        var rectangle1 = new Rectangle(3, 4, 5, 6);
        var rectangle2 = new Rectangle(5, 10, 20, 13);
        var rectangle3 = new Rectangle(11, 13, 15, 16);
        Assert.IsTrue(rectangle.IntersectsWith(rectangle1));
        Assert.IsTrue(rectangle.IntersectsWith(rectangle2));
        Assert.IsFalse(rectangle.IntersectsWith(rectangle3));
    }
```

```
[TestMethod]
public void TestIntersect()
{
    var rectangle = new Rectangle(1, 2, 10, 12);
    var rectangle1 = new Rectangle(3, 4, 5, 6);
    var rectangle3 = new Rectangle(11, 13, 15, 16);
    var intersection1 = rectangle.Intersect(rectangle1);
    var intersection3 = rectangle.Intersect(rectangle3);

    Assert.AreEqual(3, intersection1.Left);
    Assert.AreEqual(4, intersection1.Top);
    Assert.AreEqual(5, intersection1.Right);
    Assert.AreEqual(6, intersection1.Bottom);

    Assert.AreEqual(0, intersection3.Left);
    Assert.AreEqual(0, intersection3.Top);
    Assert.AreEqual(0, intersection3.Right);
    Assert.AreEqual(0, intersection3.Bottom);
    }
}
```

After compiling the unit testing project, the new unit test class and methods will appear in **Test Explorer,** so you can run or debug them. The following screenshot shows the successful execution of all of the test methods:

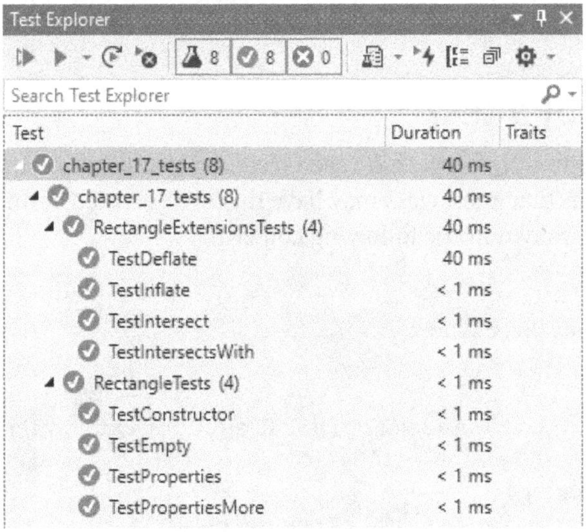

Figure 17.7 - The Test Explorer window showing the successful execution of all the unit tests, including the ones written for the Rectangle extension methods

We can also get code coverage for your code based on the unit tests you have written. You can trigger the code coverage either from **Test Explorer** or from the **Test** top-level menu. Based on the unit test we have seen so far, we get the following coverage:

Hierarchy	Not Covered (Blocks)	Not Covered (% Blocks)	Covered (Blocks)	Covered (% Blocks)
▲ 凷 chapter_17_lib.dll	1	3.03%	32	96.97%
▲ {} chapter_17_lib	1	3.03%	32	96.97%
▲ ⚙ Rectangle	0	0.00%	8	100.00%
⚙ Rectangle(int, i...	0	0.00%	1	100.00%
⚙ get_Area()	0	0.00%	3	100.00%
⚙ get_Empty()	0	0.00%	2	100.00%
⚙ get_Height()	0	0.00%	1	100.00%
⚙ get_Width()	0	0.00%	1	100.00%
▲ ⚙ RectangleExtensions	1	4.00%	24	96.00%
⚙ Deflate(chapter...	0	0.00%	2	100.00%
⚙ Inflate(chapter_...	0	0.00%	2	100.00%
⚙ Intersect(chapt...	0	0.00%	13	100.00%
⚙ IntersectsWith(...	1	12.50%	7	87.50%

Figure 17.8 - The Code Coverage Results pane in Visual Studio showing the code coverage of our unit tests

Here, we can see that the `Rectangle` class is completely covered by unit tests. However, the static class containing extensions is only covered **96%** because the extension method, `IntersectsWith()`, has one block out of eight that is not covered by the unit tests we have written. We can use this report to identify the parts of the code that are not covered by tests so that you can write more.

The anatomy of a test

In the tests we have written so far, we have seen test classes and test methods. However, there are other methods that a test class may have that are executed at different stages. A complete example is shown in the following code:

```
[TestClass]
public class YourUnitTests
{
    [AssemblyInitialize]
    public static void AssemblyInit(TestContext context) { }

    [AssemblyCleanup]
    public static void AssemblyCleanup() { }
```

```
    [ClassInitialize]
    public static void TestFixtureSetup(TestContext context) { }

    [ClassCleanup]
    public static void TestFixtureTearDown() { }

    [TestInitialize]
    public void Setup() { }

    [TestCleanup]
    public void TearDown() { }

    [TestMethod]
    public void TestMethod1() { }

    TestMethod]
    public void TestMethod2() { }
}
```

The names of these methods are irrelevant. What is important here are the attributes used to mark them. These are reflected by the testing framework and determine the order in which the methods are invoked. For this particular example, this order is as follows:

```
AssemblyInit()           // once per assembly
  TestFixtureSetup()     // once per test class
    Setup()              // before each test of the class
      TestMethod1()
    TearDown()           // after each test of the class
    Setup()
      TestMethod2()
    TearDown()
  TestFixtureTearDown()  // once per test class
AssemblyCleanup()        // once per assembly
```

The attributes used to mark these methods are listed in the following table:

Attribute	Optional	Description
AssemblyInitializeAttribute	Yes	Determines the method to be executed once per assembly, before the tests run
AssemblyCleanupAttribute	Yes	Determines the method to be executed after the tests run, once per assembly
ClassInitializeAttribute	Yes	Determines the method to be executed once for each testing class before the test methods are executed
ClassCleanupAttribute	Yes	Determines the method to be executed once for each testing class after all of the test methods have executed—there is no guarantee that the method is executed immediately after all of the test methods have finished execution
TestInitializeAttribute	Yes	Determines the method to be executed before each test method in the class
TestCleanupAttribute	Yes	Determines the method to be executed after each test method in the class
TestMethodAttribute	Required	Identifies a method of a test class containing a testing code—test methods are only considered if they belong to a class marked with the TestClass attribute
TestClassAttribute	Required	Identifies a class containing testing methods

When you want to do multiple tests for the same function with different sets of data, you can resort to retrieving them from a data source. The unit testing framework for managed code makes this possible in the ways we will see in the following section.

Writing data-driven unit tests

If you take a second look at the previous tests, such as the TestIntersectsWith() test method, you will see that we tried testing various cases, such as the intersection of one rectangle with several others, some that intersect, and some that don't. This was a simple example, and in practice, there should be many more rectangles that we should test with to cover all of the possible cases of rectangle intersection.

In general, as code evolves, so do the tests and you often have to add more to the testing datasets. Rather than writing explicitly the data in the test method, as in our previous example, you can fetch it from a data source. The test method is then executed once for each row in the data source. The unit testing framework for managed code supports three different scenarios.

Data from attributes

The first option is to provide the data in code but through an attribute called DataRowAttribute. This attribute has a constructor that allows us to specify any number of arguments. These arguments are then forwarded, in the same order, to the parameters of the test method it is used on. Let's look at an example:

```
[DataTestMethod]
[DataRow(true, 3, 4, 5, 6)]
[DataRow(true, 5, 10, 20, 13)]
[DataRow(false, 11, 13, 15, 16)]
public void TestIntersectsWith_DataRows(
    bool result,
    int left, int top, int right, int bottom)
{
    var rectangle = new Rectangle(1, 2, 10, 12);

    Assert.AreEqual(
        result,
        rectangle.IntersectsWith(
            new Rectangle(left, top, right, bottom)));
}
```

There are several things to notice in this example. First, the attribute used to indicate that this is a data-driven test method is DataTestMethodAttribute. However, for compatibility of legacy code, TestMethodAttribute is also supported, although not encouraged. The second thing to notice is the use of DataRowAttribute. We used it to provide the data for several rectangles as well as the expected result of the intersection with the reference rectangle from the test method. As mentioned before, the method is executed for each row in the data source, which, in this case, is each occurrence of the DataRow attribute.

The following listing shows the output of executing the test method:

```
Test has multiple result outcomes
    4 Passed
```

```
Results
    1) TestIntersectsWith_DataRows
       Duration: 8 ms

    2) TestIntersectsWith_DataRows (True,3,4,5,6)
       Duration: < 1 ms

    3) TestIntersectsWith_DataRows (True,5,10,20,13)
       Duration: < 1 ms

    4) TestIntersectsWith_DataRows (False,11,13,15,16)
       Duration: < 1 ms
```

If a row in the data source makes the test fail, it is reported as such, but the execution of the method is repeated for the next row in the data source.

Dynamic data

The use of the DataRow attribute is an improvement, since it makes the testing code simpler, but it is not the best alternative. A slightly better option is fetching data, dynamically, from a method or property of the class. This is possible using another attribute called DynamicDataAttribute. You must specify the name and the type of the source of data (method or property). An example is shown in the following code:

```
public static IEnumerable<object[]> GetData()
{
    yield return new object[] { true, 3, 4, 5, 6 };
    yield return new object[] { true, 5, 10, 20, 13 };
    yield return new object[] { false, 11, 13, 15, 16 };
}

[DataTestMethod]
[DynamicData(nameof(GetData), DynamicDataSourceType.Method)]
public void TestIntersectsWith_DynamicData(
    bool result,
    int left, int top, int right, int bottom)
{
    var rectangle = new Rectangle(1, 2, 10, 12);

    Assert.AreEqual(
        result,
        rectangle.IntersectsWith(
            new Rectangle(left, top, right, bottom)));
}
```

In this example, we defined a method called `GetData()` that returns an enumerable sequence of arrays of objects. We fill these arrays with the rectangle bounds and the result of the intersection with the reference rectangle. Then, on the test method, we use the `DynamicData` attribute and provide it with the name of the method that supplies the data and the type of data source (`DynamicDataSourceType.Method`). The actual test code is no different than the one from the previous example.

However, this alternative also relies on hardcoded data. The most desirable solution is to read it from an external data source.

Data from external sources

Test data can be fetched from an external source, such as a SQL Server database, a CSV file, an Excel document, or XML. For this purpose, we must use another attribute, called `DataSourceAttribute`. This attribute has several constructors that allow you to specify the connection string to the source and other necessary parameters.

> **Note**
>
> At the time of writing this book, this solution and this attribute are only available for .NET Framework and are not yet supported for .NET Core.

To write a test method that gets data from an external source, you need to be able to access information about this data source. This is possible with the help of a `TestContext` object that the framework is passing as an argument to the methods marked with either the `AssemblyInitialize` or `ClassInitialize` attributes. A simpler solution to get a reference to that object is to provide in the test class a public property called `TestContext` with the `TestContext` type as shown in the following code. The framework will automatically set it with a reference to the test context object:

```
public TestContext TestContext { get; set; }
```

We can then use the context to access data source information. In the example that follows, we rewrite the test method to fetch data from a CSV file called `TestData.csv` that resides in the same folder as the test application. The content of this file is as follows:

```
expected,left,top,right,bottom
true,3,4,5,6
true,5,10,20,13
false,11,13,15,16
```

The first column is the expected result of the intersection with the reference rectangle, and the other values on each line are the bounds of the rectangle. The test method that executes with data fetched from this CSV file is listed in the following code:

```
[DataTestMethod]
[DataSource("Microsoft.VisualStudio.TestTools.DataSource.CSV",
        "TestData.csv",
        "TestData#csv",
        DataAccessMethod.Sequential)]
public void TestIntersectsWith_CsvData()
{
    var rectangle = new Rectangle(1, 2, 10, 12);

    bool result = Convert.ToBoolean(
      TestContext.DataRow["Expected"]);
    int left = Convert.ToInt32(TestContext.DataRow["left"]);
    int top = Convert.ToInt32(TestContext.DataRow["top"]);
    int right = Convert.ToInt32(TestContext.DataRow["right"]);
    int bottom = Convert.ToInt32(
        TestContext.DataRow["bottom"]);

    Assert.AreEqual(
        result,
        rectangle.IntersectsWith(
            new Rectangle(left, top, right, bottom)));
}
```

You can see that this method, unlike the previous ones, has no parameters. Data is available through the `DataRow` property of the `TestContext` object and this method is invoked once for each row in the CSV file.

If you do not want data source information, such as the connection string, to be specified in the source code, you can use the application configuration file to provide it. To do so, you must add a custom section and then define a connection string (with name, string, and provider name) and data source (with name, connection string name, table name, and data access method). For the CSV file we used in the previous example, the `App.config` file would look as follows:

```
<?xml version="1.0" encoding="utf-8" ?>
<configuration>
   <configSections>
      <section name="microsoft.visualstudio.testtools"
               type="Microsoft.VisualStudio.TestTools.
UnitTesting.TestConfigurationSection, Microsoft.VisualStudio.
```

```
TestPlatform.TestFramework.Extensions"/>
    </configSections>
    <connectionStrings>
        <add name="MyCSVConn"
            connectionString="TestData.csv"
            providerName="Microsoft.VisualStudio.TestTools.
DataSource.CSV" />
    </connectionStrings>
    <microsoft.visualstudio.testtools>
        <dataSources>
        <add name="MyCSVDataSource"
            connectionString="MyCSVConn"
            dataTableName="TestData#csv"
            dataAccessMethod="Sequential"/>
        </dataSources>
    </microsoft.visualstudio.testtools>
</configuration>
```

With this defined, the only change we have to make to the test method is to change the
DataSource attribute, specifying the name of the data source from the .config file
(MyCSVDataSource in our example). This is shown in the following code.

```
[DataTestMethod]
[DataSource("MyCSVDataSource")]
public void TestIntersectsWith_CsvData()
{
    /* ... */
}
```

To get more information about how to provide connection strings for various types of
data sources, you should read the online documentation.

Summary

This last chapter of this book was dedicated to unit testing, which is essential for writing
quality code. We started with a basic introduction to unit testing and learned about the
Microsoft tools for writing unit tests, including the unit testing framework for managed
code. We have seen how to create unit testing projects using this framework, both for
.NET Framework and .NET Core. We then looked at the most important features of the
unit testing framework and learned how to write unit tests. In the last section, we learned
about data-driven tests and saw how to write tests with data from various data sources.

As this book concludes here, we, the authors, would like to thank you for taking the time to read it. By writing this book, we tried to provide you with everything that was essential for you to become proficient in the C# language. We hope this book proves a valuable resource for you in learning and mastering the C# language.

Test what you learned

1. What is unit testing and what are its most important benefits?

2. What tools does Visual Studio offer to help writing unit tests?

3. What functionalities does Test Explorer in Visual Studio provide?

4. How do you specify that a class in a unit testing project contains unit tests?

5. What class and methods can you use to perform assertions?

6. How do you check the code coverage of your unit tests?

7. How do you write test fixtures that execute once per test class? What about test fixtures for each method?

8. What is data-driven unit testing?

9. What does `DynamicDataAttribute` do? And what about `DataSourceAttribute`?

10. What are the supported external sources for test data?

Assessments

Chapter 1

1. The first version of the C# language, 1.0, was released in 2002, bundled with .NET Framework 1.0 and Visual Studio .NET 2002. The current version of the language, at the time of writing this book, is C# 8.

2. The CLI is a specification that describes how a runtime environment can be used on different computer platforms without being rewritten for specific architectures. The CLI describes four major components: The **Common Type System (CTS)**, the **Common Language Specification (CLS)**, the **Virtual Execution System (VES)**, and the metadata of a program's structure and content.

3. The CIL is a platform-neutral intermediate language that represents the intermediate language binary instruction set defined by the CLI. When you compile your program's source code, the compiler translates it into the CIL bytecode and produces a CLI assembly. When the CLI assembly is executed, the bytecode is passed through the Just-In-Time compiler to generate native code, which is then executed by the computer's processor.

4. To view the content of an assembly you must use a disassembler. Examples of disassemblers are ildasm.exe, distributed with .NET Framework, or ILSpy, an open source .NET assembly browser and decompiler.

5. The Common Language Runtime is. NET Framework's implementation of the VES. The CLR provides services such as memory management, type safety, garbage collection, exception handling, thread management, and others.

6. The BCL is a component of the standard libraries that provides types to represent the CLI built-in types, simple file access, custom attributes, string handling, formatting, collections, streams, and others.

7. The current major .NET frameworks are .NET Framework, .NET Core, and Xamarin. Because Microsoft plans to make .NET Core the one framework to use for building applications for desktop, server, web, cloud, and mobile; .NET Framework is put on maintenance mode and will only include security updates.

8. Assemblies are the basic unit for deployment, versioning, and security. They come in two forms: executables (`.exe`) and dynamic-link libraries (`.dll`). An assembly is a collection of types, resources, and meta-information that forms a logical unit of functionality. The identity of an assembly is composed of the name, version, culture, and a public key token.

9. The GAC is a machine-wide code cache that enables the sharing of assemblies between applications. Its default location is `%windir%\Microsoft.NET\assembly`. The Runtime Package Store is the equivalent for .NET Core applications. It enables faster deployment and lower disk space requirements. Typically, this store is available at `/usr/local/share/dotnet/store` on macOS and Linux and `C:/Program Files/dotnet/store` on Windows.

10. The minimum a C# program must contain in order to compile and execute is a class that contains a static method called `Main()`.

Chapter 2

1. The built-in integral types in C# are `byte`, `sbyte`, `ushort`, `short`, `uint`, `int`, `ulong`, and `long`.

2. The `float` and `double` types represent numbers using the inverse powers of 2 for the fractional part. Therefore, they cannot represent exactly numbers such as 1.23 or 19.99, but only an approximation of them. Although `double` has 15 digits of precision, compared to `float`, which has only 7; precision loss accumulates when performing repeated calculations. The `decimal` type uses a decimal representation of real numbers, which is much slower to compute, but provides better precision. The `decimal` type has 28 digits of precision and is suitable for categories of applications, such as financial applications, where this is key.

3. Strings can be concatenated using the + operator. Apart from concatenation, you can compose strings using the `String.Format()` static method, or with string interpolation, which is a syntactic shortcut for this method.

4. Some characters have a special meaning within a string. These are called escape sequences and are prefixed with a backlash (\). Examples include single quotes (\'), double quotes (\"), newline characters (\n), and backslashes (\\). Verbatim strings are strings that are prefixed with the @ token. For verbatim strings, the compiler does not interpret escape sequences. This makes it easier to write multi-line texts or file paths, for instance.

5. Implicitly typed variables are declared using the `var` keyword instead of an actual type and must be initialized during declaration. The compiler infers the actual type from the value or expression used for their initialization.

6. Value types and reference types are the two main categories of types in C# and .NET. A variable of a value type stores the value directly. A variable of a reference type stores a reference to (the address of) a memory location containing the actual object. Value types have value semantics (in simple terms, when you copy an object, its value is copied), and reference types have value semantics (when you copy an object, its reference is copied). Typically, value types are stored on a stack and reference types on the heap, but this is an implementation detail and not a characteristic of the types.

7. Boxing is the process of storing a value type inside an `object`, and unboxing is the opposite operation of converting the value of an `object` to a value type.

8. A nullable type is an instance of `System.Nullable<T>`, a generic value type that can represent the values of an underlying `T` type that can only be a value type, as well as an additional null value. A nullable integer variable can be declared either as `Nullable<int>` or `int?`.

9. There are three types of arrays in C#. The first type is one-dimensional arrays, which are arrays of a single dimension. An example is `int [6]`, which is an array of 6 integers. The second type is multi-dimensional arrays, which are arrays of two or more dimensions, up to a maximum of 32. An example is `int [2,3]`, which is an array of integers with 2 lines and 3 columns. The third type is jagged arrays, which are arrays of arrays. A jagged array is a one-dimensional array whose elements are other arrays, and each can be of another dimension.

10. The system-defined type conversions are implicit conversion (such as from `int` to `double`), and explicit conversion (such as from `double` to `int`). Explicit type conversions are also called casts and are necessary when conversion between two types bears the risk of losing information. User-defined conversions are possible by defining implicit or explicit operators for a certain type or with helper classes.

Chapter 3

1. The selection statements in the C# language are `if` and `switch`.

2. The `default` case of a `switch` statement can appear anywhere on the list. It is always evaluated last after all the case labels have been evaluated.

3. A `for` loop allows us to execute a block of code as long as a Boolean expression evaluates to true. A `foreach` loop allows us to iterate through the elements of a collection that implements the `IEnumerable` interface.

4. The `while` loop is an entry controlled loop. That means it executes a block of statements as long as a specified Boolean expression evaluates to true. The expression is checked before the block is executed. The `do-while` loop is an exit-controlled loop. This means the Boolean expression will be checked at the end of the loop. This ensures that the `do-while` loop will always be executed at least once, even if the condition evaluates to false in the first iteration.

5. To return from a function, you can use `return`, `yield`, or `throw`. The first two denote a normal return. The `throw` statement represents a return due to an erroneous situation in the execution flow.

6. A `break` statement can be used to exit from a `switch` case or to terminate the execution of a loop. It works for all loops: `for`, `while`, `do-while`, and `foreach`.

7. It indicates that the method, operator, or `get` accessor where it appears preceding a `return` or `break` statement is an iterator. The sequence returned from an iterator method can be consumed using a `foreach` statement. The `yield` statement makes it possible to return values as they are produced and consume them as they are available, which is especially useful in an asynchronous context.

8. You can catch all the exceptions from a function call either with `catch(Exception)`, in which case you have access to information about the exception, or with a simple `catch` statement (without specifying an exception type), in which case you do not get any information about the exception.

9. The `finally` block contains code that will execute after the `try` section. This happens regardless of whether the execution resumed normally or the control left the `try` block because of a `break`, `continue`, `goto`, or `return` statement.

10. The base class for all the exception types in .NET is the `System.Exception` class.

Chapter 4

1. A class is a template or a blueprint that specifies the form of an object. It contains both data and code that operates on that data. An object is an instance of a class. A class is introduced with the `class` keyword and defines a reference type. A structure is introduced with the `struct` keyword and defines a value type. Unlike classes, structures do not support inheritance and cannot have an explicit default constructor, and fields cannot be initialized during declaration unless they are declared `const` or `static`.

2. A read-only field is a field defined with the `readonly` specifier. Such a field can only be initialized in a constructor and its value cannot be changed later.

3. Expression body definitions are an alternative syntax, typically for methods and properties, that simply consist of evaluating an expression and perhaps returning the result of the evaluation. These have the form `member => expression`. They are supported for all class members, not just methods, but also fields, properties, indexers, constructors, and finalizers. The type of the result value of the expression evaluation must match the return type of the method.

4. A default constructor is a constructor of a class that does not have any parameters. On the other hand, a static constructor is a constructor defined with the `static` keyword that has no parameters or access modifiers and cannot be called by the user. A static constructor is called by the CLR automatically in a static class when the first static member of the class is accessed for the first time, or in a non-static class when the class is instantiated for the first time. Static constructors are useful for initializing static fields.

5. Auto-implemented properties are properties for which the compiler will provide a private field and the implementation of the `get` and `set` accessors.

6. An indexer is a class member that allows an object to be indexed like an array. An indexer defines a `get` and `set` accessor like properties do. An indexer does not have an explicit name. It is created by using the `this` keyword. An indexer has one or more parameters that can be of any type.

7. A static class is a class declared with the `static` keyword. It can only contain static members and cannot be instantiated. Static class members are accessed using the class name and not through an object. A static class is basically the same as a non-static class with a private constructor and all members are declared as `static`.

8. The available parameter specifiers are `ref`, `out`, and `in`. The `ref` specifier modifies a parameter so that it becomes an alias for an argument, which must be a variable. It allows us to create a call-by-reference mechanism, rather than the implicit call-by-value one. The `in` specifier is similar in that it causes the argument to be passed by reference, but it does not allow the function to modify it. It is basically identical to `readonly ref`. The `out` keyword also defines a call-by-reference mechanism, but it requires a function to initialize a parameter before the function returns. It guarantees that a variable is assigned a value during the specified function call.

9. A method with a variable number of arguments must have a parameter that is a single-dimensional array preceded by the `params` keyword. This does not have to be the only parameter of the function, but it must be the last.

10. An enumeration is a set of named integral constants. You must use the `enum` keyword to declare an enumeration. An enumeration is a value type. Enumerations are useful when we want to use a limited number of integral values for some particular purpose.

Chapter 5

1. Object-oriented programming is a paradigm that allows us to write a program around objects. Its core principles are abstraction, encapsulation, inheritance, and polymorphism.

2. Encapsulation allows us to hide the data inside a class from the outside world. Encapsulation is important because it reduces the dependencies between different components by defining minimal public interfaces for them. It also increases code reusability and security and makes code easier to unit test.

3. Inheritance is a mechanism through which a class can inherit the properties and functionalities of another class. C# supports single inheritance but only for reference types.

4. A virtual method is a method that has an implementation in a base class but can be overridden in derived classes, which is helpful for changing or extending implementation details. The implementation in the base class is defined with the `virtual` keyword. The implementation in a derived class is called an overridden method and is defined with the `override` keyword.

5. You can prevent a virtual member from being overridden in a derived class by declaring it with the `sealed` keyword.

6. An abstract class cannot be instantiated, which means we cannot create the object of an abstract class. An abstract class is declared using the `abstract` keyword. They can have both abstract and non-abstract members. An abstract member cannot be private and cannot have an implementation. An abstract class must provide an implementation for all the members of all the interfaces it implements (if any).

7. An interface defines a contract that is supported by all the types that implement the interface. An interface is a type introduced with the `interface` keyword and contains a set of members that must be implemented by any class or struct that implements the interface. Typically, an interface contains only declarations of members, but not implementations. Beginning with C# 8, interfaces can contain default methods.

8. There are two types of polymorphism: compile-time polymorphism, represented by method overloading, and runtime polymorphism. Runtime polymorphism has two aspects. On one hand, objects of derived classes can be seamlessly used as objects of base classes in arrays or other types of collections, method parameters, and other places. On the other hand, classes can define virtual methods that can be overridden in derived classes. At runtime, the CLR will invoke the implementation of the virtual member corresponding to the runtime type of the object. An object's declared type and its runtime type differ when objects of derived classes are used in places of objects of base classes.

9. Overloaded methods are methods with the same name but with parameters of different types or different numbers of parameters. The return type is not considered for method overloading. Operators can also be overloaded. A type can provide a custom implementation for an overloadable operator when one or both operands are of that type. The `operator` keyword is used to declare an operator. Such methods must be `public` and `static`.

10. The SOLID principles are the following: **Single responsibility principle (S), Open-close principle (O), Liskov substitution principle (L), Interface segregation principle (I)**, and **Dependency injection principle (D)**.

Chapter 6

1. Generics are types parametrized with other types. Generics provide reusability, promote type safety, and can provide better performance (by avoiding the need for boxing and unboxing for value types).

2. A type used for parameterizing a generic type or method is called a type parameter.

3. Generic classes are defined in the same way as non-generic classes except for a list of one or more type parameters, specified within angle brackets (such as `<T>`) after the class name. The same is true for generic methods; the type parameters are specified after the class name.

4. Classes can be derived from generic types. Structures do not support explicit inheritance, but they can implement any number of generic interfaces.

5. A constructed type is a type that is constructed from a generic type by replacing the type parameters with actual types. For instance, for a `Shape<T>` generic type, the `Shape<int>` is a constructed type.

6. A covariant type parameter is a type parameter declared with the `out` keyword. Such a type parameter allows an interface method to have a return type that is more derived than the specified type parameter.

7. A contravariant type parameter is a type parameter declared with the `in` keyword. Such a type parameter allows an interface method to have a parameter that is less derived than the specified type parameter.

8. Type parameter constraints are restrictions specified for type parameters that inform the compiler about what kind of capabilities the type parameters must have. Applying a constraint limits the types that can be used for constructing a type from a generic one.

9. The `new()` type constraint specifies that a type must provide a public default constructor.

10. The type parameter constraint introduced in C# 8 is `notnull`. It can only be used in a nullable context, otherwise the compiler generates a warning. It specifies that the type parameter must be a non-nullable type. It can be a non-nullable reference type (in C#8) or a non-nullable value type.

Chapter 7

1. The BCL namespace containing the generic collections is
   `System.Collections.Generic`.

2. The base interface for all the other interfaces that define functionalities for generic
   collections is `IEnumerable<T>`.

3. Generic collections are preferred over non-generic ones because they offer the
   benefit of type safety, have better performance for value types (because they avoid
   boxing and unboxing), and, in some cases, they provide functionalities not available
   in the non-generic collections.

4. The `List<T>` generic class represents a collection of elements that can be accessed
   by their index. `List<T>` is very similar to arrays, except that the size of the
   collection is not fixed but is variable and it can grow or decrease as elements are
   added or removed. You add elements with `Add()`, `AddRange()`, `Insert()`,
   and `InsertRange()`. You can remove elements with `Remove()`, `RemoveAt()`,
   `RemoveRange()`, `RemoveAll()`, and `Clear()`.

5. The `Stack<T>` generic class represents a collection with last-in, first-out semantics.
   Elements are added to the top with the `Push()` method and removed from the top
   with the `Pop()` method.

6. The `Queue<T>` generic class represents a collection with first-in, first-out
   semantics. The `Dequeue()` method removes and returns the item from the front
   of the queue. The `Peek()` method returns the item from the front of the queue
   without removing it.

7. The `LinkedList<T>` generic class represents a double linked list. Its elements are
   of the `LinkedListNode<T>` type. To add elements to the linked list you can use
   the `AddFirst()`, `AddLast()`, `AddAfter()`, and `AddBefore()` methods.

8. The `Dictionary<TKey, TValue>` generic class represents a collection
   of key-value pairs that allows fast lookup based on a key. The elements of this
   dictionary class are of the `KeyValuePair<TKey, TValue>` type.

9. The `HashSet<T>` generic class represents a set of distinct items that can be in
   any order but are stored contiguously. A hash set is logically similar to a dictionary
   where the values are also the keys. However, unlike `Dictionary<TKey,
   TValue>`, `HashSet<T>` is a non-associative container.

10. `BlockingCollection<T>` is a class that implements the producer-consumer pattern defined by the `IProducerConsumerCollection<T>` interface. It is actually a simple wrapper over the `IProducerConsumerCollection<T>` interface and does not have internal underlying storage but must be provided with one (a collection that implements the `IProducerConsumerCollection<T>` interface). If no implementation is provided, it uses the `ConcurrentQueue<T>` class by default. It is suitable for scenarios when bounding and blocking are necessary.

Chapter 8

1. A callback is a function (or more generally, any executable code) that is passed as a parameter to another function in order to be called immediately (synchronous callbacks) or at a later time (asynchronous callbacks). A delegate is a strongly typed callback.

2. A delegate is defined using the `delegate` keyword. The declaration looks like a function signature, but the compiler actually introduces a class that can hold references to methods whose signatures match the signature of the delegate. Events are variables of a delegate type declared with the `event` keyword.

3. There are two kinds of tuples in C#: reference tuples, represented by the `System.Tuple` class, and value tuples, represented by the `System.ValueTuple` structure. The reference tuples can only hold up to eight elements, while the latter can hold a sequence of any number of elements, although at least two are required. Value tuples may have compile-type named fields, and have a simpler but richer syntax for creating, assigning, deconstructing, and comparing values.

4. Named tuples are value tuples that have names for their fields. These names are synonyms for the fields `Item1`, `Item2`, and so on, but are only available at source-code level.

5. Pattern matching is the process of checking whether a value has a particular shape as well as extracting information out of the value when the matching is successful. It can be used with `is` and `switch` expressions.

6. A null value does not match a type pattern, regardless of the type of the variable. A `switch` case label with a pattern matching for null can be added in a `switch` expression with type pattern matching to specifically handle null values. When using the `var` pattern, a null value always matches. Therefore, when using the `var` pattern, you must add an explicit null check because the value may be null.

7. The .NET class that provides support for working with regular expressions is the `Regex` class from the `System.Text.RegularExpressions` namespace. By default, it uses the UTF-8 encoding for the string to match.

8. The `Match()` method checks an input string for substrings that match a regular expression and returns the first match. The `Matches()` method does the same search but returns all the matches.

9. Extension methods are methods that extend the functionalities of a type without changing its source code. They are useful because they allow extensions without changing the implementation, creating a derived type, or recompiling the code, in general.

10. Extension methods are defined as static methods of a static, non-nested, non-generic class and their first parameter is of the type they extend, preceded by the `this` keyword.

Chapter 9

1. The stack is a relatively small segment of memory allocated by the compiler that keeps track of the memory necessary for running the application. The stack has LIFO semantics and grows and shrinks as the program execution is invoking functions or returning from functions. The heap, on the other hand, is a large segment of memory that the program may use to allocate memory at runtime, and which, in .NET, is managed by the CLR. Objects of value types are, typically, allocated on the stack, and objects of reference types are allocated on the heap.

2. The managed heap has three memory segments called generations. They are named generation 0, 1, and 2. Generation 0 contains small, and usually short-lived, objects such as local variables or objects instantiated for the lifetime of a function call. Generation 1 contains small objects that have survived a garbage collection of memory from generation 0. Generation 2 contains long-lived small objects that have survived a garbage collection of memory from generation 1 and large objects (which are always allocated on this segment).

3. Garbage collection has three phases. First, the garbage collector builds a graph of all live objects in order to figure out what is still in use and what may be deleted. Second, references to objects that will be compacted are updated. Third, the dead objects are removed, and the surviving objects are compacted. Typically, the large object heap containing large objects is not compacted because moving large chunks of data incurs performance costs.

4. A finalizer is a special method of a class (has the same name as the class but prefixed with ~) that should dispose of unmanaged resources that the class has ownership of. This method is called by the garbage collector when the object is collected. This process is non-deterministic, which is the key difference between finalization and disposal. The latter is a deterministic process that occurs during the explicit invocation of the `Dispose()` method (for classes that implement the `IDisposable` interface).

5. The `GC.SuppressFinalize()` method requests the CRL not to invoke the finalizer of the specified object. This is typically called when implementing the `IDisposable` interface, so that unmanaged resources are not disposed of twice.

6. `IDisposable` is an interface with a single method called `Dispose()` that defines a pattern for the deterministic disposal of objects.

7. The `using` statement represents short-hand syntax for the deterministic disposal of objects of types that implement the `IDisposable` interface. The `using` statement introduces a scope for the variable defined in the statement and ensures the object is properly disposed of before the scope is exited. The actual disposal details depend on whether the resource is a value type, a nullable value type, a reference type, or a dynamic type.

8. A function from a native DLL can be invoked in C# using Platform Invocation Services, or P/Invoke. To do so, you must define a `static extern` method that matches the signature of the native function (using equivalent managed types for its parameters). This managed function must be decorated with the `DllImport` attribute, which defines the necessary information for the runtime to call the native function.

9. Unsafe code is code for which the CLR cannot verify its safety. Unsafe code enables the use of pointer types and supports pointer arithmetic. Unsafe code is not necessarily dangerous, but it is your entire responsibility to ensure that you do not introduce pointer errors or security risks. The typical scenarios for using unsafe code are calling functions exported from a native DLL or COM server that require pointer types as parameters, and optimizing some algorithms where performance is critical.

10. Unsafe code is defined with the `unsafe` keyword, which can be applied to types (classes, structures, interfaces, and delegates), type members (methods, fields, properties, events, indexers, operators, instance constructors, and static constructors), and statement blocks.

Chapter 10

1. The main characteristics of functional programming are immutability (objects have states that do not change) and side-effect free functions (functions do not modify values or states outside their local scope). Advantages of functional programming include the following: first, the code is easier to understand and maintain because functions do not change states and only depend on the arguments they receive. Second, the code is easier to test for the same reason. Third, it is simpler and more efficient to implement concurrency because data is immutable and functions don't have side effects, which avoids data races.

2. A higher-order function is a function that takes one or more functions as arguments, returns a function, or both.

3. C# provides the ability to pass functions as arguments, return functions from functions, assign functions to variables, store them in data structures, define anonymous functions, nest functions, and test references to functions for equality. All these characteristics make C# a language that is said to treat functions as first-class citizens.

4. Lambda expressions are a convenient way to write anonymous functions. This is a block of code, either an expression or one or more statements that behave like a function and can be assigned to a delegate. As a result, a lambda expression can be passed as an argument to a function or returned from a function. They are a convenient way to write LINQ queries, pass functions to higher-order functions (including code that should be executed asynchronously by `Task.Run()`), and create expression trees. A lambda expression has two parts separated by the lambda declaration operator, `=>`. The left part is the list of parameters, and the right part is an expression or a statement. An example of a lambda expression is `n => n%2==1`.

5. The rules that apply to variable scope in lambda expressions are as follows: first, the variables that are introduced in a lambda expression are not visible outside the lambda. Second, a lambda cannot capture `in`, `ref`, or `out` parameters from the enclosing method. Third, variables that are captured by a lambda are not garbage collected until the delegate that the lambda is assigned to is garbage collected, even if they would otherwise go out of scope. Fourth, and last, a return statement of a lambda expression refers solely to the anonymous method that the lambda represents and does not cause the enclosing method to return.

6. LINQ is a set of technologies that enable developers to query a multitude of data sources in a consistent manner. The LINQ standard query operators are a set of extension methods that operate on sequences that implement either `IEnumerable<T>` or `IQueryable<T>`. LINQ query syntax is basically syntactic sugar for the standard query operators. The compiler transforms queries written in query syntax into queries using the standard query operators. Query syntax is simpler and easier to read than the standard query operators, but they are semantically equivalent. However, not all the standard query operators have an equivalent in query syntax.

7. The `Select()` method projects each element of a sequence into a new form. This requires a selector, which is a transformation function, to produce a new value for each element of the collection. However, when the elements of the collection are themselves collections, it is often necessary to flatten them to a single collection. This is what the `SelectMany()` method is doing.

8. Partial function application is the process of taking a function with *N* parameters and one argument and returning another function with *N-1* parameters after fixing the argument into one of the function's parameters. This technique is the opposite of currying, which is the process of taking a function with *N* arguments and decomposing it into *N* functions that take one argument.

9. A monoid is an algebraic structure with a single associative binary operation and an identity element. Any C# type that has those two elements is a monoid.

10. A monad is a container that encapsulates some functionality on top of the value that it wraps. A monad has two operations: the first one that transforms a value, `v`, into a container that wraps it (`v -> C(v)`). In functional programming, this function is called a return. The second one that flattens two containers into a single container (`C(C(v)) -> C(v)`). In functional programming, this is called a bind. An example of a monad is `IEnumerable<T>` with the LINQ query operator `SelectMany()`.

Chapter 11

1. The unit of deployment in .NET is the assembly. An assembly is a file (either an executable or a dynamic-link library) that contains the MSIL code, as well as metadata about the content of the assembly, and, optionally, resources.

2. Reflection is the process of runtime type discovery and the ability to make changes to them. This means that we can retrieve information about types, their members, and their attributes at runtime. Reflection makes it possible to easily build extensible applications; to execute types and members that are private or have other access levels that makes them inaccessible otherwise, which is useful for testing; to modify existing types or creating entirely new types at runtime and execute code using them; and, in general, to change a system behavior at runtime, usually with the use of attributes.

3. The type that provides meta-information about types is System.Type. An instance of this type can be created with the GetType() method, the Type.GetType() static method, or with the C# typeof operator.

4. A shared assembly is intended to be used by several applications and is usually located under the **Global Assembly Cache (GAC)**, a system repository for assemblies. A private assembly is intended to be used by a single application and is stored in the application directory or one of its sub-directories. Shared assemblies must be strongly named and enforce version constraints; these requirements are not necessary for private assemblies.

5. In .NET, an assembly can be loaded in one of the following contexts: the load context (which contains assemblies loaded from the GAC, the app directory, or its subdirectories), the load-from context (which contains assemblies loaded from other paths than the previously mentioned), the reflection-only context (which contains assemblies loaded for reflection purposes only), or no context at all (such as when an assembly is loaded from an array of bytes).

6. Early binding is the process of creating an assembly dependency (reference) during compile time. This offers the compiler full access to the types available in the assembly. Late binding is the process of loading assemblies at runtime, in which case the compiler has no access to the content of the assembly. However, this is important for building extensible applications.

7. The Dynamic Language Runtime is a component of the .NET platform that defines a runtime environment that adds a set of services on top of the CLR in order to enable dynamic languages to run on the CLR and to add dynamic features to statically typed languages.

8. The `dynamic` type is a static type, meaning variables of this type are assigned the `dynamic` type at compile time. However, they bypass static type checking. That means the actual type of the object is only known at runtime and the compiler cannot know and cannot enforce any checks on operations performed on objects of this type. You can invoke any methods with any parameters and the compiler will not check and complain; however, if the operation is not valid, an exception will be thrown at runtime. The `dynamic` type is often used to simplify the consumption of COM objects when an interop assembly is not available.

9. Attributes are types that derive from the `System.Attribute` abstract class and provide meta-information about assemblies, types, and members. This meta-information is consumed by the compiler, the CLR, or tools that use reflection services to read them. Attributes are specified in square brackets, such as in `[SerializableAttribute]`. The naming convention for attributes is that the type names are always suffixed with the word `Attribute`. The C# language provides a syntactic shortcut that allows specifying the name of the attribute without the suffix `Attribute`, such as in `[Serializable]`.

10. To create user-defined attributes you must derive from the `System.Attribute` type and follow the naming convention of suffixing the type with the word `Attribute`.

Chapter 12

1. When you need to execute some long-running, CPU-intensive code, manually creating a dedicated thread is the preferred choice. Another option is to create a Task with `TaskCreationOptions.LongRunning` or, in most advanced scenarios, to write a custom task scheduler.

2. The most performant synchronization techniques are those not using kernel objects but user-mode objects. In order to atomically write both a file and some value in memory, the Critical Section is the most appropriate technique and is available through the `lock` keyword of the C# language.

3. The `Task.Delay` API is the most appropriate delay because it *schedules* the code in the continuation after the specified number of milliseconds, letting the thread be reused in the meantime. Conversely, the operating system `Sleep` API is exposed in .NET as `Thread.Sleep`, which suspends the thread execution for the given number of milliseconds, but it makes the thread unavailable from being reused.

4. The Task library offers the `WaitHandle.WaitAny` and `WaitHandle.WaitAll` methods, which respectively call the continuation code as soon as *any* or *all* of the operations have completed. The task results can be accessed as soon as the returned tasks have completed.

5. The `TaskCompletionSource` is a class used to create and control the `Task`. It can be used to transform any asynchronous behavior, such as a CLR event, in a Task-based operation. The client code, instead of subscribing to the event, can therefore await the task obtained from the `TaskCompletionSource`.

6. The `Task` library provides the pre-built `Task.CompletedTask` to return an empty `Task`, and the methods `Task.FromResult`, `Task.FromCanceled` and `Task.FromException` to create tasks that either return a result, report a cancellation, or throw an exception.

7. Long-running tasks may be created by specifying `TaskCreationOptions.LongRunning` in the `Task` constructor.

8. The need to use `Control.Invoke` (or `Dispatcher.Invoke` in WPF) can be verified with `Control.InvokeRequired` (or `Dispatcher.CheckAccess()` in WPF) and depends on whether the library used to access the resource already marshaled the result in the main thread. If the library already embraced the tasks and the library author did not call `Task.ConfigureAwait(false)`, you can consume the result directly because the continuation executed after the `await` keyword is invoked in the main thread thanks to the synchronization context provided by the UI framework.

9. The `ConfigureAwait` method is useful to avoid useless marshaling operations that would occur when a synchronization context is in use in the process. This is normally created by UI frameworks and ASP.NET applications. The primary users of `ConfigureAwait` are library developers who don't need to access the application objects that can only be used from the main thread.

10. You have to verify whether the asynchronous operation has completed in the main thread first (for example, by using `Control.InvokeRequired` in Windows Forms or `Dispatcher.CheckAccess()` in WPF). If it completed in a different thread, you need to access the UI by means of `Control.Invoke` or `Dispatcher.Invoke`.

Chapter 13

1. The most important classes in the `System.IO` namespace for working with system objects are `Path` for paths, `File` and `FileInfo` for files, and `Directory` and `DirectoryInfo` for directories.

2. The preferred way of concatenating paths is by using the `Path.Combine()` static method.

3. The path of the temporary folder of the current user can be retrieved with the `Path.GetTempPath()` static method.

4. The `File` and `FileInfo` classes provide similar functionalities but `File` is a static class and `FileInfo` is a non-static class. Likewise, `Directory` is a static class and `DirectoryInfo` is a non-static class, although their functionalities are similar.

5. To create directories, you can use the `Create()` and `CreateSubdirectory()` methods. The former creates a directory when its direct parent exists. The latter creates a subdirectory and all the other subdirectories in a hierarchy up to the root, if necessary. To enumerate directories, use the `EnumerateDirectories()` method, which retrieves an enumerable collection of directories that can be enumerated before the whole collection is returned. There are multiple overloads for the various search options.

6. The three categories of streams in .NET are backing stores (streams that represent a source or destination of a sequence of bytes), decorators (streams that read or write data from or to another stream, transforming it in some way), and adapters (not actually streams, but wrappers that help us work with sources of data at a higher level than bytes).

7. The base class for streams in .NET is the `System.IO.Stream` class. This is an abstract class that provides methods and properties for reading from and writing to a stream. Many of these are abstract and are implemented in derived classes.

8. By default, both `BinaryReader` and `BinaryWriter` handle strings using the UTF-8 encoding. However, they both have overloaded constructors that allow the specifying of another encoding using the `System.Text.Encoding` class.

9. The `XmlSerializer` class, from the `System.Xml.Serialization` namespace, can be used to serialize and deserialize data. `XmlSerializer` works by serializing to XML all the public properties and fields of a type. It uses some default settings, such as types becoming nodes, and properties and fields becoming elements. The name of a type, property, or field becomes the name of the node or element and the value of a field, or property, its text.

10. The JSON serializer shipped with .NET Core is called `System.Text.Json`. For .NET Framework and .NET Standard projects, it is available as a NuGet package, with the same name. You can use the `JsonSerializer.Serialize()` static method to serialize data and the `JsonSerializer.Deserialize<T>()` static method to deserialize data. You can use specific attributes to control the serialization process. On the other hand, if you want more control over what is written or read, you can use the `Utf8JsonWriter` and `Utf8JsonReader` classes.

Chapter 14

1. The code that may potentially throw an exception must be put inside a `try` block.

2. Inside the `catch` block, you may primarily want to try to recover the error. The recovery strategy may be very different and may vary from reporting a friendly error to the user to repeating the operation with different parameters. Logging is another typical operation done in the `catch` block.

3. The exception type specified in the `catch` block captures exceptions matching the same type or any derived types. For this reason, the ones lower in the hierarchy must be specified last. In any case, the C# compiler will generate an error whenever the order is not correct.

4. By specifying the variable name in the `catch` statement, you get access to the exception object. It provides important information such as the message and other information that is very precious when logging an error. The exception object can also be used as the inner exception parameter when creating a new, more specific exception.

5. After examining the exception object, you may realize that you can't do anything to recover the operation. In this case, it is more appropriate to let the exception continue bouncing to the callers. This can be done with the use of the parameterless `throw` statement, or by creating and throwing a new exception by passing the exception object in the constructor.

6. The `finally` block is used to declare a block of code that must be executed regardless of whether the code specified in the `try` block failed or completed successfully.

7. You can specify a `finally` block without `catch` whenever you don't need to be notified about the failure of the code inside the `try` block. The `finally` code will be executed in any case.

8. First-chance exceptions represent the exceptions at a very early stage, as soon as they are thrown and before jumping to their handlers, if any. The debugger may stop at them, giving a more accurate indication about a potential bug.

9. The Visual Studio debugger allows us to select the first-chance exceptions we want to stop at. This can be done using the **Exception Settings** window.

10. The `UnhandledException` event is fired right before the application is going to crash. This event can be used to provide better advice to the user, to log the error, or even to automatically restart the application.

Chapter 15

1. By enabling the C# 8 nullable reference types feature and decorating the reference types in your code, you will dramatically reduce the occurrence of `NullReferenceException` exceptions in your code.

2. The new succinct syntax to access the last item in an array is `[^1]`, which makes use of the `System.Index` type.

3. In a switch expression, the discard (`_`) character is equivalent to `default`, which is typically used in the switch statement.

4. C# 8 introduced the asynchronous dispose feature to provide an asynchronous behavior when disposing resources. This way, we can await the asynchronous closing operation from the `DisposeAsync` method and avoid the danger of using the `Task.Wait` method inside `Dispose`.

5. The null coalescing assignment `??=` is used to avoid the execution of the code on the right side (in our example, the `GetOrders()` method) of the assignment when the left side (`orders`) is not null.

6. In order to be iterated with `async foreach`, a sequence must exhibit an asynchronous behavior that cannot be done using the `IEnumerable` and `IEnumerator` interfaces and their generic counterparts. The new `IAsyncEnumerable<T>` and `IAsyncEnumerator<T>` interfaces were specifically designed to support the asynchronous behavior that is used by the `async foreach` statement.

Chapter 16

1. The `global.json` file is used to determine which SDK will be used in a given directory tree. You can create this file in the solution root folder (or any parent folders) by using the `dotnet new globaljson` command and editing it manually to match one of the versions returned by the `dotnet --info` command.

2. The `Path.Combine` method is the best way to concatenate paths on both Windows and Linux, both of which use different path separators. This method is also very convenient to avoid mistakes when concatenating relative paths and doubling or omitting the separators.

3. Libraries conforming to the .NET Standard specification are binary compatible with any framework supporting it. When you need to share code among different frameworks, verify which is the most recent version of .NET Standard supported by them and create a library that uses it. If the APIs you need to use are not supported by the required version of .NET Standard, you can change strategy and create separate libraries and package them together in a single NuGet package. The package manifest will need to associate each assembly to the specific framework, platform, or architecture the library can run on.

4. Thanks to the new project file format, it is now possible to copy the desired `PackageReference` tags from one project to another. This can also be done in Visual Studio when the solution is opened and, as soon as the file is saved, the NuGet packages will be restored automatically.

5. After analyzing the architectural implications, the very first step is upgrading the current solution to the latest version of .NET Framework, at least version 4.7.2.

6. To minimize the startup time, .NET Core 3 offers two new publishing options. The first is **AOT** compilation, which immediately generates the assembly code, dramatically reducing the need for the **JIT** compiler. The second is enabling the **Quick JIT** compiler, which is used at runtime and is faster than the traditional **JIT** compiler, but generates less-optimized code.

Chapter 17

1. Unit testing is a type of software testing where individual units of code are tested in order to validate whether they are working as they were designed to work. Unit testing helps to identify and fix bugs early in the development cycle, therefore helping to save time and money. It helps developers to better understand the code and allows them to make changes easier. It helps with code reuse by requiring the code to be more modular in order to test it better. It can act as project documentation. It also helps with debugging because when tests fail, only the latest changes need to be checked and debugged.

2. Visual Studio tools for unit testing are the **Test Explorer** (where you can view, run, debug, and analyze tests), the Microsoft unit testing framework for managed code, code coverage tools (which determine the amount of code that unit tests are covering), and the Microsoft Fakes isolation framework (which allows you to create substitutes for classes and methods).

3. The **Test Explorer** in Visual Studio allows you to view available unit tests, grouped by different levels (projects, classes, and so on). You can run and debug the unit tests from the **Test Explorer**, and you can view the results from their execution.

4. To specify that a class contains unit tests, you must decorate it with the `TestClass` attribute. Methods containing unit tests must be decorated with the `TestMethod` attribute.

5. The class to use for performing assertions is called `Assert` and is available in the `Microsoft.VisualStudio.TestTools.UnitTesting` namespace. It contains many static methods, such as `AreEqual()`, `AreNotEqual()`, `IsTrue()`, `IsFalse()`, `AreSame()`, `AreNotSame()`, `IsNull()`, and `IsNotNull()`.

6. Code coverage can be determined based on the available unit tests from the **Test Explorer** or from the **Test** top-level menu. The results are available in the **Code Coverage Results** pane.

7. You can provide fixtures that execute once per class by providing methods decorated with the `ClassInitialize` and the `ClassCleanup` attributes. The former executes once per class before all the tests are executed, and the latter once after all the tests are executed. For fixtures that execute before and after each unit test, you must provide methods decorated with the `TestInitialize` and `TestCleanup` attributes.

8. Data-driven unit testing means writing unit tests that fetch testing data from an external source (such as a file or a database). The test method is then executed once for each row in the data source.

9. The `DynamicData` attribute allows you to specify a method or property of the unit testing class as the source of data. The `DataSource` attribute allows you to specify an external source of data.

10. The external sources of data supported by the Microsoft unit testing framework for data-driven tests are SQL databases, CSV files, Excel documents, and XML documents.

Other Books You May Enjoy

If you enjoyed this book, you may be interested in these other books by Packt:

Hands-On Microservices with C# 8 and .NET Core 3 - Third Edition

Gaurav Aroraa, Ed Price

ISBN: 978-1-78961-794-8

- Package, deploy, and manage microservices and containers with Azure Service Fabric
- Use REST APIs to integrate services using a synchronous approach
- Protect public APIs using Azure Active Directory and OAuth 2.0
- Understand the operation and scaling of microservices using Docker and Kubernetes
- Implement reactive microservices with Reactive Extensions
- Discover design patterns and best practices for building enterprise-ready apps

Hands-On Software Architecture with C# 8 and .NET Core 3

Francesco Abbruzzese, Gabriel Baptista

ISBN: 978-1-78980-093-7

- Overcome real-world architectural challenges and solve design consideration issues
- Apply architectural approaches like Layered Architecture, service-oriented architecture (SOA), and microservices
- Learn to use tools like containers, Docker, and Kubernetes to manage microservices
- Get up to speed with Azure Cosmos DB for delivering multi-continental solutions
- Learn how to program and maintain Azure Functions using C#
- Understand when to use test-driven development (TDD) as an approach for software development
- Write automated functional test cases for your projects

Leave a review - let other readers know what you think

Please share your thoughts on this book with others by leaving a review on the site that you bought it from. If you purchased the book from Amazon, please leave us an honest review on this book's Amazon page. This is vital so that other potential readers can see and use your unbiased opinion to make purchasing decisions, we can understand what our customers think about our products, and our authors can see your feedback on the title that they have worked with Packt to create. It will only take a few minutes of your time, but is valuable to other potential customers, our authors, and Packt. Thank you!

Index

V

U

9 781789 805864